Luci Yamamoto &
Conner Gorry

HAWAI
THE BIG ISLAND

CONTENTS

Our authors are independent, dedicated travelers. They don't research using just the internet or phone, and they don't take freebies, so you can rely on their advice being well researched and impartial. They travel widely, visiting thousands of places, and take great pride in getting all the details right and telling it like it is.

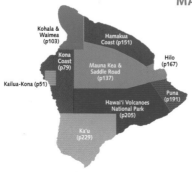

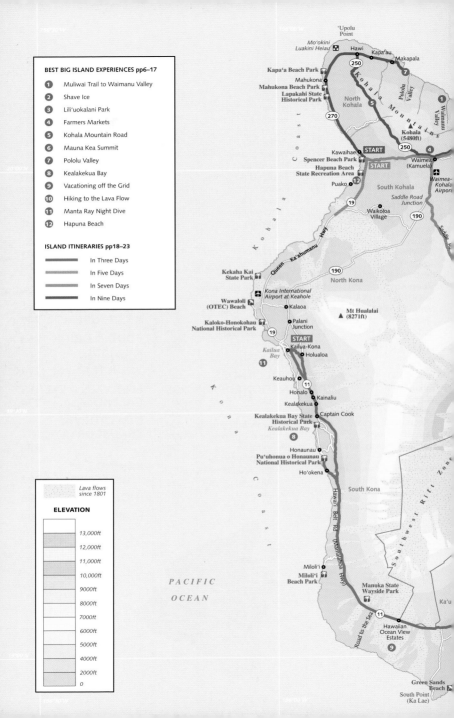

BEST BIG ISLAND EXPERIENCES pp6–17

1. Muliwai Trail to Waimanu Valley
2. Shave Ice
3. Lili'uokalani Park
4. Farmers Markets
5. Kohala Mountain Road
6. Mauna Kea Summit
7. Pololu Valley
8. Kealakekua Bay
9. Vacationing off the Grid
10. Hiking to the Lava Flow
11. Manta Ray Night Dive
12. Hapuna Beach

ISLAND ITINERARIES pp18–23

In Three Days
In Five Days
In Seven Days
In Nine Days

Lava flows since 1801

ELEVATION

13,000ft
12,000ft
11,000ft
10,000ft
9000ft
8000ft
7000ft
6000ft
5000ft
4000ft
2000ft
0

PACIFIC

OCEAN

'Upolu Point
Mo'okini Luakini Heiau
Hawi
Kapa'au
Makapala
250
7
Kapa'a Beach Park
Mahukona
Mahukona Beach Park
Lapakahi State Historical Park
270
North Kohala
5
Pololu Valley
Kohala Mountains
Waimanu Valley
1
Kohala (5480ft)
Kawaihae
Spencer Beach Park
Hapuna Beach State Recreation Area
Puako
12
START
250
Waimea (Kamuela)
4
Waimea-Kohala Airport
South Kohala
Saddle Road Junction
19
Waikoloa Village
190
Saddle Rd
Queen Ka'ahumanu Hwy
Kekaha Kai State Park
Kona International Airport at Keahole
190
North Kona
Wawaloli (OTEC) Beach
Kaloko-Honokohau National Historical Park
Kalaoa
Palani Junction
Mt Hualalai (8271ft)
19
START
Kailua-Kona
Holualoa
11
Kailua Bay
Keauhou
11
Honalo
Kainaliu
Kealakekua
Kealakekua Bay State Historical Park
Kealakekua Bay
Captain Cook
8
Honaunau
Pu'uhonua o Honaunau National Historical Park
Ho'okena
South Kona
Southwest Rift Zone
Mamalahoa Hwy
Hawaii Belt Rd
Miloli'i
Miloli'i Beach Park
Manuka State Wayside Park
Ka'u
Road to the Sea
11
Hawaiian Ocean View Estates
9
Green Sands Beach
South Point (Ka Lae)

BEST BIG ISLAND EXPERIENCES

Hawai'i ain't just another pretty face. Sure, she's a knockout with glorious sun, sand and surf. But the youngest Hawaiian Island will also challenge you, surprise you and take you to extremes. Witness the stark terrain of lava-rock desert and the smoldering glow of molten lava. Climb Hawaii's highest and largest volcanic mountains, majestic and perhaps capped with fresh snow. Visit old plantation towns – sans high-rises and fast-food chains – and misty valleys, weathered by rain, waves and time. Meet Native Hawaiians, the remaining keepers of ancient island culture, and nouveau hippies who've flocked here seeking a life 'off the grid.' Hawai'i is vast, diverse and impossible to pigeonhole. Honor her, and she'll fascinate you to no end.

The following pages contain, in no particular order, our recommendations for the top, most genuine and most memorable Big Island experiences.

❶ **BEST HIKE:** Muliwai Trail to Waimanu Valley (p162)

Hiking is kind of like ice cream: it depends what flavor floats your boat. So 'best hike' is relative. What makes this one a highlight is that a) the switchback Z-trail will kick your butt, and b) you're almost guaranteed to have this emerald valley all to yourself. With two days romping on the black-sand beach and exploring waterfalls and pools few visitors have ever experienced, you might forget the grueling hike back that's waiting for you. Pray for good weather or you're in for a slippery slog. If you're not up for the entire hike, at least hoof it to the third, deep switchback on the Z-trail for valley views that'll make you weep. If this all sounds like too much exertion or you're traveling with kids, you can inch your way down the super steep road to Waipi'o Beach. Once down, there are waterfalls to explore, wild Waipi'o horses munching on green grass and surfable waves. The last is for experts only.

1

GREG ELMS

❷ BEST HEAT-BEATING REFRESHMENT: Shave ice (p184)

Ice. Syrup. What's the big deal? Ah, to those uninitiated with the wonders of shave ice, prepare for sweet relief. This local treat is made with finely shaved (not crushed, grated or scraped) ice, topped by Day Glo–colored syrups. The ice resembles powdery snow, which distinguishes it from the coarser mainland sno-cone or Italian granita. Shave ice originated from a similar Japanese treat called *kakigori*, brought to Hawaii by plantation-era immigrants. Back in the day, shave ice was served in a white paper cone, but today Styrofoam cups are woefully ubiquitous. Likewise, traditional fruit flavors have made way for dozens of novelties, from guava to butterscotch. The ingredients are simple, but locals are finicky about quality. Gritty ice is unacceptable, while too much or too little syrup can ruin the whole shebang. Nowadays genuine mom-and-pop sellers are rare, but you can still find paper cones, wooden spoons and $1.50 servings at Itsu's Fishing Supplies (p184) in Hilo (where locals call it 'ice shave').

ANN CECIL

❸ BEST PICNIC SPOT:
Liliʻuokalani Park (p174)

There are no *bad* picnic spots on Hawaiʻi. A vacant bench, a patio table, a patch of sand on the beach. They're everywhere. But sprawling Liliʻuokalani Park is tailor-made for an afternoon of picnicking, strolling, tossing a football and any other kick-back fun. With a sweeping view from Hilo Bay to Mauna Kea, this park encompasses 30 acres of Japanese-style gardens, with grassy lawns, serene ponds and charming pagoda bridges. Under leafy shower trees and stately ironwood pines, you'll find countless private picnic spots. While here, walk across the footbridge to Mokuola (Coconut Island; p175), a kid's-fantasy miniature island.

❹ BEST PLACE TO MEET LOCALS: Farmers markets (p133)

Oyster mushrooms by the bagful. Jaboticaba, mamey, rambutan and other strange fruit you've never heard of. Barbies in Hawaiiana haute couture. Novels for 25¢ and lomilomi massages for $1 a minute. You can find almost anything at a Big Island farmers market, but what you'll come away with (in addition to pin-cushion proteas and jerked ʻahi) is that warm fuzzy aloha feeling. Whether you're buying, browsing or just chatting about yesterday's vog (volcanic fog), jumping into the community starts at these markets-cum-church-socials. In Wai-

mea (p133), farmers in muddy boots offer radicchio recipes and aunties compare notes on harvesting wild ʻohelo berries. Volcano's market (p226) brings out the whole town for killer organics, rain or shine. In Hilo, the island's oldest market (p175) exemplifies diversity. Got kids? They'll love playing tag with the local *na keiki* in Waimea or hitting the skate park in Volcano. So come on down, sip some ʻawa (kava), nibble on samples of organic goat cheese and talk story. But before you do, hit the ATM – it's impossible to walk away empty-handed.

GREG ELMS

There's one scenic drive that's truly epic: the winding two-lane highway called Kohala Mountain Road

○5

© PHOTO RESOURCE HAWAII / ALAMY

❺ **BEST SCENIC DRIVE:**
Kohala Mountain Road (p124)

A boring Big Island drive? No such thing. Here, even a trip to the supermarket might warrant your high-res camera, while journeys past an unobstructed horizon or lava desert might leave you speechless. But there's one scenic drive that's truly epic: the winding two-lane highway called Kohala Mountain Rd, between Hawi and Waimea. Even control freaks might prefer the passenger seat, to fully absorb the monumental panorama splayed below: in the foreground, windblown grasses carpet far-flung slopes, where grazing cows look too picturesque to be real. Further down, rugged fields of ancient lava meet the sandy beaches of South Kohala. Still further, the triumvirate of Mauna Kea, Mauna Loa and Hualalai is colossal (never mind the distance), while the blue palette of big-sky country overlooks it all. More than any other, this drive shows off why the Big Island deserves its name.

❻ BEST ISLAND VIEW: Mauna Kea summit (p143)

It is breathless *and* breathtaking up here in the rarefied air of Hawai'i's most sacred and lofty spot, with the setting sun bouncing halos off the surrounding cinder cones. Look for the mountain shadow framing Hilo in a purple triangle when it's clear. When it's cloudy, the view is just as spectacular, only different; it's like looking down on heaven, so thick is the layer of marshmallow fluff blanketing the island. Southward, massive Mauna Loa taunts 'climb me if you dare.' With a cloud tutu hugging its gently sloping summit, it actually looks doable. Once the sun goes down, the stars come up, and the best island view transitions to the best view in the universe.

GREG ELMS

➐ **BEST SHORT HIKE:**
Pololu Valley (p128)

The surefooted can hoof it down in 10 minutes. But why hurry? Trek leisurely to drink in the magnificent views. Created by the ancient Kohala volcano, Pololu Valley reveals a lushly weathered patina, possible only by the passage of time. Along the easterly coast, a lineup of melancholy valleys looms, fading from black to gray to sheer silver faraway. Inland, the valley slopes converge, green and misty above Pololu Stream. The black-sand beach, strewn with driftwood, is too rough for casual swimmers, but intrepid surfers paddle out with gusto, oblivious to onlookers, into the unforgiving whitecaps.

© V1 / ALAMY

© PHIL DEGGINGER / ALAMY

❽ BEST SNORKELING: Kealakekua Bay (p87)

It's all true. Teeming, Technicolor fish in 3ft of water. Spinner dolphins lazily circling your kayak. Green-studded cliffs soaring 600ft above you. Water so clear you can see your fins and the cleavage of the woman nearby. OK, maybe you don't need to see that. The point is, the tourist brochures hype this as the best snorkeling in the state, and, in this case, you can believe it. But it's not just the fish, it's the whole experience. You hike down the cliffs or paddle past a heiau (ancient stone temple) to the Ka'awaloa Cove snorkeling grounds,

where circumnavigator Captain James Cook first landed on Hawai'i and drew his last breath, captured for posterity with a white obelisk surrounded by palm trees. You'll see the fish before you're even wet, including the iconic *humuhumunukunukuapua'a* (Hawaiian triggerfish). Swim out 150ft and you'll be hovering over the dark depths with nothing but blue as far as the eye can see, except if you're really lucky – sometimes whales lumber through these waters, and green sea turtles, too.

GREG ELMS

❾ BEST LOW-IMPACT EXPERIENCE: Vacationing off the grid (p239)

Across the island, locals are choosing to live off the grid by harnessing the sun, rain, wind and whatever other alternative energy their ingenuity devises. Vacationers can participate in this positive, environmentally friendly cycle, too. Learn firsthand what it's like to rise and sleep according to the sun rather than a clock, how solar showers and wind-up gadgets can liberate you from batteries and fossil fuels, and why you don't have to sacrifice hot coffee or wi-fi. A couple of our favorite sustainable sleeps include Lova Lava Land (p239) and Waianuhea B&B (p157).

❿ BEST LAND ADVENTURE: Hiking to the lava flow (p217)

Kilauea is churning out 50,000 gallons of lava a minute, people, and you need to see the action to believe it. There are so many revelatory experiences on this magic isle, but nothing rivals skipping and tripping over crunchy old lava to get to where hot ribbons of the new stuff flow into the ocean, boiling it on contact (in Puna, at the end of Chain of Craters Rd near Kalapana, at the time of writing). Sometimes the lava isn't accessible on foot, in which case the only way to see it is from the air. If that's not in the budget, buy the screensaver and enjoy some of the world's longest lava tubes – another great Big Island adventure.

JOHN ELK III

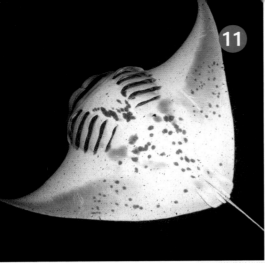

© RHK UW PRODUCTIONS / ALAMY

⓫ BEST OCEAN ADVENTURE:
Manta ray night dive (p60)

Even the island's baddest, bravest divers get teary-eyed reminiscing about this night dive with the sea's most graceful beasts. Diving at night is a thrill in itself, but once you turn on your lights and attract a corps de ballet of Pacific rays, some with wing spans of 10ft or wider and tails like javelins, your life becomes re-segmented: before diving with mantas and after. If you're not certified, you can do it with a snorkel, but looking down at them isn't the same as looking up. Book this tour early – everyone is hot to do it and boats fill fast.

Even the island's baddest, bravest divers get teary-eyed

⓬ **BEST MULTIPURPOSE BEACH:** Hapuna Beach (p117)

With its half-mile sweep of powdery sand, Hapuna Beach is a classic beauty, revered by locals and tourists alike. It's a drive-up hot spot, drenched with South Kohala sun all year round. During calm summer months, gentler waves allow swimming and snorkeling. Come winter, the surf swells, attracting daredevil bodyboarders and surfers. Hapuna Beach is ranked among the premier US beaches – so it's always jammed with suntanned (or burnt, we'd reckon) revelers. Certainly, off-road beaches are pristine and private, but without a 4WD or the energy for a sweaty hike, they could very well be 1000 miles away.

GREG ELMS

ISLAND
ITINERARIES

With limited time, don't try to go *everywhere*. You'll spend too much time driving and have too little time to actually experience this *big* (4028 sq mile) island. Due to limited space, we omitted two regions here – **Puna** (p191) and **Ka'u** (p229) – each unique and worth visiting.

See the itineraries at the beginning of each regional chapter for more detailed routes.

IN THREE DAYS *This leg: 100 miles*

❶ KAHALU'U BEACH (p71) Ease right into 'Hawaiian time' at Kahalu'u Beach, a roadside **snorkeling** hot spot, where tropical fish and *honu* (sea turtles) glide by before the water even covers your head!

❷ HOLUALOA (p75) In the afternoon, go upcountry to retro Holualoa, where you can browse **fine-art galleries**, sample Kona coffee and catch a spectacular sunset.

❸ MANTA RAY NIGHT DIVE (p59) Certified divers, skip Holualoa and book a night dive to see giant, gentle manta rays.

❹ KEALAKEKUA BAY (p86) Although shore snorkeling is convenient, it's just a foretaste of the deeper waters accessible only by boat. On day two, book a morning **snorkeling cruise (p58)** or paddle a **kayak (p88)**

to the glassy waters near the Captain Cook Monument.

❺ PU'UHONUA O HONAUNAU (p91) Toward sundown, visit this ancient *pu'uhonua* (place of refuge), with nicely replicated artifacts and an easy **coastal hike**.

❻ HAWAI'I VOLCANOES NATIONAL PARK (p205) On day three, hit the road to the world's most active volcano. Hike down the 4-mile **Kilauea Iki Trail (p218)**, an intriguingly varied trek across ohia forest and the vast crater floor.

❼ VOLCANO ART CENTER (p211) By day, browse the gallery's impressive collection of Hawaii-made arts and crafts, all for sale. By night, catch outstanding dance and music performances.

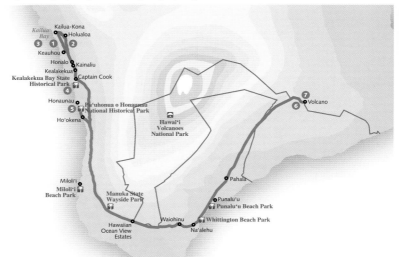

IN FIVE DAYS *This leg: 80 miles*

⑧ HILO (p167) On day four, kick back in Hawai'i's capital town, which charms 'em all with its scenic bay, retro downtown, lush greenery and genuine community. Hilo is a great home base to explore East Hawai'i. If it's Saturday or Wednesday, rise early for the Hilo Farmers Market (p175), where $1 will buy you four succulent papayas. Or simply stroll around downtown, where minimuseums, art galleries and indie shops are modest but charming, just like Hilo.

⑨ 'IMILOA ASTRONOMY CENTER OF HAWAI'I (p176) This fascinating museum presents the convergence of ancient Hawaiian seafaring, modern astronomy and the Islands' volcanic origins. Highly recommended if you're headed to Mauna Kea (p137).

⑩ LILI'UOKALANI PARK & MOKUOLA (COCONUT ISLAND) (p174) In the afternoon, enjoy a picnic amid serene Japanese-style ponds and lawns. Or join the locals for a sunset jog or stroll. For dinner, discriminating palates will appreciate foodie-darling Hilo Bay Café (p184), while nostalgia buffs (and fish eaters) must experience no-frills, family-run Seaside Restaurant (p185).

⑪ HAMAKUA COAST (p151) On day five, head out along the Hamakua Coast, where you'll wind through steep coastal gulches, foliage growing wild and miles of open cane land. Detour onto the Pepe'ekeo 4-Mile Scenic Drive (p165), which winds through storybook tropical rain forest (and past a scrumptious fruit-smoothie stand). Further along the highway, stop at gorgeous Akaka Falls (p165).

⑫ HONOKA'A (p154) Amid idyllic pastureland and the sweeping coast, this cowboy town can make a lovely rural home base. Day trippers can browse the indie shops and down a couple of fresh *malasadas* (Portuguese fried doughnuts) at Tex Drive-In (p155).

⑬ WAIPI'O VALLEY (p158) If you think you know the color green, you ain't seen nothin' yet! The walk to the valley floor is steep, but paved and short. For outdoorsy types, the Muliwai Trail (p162) to Waimanu Valley is a challenging (think *slippery*) trek, but the reward is astounding panoramic views.

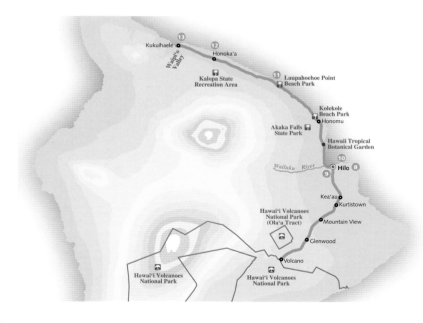

IN SEVEN DAYS *This leg: 70 miles*

⑭ SOUTH KOHALA BEACHES (p107) If your fantasy Hawai'i is all sun, sand and surf, enjoy day six at South Kohala's famous beaches. Seemingly endless **Hapuna Beach (p117)** is a phenomenally popular beach, ideal for bodyboarding except during high winter surf. **Spencer Beach Park (p118)** is great for tots, while perfectly curved **Kauna'oa Bay (p116)** is arguably the island's prettiest.

⑮ PUAKO PETROGLYPH PRESERVE (p112) Refuel with a picnic lunch at **Holo- holokai Beach Park (p111)**, a salt-and-pepper pebble beach. There are no bikinis or body- boards in sight, but shaded picnic tables spell relief from the mighty Hapuna sun. From the beach, walk to one of the state's largest collections of **petroglyphs**, carved on smooth plates of ancient lava. Also worth a stop is **Pu'ukohola Heiau National Historic Site (p119)**, the massive ruins of a heiau (ancient temple) built by King Kamehameha.

⑯ RESORT GOLF (p109) In the late after- noon, snag the twilight discount at the **Waikoloa Beach & Kings' Courses (p109)**, **Mauna Kea &** **Hapuna Golf Courses (p117)** or **Francis I'i Brown North & South Courses (p113)**. If golf isn't your thing, pamper yourself at a luxury **spa (p113)**.

⑰ MAUNA KEA SUMMIT TRAIL (p146) On day seven, visit the island's tallest mountain, sacred to Native Hawaiians, stunning from afar and otherworldly up close. If (and only if) you're fit and adventurous, the 6-mile trail to the summit is a worthy challenge. Start at the crack of dawn to complete the eight-hour journey before dark.

⑱ MAUNA KEA (p137) If the summit trail sounds insanely grueling, no problem: drive up or join a tour. Most tours depart in the mid-afternoon from Waikoloa, timed for the sunset and stargazing. Rest up in the morning, and eat lightly to alleviate po- tential altitude sickness. After nightfall, go **stargazing (p145)** at the Onizuka Visitor In- formation Station. At 9200ft, the air is ex- ceptionally clear, dry and dark. If you have no eye for constellations, here's your chance to finally identify that Orion or Leo!

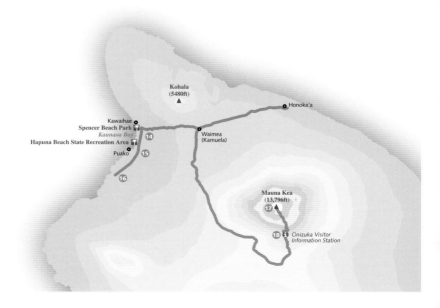

IN NINE DAYS *This leg: 50 miles*

⑲ NORTH KOHALA (p120) On your eighth day, visit Hawai'i's rural northern tip. Circle the coast on the Akoni Pule Hwy, stopping at **Lapakahi State Historical Park (p121)** and (calling ahead for access) **Mo'okini Luakini Heiau (p122)**. Save your appetite for **Hawi (p124)**, a tiny plantation village with a remarkable number of destination eateries.

⑳ KENJI'S HOUSE (p125) Despite its humbleness, the seashell 'art' of the late Kenji Yokoyama is touchingly memorable. On his lifelong homestead, find a **bistro**, an **art co-op** and a **minimuseum**.

㉑ POLOLU VALLEY (p127) End the day with a steep but short **hike** down into this valley, which shows another face of Hawai'i: rugged, mysterious and ancient.

㉒ KOHALA MOUNTAIN ROAD (p124) On day nine, wind down this rural highway, with stupendous views of West Hawai'i. You'll wish for more than the single lookout stop.

㉓ WAIMEA (p129) Check out this three-stoplight *paniolo* (cowboy) town that boasts big-name **restaurants** and **fine-art galleries** amid mainstream strip malls. While away the morning amid art exhibits at **Isaacs Art Center (p130)**.

㉔ MERRIMAN'S CULINARY & FARM ADVENTURE TOUR (p131) For fans of the 'locavore' movement, organic farming and fresh gourmet cuisine, this tour will satisfy all senses. You'll visit local farms that supply the ingredients for the highlight of the tour: a scrumptious four-course meal.

㉕ KOHALA FOREST RESERVE TRAIL (p135) For a final look at the island's natural beauty, **hike** through this fairytale forestland, lush and green. Another memorable Waimea adventure is **horseback riding (p131)**, which you'll long to do once you glimpse Waimea's breezy ranchland.

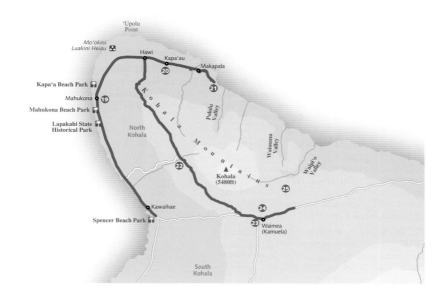

BIG ISLAND MIXED PLATE

❶ CEVICHE DAVE'S (p96) After a morning snorkel or afternoon carving at **Pine Trees (p98)**, pull up a stool at Dave's wooden bar for his wild and wonderfully fresh ceviche.

❷ HUALALAI GRILLE BY ALAN WONG (p100) The best meal of your vacation, if not your life, might be the exquisite tasting menu crafted by one of the giants of Hawaii Regional Cuisine.

❸ SUSHI ROCK (p124) Intimate and local, this innovative sushi joint is as charming as little Hawi itself. Plus there's a full bar. Sidle up.

❹ MERRIMAN'S (p133) Waimea is foodie central thanks to pioneer chef Pete Merriman. Not in the budget? Try Sunday brunch at **Daniel Thiebaut (p133)**.

❺HILO FARMERS MARKET (p175) *Warabi* (fern shoots), *'opihi* (limpet) and lychee: foodies know hitting the local market is as much cultural as culinary experience. So true at Hawai'i's oldest farmers market.

❻ LA BOURGOGNE (p65) Odd minimall location notwithstanding, this is the place to get cozy with your sweetheart around hearty plates of fine French fare.

❼ KONA BREW FESTIVALS (p64) For a liquid diet, the **Kona Brewers Festival** each March and **Kona Coffee Cultural Festival** in November get Hawai'i buzzing.

BACKROADS: THE BIG ISLAND UNPLUGGED

❶ KOHALA MOUNTAIN ROAD (p124) This is one of Hawai'i's most glorious drives – the bearded, leather-clad dudes taking curves with wild smiles seem to think so, too. Soundtrack: Stevie Wonder, *Songs in the Key of Life*.

❷ OLD MAMALAHOA HIGHWAY, WAIMEA TO HONOKA'A (p136) You'll wish you were staying in one of Ahualoa's **secluded B&Bs (p156)** after this lovely drive. Soundtrack: Ozomatli, *Live at the Fillmore.*

❸ OLD MAMALAHOA HIGHWAY, WAIKAUMALO PARK TO UMAUMA (p166) Off-the-beaten-track Hawai'i is not an oxymoron. For proof, take this forested and largely forgotten road north of Hilo. Soundtrack: Ledward Ka'apana, *Kiho'alu: Hawaiian Slack Key Guitar.*

❹ PEPE'EKEO 4-MILE SCENIC DRIVE (p165) Locals love poking around this jungle-festooned back road, smoothie from **What's Shakin' (p166)** in hand. You will, too. Soundtrack: Jake Shimabukuro, *Gently Weeps.*

❺ RED ROAD (p201) Hot springs, a **black-sand beach**, the island's best **tide pools**…careful your whole vacation isn't swept away exploring this winding road. Soundtrack: Bob Marley, *Rastaman Vibration.*

❻ HILINA PALI ROAD (p215) From your bucket or bicycle seat, behold Mauna Kea, Mauna Loa and jet-black lava flows all around. Soundtrack: Led Zeppelin, *Led Zeppelin II.*

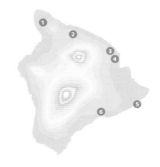

ON LAND, AT SEA

❶ KAYAKING & SNORKELING KEALA-KEKUA BAY (p87) Start your ocean itinerary paddling this unbelievably blue bay teeming with underwater life, including **spinner dolphins** and **sea turtles**.

❷ MANTA RAY DIVE (p60) By day, romp on one of the **Kekaha Kai State Park (p99)** beaches. By night, dive with mantas – ranked among the world's top 10 dives by *National Geographic*.

❸ ROAD TO THE SEA (p240) If off-the-beaten-track coastal adventure is your speed, get a 4WD, gas up and go here. Today.

❹ MAUNA KEA SUNSET & STARGAZING (p142) There's no better place to begin the land portion of your trip than atop Hawaii's most sacred mountain. Once night falls, you're in for the world's best **stargazing (p145)**.

❺ HIKING TO THE LIVE LAVA FLOW (p217) Watching land being created and destroyed by rivers of hot lava is the Big Island's main event.

❻ EXPLORING A SECRET LAVA TUBE (p219) Enter into the dark and curious depths of the national park and you'll see lava formations that still baffle the experts.

❼ WAIPI'O BEACH & VALLEY (p161) This day trip combines the best of both worlds – a **black-sand beach** at the foot of one of Hawaii's most majestic valleys.

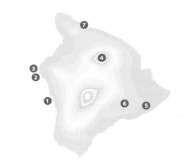

LOW-IMPACT HIGHS

❶ SOUTH KONA COAST WILDLIFE WATCHING (p87) Paddling to **Captain Cook Monument** for kickin' snorkeling is a trip highlight – even for the worldliest travelers. Continue south to **Two-Step (p93)** for more wild marine life.

❷ BACKCOUNTRY IN HAWAI'I VOLCA-NOES NATIONAL PARK (p221) It's hard, hot and kinda heinous walking over all that lava, but it's worth it to camp between the lofty cliffs and white-sand beaches of **Halape's** or **Keauhou's (p223)** raw, savage beauty.

❸ SUMMITING MAUNA LOA (p220) Bust out the winter gear if you want to climb this 13,677ft beauty. There are three routes: the 'easy' way, the 'OK, so you can hike' way and the 'where do we send the medal?' way. Which is yours?

❹ WAIPI'O VALLEY, TOP TO BOTTOM (p158) Hike to the top, **back end of Waipi'o Valley (p135)** for jaw-dropping views. Then head into the valley from the Waipi'o **scenic**

lookout (p161) for totally different, equally outstanding views.

❺ MO'OKINI LUAKINI HEIAU (p122) Explorations in North Kohala abound, but this heiau, the most sacred site in all the Hawaiian Islands, is awe inspiring. The hike down into nearby **Pololu Valley (p127)** ain't half bad either.

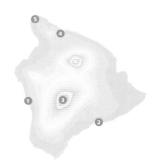

OUTDOOR ACTIVITIES & ADVENTURES

If you're after monster swells and skydiving free falls, head to Oʻahu. But if you want the world's best for almost everything else, the Big Island is where it's at. Here you can hike the world's most active volcano and stargaze (or snowboard!) atop the Earth's clearest summit. How about strolling on the planet's newest black-sand beaches and diving with giant manta rays at night? Exploring Hawaii's most sacred heiau (ancient stone temples) and valleys is another draw for culture vultures and adventure junkies; those in the latter category will pass days kayaking clear, wildlife-filled bays, snorkeling with sea turtles or horseback riding in greener pastures. In winter, you can watch humpback whales calving or bird-watch in Hawaiʻi Volcanoes National Park. Hardcore readers are probably already training for the famous Ironman Triathlon, held each fall. When planning your adventures, build in flexibility – what you can do when will be determined by the island's fickle weather.

AT SEA

In case you've forgotten, Hawaiʻi is 2500 miles from the closest landmass. With so much water around and a long, strong tradition of communing with the ocean, your vacation here is sure to be a wet dream. Even if you've never snorkeled or surfed, this is a great place to try, since experienced outfitters abound on both sides of the island. And in typical Hawaiian style, you don't need much advance planning save a check on the weather – just get up, get psyched and *go*.

BODYSURFING & BODYBOARDING

Boogie boarding or bodyboarding – whatever you want to call it, this fun sport has surpassed surfing as the most popular way to wave-ride. Top Big Island spots for bodyboarding and bodysurfing

BIG ISLAND ACTIVITIES

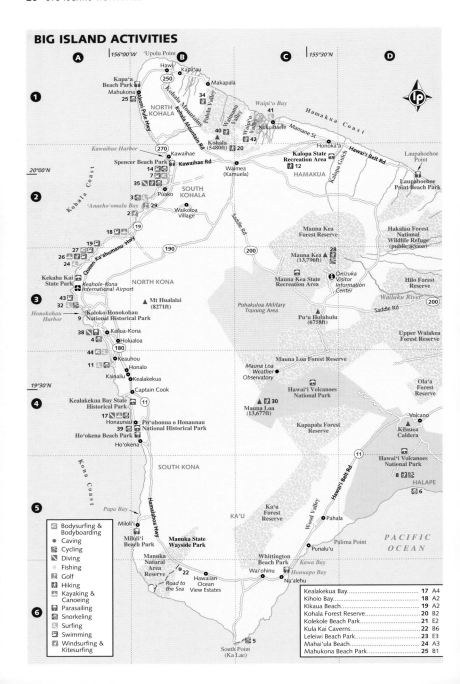

Legend:
- Bodysurfing & Bodyboarding
- Caving
- Cycling
- Diving
- Fishing
- Golf
- Hiking
- Kayaking & Canoeing
- Parasailing
- Snorkeling
- Surfing
- Swimming
- Windsurfing & Kitesurfing

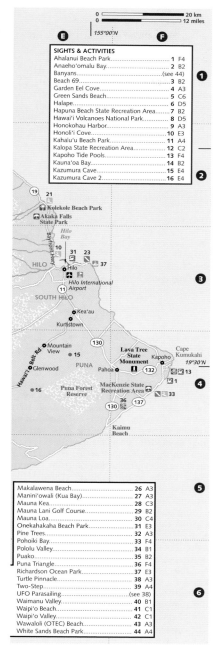

include Hapuna Beach (p117), White Sands Beach (p57), and the Kekaha Kai State Park beaches, especially in winter and especially at Manini'owali (p99). Board rentals typically run $4/16 per day/week. Spongers unite!

DIVING

Most Big Island diving happens in warm, calm Kona Coast waters, where 100ft visibility is the norm and conditions are good year-round (September and October are best). From shallow beginner dives to challenging nighttime and lava tube explorations, there's something for everyone. One of the best spots is Ka'awaloa Cove, in the Kealakekua Bay State Historical Park (p86). Other good leeward sites include Harlequin, Aquarium and Suck 'Em Up, all near the Four Seasons in North Kona, Puako (p112) further north, and Turtle Pinnacle (p95) outside Kailua-Kona. The manta ray night dive (p60) is a must, so book early in your stay. River runoff on the Hilo side usually means cloudy visibility, but Pohoiki (p137) – East Hawai'i's best site – teems with marine life.

About 700 fish species (nearly one-third endemic!), plus spinner dolphins, green sea turtles and moray eels, call Hawaiian waters home. Expect to travel only 30 minutes, tops, on boat dives. For more insight, check out Lonely Planet's *Hawaii: Diving & Snorkeling Guide.*

If you've dreamt of diving, the Kona Coast is a world-renowned spot to learn, with a smorgasbord of dive operators (see the table on p29) and sites. Introductory courses usually include three hours of class, followed by a shallow beach or boat dive. Full-on open-water certification usually takes around four days. The underwater wary can try snuba, whereby divers breathe through a long hose attached to an air tank, which floats on a raft at the surface. This is also great for kids (ages four and up).

FISHING

The Kona Coast is a deep-sea fishing fantasy, with the world's biggest marlin caught here regularly. How big? At least one 'grander' (1000lb or more) is reeled in every year, just two to five miles offshore. The next

RESPONSIBLE DIVING

The popularity of diving places immense pressure on many sites. Help preserve Hawai'i's reef and marine ecosystems with these tips.

- Respect Native Hawaiian cultural practices and sacred places, including fishing grounds.
- Do not use reef anchors or ground boats on coral (anchoring in sand is better). Encourage dive operators to establish permanent moorings at popular sites.
- Avoid touching living marine organisms or dragging equipment across the reef. Even the gentlest contact can damage polyps. *Never* stand on coral. If you must hold on to the reef, touch only exposed rock or dead coral.
- Be fin conscious. Even without contact, heavy fin strokes near the reef can damage delicate organisms. When treading water in shallow reef areas, take care not to kick up clouds of sand, which can smother fragile reef life.
- Spend as little time in underwater caves as possible – your air bubbles may be trapped within the roof, leaving previously submerged organisms high and dry.
- Collecting live coral or rock is illegal!
- Resist the temptation to buy coral or shells. It's ecologically damaging and depletes the beauty of a site.
- Carry out all trash, including found litter. Plastics, especially, are a serious threat to marine life. Turtles can mistake plastic for jellyfish and eat it.
- Collect any abandoned fishing gear you find (hooks, lines, nets), which can harm marine life and other divers.
- Don't feed the wildlife or disturb marine animals. It's illegal to come within 30ft of turtles and 150ft of whales, dolphins and Hawaiian monk seals. Do not ride on the backs of turtles, as this causes them great anxiety. Limit your observation of an animal to 30 minutes.
- Tip your dive guide!

one could be yours, with over 100 charter companies leaving from Honokohau Harbor (see p60). June to August typically sees the biggest hauls for blue and black marlin, while January to June is best for striped marlin. These waters are also rich with 'ahi (yellowfin tuna) and aku (bonito or skipjack tuna), swordfish, spearfish, mako sharks and mahimahi. Some questions to ask your charter: Can I keep my catch or is it tag and release? Is there a shaded cabin? What's the maximum number of people on a shared charter?

KAYAKING

The warm, calm seas hugging the Kona Coast combined with hidden coves and turquoise, fish-filled waters make Hawai'i prime sea kayaking turf. (Forget rivers – there are none.)

Kealakekua Bay (p88), with its smooth, accessible waters and abundance of fish and spinner dolphins, is the jewel in the underwater crown. It can get crowded, so start early. Up north, pristine coastline along Kekaha Kai (eg Makalawena; p99) and Kiholo Bay (p101) provides solitude.

A northern island start in the summer makes a spectacular kayak from 'Upolu Point to the Waipi'o Valley. Down Hilo way, the most popular put-in is at Richardson Ocean Park (p173).

Single/tandem kayaks rent for around $35/60 for 24 hours ($160/210 weekly) along Hwy 11 between Honaunau and Honalo. Though pricier than most Hwy 11 outfits, we like Kona Boys (p88) for its sustainable policies and off-the-beaten-track kayaking/camping trips, and Plenty Pupule Adventure Sports (p120) in Kawaihae for its quality gear (the 'tri-yak' holds two adults and a child) and vision/philosophy. The Aloha Kayak Company (p88) has glass-bottomed kayaks if you can't snorkel.

Island Insights

Kona is the only place in the world where both blue and black marlin 'granders' – fish weighing 1000lb or more – have been caught.

DIVING & SNORKELING OUTFITTERS

Company	Page	Tours	Price	Departs	Dive/snorkel spots
our pick Aloha Dive Company (☎ 325-5560, 800-708-5662; www.alohadive.com)	p60	Near Kona & remote dives	$110 (2-tank local), $140/200 (2-/3-tank remote)	Kawaihae, Honokohau, Keauhou	Mahukona to South Point
Big Island Divers (☎ 329-6068, 800-488-6068; www.bigisland divers.com)	p60	Boat dives, manta dives & snorkel tours, black water dives	$120/200 (2-/3-tank), $80/100/130 (manta snorkel/1-tank/ 2-tank), $150 black water dive	Honokohau	Kona Coast from Old Kona Airport to Pentagon
our pick Dive Makai (☎ 329-2025; www.dive makai.com)	p60	Boat, remote, manta & night dives	$120 (2-tank), $137 (2-tank manta dive)	Honokohau	Kona Coast
our pick Dive Tek Hawaii (☎ 329-1004, 877-885-3483; www.divetekadventures.com)	p60	Recreational & technical dives, PADI cert	$165 (2-tank recreational), from $165 (2-tank technical)	Honokohau	Kona Coast from Bandit Ledge to Hammerhead
Jack's Diving Locker (☎ 329-7585, 800-345-4807; www.jacksdivinglocker.com)	p60	Boat, shore & pelagic dives; snorkel tours; classes	$125 (2-tank), $175/225 (advanced 2-/3-tank), $95/145 (manta snorkel/2-tank), $295 (PADI cert)	Honokohau	Kona Coast from Ridges to Black Point South
Nautilus Dive Center (☎ 935-6949; www.nautilus divehilo.com)	p179	Shore & hot-lava dives, classes	$85 (2-tank dive), $440 (PADI cert)	Hilo	Leleiwi, Richardson, Pohoiki, Punalu'u
Ocean Eco Tours (☎ 324-7873; www.oceanecotours.com)	p95	Boat & shore dives, classes	$85 (shore dive), $95 (2-tank)	Honokohau	Kona Coast
our pick Sandwich Isle Divers (☎ 329-9188; www.sandwich isledivers.com)	p60	Boat dives (max 6 people), manta night dives, classes	$125 (2-tank), $150 (2-tank manta dive), $300 (cert)	Kailua-Kona shop	Kona Coast
Sea Paradise (☎ 800-322-5662; www.seaparadise.com)	p59	Boat dives (max 6 people), manta dives & snorkel tours, classes	$110 (2-tank or 1-tank manta), $85/60 (adult/ child manta snorkel), $550 (PADI cert)	Keauhou Bay	35 sites on Kona Coast

KITESURFING

Kitesurfing (aka kiteboarding) is hot wherever wind and thrill seekers collide, which on the Big Island means 'Anaeho'omalu Bay in the Waikoloa Resort area. It's kind of like surfing with a two-string kite that launches you skyward; imagine snowboarding but with water and whipping wind. See how the pros get wicked big air at www .kiteflix.com (which may be as close as you get to kitesurfing on Hawai'i, where it's very expensive and DIY).

PARASAILING

Risk averse? You'll like parasailing because you're strapped into a harness and parachute attached to a 400ft to 1200ft line that's trailed by a boat. At its best, parasailing offers a peaceful float followed by an exhilarating free fall. **UFO Parasailing** (www.ufoparasailing .com), the only parasailing outfit on the island, offers seven-/10-minute single or tandem rides from Kailua-Kona for $65/75.

Island Insights

What a trip! Imagine circumnavigating the Big Island in a kayak: the swells and sea caves, moonbows and islandwide 'ohana (families). Now imagine you're the first to attempt it and your one-legged partner has never paddled a kayak. Read Kelly Harrison's story: www.plentypupule.com.

SAILING

There are plenty of catamaran/snorkel tours available where you motor about in clear Kona waters, but to really *sail*, try intimate Kamanu Charters (p59) out of Honokohau Harbor. Old salts will want to reserve the Maile (www.adventuresailing.com; 3½hr cruises from $890), a 50ft sloop sailing from Kawaihae. The best spots? Up North Kohala way or around Old A's (aka Old Kona Airport; p57). Red Sail Sports (www.redsailhawaii.com) does a sunset cruise (adult/child $76/46) and a dinner sail ($87/53).

SNORKELING

Talk about instant gratification! On Hawai'i, you can literally step off the lava or beach into clear tropical waters teeming with vibrant corals and reef fish. Unfortunately, sometimes the best haunts are also teeming with tourists. To escape the crowds, go early, go further up (or down) the coast (Beach 69 is a good choice; p115), or hike or kayak to remote spots such as Halape (p223).

While East Hawai'i has a few worthwhile spots (think Kapoho Tide Pools; p201), the real deal is in west-side waters, where good visibility and warm conditions prevail. Even so, consider a 3mm neoprene shirt for winter explorations. Also, you'll kiss your reef shoes after a walk along these lava-lined shores.

Top Picks

SNORKELING SPOTS

- **Kealakekua Bay** (p87)
- **Pu'uhonua o Honaunau National Historical Park** (p93)
- **Kahalu'u Beach Park** (p71)
- **Kapoho Tide Pools** (p201)
- **Puako Bay** (p116)

Gear rental prices are around $8/32 per day/week. Most places rent prescription masks, which are essential for the myopic (contacts get irritated underwater). Snorkeling tours, typically from $80 to $120 for four hours, transport you to prime spots and provide gear and food. Most depart from Keauhou Bay, Kailua Pier or Honokohau Harbor; see the table on p29 for a list of operators. It's best to book in advance, especially during the high season.

Offshore

You don't have to go far for kick-ass underwater eye candy. Terrific, convenient offshore spots include Two-Step (p93); Mahukona Beach Park (p121), north of Kawaihae; and Kahalu'u (p71), called Turtle Beach by locals – a great place for first timers. More experienced folks will want to check out Garden Eel Cove (p57), north of the Old Kona Airport, and Kauna'oa Bay (p116).

Snorkeling at Kikaua Beach, in Ka'upulehu on the North Kona Coast

CONNER GORRY

ENDLESS SUMMER

It took a culture deeply steeped in the sea to invent **he'enalu** (wave sliding). From the start, the Polynesians crisscrossed the Pacific following the stars and riding the waves – a way of life that transferred seamlessly to the early Hawaiians. Surfing has always been sacred, from the kahuna's selection of the tree and carving of the board, to the special chants to christen the board and instil courage in those challenging the waves. Then, now and forever, surfing embodies the Hawaiians' profound love and knowledge of the ocean.

The high status of *he'enalu* as a Hawaiian pastime was evidenced in its strict *kapu* (taboos), especially in relation to the shape and size of the board. Children tended to ride the *paipo* or *kioe* (belly board) measuring 2ft to 4ft long, not unlike the bodyboards of today. Common-ers generally used two different-sized boards made from koa: the 9ft *alaia* or *omo* (stand up board), and the longer *kiko'o*, which could reach up to 18ft. Sometimes weighing 100lb, it took a real master to surf these planks! The *ali'i* (chiefs, royalty) on the other hand rode *olo* boards, longer still (up to 24ft) and specially made from *wili wili*, a light balsa-like wood. Certain beaches and breaks were *kapu* to all but the *ali'i*. (As a visitor to these breaks, you're the modern-day commoner, while the locals are the *ali'i*, protecting their surf turf.)

But the fun stopped shortly after contact with the Europeans, who brought disease and death to the Hawaiians. With populations decimated, the Islands came under a new Calvinis-tic morality. Replacing the *kapu*, this new set of rules banned surfing, music and hula in the interest of modesty, industry and religion. By 1820 surfing, like much of Hawaiian culture, had almost vanished.

He'enalu continued, but was driven underground for the most part, until the turn of the 20th century, when the sport started to come back big time. The father of this modern revolution was **Duke Kahanamoku**, a Native Hawaiian who was one of the few to ride and master the 'bluebirds' (big swells). Following in his ancestral tradition he was the consum-mate waterman, winning a 1912 Olympic gold medal in swimming. He soon took his noto-riety around the world and became known as the ambassador of surfing, a local hero and a legend in his own time.

Boat Trips

Hopping on a boat or paddling to fertile snorkeling grounds expands your possi-bilities. The 1-mile Kealakekua Bay paddle is insanely popular for good reasons: the spinner dolphins en route and the superla-tive snorkeling upon arrival (paddling also leaves minimal imprint on the environ-ment). Catamaran trips to this spot with outfits such as Fair Wind (p59) or Sea Paradise (p59) are also possible (both leave from Keauhou Bay, allowing more snorkel-ing time than Honokohau Harbor boats). The nighttime manta ray snorkel – led by most of the same dive operators listed in the table on p29 – is unforgettable. Tours start at $80.

SURFING

The ubiquitous lunar lava landscape ex-tends to beneath the sea, where spiny nas-ties called *wana* (sea urchins) lurk below the swells. Not ideal surfing conditions, but

no matter for dedicated Big Island surfers: they're out there braving crowded breaks and bloody limbs to pursue 'the sport of kings.'

Generally winter northern swells are big-ger, but conditions can be good anywhere, anytime (follow that surfboard-toting car!). Leeward breaks are generally cleaner. Check local tides, weather and swell size with the daily Big Island Surf Report (www.hawaiisurfnews .com). Surf Adventures (www.surfadventures.com) sells a *Big Island Surf Map* ($7.95) with de-tails of the island's 69 breaks.

Consistent east-side spots are Honoli'i Cove (p173), Kolekole Beach Park (p165) and Waipi'o Beach (p161), all north of Hilo. Pohoiki Bay (p202) is a bit heavier, but ex-perienced surfers will enjoy this lava reef.

Along the Kona Coast, try Kahalu'u Beach (p71) in Keauhou, Banyans (p61), and Pine Trees (p98), near Wawaloli (OTEC) Beach. Beach 69 (p115) has been called 'the Pipeline of the Big Island' – you be the judge.

Surfboard rentals (short/long board $15/20) are available in Kailua-Kona (p61) and Hilo (p179). Beginners might try lessons (see Kona Boys, p88, and Ocean Eco Tours, p95). Expect to pay between $95 and $125 for a couple of hours in a group class, or $150 to $180 (ouch!) for a private lesson.

SWIMMING

Since the lava landscape extends to the blue depths, Big Island shores are mostly lava rock – except for the Kona Coast, of course, which has postcard-perfect palm-lined beaches.

The west side is the best side for swimming, including Hapuna Beach (p117) and perfect, crescent-shaped Kaunaʻoa Bay (p116), known as Mauna Kea Beach. Meanwhile, Maniniʻowali Beach (aka Kua Bay; p99) has brilliant turquoise water and white sand, and is an excellent, but crowded swimming spot when calm.

East Hawaiʻi is rougher and, in large part, only for strong swimmers. Nevertheless, unique swimming opportunities run the length of Puna, with a hot pond at Ahalanui

Island Insights

Lots of secret pockets of sand (black, green and in between) grow when the tide goes out. When the tide comes in, snorkeling spots are flooded with fish. To enhance your beach experience, use the tide charts (under Current Big Island Weather) at www.instanthawaii.com.

Beach Park (p201) great for moonlit skinny dipping, and rich lava tide pools (p201).

For lap addicts, there are public pools in county parks islandwide. For locations and schedules, contact the Aquatics Division (☎ 961-8694; www.hawaii-county.com/parks/aquatics _program_guide.htm). The HPA pool (p131) in Waimea is big and clean, and you'll have your own lane. For a thrill, try a short lap in the freshwater lava tube at Kiholo Bay (p101).

WHALE WATCHING

Humpback whales (*na kohola* in Hawaiian) mate and calve here from December

BIG ISLAND SURF BEACHES & BREAKS *Jake Howard*

Because Hawaiʻi is the youngest island in the chain and the coastline is still quite rugged, it's often assumed there isn't much in the way of surfable waves. As a result, places such as Oʻahu and Kauaʻi have stolen the surf spotlight in recent years, but archaeologists and researchers believe that Kealakekua Bay (p86) is probably where ancient Polynesians started riding waves. Today a fun little left-hander called Keʻei breaks near the bay.

Unlike its neighboring islands, whose north and south shores are the primary centers of swell activity, the east and west shores are the Big Island's focal points. Because swells are shadowed by the other islands, as a general rule the surf doesn't get as big here. The Kona Coast offers the best opportunities, with north and south swell exposures as well as the offshore trade winds. Kawaihae Harbor (p118) is surrounded by several fun, introductory reefs near the breakwall, while further south, around Kekaha Kai State Park (p99) is a considerably more advanced break that challenges even the most seasoned surfers. If you have a 4WD vehicle or don't mind an hour-long hike, be sure to check out heavy reef breaks such as Mahaiʻula (p99) and Makalawena (p99). They break best on northwest swells, making the later winter months the prime season.

On East Hawaiʻi, just outside Hilo, are several good intermediate waves. Richardson Ocean Park (p173) is a slow-moving reef break that's great for learning, and just north of town is Honoliʻi (p173), a fast left and right peak breaking into a river mouth. Further up the Hamakua Coast is Waipiʻo Bay (p161), and while access to myriad beaches requires a long walk or a 4WD vehicle, the waves and scenery are worth the effort.

Top bodyboarding and bodysurfing spots include Hapuna Beach (p117), White Sands Beach (p57) and the beaches at Kekaha Kai State Park.

Jake Howard is a senior writer at Surfer *magazine and lives in San Clemente, CA*

Richardson Ocean Park is Hilo's best beach, replete with lava-rock swimming holes   GREG ELMS

to April during their 6000-mile round-trip migration between Alaska and Hawaii – one of the longest of any of Earth's creatures (except maybe traveling Aussies). Over 60% of the North Pacific humpback population winters here, so you'll have a good chance of seeing their acrobatics on a cruise or even from shore – don't forget binoculars. For boat tours, everyone agrees Captain Dan McSweeney (p61), with years of specialized research and experience, is the man. Another option is Fair Wind (p59). A three-hour tour costs around $75.

WINDSURFING

Wimpy wind, coupled with the higher adrenaline offered by kitesurfing means pickings are slim for windsurfing here. The best area is 'Anaeho'omalu Bay (p107), where wind consistently funnels down from Waimea; lessons and equipment are available. Winter storms bring winds from 18 to 35 knots and things get a little more exciting when the 'Kona winds' kick up in spring; novices are warned off at that time.

ON LAND

Hawai'i has 11 of the world's 13 ecosystems, filled with exotic flora and fauna waiting to be seen by the likes of you. If hiking gets you high, you'll likely overdose here. While coming down, you can horseback ride, snowboard (yes, in Hawaii! See p147), cycle or stargaze. First, though, check the weather (☎ 961-5582), since variable conditions and road closures can foil the plans of even the most gung ho.

CAVING

Strap on a head lamp, limber up and you're good to go. Once again, the Big Island has some of the world's best, with six of the 10 longest lava tubes in the world and many still 'sleeping' (yet to be explored). In Puna you can explore parts of the Kazumura Cave (see the box on p196), the world's longest lava tube, and in Ka'u, the Kula Kai

MEN OF STEEL, WOMEN OF TITANIUM

When thousands of athletes and fans swoop into Kailua each October (second Saturday), locals gripe about traffic and crowds. But nobody can deny the awesome spectacle of the Ford **Ironman Triathlon World Championship** (☎ 329-0063; www.ironman.com/worldchampionship). The granddaddy of triathlons is a grueling combination of a 2.4-mile ocean swim, 112-mile bike race and 26.2-mile run. And it all has to be done in 17 hours. Belgian Luc Van Lierde set the current men's record at eight hours and four minutes in 1996, while the women's record, set by Paula Newby-Fraser of the USA in 1992, is eight hours and 55 minutes.

Harsh *kona* (leeward) conditions make the event the ultimate endurance test. Heat bouncing off the lava commonly exceeds 100°F, making dehydration and heat exhaustion major challenges. Many contenders arrive weeks before the race just to acclimatize. On race day, over 5500 volunteers line the 140-mile course to hand out 26,000 gallons of fluid to the world's toughest athletes pushed to the max – this includes a 76-year-old nun, an Iraq war veteran amputee and other superhumans.

Begun in 1978 by Navy SEALS on a dare, the Ironman was labeled 'lunatic' by *Sports Illustrated*. A few years later, the lead athlete crawled to the finish line, but lost by a few seconds. With that drama, the sports world was hooked. Today the event draws up to 2000 athletes from over 50 countries. Whaddya win if you win? Who cares? It's all about the challenge (and the bragging rights).

Caverns (p239) await. For something extra special, you can take the secret lava tube tour in Hawai'i Volcanoes National Park (p219) – if you're lucky (tours are limited to 12 people per week).

CYCLING & MOUNTAIN BIKING

Road cycling is tricky here, with narrow roads sporting lava-lined or (worse?) no shoulders. The Ironman route on Hwy 19 north of Kailua-Kona is an exception. Mountain biking Hawai'i Volcanoes National Park's Escape Rd is forested and fun, and the Puna Triangle (Hwys 132, 130 and 137) is remarkable for its natural and human elements. If you're down South Point way, you can rock hop to Green Sands Beach. Established routes include the beautiful, but tough Waimea–Hawi trip over the Kohala Mountains (21.5 miles) and the 6.5-mile beach trail to Pine Trees (p98) on the Kona Coast.

For rentals, head to Hilo (p190) or Kailua-Kona (p71). The following organizations offer tours and information:

Inside the Kula Kai Caverns in Ka'u   GREG ELMS

Big Island Mountain Bike Association (☎ 961-4452) Trail descriptions and maps from Hilo-based organization.
Big Island Race & Training Schedule (www.big islandraceschedule.com) For volunteering, joining a ride or exploring independently, this is the go-to source.
🌿 **Common Circle Expeditions** (☎ 503-239-8426; www.commoncircle.com) Low-impact Big Island cycling trips from this Oregon-based outfit rate high with participants.
Orchid Isle Bicycling (☎ 327-0087, 800-219-2324; www.orchidislebicycling.com) Kona outfit with tours through the Kohala Mountains, to South Point and more.
People's Advocacy for Trails Hawaii (☎ 936-4653; www.pathhawaii.org) Nonprofit cyclist organization with online islandwide bike routes.

GOLF

We're with Samuel Clemens on this one: golf is a good walk spoiled (not to mention the environment), but it's undeniably one helluva popular game. If it's yours, never fear: the Big Island boasts over 20 golf courses, including world-class links at the South Kohala resorts. For local flavor, try the Hilo Municipal Golf Course (p179). If you like your greens truly green, go to the eco-friendlier links at Mauna Lani Bay Hotel & Bungalows (p113). Ask about discounts – greens fees are usually slashed by

Top Picks
BEACHES FOR KIDS
■ **Manini'owali** (Kua Bay; p99)
■ **Kikaua Beach** (p100)
■ **Makalawena's keiki pool** (p99)
■ **Kauna'oa Bay** (Mauna Kea Beach; p116)
■ **Hapuna Beach** (p117)
■ **Onekahakaha Beach Park** (p173)

50% if you take an afternoon tee time. For course descriptions and book-ahead tee times for a dozen courses, check out www.teetimeshawaii.com.

HELICOPTER & AIRPLANE TOURS

There's something to be said for the bird's-eye view. Especially when you're gazing upon the world's most active volcano, plus live lava and gushing waterfalls. These tours (see below for operators) aren't cheap, but it's all about the memories, right? Although helicopter tours are what's hyped, fixed-wing planes offer a smoother, quieter ride; have the fuel capacity to circle the island; and are less expensive. Still, the

HELICOPTER & AIRPLANE TOURS

Company	Tours	List prices	Extras
our pick Blue Hawaiian (☎ 961-5600, 800-786-2583; www.bluehawaiian.com)	Circle island, Kohala Coast, volcanoes & waterfalls, Big Island & Maui	per person $178-430	Eco-Star helicopter has more room & visibility; only departure from Waikoloa
our pick Island Hoppers (☎ 329-0018, 800-538-7590; www.iolaniair.com)	Volcanoes & waterfalls, volcano sunset, circle island, flight lessons	tours $150-290, 1hr flight lesson $230	Flies 3- & 6-passenger planes; every seat has a 360-degree view; Japanese-speaking pilot available; flies from Hilo & Kona
Paradise Helicopters (☎ 866-876-7422; www.paradisecopters.com)	Volcanoes & waterfalls (with doors-off option), volcano & valley landing, Hawaii experience	$180-477	Unique doors-off option & valley landing; only 5 of 6 are window seats
Safari Helicopters (☎ 969-1259, 800-326-3356; www.safarihelicopters.com)	Volcano, volcano deluxe	$135-151	Skylight provides vertical waterfall views
Sunshine Helicopters (☎ 270-3999, 866-501-7738; www.sunshinehelicopters.com)	Volcano, volcano deluxe	$200, $430	Also offers helicopter & snorkel packages
Tropical Helicopters (☎ 961-6810, 866-961-6810; www.tropicalhelicopters.com)	Volcano, volcanoes & waterfalls (with doors-off option)	custom charters from $142	Flies from Hilo & Kona; flies 4- & 6-passenger helicopters

Big Island trails cross stark lava fields, lush valleys and coastal beaches

GREG ELMS

allure of some 'doors-off' helicopter tours is undeniable. Either way, these tours are an excellent way for travelers (including those with disabilities) to experience Hawai'i's grandeur.

Standard helicopter volcano/waterfall tours are 45 minutes; circle-island tours are two hours. If you're lava-chasing, volcano tours are cheaper from Hilo than Kona. The best photography opportunities are on later afternoon flights – wear a dark shirt to cut down on window glare. Check out what type of aircraft your tour flies, how many window seats there are, if there are two-way headsets (so you can hear and talk to the pilot) and the outfit's safety record. Weather is a factor, so wait for a crystal-clear day if you can. Most outfits offer on-line discounts.

HIKING & CAMPING

From an afternoon stroll through a lava tube to a multiday summit attempt, the Big Island has all flavors of superlative hiking. Hit the trail and you'll be best able to appreciate the abundance of ecosystems.

Obviously, Hawai'i Volcanoes National Park has the widest variety of hiking. Don't miss the half-day Kilauea Iki Trail (p218), which crosses the steaming crater floor. For views, the short Pu'u Huluhulu (p216) hike is a winner. With more time, check out backcountry camping in the park's coastal shelters (p223), the arduous Observatory Trail (p220) to Mauna Loa's summit or the equally taxing Mauna Kea Summit Trail (p146).

The short knee-quaker into Waipi'o Valley (p161) should be on everyone's itinerary, but for a different angle, try the Kohala Forest Reserve Trail (p135) to the valley's topside. A bigger commitment (for bigger payoff) is needed to reach remote Waimanu Valley (p162), beyond Waipi'o.

North of Kailua-Kona, you can hike in from the highway to secluded beaches (try Makalawena; p99) or explore petroglyph

RESPONSIBLE HIKING

To help preserve the ecology and beauty of the Big Island, consider the following when hiking. For all you cynics, yes, we practice what we preach (including the toilet paper business).

Trash

■ Carry out *all* your trash, including (and especially) cigarette butts, orange peels and plastic wrappers. Make an effort to carry out garbage left by others. Burning garbage is discouraged.

■ Never bury your trash: digging disturbs soil, encourages erosion and can attract feral animals (cats, pigs), thereby contributing to an unhealthy ecological cycle.

■ Pack out sanitary napkins, tampons, condoms and toilet paper. Yucky, but necessary.

Human Waste Disposal

■ Contamination of water sources by human waste can lead to the transmission of all sorts of nasties such as Hepatitis B, which resulted in the closure of the Waipi'o Valley campground. Where there's a toilet, use it. Where there is none, bury your business. Dig a small hole 6in deep and at least 320ft from any watercourse. Cover the waste with soil and a rock. In snow, dig down to the soil.

■ The jury is split on urinating in the ocean; we say only if absolutely necessary, such as on an extended sea kayaking trip.

Washing

■ Don't use detergents or toothpaste in or near watercourses, even if they're biodegradable.

■ For personal washing, use biodegradable soap and a water container at least 160ft away from the watercourse. Disperse the waste water widely to allow the soil to filter it fully.

■ Wash cooking utensils 160ft from watercourses using a scourer, sand or snow instead of detergent.

Erosion

■ Hillsides and mountain slopes, especially at high altitudes, are prone to erosion. Stick to existing trails and avoid shortcuts.

■ If a well-used trail passes through a mud patch, walk through the mud so as not to increase the size of the patch.

■ Avoid removing the plant life that keeps topsoils in place. Likewise, don't pick any flora, including 'ohelo berries.

Fires & Low-Impact Cooking

■ Most Big Island campsites prohibit open fires for cooking. Instead, cook on a lightweight kerosene, alcohol or white-gas stove, and avoid those powered by disposable butane gas canisters.

■ Fruits, grains and canned foods are good alternatives to cooking. Just be sure to pack out what you pack in.

Wildlife Conservation

■ Don't buy items made from endangered species, including tortoiseshell, coral and 'opihi (limpets) smaller than 1.5in in diameter (it is illegal to collect 'opihi smaller than this size).

■ Don't feed the nene (native Hawaiian geese) and drive carefully in areas they frequent, such as the parking lots sprinkled around Crater Rim Dr in Hawai'i Volcanoes National Park.

■ Discourage the presence of wildlife by not leaving food scraps behind and tying packs to rafters or trees.

■ Certain fishing grounds, such as those east of Halape campground in Hawai'i Volcanoes National Park, are off-limits to everyone except 'Native Hawaiian residents and visitors under their direct guidance.'

Camping & Walking on Private Property

■ Observe *kapu* (technically 'prohibited' but universally understood as 'no trespassing') signs when hiking. Residents of Waipi'o Valley are particularly sensitive about this.

■ Always seek permission to camp from landowners.

fields near Puako (p112). For trail maps to hikeable sections of the coastal Ala Kahakai (a National Historic Trail), plus other possibilities, consult **Na Ala Hele** (☎ 974-4382; www .hawaiitrails.org).

For tours, try these recommended outfits:

🌿 **Big Island Moku Loa Group** (☎ 965-5460; www .hi.sierraclub.org/Hawaii/outings.html; suggested donation for nonmembers $3)

🌿 **Hawai'i Forest & Trail** (☎ 331-8505, 800-464-1993; www.hawaii-forest.com) These folks penetrate remote spots including Hakalau Forest Wildlife Refuge and off-limits Mt Hualalai.

🌿 **Hawaiian Walkways** (☎ 775-0372, 800-457-7759; www.hawaiianwalkways.com)

Hawai'i is a stellar camping destination, with facilities of all types sprinkled around the island, from A-frame cabins at Hapuna Beach (p117) to campsites in native forest at Kalopa State Recreation Area (p163). In Hawai'i Volcanoes National Park, you'll find some of the island's most picturesque camping (we like the coastal sites from 'Apua Point to Ka'aha). Technically, you need permits to camp at county, state and certain private sites (see p273).

You can buy all your supplies on-island – Wal-Mart in Kailua-Kona has a good selection, but for professional gear, from topographical maps to backpacks, Hawai'i Forest & Trail (p148) is the ticket.

Hiking Safety

You don't have to worry about snakes, wild animals or poison ivy here. What you *do* have to worry about is lava – from ankle-twisting 'a'a (slow-flowing rough and jagged lava) and toxic fumes to collapsing lava benches and hellishly hot conditions. Heed all posted warnings and hike with a buddy.

Flash floods are a real danger in many of the steep, narrow valleys that require stream crossings (yes, including Waipi'o). Warning signs include a distant rumbling, the smell of fresh earth and a sudden increase in the river's current. If the water begins to rise, get to higher ground immediately. Walking sticks are good for steadying yourself and testing river depths; look for them at trailheads.

Island Insights

Can I camp at Kolekole? Is there potable water at Miloli'i? A pool at Pahala? How do I get a camping permit? Get answers to these questions and more about island-wide county park facilities at www.hawaii -county.com/parks/parks.htm.

Darkness falls fast once the sun sets and ridge-top trails are no place to be caught unprepared in the dark. *Always* carry a flashlight just in case (good for exploring lava tubes, too). Long pants offer nettle and sun protection, and sturdy, ankle-high footwear with good traction is a must. If you plan to hike the summits, you'll need to prepare for winter mountaineering conditions. Pack 2L of water per person for a day hike, carry a whistle and something bright to alert rescue workers, wear sunscreen, tote a first-aid kit and, above all, start out early.

HORSEBACK RIDING

In addition to deep blue waters and red-hot lava, the Big Island has rolling green pastures where *paniolo* (cowboys) wrangle cattle and rodeo time. Up in North Kohala and Waimea especially, you can arrange trail rides, cattle drives and customized tours. Prices range from $60 for a 1½-hour beginner's ride to $160 for a four-hour cross-the-plains odyssey. For tours in Waimea, see p131; in North Kohala, p126; and in Waipi'o Valley, p163.

RUNNING

Ancient Hawai'i was big on running, with sprinters and long-distance runners trained since childhood for *kukini* – foot racing. The Big Island has taken the tradition to the next level with the famous Ironman Triathlon held each October (see the box on p34).

The craters and calderas of Hawai'i Volcanoes National Park make a unique running circuit. The Kilauea Volcano Wilderness Runs organized by the **Volcano Art Center** (www.volcanoartcenter.org) are a terrific way to get in on the action.

SPAS

Healing and wellness are virtually synonymous with Hawai'i, where traditional lomilomi massage (a rhythmic elbow action combined with prayer), Reiki, herbal scrubs, plus more intense treatments, including sweat baths and ayurvedic medicine, are available.

For an array of traditional treatments, try Hale Ho'ola in Volcano (p91), especially after a grueling hike. Stargazing from one of the soaking tubs at Kealakekua's Mamalahoa Hot Tubs & Massage (p84) is absolutely divine, as are the $30, one-hour massages at Akalani (p84), the local massage school. Of course, the top Kohala Coast resorts also have fabulous on-site spas, especially Spa Without Walls (p113) and Mauna Lani Spa (p113).

STARGAZING

From atop Mauna Kea, where international superpowered telescopes are trained on the heavens, scientists explore our universe. You can too, either on Mauna Kea itself with the eye-opening nightly stargazing program (p145) or, if you're more a DIYer, lying under the stars with the monthly star chart published by the **Ka'u Calendar** (www .kaucalendar.com).

TENNIS

There are some 40 municipal courts on the Big Island with fresh nets and night lighting. Call the **Department of Parks & Recreation** (☎ 961-8740) for a list of public tennis courts. Also, many of the large hotels allow nonguests to rent court time.

YOGA

A beautiful, centering place to practice your downward-facing dog and *pranayama* (breath control), the Big Island has everything from drop-in yoga classes to week-long retreats. There are studios all over, but we especially like the long-standing Big Island Yoga Center (p84) in Kealakekua, Yoga Centered and Balancing Monkey (p179) in Hilo, and Kona Yoga (p62) in Kailua-Kona.

Hiking the steaming Kilauea Iki Trail in Hawai'i Volcanoes National Park   CONNER GORRY

GREEN
BIG ISLAND

The saturated greens of Waipi'o

Valley, Kilauea's red-hot lava, and those Kona Coast blues: this island is that *Wizard of Oz* moment when your screen bursts into color – suddenly Dorothy's dress is blue and white, and the yellow brick road is just that. It's beautiful, theatrical, but something evil lurks…

On vivid-as-Oz Hawai'i, lurking evils include competing priorities, population growth and invasive species. Meanwhile, the infrastructure slowly decays, and dependency on imports and tourism sketches a volatile scenario beholden to world markets and the weather. What's a little (big) island to do?

Raise standards, awareness and some hell. All is afoot here, with various projects underway, from the statewide Hawaii 2050 Sustainability Plan (drafted in 2007; www.hawaii2050.org) to the grassroots Big Island Reef Fund (www.malama-kai.org/birf/index.htm). Being green here means both ecological and cultural conservation, and you'll find ample opportunity to participate in both. Fortunately, stewardship of natural and cultural resources is a pillar of Native Hawaiian philosophy, reflected in *aloha 'aina* – that simple, yet profound, love of the land.

THE BIG ISLAND GOES GREEN

Historically, two factors are responsible for the lion's share of Hawai'i's environmental woes: land use and invasive species. The most controversial, land use pits stakeholders against each other in an ongoing battle that dates back centuries. What's ironic is that all sides claim to share the same mission: doing what's best for the island.

The military and big business (tourism) argue their presence brings employment, which it does, and mightily. Many activists counter: what kind of jobs and at what cost? Furthermore, say Native Hawaiians and like-minded allies, the lands appropriated by these two economic giants are usually the

❁ SUSTAINABLE ICON

It seems like everyone's going 'green' these days, but how can you know which Big Island businesses are genuinely eco-friendly and which are simply jumping on the sustainable bandwagon? Throughout the book, this Sustainable icon indicates listings that we are highlighting because they demonstrate an active sustainable-tourism policy. Some are involved in conservation or environmental education, while others maintain and preserve Hawaiian identity and culture, and many are owned and operated by local and indigenous operators. For quick reference, these listings are compiled in the GreenDex (p303).

most productive, sacred, endangered or a combination. And these industries tend to leave deep, sometimes indelible, imprints – detection of depleted uranium (DU) at the Pohakuloa Training Area in August 2007 is a case in point. Like the Superferry and Wal-Mart expansion, DU is a hot-button issue on the island.

Whether it's plants, bugs or animals (some append tourists to the list), as a self-contained ecosystem, Hawaii is extraordinarily vulnerable to invasive species. Taken together, alien species enter the state at a rate that's two million times faster than what occurs naturally, causing millions of dollars in annual losses. Things are so bad, the US Office of Technology Assessment declared Hawaii's alien species problem the worst in the country (this means you, coqui frog!).

Intolerable (for Hawai'i) traffic, wild land speculation and resource depletion are also ingredients in the island's cultural-environmental pressure cooker. Finding ways to let the steam escape – while balancing environmental protection, Native Hawaiian rights and economic interests – is critical for the island's survival. Luckily survival is part of the vernacular here: already 20% of Hawai'i's power (that's 25 to 30 megawatts) is geothermal, and the Slow Food Movement, aquaculture and permaculture, emphasizing locally grown products, are gaining traction at lightning speed. Agritourism is also hot. Restricting road use to

ease traffic, a burgeoning recycling program and conserving more land (Hawai'i Volcanoes National Park recently purchased 116,000 acres, and the Place of Refuge more than doubled in size) are all in the green mix here.

Working together, the government, NGOs, local conservation organizations, communities and individuals have successfully protected some of the largest swaths of native ecosystems in the state. Top places to get intimate with the work of these green stewards include Hawai'i Volcanoes National Park (p205), Pu'uhonua o Honaunau ('Place of Refuge'; p91), Kealakekua Bay (p86), Kona Cloud Forest Sanctuary (p56) and the Amy BH Greenwell Ethnobotanical Garden (p84).

The Sierra Club (www.hi.sierraclub.org/Hawaii/outings.html; donation for nonmembers $3) has killer outings, including full-moon kayaking in Hilo and mountain biking on Mauna Kea. Birders will want to check out field trips offered by the Hawaii Audubon Society (www.hawaiiaudubon.com/trips.html). To donate sweat equity, you can volunteer to count turtles or work on an organic farm (p47). Patronizing businesses listed by the Hawaii Ecotourism Association (www.hawaiiecotourism.org), such as the award-winning Hawai'i Forest & Trail (p148) with its unique adventures deep into the island's supremely pristine pockets, is another way to go green here.

SUSTAINABLE BIG ISLAND

Environmentalist ideologues should travel elsewhere: the fuel alone used to jet here will compromise your commitment (carbon offsetting schemes notwithstanding). From gas-guzzling 4WDs to helicopter rides, as a

Island Insights

Genetically modified organism (GMO) research is a tinderbox issue here, with farmers and activists tangling with politicians and business interests. *Kalo* (taro) farmers, especially, are fighting for strict regulation as part of the Save Haloa movement. To learn all you need to know (and probably more!), visit www.kahea.org/gmo.

Symbolic of Hawaii, the green sea turtle (*honu*) is a protected species

destination, Hawai'i is a resource-sucker – no point in greenwashing it – but there *are* many ways to contribute to (or at least not damage) the ecological and cultural health of the island.

You're headed to explore land pulsing with mana (spiritual essence), where spells were cast, humans were roasted and hula was born. A Hawaiian adventure goes beyond erupting volcanoes and 400ft waterfalls, and learning a little something about Hawaiian culture will greatly enrich your experiences. Luckily, the renaissance in native culture means you can weave a lei (see Kalaekilohana, p237), see the planet's best hula at the Merrie Monarch Festival (see the box on p182) or learn about wayfinding at the 'Imiloa Astronomy Center (p176). Traditional culture comes alive at sacred heiau (ancient stone temples), including Mo'okini Luakini (p122), one of Hawai'i's most revered in North Kohala. Outside Kailua-Kona, Kaloko-Honokohau National Historical Park (p97) is an amazing example of Hawaiian ingenuity.

Then there's aloha – the spirit-philosophy that at its core is a humanistic, harmonic way of being. Letting a car pull out in front of you elicits a *shaka* (the universal sign of thanks in Hawaii), and the next time you're fighting to merge into traffic someone will probably let you in, in a self-perpetuating,

good karma cycle. As a visitor to Hawai'i, you become part of that cycle. Soon you'll be bagging groceries for a young mom or helping an older gentleman from the curb. Keeping that good vibe going is part of responsible travel here; to get into the spirit, tune to KAPA 100.3FM. If you're lucky, some of that aloha will go home with you.

Striking a balance between fun and responsible, minimizing your impact and finding ways to give back to the land are keys to the approach. Protecting Hawai'i's land and culture is a process that begins with respect. Lead, follow or get out of the way.

ON THE GROUND

Unfortunately, being green is kind of like being communist: it's great in theory, but gets tricky in practice. Here are some ideas to bring the ideal closer to reality.

Since Big Island buses are as rare as hoary bats, a rental car is the way to go. Opt for a compact car and the environment (and your wallet) will thank you. Although determined cyclists and hitchhikers can get around by pedal or thumb, neither is for the risk averse. Common Circle Expeditions' low-impact bicycle tours (p34) are a recommended alternative. Alternative energy is all the rage at progressive B&Bs, such as the completely solar-powered Waianuhea B&B (p157), proving that luxury and ecology aren't mutually exclusive. At the other end of the spectrum is off-the-grid lodging (no public electricity or water), where a gentle imprint is the point, such as the rustic Ohana House Rural Retreat (p240). Getting intimate with Mother Nature is easy with a tent; top camping spots include Waimanu Valley (p162) and Halape (p221). It's hard to make a green case for resorts, with their golf courses and dry cleaners, but Mauna Lani Bay Hotel & Bungalows (p114) leads the green pack by a mile.

Walking the walk *and* talking the talk means considering carefully how you do what you do here. Many enthusiasts wax environmental about swimming with dolphins in captivity ('the dolphins seem pretty happy'), but are you convinced? The dolphin issue is contentious, as more folks learn where they hang out and are eager to commune with them in the wild, posing a possible threat to their habitat. Horseback riding, hiking, kayaking, surfing and snorkeling are all low-impact, high-excitement alternatives on the Big Island.

A key component of sustainability is personal responsibility (*ho'okuleana* in Hawaiian). First, conserve water: turn off the tap when shaving or brushing your teeth. If your hotel offers to wash linens only when requested instead of daily, jump on it; if it doesn't, ask the staff to implement this easy conservation measure. Individual bottles of water are hell on the planet; take your own water bottle and refill instead. Buying local is an effective way to sustain the local

ISLAND VOICES

NAME: JESSE LAW
OCCUPATION: FOUNDER, SUSTAINABLE ISLAND PRODUCTS
RESIDENCE: HILO

It's brilliant: 100% compostable packaging and tableware. Why did you start this business here? I was looking for something that could function as a solution to an existing problem. Per capita, Hawaii is the largest consumer of 'to go' packaging in the country and 30% of this island's landfill is packaging. There's a landfill crisis here – Hilo is overflowing, Kona is almost full.

So it's about garbage. That's what gets people talking. But the case I'm making is for zero waste. This packaging can be locally manufactured, locally used and locally reprocessed into a reusable resource. We can employ people to grow and process the sugarcane for it. In 30 days, this clamshell box is composted. These spoons are roach food.

But are people willing to pay more for it? People love it! They're acutely aware that we're on an island and want alternatives to landfills, shipping garbage off-island and incinerators – the newest proposal. We're seeing people choosing businesses using this packaging over others that don't. I'm a firm believer that the market will drive this.

What can travelers do to minimize their impact on the Big Island? Bring a reusable dining set – it's as easy as a pair of chopsticks, a plate and a cup. Some places even give you a discount for using your own. Support farmers markets and the local economy. Keep it local. People say 'it's cheaper at Wal-Mart,' but it's not. When you do a true cost assessment of the health and environmental costs, it's not cheaper.

economy – think Main St instead of Wal-Mart, farmers market instead of supermarket. Look for the Mountain Apple Brand, denoting local products, sold in all KTA Super Stores. Products labeled with 'Island Fresh' or the 'Hawaii Seal of Quality' are also local. At the very least, read *50 Simple Things You Can Do to Save Hawai'i*, by Gail L Grabowsky.

HELPFUL ORGANIZATIONS

Hawaii is one of the world's most eco-conscious destinations, thanks in part to the work of many organizations, including the following:

Big Island Reef Fund (www.malama-kai.org/birf/index.htm) Part of CCN.

Community Conservation Network (CCN; ☎ 528-3700; www.conservationpractice.org) CCN promotes responsible use of ocean resources through traditional fishing and stewardship practices.

Hawaii Ecotourism Association (HEA; ☎ 877-300-7058; www.hawaiiecotourism.org) HEA's *Green Travel Directory* lists over 700 eco-responsible businesses exhibiting environmental and cultural stewardship.

Hawaii Organic Farmers Association (HOFA; ☎ 969-7789; www.hawaiiorganicfarmers.org) This certification agency is the go-to organic source. Get proactive with its apprenticeship program (free room and board!) and *Organics Product Directory*.

Kahea – The Hawaiian-Environmental Alliance (www.kahea.org; PO Box 270112, Honolulu, HI 96827) Activist organization dedicated to protecting Mauna Kea, preventing genetic engineering, monitoring depleted uranium and other issues. Check its links for valuable resources.

Nature Conservancy of Hawaii (☎ 885-1786; www.nature.org) Explore limited-access areas on its tours.

Sierra Club (☎ 965-5460; www.hi.sierraclub.org) This green-movement giant keeps the bulldozers at bay, fights invasive species and scrutinizes the military's enviro-compliance.

Slow Food Hawai'i Convivium (☎ 885-6085; www.slowfoodhawaii.org) Online 'Slow Food's Guide to Hawai'i Island Grown Food' is handy.

Hawai'i is home to the world's only known blonde, blue-eyed zebra

ENVIRONMENT

Geologically speaking, the Big Island is like a small child – young, growing and rambunctious. This enviable state is largely due to mighty Kilauea, Hawaii's only currently erupting volcano. Calling this baby active is like calling David Blaine deft: Kilauea has generated more than 2.5 billion cubic yards of lava since the eruption began in 1983 and probably won't quit anytime soon (not before your trip, anyway). The lava oozing from Kilauea, which eventually hardens into rock or shatters into black grains to create those glorious beaches, has added over 600 acres to the island in the past 25 years. Here lava moves slowly, and usually at a safe distance; beholding the live flow under a starry sky is certain to be among your most indelible travel memories or your money back. Just kidding. What isn't a joke is the rates at which alien species are overtaking natives and resources are being depleted. Preserving the island's resources requires an ever-mindful relationship with the land, even if it's for a 10-day whirlwind or once-in-a-lifetime honeymoon.

THE LAND

Myth, science and motion meet in a mesmerizing tango on the Big Island, with plate tectonics, a geologic 'hot spot' and the goddess Pele conspiring to create a powerfully majestic landscape. The youngest of the Hawaiian Islands (and, of course, the biggest, with 4028 sq miles of land and some 250 miles of coastline), the Big Island is a cluster of seven volcanoes (five above sea level) at the end of a long volcanic chain made up of the state's main islands, plus the far-reaching Northwestern Hawaiian Islands (which were proclaimed the Papahānaumokuākea Marine National Monument in 2006). Each island was created when a column of rock some 2200 miles below the Earth's surface slowly began moving upward, eventually piercing the ocean's surface as a volcano. When that volcano passes over a hot spot due to plate tectonics, lava ensues. The Big Island is hovering over that hot spot as you read this. The next volcano slated to emerge

GET ENGAGED: VOLUNTEER OPPORTUNITIES

- **Hawai'i Forest & Trail** (www.hawaii-forest.com)
- **Hawai'i Volcanoes National Park** (www.nps.gov/havo/supportyourpark/volunteer.htm)
- **Hawai'i Wildlife Fund** (http://wildhawaii.org/volunteer.html)
- **Hawaii Organic Farmers Association Apprenticeship Program** (www.hawaiiorganicfarmers.org /appren.htm)
- **Kalani Oceanside Retreat** (www.kalani.com/community/volunteer/index.php)
- **Mauna Kea Volunteer Program** (www.ifa.hawaii.edu/info/vis)
- **Sierra Club Trail Service** (www.hi.sierraclub.org/Hawaii/outings.html)
- **The Nature Conservancy** (www.nature.org/wherewework/northamerica/states/hawaii/volunteer)
- **US Fish & Wildlife Service** (www.fws.gov/volunteers)
- **USGS Hawaiian Volcano Observatory** (http://hvo.wr.usgs.gov/volunteer)

from the ocean is the Lo'ihi Seamount: most experts agree it will take at least 30,000 years for the volcano to traverse the 900yd it still has to go. Plate tectonics also cause earthquakes, such as the 6.7 rocker that caused over $200 million in damage on October 15, 2006.

The sights, sounds and smells of this subterranean party are all around you on Hawai'i. If you've only a day, meander along Crater Rim Dr in Hawai'i Volcanoes National Park (p211) to behold the hardened lava flows pierced by steam vents belching malodorous sulfur. If the live lava is cooperating, you might see the glowing flow (see the box on p217). If not, get the aerial view on a helicopter tour (p35).

Can you imagine what that molten magma would do to a whole town? Travel deep into Puna to the former village of Kalapana (p203) to find out. But lava isn't all bad: consider the spectacular lava tubes

formed when the outermost layer of a lava river cools off and hardens. With six of the world's 10 longest lava tubes, including the Kazumura Cave (p196), the world's longest, the Big Island is renowned for these geological oddities.

WILDLIFE

The Big Island isn't a misnomer: Hawai'i has twice the land area of the other Hawaiian Islands combined, and 11 of the world's 13 climatic zones to go with it (more than Brazil!). This is where macho travelers nab bragging rights by snorkeling in the morning and snowboarding in the afternoon. So diverse is the island, its desert, montane and tropical forests, bogs and other ecosystems support the highest concentration of life-zone types on Earth.

Millions of years ago, the first spores and seeds arrived on the three Ws – wind, water and wings – to take root on the new volcanic island. Over time, more plants and animals washed up here so that today the island supports some 10,000 indigenous species. Many of them (insects, snails and other creepy crawlies) are the size of this upcoming comma, so don't get too excited. Stowaways in the canoes of the first settlers, and critters underneath the bark of giant logs that eventually ran aground here added to the mix.

While there are no monkeys or jungle cats to entice travelers to Hawai'i's shores, there are playful marine animals in abundance, endangered plants and bats, and even an animal sanctuary with the world's only known blonde, blue-eyed zebra (see the boxed text on p48).

Top Picks

THE GREEN PARTY

- Lova Lava Land eco-resort (p239)
- Sustainable Island Products (p44)
- Hawaii Gateway Energy Center (p98)
- Camping in Hawai'i Volcanoes National Park (p221)
- Apprenticing on an organic farm (above)
- East Hawai'i Cultural Center (p177)
- 'Imiloa Astronomy Center (p176)
- Kona Cloud Forest Sanctuary (p56)
- Tara Yoga Center (p165)

Animals

If you flew over on Hawaiian Airlines, you probably saw lots of in-flight footage of whales breaching and romping; now go for the real thing. Whale watching is not to be missed here during the winter calving of Pacific humpback whales (from mid-January to early April) – up to 10,000 pass through Hawaiian waters every season (see p32). Good bets are along the northwest coast, off Ka Lae (p237) or on a tour out of Honokohau Harbor (p61).

Any time of year off the Kona Coast you might see sperm, melon-headed, pilot and pygmy killer whales, plus rough-toothed, spotted, bottlenose or spinner dolphins. The last are particularly fun and frisky, but don't approach them since law and traveling best practices say you must stay 50yd away. You must also keep your distance from any hawksbill or green turtles you may encounter.

Recently the Hawaiian monk seal population has been rebounding and these mammals (the most endangered of any US marine mammal) have started visiting some of Hawai'i's more remote beaches to come ashore to sun themselves. Linger on the shores of Onomea Bay (p166) and you might get a lucky sighting.

Aside from birds and bugs, Hawai'i isn't known for its land wildlife, as animals such as mouflon sheep, feral cats, pigs and donkeys (the latter are lampooned as 'Kona nightingales' for their evening bray fests) have wreaked havoc on native flora and fauna. Some wilderness areas have a zero-tolerance policy for these beasts and their habitat destruction.

If you're into airborne animals, the Big Island has a lot to offer, including the only native Hawaiian land mammal, the 'ōpe'apēa (Hawaiian hoary bat). About the size of a *malasada,* this insect-eating bat roosts in trees during the day, swooping out at dusk to feed on moths and the like. This reddish-brown bat sometimes has pale hairs that give it a frosted, hoary look (hence the name).

If you're a birder, Hawai'i is likely already on your to-do list, since it's home to many species that can't be seen anywhere else. For a nice day hike, try one of the many hiking trails around Kilauea Volcano in the national park (p218), where you might catch sight of native forest birds, such as the

DR DO-A-LOT

Dr Dolittle talked to the animals. Dr Ann Goody communes with them, fixes their broken bones and psyches, coaxes them back into their natural behavior and sets them free. Or not – some rescued and exotic animals just can't cut it in the wild. That's when they become residents of the **Three Ring Ranch Exotic Animal Sanctuary** (www.threeringranch.org) on five lovely acres in upland Kona.

Licensed by the US Department of Agriculture and accredited by the American Association of Sanctuaries (the only sanctuary in the state and one of only 38 nationally with this distinction), Three Ring currently hosts South African crowned cranes, lesser flamingos, David and Goliath (a pair of gigantic African spur thigh tortoises) and much more, including native endangered species such as the Hawaiian owl. Like the very best mentors, healers and caretakers, it's clear Dr Goody doesn't play favorites, but zebra Zoe is something special: rescued from the failed Moloka'i Ranch Safari Park, Zoe has 'amelanosis,' meaning her stripes are the color of Hapuna Beach sand and her eyes the color of the water.

Dr Goody – who has been struck by lightning, tossed by a shark and is a breast cancer survivor – is as good with people as she is with animals. This, along with the unflagging support of her husband and business partner Dr Norm Goody, has led to enormously successful educational initiatives, including an after-school program, a resident intern program and a residency placement program for preveterinarian students (more competitive than medical residencies, it's a testament to the sanctuary's curriculum that it has successfully placed over a dozen residents). Since the sanctuary's primary commitment is to the animals, it generally isn't open for tours. But that could change; to get the latest, drop the good doctors an email at animals@3rr.org.

The ohia, the island's official flower

GREG ELMS

bright red *'apapane* and the green *'amakihi*. For these and rarer species, stroll the 1-mile loop hike through 'Bird Park' (p216).

Plants

Even in the plant world, there's tension between those who were here first and those who followed. And the latter have eclipsed the former: there are about 1200 native plants and ferns on the Big Island, but some 1500 non-native plants and they're all competing for the same limited resources, just like the humans around them. In densely populated areas such as Kailua-Kona and Hilo, the aliens dominate and you'll see all the flowering plants you'd see if you were in Havana or Burbank (bird of paradise, hibiscus, calla lily etc). But head up above 2000ft and it's a different story. Here's where the natives begin to take hold: whimsical tree ferns and the ubiquitous red puffs of the ohia tree, the island's official flower and symbol of Ku, the Hawaiian god of war and patron of the forest.

Near Mauna Kea, there's Pu'u Huluhulu (p150), a cinder cone of luxuriant forest in an otherwise sere lava setting. Here, mighty koa trees and red-blossomed ohia form a canopy over a mix of native shrubs, vines and ferns. Out on the lava flows, you'll also see low-lying shrubs bursting with what looks like a cranberry but is in fact the native *'ohelo* berry, delicious in jams or drizzled over ice cream. Climb higher, above 9000ft, and you'll behold distinctive flora providing the building blocks of the island's subalpine ecosystem, such as the yellow-flowered *mamane* tree, which is a food staple for the endangered *palila,* a Hawaiian honeycreeper. Be on the lookout for these and other natives, such as the tiny-leafed *pukiawe* shrub, with red, pink or white berries (ingested by ancient Hawai'i's high chiefs to nullify their power so they could relate to the hoi polloi) as you head up to Mauna Kea.

NATIONAL, STATE & COUNTY PARKS

About 13% of the Big Island is protected as national, state and county parks, with additional land set aside as nature and marine preserves, botanical gardens and more. National Wildlife Refuges (NWR; www.refugenet.org), such as the Hakalau Forest National Wildlife Refuge, due east of Mauna Kea and most easily accessed with Hawai'i Forest & Trail (p96), also afford protection for natural resources, from koa to endangered birds.

Different stakeholders hold different opinions on how or how much land should be protected, by whom and to what end. A case in point is the Cave Conservancy of Hawai'i, which set out to preserve the Kipuka-Kanohina cave system within which are the Kula Kai Caverns (p239), but met resistance from Native Hawaiians who felt the caves should remain untouched out of respect for their cultural heritage. Eventually consensus was reached to preserve the caves and draft Department of Land and Natural Resources statutes for further protection. Forging agreements such as these between multiple interests holds great possibilities for a sustainable future of Hawai'i's wilderness and parklands.

THE BIG ISLAND'S TOP PROTECTED AREAS

Whether you're looking to jump on the green bandwagon or are already driving it, you've come to the right place. The following are some of our favorite nature opportunities, good for a visit any time of year.

Nature Area	Features	Activities	Page
Ahalanui Beach Park	lava-rock hot pond	soaking, swimming	p210
Akaka Falls State Park	lush rain forest with two impressive waterfalls	walking	p165
Hapuna Beach State Recreation Area	white-sand beach	bodyboarding, camping, swimming	p117
Hawai'i Volcanoes National Park	vast lava landscape, active volcanoes, forest, petroglyphs, museum	sightseeing, hiking, camping	p205
Honoli'i Beach Park	consistent surf break near Hilo	surfing	p173
Kahalu'u Beach Park	underwater aquarium, lots of turtles	snorkeling, surfing	p71
Kealakekua Bay State Historical Park	abundant marine life in clear, protected waters	snorkeling, kayaking, diving	p86
Kekaha Kai State Park	remote beaches	swimming, bodysurfing, bodyboarding, kayaking, snorkeling, hiking	p99
Mauna Kea	Hawaii's highest peak, world-class astronomy site	stargazing, hiking	p137
Mo'okini Luakini Heiau	ruins of ancient sacrificial temple, spectacular view of horizon & Maui	hiking, whale watching	p122
Onekahakaha Beach Park	shallow waters, tide pools	swimming, exploring, picnicking	p173
Pololu Valley	mystical valley at island's northernmost tip	hiking	p127
Pu'uhonua o Honaunau National Historical Park	ancient Hawaiian 'place of refuge'	walking, snorkeling, sightseeing	p91
South Point	green-sand beach at USA's southernmost point	hiking, swimming, cliff jumping	p236
Waipi'o Valley	spectacularly lush valley, taro fields, waterfalls	hiking, surfing	p158

KAILUA-KONA

Talk about multiple personalities! Kailua-Kona
is foremost a quintessential tourist town, with a relentless lineup of coastal
condos, souvenir shops and sunburnt pleasure-seekers trolling for a meal or
a drink. Further upland, it's old-time Kona in Holualoa, an art mecca in the
cool, misty Coffee Belt. All the while, the natural beauty of Kailua Bay recalls its
original role as an idyllic retreat for Hawaiian royalty. To visitors, Kailua-Kona is a
sunny delight and a hub for ocean sports. To locals, it's now a sprawling suburb,
with pricey subdivisions blanketing the slopes of Mt Hualalai and nightmare
rush-hour traffic. In sum, it's either for you or it's not. Stop in to find out.

KAILUA-KONA
ITINERARIES

IN TWO DAYS *12 miles*

❶ KAHALU'U BEACH PARK (p71) Ease into 'Hawaiian time' at this crowded but beginner-friendly snorkeling beach teeming with tropical fish and *honu* (sea turtles).

❷ ALI'I DRIVE (p55) Afterward, stroll along lively Ali'i Dr, where you can sample mildly sedative kava at Kanaka Kava (p65) or indulge your sweet tooth with the best locally made ice cream (p64).

❸ HULIHE'E PALACE (p57) Wind down in the afternoon at this museum, once a royal retreat, where you can glimpse ancient artifacts such as King Kamehameha's personal war spears.

❹ FUJIMAMAS (p65) For dinner, scads of oceanfront restaurants will vie for your attention, but the coolest is this Asian-fusion hot spot. Also excellent, despite its shopping mall setting, is O's Bistro (p65), with eclectic Hawaii Regional Cuisine from dressed-up comfort food to vegetarian masterpieces.

❺ ISLAND LAVA JAVA (p64) The next morning, wake up to café culture, Kona style. Go early to snag a ringside people-watching seat.

❻ SOUVENIRS (p67) After breakfast, browse souvenirs along Ali'i Dr, which is chockablock full of gift shops. Alas, most specialize in touristy doodads. Instead, buy a cool, retro, genuine-logo tee at Destee Nation.

❼ HOLUALOA ART GALLERIES (p76) Cool off by heading upland to Holualoa, a historic coffee community, now home to art galleries. Plan to return on a Wednesday evening, so you can catch the *kanikapila* (jam session) at Holualoa Ukulele Gallery.

❽ KIMURA LAUHALA SHOP (p77) Stop for more souvenirs at this family-run shop. Handmade *lauhala* (pandanus leaf) crafts are ideal gifts: lightweight, useful and 100% Hawaiian.

❾ KONA COFFEE TASTING (p76) In the afternoon, wake up with free coffee samples offered by several plantations in Holualoa, the north end of the Kona Coffee Belt.

❿ GIANT MANTA RAYS (p59) After dark, the best nightlife is found underwater: giant manta rays! The waters off Kailua-Kona are notable for these mesmerizing creatures.

Handcrafted instruments at Holualoa Ukulele Gallery

GREG ELMS

FOR HAWAIIAN CULTURE

❶ HULIHE'E PALACE (p57) To learn about Hawaiian history, a good starting point is this palace and royal retreat.

❷ MOKU'AIKAUA CHURCH (p57) Across the street from the palace, visit the first Christian church in Hawaii.

❸ AHU'ENA HEIAU (p58) Compare the church with this replica of King Kamehameha's personal heiau (temple), where he worshipped in his last days. Highly recommended is the Kona Historical Society's **walking tour (p62)**.

❹ ANCIENT HAWAIIAN SITES & TIDE POOLS (p72) Although a large hotel now dominates the property, this area in Keauhou still has intact sites and a gorgeous tide pool, home to green sea turtles. Enjoy a leisurely stroll and drink at the **Verandah Lounge (p74)**.

❺ HOLUALOA (p75) A throwback to the old-time plantation days, this tiny village is now a well-known art community. **Ipu Hale Gallery (p76)** shows off the little-known ancient art of dyeing traditional designs on gourds.

❻ KONA CLOUD FOREST SANCTUARY (p56) Just 15 minutes from Kailua-Kona, this lush, jungly, 70-acre preserve shows the natural side of Kona. On a 3-mile walk, you'll see Hawaiian koa and ohia living harmoniously with palms and bamboo from around the world.

KAILUA-KONA

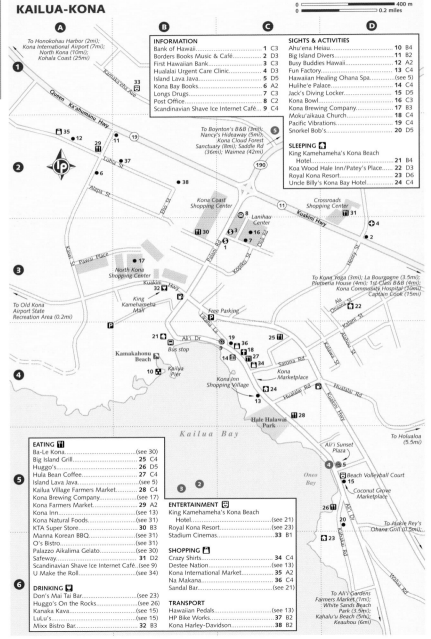

INFORMATION
Bank of Hawaii	**1**	C3
Borders Books Music & Café	**2**	D3
First Hawaiian Bank	**3**	C3
Hualalai Urgent Care Clinic	**4**	D5
Island Lava Java	**5**	D3
Kona Bay Books	**6**	A2
Longs Drugs	**7**	C3
Post Office	**8**	C2
Scandinavian Shave Ice Internet Café	**9**	C4

SIGHTS & ACTIVITIES
Ahu'ena Heiau	**10**	B4
Big Island Divers	**11**	B2
Busy Buddies Hawaii	**12**	A2
Fun Factory	**13**	C4
Hawaiian Healing Ohana Spa	(see 5)	
Hulihe'e Palace	**14**	C4
Jack's Diving Locker	**15**	D5
Kona Bowl	**16**	C3
Kona Brewing Company	**17**	B3
Moku'aikaua Church	**18**	C4
Pacific Vibrations	**19**	C4
Snorkel Bob's	**20**	D5

SLEEPING
King Kamehameha's Kona Beach Hotel	**21**	B4
Koa Wood Hale Inn/Patey's Place	**22**	D3
Royal Kona Resort	**23**	D6
Uncle Billy's Kona Bay Hotel	**24**	C4

To Honokohau Harbor (2mi);
Kona International Airport (7mi);
North Kona (10mi);
Kohala Coast (25mi)

Kamaka'eha Ave

Queen Ka'ahumanu Hwy

To Boynton's B&B (3mi);
Nancy's Hideaway (5mi);
Kona Cloud Forest
Sanctuary (8mi); Saddle Rd
(36mi); Waimea (42mi)

190

Luhia St

Alapa St

Eho St

Palani Rd

Kona Coast
Shopping Center

Lanihau
Center

Kuakini Hwy

Crossroads
Shopping Center

Kaiwi

Pawai Place

North Kona
Shopping Center

Kuakini

King
Kamehameha
Mall

Hwy

To Kona Yoga (3mi); La Bourgogne (3.5mi);
Plumeria House (4mi); 1st Class B&B (4mi);
Kona Community Hospital (10mi);
Captain Cook (15mi)

Ala
Onaona St

Kalani St

To Old Kona
Airport State
Recreation Area (0.2mi)

Free Parking

Kuakini Hwy

Henry St

Kaiwa St

Ali'i Dr

Bus stop

Alahou St

Kamakahonu
Beach

Kailua
Pier

Kona Inn
Shopping Village

Sarona Rd

Kona
Marketplace

Hualalai Rd

Hualalai Rd

Kuakini Hwy

Hale Halawai
Park

Kailua Bay

To Holualoa
(5.5mi)

Ali'i Sunset
Plaza

Oneo
Bay

Beach Volleyball Court

Coconut Grove
Marketplace

EATING
Ba-Le Kona	(see 30)	
Big Island Grill	**25**	C4
Huggo's	**26**	D5
Hula Bean Coffee	**27**	C4
Island Lava Java	(see 5)	
Kailua Village Farmers Market	**28**	C4
Kona Brewing Company	(see 17)	
Kona Farmers Market	**29**	A2
Kona Inn	(see 13)	
Kona Natural Foods	(see 31)	
KTA Super Store	**30**	B3
Manna Korean BBQ	(see 31)	
O's Bistro	(see 31)	
Palazzo Aikalima Gelato	(see 30)	
Safeway	**31**	D2
Scandinavian Shave Ice Internet Café	(see 9)	
U Make the Roll	(see 34)	

ENTERTAINMENT
King Kamehameha's Kona Beach Hotel	(see 21)	
Royal Kona Resort	(see 23)	
Stadium Cinemas	**33**	B1

SHOPPING
Crazy Shirts	**34**	C4
Destee Nation	(see 13)	
Kona International Market	**35**	A2
Na Makana	**36**	C4
Sandal Bar	(see 21)	

TRANSPORT
Hawaiian Pedals	(see 13)	
HP Bike Works	**37**	B2
Kona Harley-Davidson	**38**	B2

DRINKING
Don's Mai Tai Bar	(see 23)	
Huggo's On the Rocks	(see 26)	
Kanaka Kava	(see 15)	
LuLu's	(see 15)	
Mixx Bistro Bar	**32**	B3

To Ali'i Gardens
Farmers Market (1mi);
White Sands Beach
Park (3.5mi);
Kahalu'u Beach (5mi);
Keauhou (6mi)

To Jackie Rey's
Ohana Grill (0.5mi)

Ali'i Dr

Kuhakahi Rd

Walua Rd

0   400 m
0   0.2 miles

HIGHLIGHTS

❶ **BEST BEACH:** Kahalu'u Beach (p71)
❷ **BEST VIEW:** From a cruise ship (p58)
❸ **BEST ACTIVITY:** Manta ray night dive (p60)
❹ **BEST PEOPLE-WATCHING SPOT:** Island Lava Java (p64)
❺ **BEST ECO EXPERIENCE:** Kona Cloud Forest Sanctuary (p56)

Highlights are numbered on the maps on p54 and p72.

pop 10,000

HISTORY

Kamehameha the Great lived his last years in Kailua-Kona, worshipping at Ahu'ena Heiau, his own temple. Soon after his death in 1819, his son Liholiho broke an important *kapu* (taboo) by dining with women. He suffered no godly wrath, so when the first missionaries sailed into Kailua Bay in 1820, they easily converted the Hawaiians to Christianity.

In the 19th century, the town was a leisure retreat for Hawaiian royalty. Hulihe'e Palace (p57) was a favorite getaway for King David Kalakaua, a talented patron of the arts, including hula, music and literature.

Since the 1970s Kailua-Kona has been the island's economic powerhouse, fueled by tourism, retail and real estate. But Hilo is the governmental seat of the island and still tends to control public investments. Don't be surprised to hear Kailua-Kona folks griping about Hilo's ample road improvements in light of Kona's highway gridlock.

ORIENTATION

Kailua-Kona is located south of the airport along the Queen Ka'ahumanu Hwy (Hwy 19). The main entry road is Palani Rd. Note that the highway confusingly becomes the Kuakini Hwy (Hwy 11) at the intersection with Palani Rd. Note also that this highway connects with the historic Kuakini Hwy closer toward the ocean. In other words, for a short stretch, there are two Kuakini Hwys!

Ali'i Dr is Kailua's main tourist thoroughfare: the best pedestrian stretch starts at the north end and runs for a half-mile. From there, a seemingly endless row of condos lines the road for 5 miles to Keauhou. Near the highway, you'll find the everyday shopping malls and supermarkets popular with locals.

INFORMATION
Bookstores

Borders Books Music & Café (☎ 331-1668; 75-1000 Henry St, at Hwy 11; ⊙ 9am-9pm Sun-Thu, to 10pm Fri & Sat) Largest bookseller in Kailua-Kona, with many US and foreign newspapers.
Kona Bay Books (☎ 326-7790; www.konabaybooks .com; 74-5487 Kaiwi St; ⊙ 10am-6pm) Awesome selection of used books, CDs and DVDs, near Kona International Market.

Emergency

Police (☎ 935-3311) For nonemergencies.
Police, fire and ambulance (☎ 911) For emergencies.
Sexual Assault Hotline (☎ 935-0677)

Internet Access

Island Lava Java (☎ 327-2161; Ali'i Sunset Plaza, 75-5799 Ali'i Dr; per 20min $4; ⊙ 6am-10pm) Free wi-fi with purchase, plus three computers for paid access. Patio seating always packed, but avoid sweltering heat inside café.
Scandinavian Shave Ice Internet Café (☎ 331-1626; 75-5699 Ali'i Dr; per 15/60min $2.25/8; ⊙ 8am-9pm) Cavernous space next door to café (see p64).

Internet Resources

Big Island Visitors Bureau (www.bigisland.org) Basic info geared toward mainstream travelers; handy calendar of events.

Island Insights

Kailua was renamed Kailua-Kona so that the post office could distinguish it from another Kailua on O'ahu. While it's common to interchange Kailua-Kona, Kailua and Kona in casual conversation, be aware that the Kona region covers much more than just Kailua town.

KAILUA-KONA

KONA CLOUD FOREST SANCTUARY

🌿 our pick Escape the heat and head upland to Kaloko Mauka, a subdivision containing a spectacular botanical ecosystem unknown even to most locals. The **Kona Cloud Forest Sanctuary** (www.konacloudforest.com) is a privately owned 70-acre collection of plant species, both native (such as koa, ohia and *hapu'u*) and introduced (including spectacular palms, bromeliads, orchids, ferns and bamboo) from around the world. At 3000ft above sea level, the climate is cool and moist. Here, in a cloud forest, plants absorb moisture not only from rain (as in rain forests) but from mist and clouds.

Norm Bezona, the sanctuary director, is an expert on tropical horticulture and sustainable agriculture. Much of the Kaloko Mauka subdivision has already been destroyed by property owners who clear the land and add a cow to snag the agricultural-zone tax break. Bezona helped to establish a tax break for property owners who maintain their forestland instead of clearing it. When he leads tours for school kids, he asks them for a moment of silence to hear the birds, insects and other forest sounds in the vast, often-unseen ecological web.

To book a three-hour walking tour, contact **Hawaiian Walkways** (☎ 800-457-7759; www .hawaiianwalkways.com; adult/child $95/75; ☼ 8:30am-1pm). Guides are knowledgeable on botany and geology, and the tour ends with a visit to the adjacent **Mountain Thunder Coffee Plantation** (p76). Nonprofit groups, such as scouts, schools and environmental clubs, receive free tours, often given by Bezona himself. Wear sturdy shoes.

KonaWeb (www.konaweb.com) Founded in 1995 by Konabob and Shirley Stoffer, this homespun website provides condo listings, restaurant picks, webcam views and more.

Media

West Hawaii Today (www.westhawaii today.com) is Kailua-Kona's daily newspaper; also see the Hilo-based papers (p172). Due to the Big Island's size and mountainous terrain, West Hawai'i stations broadcast only in the vicinity. Often a station will simulcast shows at different frequencies on either side of the island. Check out http:// archive.hawaiiradiotv.com/HIRATV/Big IsleRadio.html for a complete listing.

KAGB 99.1FM (www.kaparadio.com) Traditional and contemporary island music.

KAOY 101.5FM (www.kwxx.com) Island and pop hits.

KKON 790AM ESPN sports.

KLEO 106.1FM (www.kbigfm.com) Contemporary pop hits.

KLUA 93.9FM (www.dabeatfm.com) Hawaii hits.

Medical Services

Hualalai Urgent Care Clinic (☎ 327-4357; 75-1028 Henry St; ☼ 8am-5pm Mon-Fri, 9am-5pm Sat) For nonemergency medical care. Call for appointments.

Kona Community Hospital (Map p85; ☎ 322-9311; www.kch.hhsc.org; 79-1019 Haukapila St, Kealakekua) Located about 10 miles south of Kailua-Kona.

Longs Drugs (☎ 329-1380; Lanihau Center, 75-5595 Palani Rd; ☼ 8am-9pm Mon-Sat, to 6pm Sun) A centrally located drugstore and pharmacy.

Money

Bank of Hawaii (☎ 326-3903; Lanihau Center, 75-5595 Palani Rd) With 24-hour ATM.

First Hawaiian Bank (☎ 329-2461; Lanihau Center, 74-5593 Palani Rd) With 24-hour ATM.

Post

Post office (☎ 331-8307; Lanihau Center, 74-5577 Palani Rd, Kailua-Kona, HI 96740) Holds general-delivery mail for 10 days. See p284 for instructions.

Tourist Information

There's no official tourist information center in town. Your best sources are local proprietors and publications, as well as the internet.

DANGERS & ANNOYANCES

Be wary of 'tourist information' or 'discount activities' booths along Ali'i Dr, as some may be fronts for timeshare salespeople.

While in-town traffic is generally light, roads to and from Kailua-Kona are jammed during peak periods.

BEACHES

Kailua-Kona might *act* like a beach town, but its three beaches are not among the Kona Coast's showstoppers. The only swimmable in-town beach is Kamakahonu Beach, a teeny-tiny beach at the north end of Ali'i Dr. You'll be on display to car traffic and passersby, but the waters are calm and safe for children.

OLD KONA AIRPORT STATE RECREATION AREA

Forget swimming at this sandy but rock-strewn beach; however, the spacious 100-acre grounds are ideal for picnicking, exploring tide pools and experiencing a locals' beach. At low tide, tiny sea urchins, crabs and bits of coral resemble mini lava-rock aquariums. The old Kona airport was once located here, hence the unfortunate but apt name.

From the north end, a short walk leads to Garden Eel Cove, a good area for scuba divers and confident snorkelers. When the surf's up, local surfers catch an offshore break at 'Shark Rocks.'

Facilities include restrooms, showers, covered picnic tables, a popular running track and ample parking. To the south, Kailua Park Complex (☎ 327-3553; ⏰ 12:15-9pm Mon-Thu, 7:45am-9pm Fri) offers a pool, gym, kiddie playground, tennis courts, and soccer, football and baseball fields. To get here, take the Kuakini Hwy to its end, 1 mile north of downtown.

WHITE SANDS BEACH PARK

Located along Ali'i Dr south of Kailua-Kona, this popular beach is nicknamed Magic Sands or Disappearing Sands for good reason: the sand can wash offshore literally overnight during high surf, exposing dangerous rocks and coral. When the surf calms down, however, the sand magically returns. Also known as La'aloa Beach, this compact, roadside beach is always lively and a hot spot for bodyboarding, surfing or just watching the action. Facilities include restrooms, showers, picnic tables and a volleyball court; a lifeguard is on duty.

SIGHTS

Ali'i Dr might bombard you with surf shops and ABC stores, but amid the tourist kitsch are a handful of historic buildings and landmarks. The farmers markets (p66) are also worth a look.

HULIHE'E PALACE

☎ 329-1877; www.huliheepalace.org; 75-5718 Ali'i Dr; adult/child/senior $6/1/4; ⏰ 9am-4pm Mon-Fri, 10am-4pm Sat & Sun

Imagine the life of Hawaiian royalty in this palace, a simple island manor constructed in 1838 by Hawaii's second governor, John Adams Kuakini, as his private residence. It was originally built with lava rock, but in 1885 King Kalakaua preferred a more polished style after his travels abroad and plastered it over.

The two-story palace contains Western antiques collected on royal jaunts to Europe, Hawaiian artifacts and a number of Kamehameha the Great's personal war spears.

Admission includes a 40-minute tour, which provides interesting anecdotes about past royal occupants. The walking tour (p62) offered by the Kona Historical Society also includes museum admission.

After sustaining major earthquake damage in 2006, the palace was closed for repairs, but should reopen in late 2008.

MOKU'AIKAUA CHURCH

☎ 329-1589; www.mokuaikaua.org; 75-5713 Ali'i Dr; admission free; ⏰ services 8am & 10:30am Sun

When the first Christian missionaries landed in Kailua Bay on April 4, 1820, their timing couldn't have been better. King Liholiho

Moku'aikaua Church
GREG ELMS

had abolished the traditional religion on that very spot just a few months before. He gave them this site, just a few minutes' walk from Kamehameha's Ahu'ena Heiau, to establish Hawai'i's first Christian church.

Completed in 1836, Moku'aikaua Church matches its island setting, with walls of lava rock held together by a mortar of sand and coral lime. The posts and beams, hewn with stone adzes and smoothed down with chunks of coral, are made from resilient ohia, and the pews and pulpit are made of koa, the most prized native hardwood. The steeple tops out at 112ft, making the church the tallest structure in Kailua.

KONA BREWING COMPANY
☎ 334-2739; www.konabrewingco.com; North Kona Shopping Center, 75-5629 Hwy 11; admission & tour free; ☉ 11am-10pm Mon-Thu, to 11pm Fri & Sat, tours 10:30am & 3pm Mon-Fri

Since opening in 1994, this company has been Hawai'i's mainstay in the microbrewery phenomenon. The once-small, family-run operation now distributes its beers in other states and Japan, and established a second pub in Honolulu. Tours include samples. Enter the parking lot from Kaiwi St.

AHU'ENA HEIAU
near King Kamehameha's Kona Beach Hotel (p67); admission free

On the north side of Kailua Bay, Kamehameha the Great lived his last years at Kamakahonu (Eye of the Turtle). Today, you can view the remains of Kamehameha's personal temple: rock walls and a replica thatched hut.

KAILUA PIER
While not a major attraction, the pier and bay are historically significant. Kailua Bay was once a major cattle-shipping area, where the animals were stampeded into the water and forced to swim out to steamers waiting to transport them to Honolulu slaughterhouses.

Built in 1915, the pier was the center of sportfishing until it got too crowded and charter fishing boats moved to the larger Honokohau Harbor. Today Kailua Pier marks the start and finish of the Ironman Triathlon, is the dock for cruise ships, and serves dive and cruise boats.

ACTIVITIES

For swimming, head to Kahalu'u Beach Park (p71), or to further hot spots, from Kekaha Kai State Park (p99) to Hapuna Beach State Recreation Area (p117). With rocky shores and rough waters, Kailua-Kona isn't ideal for swimming. Note that snorkeling cruises only launch from Kailua-Kona; the actual snorkeling is done in South Kona's glassily calm waters.

Snorkeling

For shore snorkeling, Kahalu'u Beach Park is your closest and best option. Rent gear from Snorkel Bob's (☎ 329-0770; www.snorkelbob .com; 75-5831 Kahakai Rd; ☉ 8am-5pm), near the Royal Kona Resort.

Snorkeling cruises aren't cheap, but they offer regular folks a chance to enter deeper waters, sail along the panoramic coast and learn from longtime seamen. Opt for a morning departure because water conditions are best then. Cruises depart from either Keauhou Pier or Honokohau Harbor. Book online for frequent discounts.

Most tours head south to Kealakekua Bay (p86), but other coves can be just as scenic and less crowded. The coast south of Kailua features beautiful lava cliffs and caves, while the northern coast is a flat lava shelf with ample marine life. Ultimately, the captain decides the best destination for the day's conditions.

There are two types of cruises. Zodiac rafts are zippy and thrilling, capable of exploring sea caves, lava tubes and blowholes, but you must expect a bumpy ride and no shade or toilets. Catamarans are much larger, smoother and comfier, but you can't go as close into coves as the rafts can. Also, if you're a nondiver who wants to see manta rays, note that some diving outfits allow snorkelers aboard for $80 to $95.

Recommended Zodiac outfits include the following:

Captain Zodiac (☎ 329-3199; www.captainzodiac.com; adult/child 4-12yr half-day cruise $90/75) Offers daily trips to Kealakekua Bay in 24ft rigid-hull inflatable Zodiacs with up to 16 passengers. Departs from Honokohau Harbor, with pickups possible at the Kailua-Kona and Keauhou Piers.

Sea Hawaii Rafting (☎ 325-7444; www.seahawaii rafting.com; adult/child $95/75) With over 13 years of experience in Kona's waters, excellent guide Kris Henry can tailor trips to your preferences. His rigid-hull, inflatable Zodiac can accommodate up to 20 passengers, with a trip minimum of four. Personalized, friendly owner. Departs from Honokohau Harbor.

our pick **Sea Quest** (☎ 329-7238, 888-732-2283; www.seaquesthawaii.com; adult/child morning cruise $89/72, afternoon cruise $69/59) Sea Quest is distinct with its small groups of either six or 12 (on 22ft and 26ft rigid-hull inflatable rafts). The recommended morning cruise includes both Honaunau and Kealakekua Bays, while the afternoon cruise concentrates on Kealakekua Bay. Departs from Keauhou Bay.

For catamarans, try the following:

Fair Wind (☎ 345-0268, 800-677-9461; www.fair -wind.com; adult/child Fairwind II $75/45, incl meal from $109/69, Hula Kai per person incl meal $125-155) The *Fairwind II*, a scrappy 100-passenger catamaran with a 15ft slide, sails daily to Kealakekua Bay. Cruises on the luxury hydrofoil catamaran *Hula Kai* are longer and explore less-trafficked waters; minimum age is 18. Divers are welcome. Departs from Keauhou Bay.

Kamanu Charters (☎ 329-2021, 800-348-3091; www .kamanu.com; adult/child $80/50) Snorkel in uncrowded Pawai Bay, just north of the protected waters of the Old Kona Airport State Recreation Area. The 36ft catamaran, which motors down and sails back, maxes out at 24 people. Departs from Honokohau Harbor.

our pick **Sea Paradise** (☎ 322-2500, 800-322-5662; www.seaparadise.com; adult/child snorkel cruise incl 2 meals $95/59, 2-tank dive $125, adult/child manta snorkel $85/59, manta dive $110) Highly recommended Sea Paradise offers morning snorkel cruises to Kealakekua Bay and dive trips (including a bargain-priced manta ray night dive) on a 46ft catamaran with a friendly, professional crew. Departs from Keauhou Bay.

Diving

The Kona Coast is known for calm, clear waters, unique lava formations and coral reefs. Near the shore, divers can see steep drop-offs with lava tubes, caves and diverse marine life. In deeper waters there are 40 popular boat-dive areas, including an airplane wreck off Keahole Point.

Ahu'ena Heiau

GREG ELMS

KAILUA-KONA

Island Insights

A signature experience is a night dive with Pacific manta rays. With wingspans of 8ft to 12ft, these gentle giants will leave you speechless. If you're certified but rusty, the two-tank dive allows practice time during the first afternoon dive (especially if this is your first night dive). Note that afternoon dives are generally mundane, with day fish settling into hiding places and night fish not yet out. Manta ray sightings are not guaranteed, no matter what dive operators promise. For more on manta rays, see www.mantapacific.org.

The best outfits for manta ray dives (and amateur-level tours) are Dive Makai, Big Island Divers, Sandwich Isle Divers and Sea Paradise. The best outfits for experi-enced divers are Dive Tek and Aloha Dive Company.

Most dive tours launch from Honokohau Harbor (p95) but either do business from Kailua-Kona or have no bricks-and-mortar location whatsoever. Including all gear, the cost of a standard two-tank dive ranges from $110 to $150, while a two-tank night dive to see manta rays costs between $130 and $150. PADI Open Water certification programs cost about $500.

Aloha Dive Company (☎ 325-5560, 800-708-5662; www.alohadive.com) 'Remote' dives (for certified divers) beyond the well-trafficked Kailua-Kona waters are the specialty of this small, Hawaiian-owned operation. Owner and local guy Mike Nakachi is a hands-on guide who will tailor unique trips and impart much historical, geological and cultural info. Reasonable rates (two-tank dives are $110 for local and $140 for remote). No manta ray night dives. Groups max out at six on a 28ft boat.

Big Island Divers (☎ 329-6068, 800-488-6068; www.bigislanddivers.com; 74-5467 Kaiwi St; ☾ 8am-6pm) This large, well-stocked shop in the industrial area offers reasonably priced dives (including manta ray night dives), top-quality gear and the full range of certifications.

Dive Makai (☎ 329-2025; www.divemakai.com) This longtime husband-and-wife operation changed hands in 2005, but the new owners (another hands-on couple) are successfully maintaining the company's excellent reputa-tion for thorough instructions, flexible dives and small groups (up to 12 but average eight). Best-value rates with discounts for multiple-day bookings.

Dive Tek Hawaii (☎ 329-1004, 877-885-3483; www.divetekhawaii.com) This highly competent outfit offers personalized advanced dives, thus the website shows no set packages or prices (it falls in the upper-middle range). The longtime guides are passionate about their sport and, although they might train advanced pros, are patient and unpretentious in all levels of certification courses. Kids can ride along and on-board childcare is offered.

Jack's Diving Locker (☎ 329-7585, 800-345-4807; www.jacksdivinglocker.com; Coconut Grove Market-place, 75-5819 Ali'i Dr; ☾ 8am-9pm) Since its humble beginnings in 1981, Jack's has expanded to two locations, five boats, 40 employees and a huge training/retail facility. However, while impressive and professionally run, dive groups can be large (12 to 14); guide quality can range from stellar to so-so, depending on who's on staff that day. Full range of certification courses. In 2005, Jack's received a statewide Living Reef Award for helping to protect Hawaii's coral reefs from anchor damage.

Sandwich Isle Divers (☎ 329-9188; www.sandwichisledivers.com; 75-5729 Ali'i Dr) Owned by a husband-and-wife team, this small outfit offers personalized tours (six-passenger max; two guides; small boat) and a wealth of

Boats at Honokohau Harbor   GREG ELMS

PORTRAIT OF A GROM

In surf lingo, a 'grommet' or 'grom' is a young surfer, male or female, under age 15 (although the age max sometimes creeps up to 18 or even 20). Kailua-Kona is a hotbed for talented groms, such as superstar **Tonino Benson**, born in 1989, who started competing at age eight. In 2005 he won the Boys Under 16 division of the prominent Quiksilver World Junior Championships, after preparing daily at Banyans. His father would film his practice sessions and they'd study the footage and score his waves. In competitions, surfers can't control the quality of their waves, but the true phenoms can look awesome on any wave.

Like other serious groms, Benson's childhood revolved around surfing. His parents enrolled in home school so he could practice during the day, and by age 16 he was sponsored by numerous major surf labels, including Reef, Dakine and Bubble Gum Surf Wax.

In 2007 he won the most prestigious amateur title, the National Scholastic Surfing Association Open Men's Championship. Look for Benson's name in the pro circuits anytime now.

experience in Kona waters. Rates are in the upper-middle range, but the small-group atmosphere feels almost like a private charter. It also offers certification courses and reasonably priced rental gear.

Bodyboarding & Surfing

White Sands Beach Park (p57) is a favorite spot for bodyboarding, while board surfers like Kahalu'u Beach Park (p71), Banyans (near the banyan tree north of White Sands Beach) and Pine Trees (p98), near Wawaloli (OTEC) Beach.

For board rentals and expert advice, visit Pacific Vibrations (☎ 329-4140; pacvibe@hawaii.rr.com; 75-5702 Likana Lane; ⚑ 10am-5:30pm Mon-Fri, to 3:30pm Sat), the first surf shop in West Hawai'i.

Whale Watching

Although snorkeling, diving or fishing tours often also offer whale watching during humpback season, we recommend marine-mammal biologist Dan McSweeney's ❀ **our pick** Whale Watch (☎ 322-0028, 888-942-5376; www.ilovewhales.com; adult/child 3hr cruise $69/59; ⚑ Jul-Apr) excursions. His tours are not offhand add-ons but focus on whale sightings and education. In other words, whales are the main event! While humpbacks are present only from December to April, many other types of whales live in Kona waters year-round. Hydrophones allow passengers to hear whale songs.

Fishing

Kailua is legendary for big-game fishing, so it's no surprise that over 100 charter boats are available to take you aboard. The standard cost for joining an existing party starts at $80 per person for a half-day (four-hour) trip. If you charter a whole boat, you can take up to six people for $300 to $600 for a half-day (four hours), and between $500 and $900 for a full day. Ask whether the captain shares the catch.

Agencies book for so many boats that it's impossible to guarantee quality or consistency, but Charter Desk (☎ 329-5735, 888-566-2487; www.charterdesk.com) is a reputable service. Use Charter Services Hawaii (☎ 334-1881, 800-567-2650; www.konazone.com) if Charter Desk is booked up.

Highly recommended boats include the following:

Captain Jeff's Charters (☎ 895-1852; www.fishin kona.com; exclusive 6hr charter $550-750) Longtime captain is a straight shooter who offers tailored trips, insider advice and a share of the catch. Informative website.

Hooked Up Sportfishing (☎ 960-5877; www.kona charterboat.com; exclusive 4hr charter $400) Personalized, family-oriented service on 42ft boat with proven catch record.

Island Insights

The largest **Pacific blue marlin** (1376lb) was caught in Kailua-Kona on May 31, 1982, by angler Jay de Beaubien. If you can't visualize the size of a 1-ton 'grander,' go to **King Kamehameha's Kona Beach Hotel** (p67) to see the mounted 1993 Hawaiian International Billfish Tournament Pro-Am record catch, a 1166lb marlin, and the 1986 record catch at 1065lb.

Sea Wife II (☎ 888-329-1806; tim@fishinkona.com; shared charter per person $100, exclusive 4hr charter $550) Go here if you need to join a shared charter. Nonfishing tagalongs cost $50.

Snuba

For non–scuba divers, snuba can be a fun option to descend 25ft underwater, using a breathing hose attached to a raft and your air tank. The tours by **Snuba Big Island** (☎ 326-7446; www.snubabigisland.com) are pricier than comparable snorkeling tours, however. Beach dives (1½-hour tour $89, departures 9am, 11am, 1pm and 3pm) leave from Kailua Pier and boat dives (three-hour tour, one/two dives $145/170, departures 8:30am and 12:30pm) from Honokohau Harbor. Minimum age is eight, but kids as young as four can participate by wearing a flotation device and staying at the surface.

Yoga

Kona Yoga (☎ 331-1310; www.konayoga.com; Sunset Shopping Plaza, 77-6425 Hwy 11, D202; drop-in class $15) is a no-frills studio with a limited schedule, but owner Barbara Uechi teaches Iyengar-inspired classes with lots of care and humor. Acupuncture and massage are also available.

Spas

If you can't afford the fanciest resort spas, **Hawaiian Healing Ohana Spa** (☎ 331-1050; www.hawaiihealingohana.com; Ali'i Sunset Plaza, 75-5799 Ali'i Dr; massage from $75, facial from $90; ☾ by appointment) in downtown Kailua-Kona will surely meet your pampering needs. Customized massages can combine different techniques, facials use high-end organic products, and body treatments are practically edible, featuring island sugar, coconut, *awapuhi* (Hawaiian ginger) and Kona sea salt. The location behind Island Lava Java is convenient, if rather too populated.

KAILUA-KONA FOR KIDS

Kids will probably need little cajoling to enjoy the Kailua-Kona area. Just focus on the outdoors: snorkeling at Kahalu'u Beach Park (p71), bodyboarding at White Sands Beach Park (p57) or tide pool exploring at Old Kona Airport State Recreation Area (p57). Better yet, if you can afford it, snorkeling (p58) or whale-watching cruises (p61) are thrilling for all ages.

For babysitting services, **Busy Buddies Hawaii** (☎ 334-1800, 866-305-1800; www.busybuddieshawaii.com; Kaiwi Sq, 74-5565 Luhia St; per hr $4.50-7.50; ☾ 7am-6pm Mon-Fri, 8am-9pm Sat) is a trusted daycare center open to kids aged two to 12. Drop-in kids are welcome at this squeaky-clean indoor facility, which includes a plastic-ball pit, climbing wall, games (electronic and board), quiet reading loft, crafts and toys. Each child needs proof of TB clearance and immunization record, plus parent's ID and socks (no shoes are worn inside, local style).

For more indoor fun, try these standbys: **Fun Factory** (☎ 334-1578; Kona Inn Shopping Village, 75-5744 Ali'i Dr; token 25¢; ☾ 10am-10pm Sun-Thu, to midnight Fri & Sat) It's back to the '80s in this arcade amid the thick of Ali'i Dr foot traffic.

Kona Bowl (☎ 326-2695; 75-5591 Palani Rd; adult/child per game $4.25/3; ☾ 9am-10pm Sun-Thu, to midnight Fri & Sat) Retro and slightly divey, the bowling alley features Friday- and Saturday-night 'Cosmic Bowling' (per hour $32, shoes included), which means bowling in the dark (think loud music, black lights, glow-in-the-dark pins and wild laser lights).

TOURS

The **Kona Historical Society** (☎ 938-8825; www.konahistorical.org; 75min tour incl palace admission $15; ☾ tours 9:30am & 1:30pm Tue & Fri) offers an interesting walking tour that will give more meaning to Hulihe'e Palace, Moku'aikaua Church, Kona Inn and other sites along Ali'i Dr. The tour starts at King Kamehameha's

Top Picks

KAILUA-KONA FOR KIDS

- **Kahalu'u Beach Park** (p71)
- **Sheraton Keauhou Bay Resort & Spa** (p75)
- **Premium ice cream** (p64)
- **Snorkeling or whale-watching cruises** (p58)
- **Kona Cloud Forest Sanctuary** (p56)

ISLAND VOICES

NAME: BARBARA UECHI
OCCUPATION: YOGA TEACHER, MASSAGE THERAPIST AND OWNER OF KONA YOGA
RESIDENCE: KAILUA-KONA

Has Kona changed since your childhood? I grew up in Ho'okena, which was rural then, the way Ka'u remains today. When you went to the store, everyone knew your name. When you drove around, you recognized everyone by car. You could walk across the highway anytime!

Tell me about your parents and family. My father is a second-generation Japanese who grew up in North Kohala and owned a service station and a body shop. My mother is also a *nisei*, from South Kona, and she was a longtime cafeteria manager in the public school system. I'm a *sansei* (third-generation Japanese immigrant). I have three brothers, who live in New York, Las Vegas and San Francisco. I think I could be happy in another town, but more and more I love my life in Kona.

Is there a sense of community in Kona? Yes, but it takes more effort now. In my 20s, I left for Honolulu partly because I wanted not to know everyone in town. Now, I can go to a party and meet someone who's lived here 25 years, whom I've never seen. The Kona side covers a vast area, so there's less of a community feeling than in Hilo.

What's your reaction to Kona's growth? For 10 years, starting in the mid-1980s, I was a real-estate agent. Back then, Kona was developing and I'd drive buyers around, telling them the differences between North and South Kona and so forth. I felt that I was sharing the island with potential newcomers. Now there are lots of new subdivisions with rows and rows of houses. It seems like too many, but it reminds me of a yoga class: all you really need is your mat space, if those around you are courteous and aware of their surroundings. Likewise, all the people in their houses can share and live as neighbors if they make the effort.

What do you like best about Kailua-Kona? Sunsets, sunsets, sunsets. We old-timers feign a yawn and say, 'Oh my, another Kona sunset.' But inside it thrills us every day. It's great that no jets fly directly overhead (unless you're at the old airport beach but then…you're at the beach!) and no tall billboards clamor for attention.

Kona Beach Hotel and includes a booklet with over 40 archival photos of historic Kailua.

For sedentary, rather than active, ocean tours, consider the following:

Atlantis Submarines (☎ 329-6626, 800-548-6262; www.atlantisadventures.com; adult/child 35min ride $89/45; ☼ departures 10am, 11:30am & 1pm) For folks who refuse to get wet, submarines let you descend 100ft while in your street clothes. There are 26 portholes for 48 passengers, which means that sharing is required. The overpriced excursion comprises 35 minutes underwater plus 15-minute boat rides from Kailua Pier to the sub and back. Japanese-language headsets are available.

Kailua Bay Charter Company (☎ 324-1749; www .konaglassbottomboat.com; adult/child $30/15; ☼ departures hourly from 10:30am) If you're both aquaphobic and claustrophobic, try Ralph Jewell's 36ft, 24-passenger glass-bottom boat, which departs from Kailua Pier. You'll see Kona's underwater reef and, because you're skimming the waters, you can also view the coastline and perhaps dolphins or whales. Besides the affordable cost,

COOL SCOOPS

For scrumptious premium ice cream (made by Kailua's own Big Island Ice Cream company), try two shops on Ali'i Dr. A modern, sparkling-clean shop, **Hula Bean Coffee** (☎ 329-6152; www.hulabean .com; 75-5719 Ali'i Dr; desserts $2.25-6, single scoops $3.40; ☻ 7am-9:30pm) is a coffee retailer with a cheery counter selling the most flavors in town. Follow your nose to **Scandinavian Shave Ice Internet Café** (☎ 331-1626; 75-5699 Ali'i Dr; single scoops $3.50; ☻ 8am-9pm), which constantly exudes the soothing aroma of fresh-baked waffle cones. It also makes shave ice and offers a thrilling 45 flavors.

Palazzo Aikalima Gelato (☎ 327-3388; Kona Coast Shopping Center, 74-5588 Palani Rd; single scoops $3.25; ☻ 12:30-8:30pm Mon-Fri, to 9:30pm Sat & Sun) is perhaps the only gelato maker on the island. Aficionados will sniff at the icy texture, but flavors are fun and homemade.

bonuses include an onboard naturalist and easy boarding for kiddie, elderly or mobility-impaired travelers.

FESTIVALS & EVENTS

Kona Brewers Festival (☎ 331-3033, 334-1884; www .konabrewersfestival.com; admission $55) On the second Saturday in March, the owners of the Kona Brewing Company (p58) throw an annual beer tasting to promote Hawaii's microbrew industry. Taste 30 diverse craft beers from Hawaii, California and the Pacific Northwest. Proceeds go to environmental and children's groups. Book in advance.

Hawaiian International Billfish Tournament (☎ 329-6155; www.hibtfishing.com) Hawaii's most prestigious sportfishing competition, with five days of all-day fishing followed by weigh-ins at Kailua Pier. The tourney starts in late July or early August.

Ironman Triathlon World Championship (☎ 329-0063; www.ironman.com) On the second Saturday in October, all traffic halts for this premier endurance test that finishes on Ali'i Dr; see p34.

❀ **our pick** **Kona Coffee Cultural Festival** (☎ 326-7820; www.konacoffeefest.com; admission $3, additional fees for selected events) For 10 days during the early November harvest season, the community celebrates the Kona coffee pioneers and their renowned beans. The dozens of events include a cupping competition, a recipe contest, art exhibits, farm tours, coffee tastings and a three-minute coffee-picking contest.

EATING

There are two categories of restaurants in Kailua-Kona: for tourists and for locals. The open-air, ocean-view dining options along Ali'i Dr are tourist magnets, while the hole-in-the-wall spots at shopping malls cater to local tastes (and appetites).

U MAKE THE ROLL   Sushi $
☎ 326-1322; Kona Marketplace, 75-5725 Ali'i Dr; sushi rolls $3.95-4.50; ☻ 11am-7pm Mon-Fri, to 4pm Sat

Crazy combinations and low prices make this hidden sushi stand a hit with local teens and surfers. For value, not gourmet, sushi, this is it.

MANNA KOREAN BBQ   Diner $
☎ 334-0880; Crossroads Shopping Center, 75-1027 Henry St; mains $6-9; ☻ 10am-8:30pm Mon-Sat

The beef industry owes much to Manna's popular charbroiled, marinated short ribs. Plates come with rice and a variety of sides, such as kimchi and bean sprouts. The strip mall setting means no ambience but ample parking.

ISLAND LAVA JAVA   Café $$
☎ 327-2161; Ali'i Sunset Plaza, 75-5799 Ali'i Dr; meals $7-14; ☻ 6am-9pm

Enjoy free wi-fi and people-watching at this bustling patio café – if you can snag a spot outside. Expect American classics, such as hearty pancakes, three-egg omelettes and dressed-up burgers and pastas. Avoid the inside seating area, which could double as a sauna.

BA-LE KONA   Vietnamese $$
☎ 327-1212; Kona Coast Shopping Center, 74-5588 Palani Rd; dishes $8-10; ☻ 10am-9pm Mon-Sat, 11am-7pm Sun

Come for light and healthy Vietnamese fare, not the no-frills decor and mall setting. Ba-Le offers generous, family-sized plates of the classics, from green papaya salad topped with shrimp to steaming *pho* noodle soups (with mushroom broth instead of beef broth for vegetarians).

KONA BREWING COMPANY   Pub $$
☎ 334-2739; 75-5629 Kuakini Hwy; sandwiches & salads $8-11, small/large pizzas $13/22; ☻ 11am-10pm Sun-Thu, to 11pm Fri & Sat

Expect a madhouse crowd at this sprawling brewpub, despite the poorly lit outdoor seating and lackadaisical wait staff. Everyone's here for delectable Greek, spinach and Caesar salads and handcrafted beer made on site. Pizza toppings verge on the gourmet, but crusts are soggy and bready. Enter the parking lot from Kaiwi St.

BIG ISLAND GRILL
Diner $$
☎ 326-1153; 75-5702 Kuakini Hwy; plate lunches $9, mains $13; ☺ breakfast, lunch & dinner
Big appetites are no match for the big portions served at this Denny's-style diner. The food is down-home rather than upscale, and favorites include teriyaki beef, grilled mahimahi, and giant burgers and pancakes. Friendly service can slip during busy periods.

KANAKA KAVA
Hawaiian $$
our pick ☎ 327-1660; Coconut Grove Marketplace, 75-5803 Ali'i Dr; salads $16, kava $4; ☺ 10am-10pm Sun-Wed, to 11pm Thu-Sat
This tiny, tropical café is the perfect place to try kava (the mildly relaxing juice of the 'awa plant), grown by owner/chef Zachary Gibson. His delicious organic salads are topped with a choice of fish, shellfish, chicken, tofu or poke (cubed raw fish marinated in soy sauce, oil and chili pepper).

JACKIE REY'S OHANA GRILL
Hawaii Regional $$$
☎ 327-0209; Sunset Shopping Plaza, 75-5995 Kuakini Hwy; mains lunch $10-14, dinner $22-30; ☺ lunch & dinner daily, pupu 2-5pm Mon-Fri
With warm wood furnishings and a festive, family-appropriate bar, Jackie Rey's is apt for tourists, locals and anyone's mother-in-law. The meat and seafood dishes are island interpretations of American bar classics: shrimp crab cakes with coconut curry, seared 'ahi (yellowfin tuna) with ginger glaze, New York strip steak with chili-garlic shrimp.

FUJIMAMAS
Japanese $$$
☎ 327-2125; 75-5719 Ali'i Dr; mains lunch $12, dinner $16-24; ☺ 11:30am-2:30pm & 5-10pm Mon-Sat, 5-10pm Sun
The hippest eatery on Ali'i Dr, Fujimamas is nouveau fusion Japanese. The creative sushi is outstanding, as are the Japanese touches, from duck cured in kombu (seaweed) to

miso mashed potatoes. Splurge on decadent desserts and wacky martinis (the 'Hello Kitty' blends sake and Chambord).

O'S BISTRO
Hawaii Regional $$$$
our pick ☎ 327-6565; www.osbistro.com; Crossroads Shopping Center, 75-1027 Henry St; dinner mains $24-34; ☺ lunch & dinner daily, breakfast 10am-noon Mon-Fri, 10am-2pm Sat & Sun
One of the pioneers of Hawaii Regional Cuisine, Amy Ferguson still garners raves for her eclectic, East-meets-West menu of island fish and meats, along with her signature noodle dishes and succulent grilled vegetables. Her dressed-up comfort food includes a tuna noodle casserole with orecchiette, spicy 'ahi and shiitake cream, and an outstanding 'Food Without Faces' veg menu. The only negative: a mundane mall setting. Sit inside.

LA BOURGOGNE
French $$$$
☎ 329-6711; Kuakini Plaza, 77-6400 Nalani St, at Hwy 11; mains $28-36; ☺ dinner Tue-Sat
A dining room sans view or even windows? Yes, but that's the appeal of this intimate French restaurant, where slow, lingering meals are encouraged. Highly recommended is the fresh catch in a steaming crock of bouillabaisse – but, meat eaters,

Kalua pork at Kanaka Kava   GREG ELMS

KAILUA-KONA

don't miss the outstanding rack of lamb. For an hour or three, you'll swear you're in France.

If your heart is set on oceanfront dining, the usual suspects along Ali'i Dr are overpriced but compensate with splendid views. Expect predictable but decent steak and seafood at the following places:

Huggo's (☎ 329-1493; 75-5828 Kahakai Rd; mains $25-50; ☺ lunch Mon-Fri, dinner daily) At this quintessential oceanfront restaurant, fresh fish is done up in tried-and-true ways: crab-crusted *ono* (white-fleshed wahoo), mac-nut mahimahi, grilled *'ahi*. Generous portions and well-prepared standards make this the best 'touristy' spot.

Kona Inn (☎ 329-4455; Kona Inn Shopping Village, 75-5744 Ali'i Dr; dinner mains $16-36; ☺ 11:30am-9:30pm) Find a handsome, if a bit worn, hardwood interior, full horizon views and business-class fare. Best choice is fresh fish served Cajun-style or broiled with lemon butter.

For fresh fruit and vegetables, the **Kona Farmers Market** (cnr Kaiwi & Luhia Sts; ☺ 8am-5pm Sat, to 3pm Sun) is an unassuming gathering, focused on produce rather than souvenirs. The **Kailua Village Farmers Market** (cnr Ali'i Dr & Hualalai Rd; ☺ 9am-5pm Thu-Sun) also sells local produce amid phony shell jewelry and pseudo-Hawaiian knickknacks. Don't bother with the **Ali'i Gardens Farmers Market** (Ali'i Dr; ☺ 9am-5pm Thu-Sun), run by the owners of Huggo's restaurant, unless you want touristy gift items.

Find supermarkets at the malls:

Kona Natural Foods (☎ 329-2296; Crossroads Shopping Center, 75-1027 Henry St; ☺ 8:30am-9pm Mon-Sat, to 7pm Sun) Well-stocked; pricey but within reason.

KTA Super Store (☎ 329-1677; Kona Coast Shopping Center, 74-5594 Palani Rd; ☺ 5am-midnight) The Big Island's best grocery chain, with a deli that's good but cannot compare with Hilo's.

Safeway (☎ 329-2207; Crossroads Shopping Center, 75-1027 Henry St; ☺ 24hr) Kailua's largest supermarket carries the gamut of mainstream mainland fare.

DRINKING
MIXX BISTRO BAR

our pick ☎ 329-7334; www.konawinemarket.com; King Kamehameha Mall, 75-5626 Kuakini Hwy; pupu $6-15; ☺ noon-late

A cool local joint, 'The Mixx' attracts an older crowd in the early evening for wine and tapas-style snacks. The younger set arrives later, especially for *mojitos* and salsa

dancing on Thursdays. Check the website for the live music lineup on Fridays.

HUGGO'S ON THE ROCKS
☎ 329-1493; 75-5828 Kahakai Rd; ☺ 11:30am-midnight

Livelier than Don's (if that means much), this thatched-bar hangout has the casual feel of a poolside bar. It's touristy, but most will agree that the sunset view, open-air setting, hot *pupu* (snack) menu and tropical drinks are reason to stop here. Live music till 10pm or 11pm nightly.

DON'S MAI TAI BAR
☎ 329-3111; www.royalkona.com; 75-5852 Ali'i Dr; ☺ 10am-10pm

Sure, it's pure kitsch. But where else can you shamelessly indulge your tiki-lounge fantasy, sip an umbrella drink and gaze at the great wide ocean?

Another popular option is Kona Brewing Company (p58), a clamorous venue that's a far cry from a real pub but at least offers microbrews widely considered among the state's finest. Along Ali'i Dr, the numerous patio bars are generally tourist traps, but if you can't miss that big game, grab a beer (but skip the food) at LuLu's (☎ 331-2633; Coconut Grove Marketplace, 75-5819 Ali'i Dr; ☺ 11am-10pm), an outdoor sports bar with dozens of TV screens and a no-holds-barred crowd of tourists or youngsters.

ENTERTAINMENT
Hula & Luau

Unless you're a curious first-timer, you might be disappointed by Kailua-Kona's two luau options, listed below. Both are established, entertaining shows, featuring colorful Polynesian dances and much audience participation. But neither is outstanding and the price is steep. Also consider the Kona Village luau (p101), considered the most authentic and within a reasonable distance.

King Kamehameha's Kona Beach Hotel
(☎ 326-4969; www.islandbreezeluau.com; 75-5660 Palani Rd; adult/child $72/36; ☽ 5-8:30pm Tue-Fri & Sun) Luau benefits from a scenic oceanfront setting but crowds can reach 400. Forgo if rainy because an indoor show ain't worth it.

Royal Kona Resort (☎ 329-3111; www.royalkona .com; 75-5852 Ali'i Dr; adult/child $75/29, 1 child admitted free per paying adult; ☽ 5pm Mon, Wed & Fri) The 'Lava Legends and Legacies: Journeys of the South Pacific' show is standard fare; MC can be corny but all in good fun.

Cinemas

Catch first-run movies on 10 screens at **Stadium Cinemas** (☎ 327-0444; Makalapua Shopping Center, 74-5475 Kamaka'eha Ave).

SHOPPING

Kailua-Kona shopping falls into two general categories: tourist traps and big-box chains. Sad but true. The souvenir and surf shops along Ali'i Dr can be fun, but beware of 'Made in China' fakes. Along the Queen Ka'ahumanu Hwy, you'll find Wal-Mart,

---

Don't Miss

- **Holualoa art galleries** (p76)
- **Offshore snorkeling or whale watching** (p58 and p61)
- **A walk through Kona Cloud Forest Sanctuary's lush vegetation** (p56)
- **Roadside snorkeling at Kahalu'u Beach Park** (p71)
- **Kona Coffee Cultural Festival** (p64)
- **Manta ray night dive** (p60)
- **Coffee tour at Mountain Thunder Coffee Plantation** (p76)
- **Innovative Japanese fare at Fujimamas and Kenichi Pacific** (p65 and p74)
- **Vintage logo souvenir T-shirts from Destee Nation** (above right)
- **Massage or facial at Hawaiian Healing Ohana Spa** (p62)

Macy's and other such brands. In 2009 the old industrial area will see the arrival of more biggies, including Target, Circuit City and Sports Authority.

CRAZY SHIRTS

☎ 329-2176; Kona Marketplace, 75-5719 Ali'i Dr; ☽ 9am-9pm
Once maverick, now mainstream, Crazy Shirts are pricey and nowadays worn mainly by tourists. The best designs feature natural dyes, such as coffee, chocolate and volcanic ash.

DESTEE NATION

our pick ☎ 327-4478; www.desteenation.com; 75-5744 Ali'i Dr; ☽ 9am-9pm
Hipsters will love these snug-fit tees screen-printed with genuine logos of longtime Big Island companies. Guaranteed to make you look retro cool.

KONA INTERNATIONAL MARKET

☎ 329-6262; 74-5533 Luhia St; ☽ 9am-5pm Tue-Sun
If you keep your expectations reasonable, this tourist-oriented marketplace is worth a browse. The large warehouse buildings hold numerous individual stalls selling mostly inexpensive items, such as Crocs, toiletries, beach gear, flowers and island souvenirs (check the label). Ample parking, clean bathrooms, shade and a food court add to the convenience.

NA MAKANA

☎ 326-9552; 75-5722 Likana Lane; ☽ 10am-5pm
Poke around this hole in the wall for genuine Hawaii-made souvenirs and collectibles to fit all budgets. Check out the genuine Japanese glass fishing floats (those translucent greenish spheres), which are becoming rare.

SANDAL BAR

☎ 326-2076; King Kamehameha's Kona Beach Hotel, 75-5660 Palani Rd; ☽ 9am-9pm Mon-Sat, 10am-8pm Sun
Huge selection of sandals and slippers from Reef, Teva, Crocs and more.

SLEEPING

Kailua offers the gamut of accommodations, predominantly in a string of seemingly indistinguishable condominiums along Ali'i Dr. Remember that 'oceanfront' does not necessarily mean 'beachfront' on the Big Island, where sandy beaches are not the norm.

B&Bs, Inns & Hostels

Parking is no problem at the following.

KOA WOOD HALE INN/PATEY'S
PLACE Hostel $
☎ 329-9663; www.alternative-hawaii.com/afford able/kona.htm; 75-184 Ala Ona Ona St; dm/s/d from $25/55/65; 💻

Don't confuse this well-managed hostel with the former Patey's Place (a notorious dive). No-frills rooms (all with shared bathrooms) are decently clean, with shared kitchens and living rooms, and attract the under-35 set. Max capacity is 25 guests. No drugs, no alcohol and no shoes indoors.

PLUMERIA HOUSE Inn $$
our pick ☎ 326-9255; www.plumeriahouse.com; Kilohana St; 1br $90-120; 💻

Shh, this immaculate 800-sq-ft one-bedroom deal is a downright steal for longer stays (five-night minimum). Located in an upland residential neighborhood, the unit features many convenient touches: full kitchen, filtered water, patio tables and use of washer-dryer. Wheelchair accessible; $50 cleaning fee.

BOYNTON'S B&B B&B $$
☎ 329-4178; www.konabandb.com; Palani Rd; 2br incl breakfast $120, extra guest $15; 💻

Seeking a home away from home? You got it: two bedrooms, deck with hot tub, full kitchen and sitting room. Spread out and get comfy! Located 3 miles upland, the in-law unit comprises the entire ground floor, which has a lovely view of Kailua Bay. Hosts are gracious longtime residents who stock your kitchen with breakfast fixings (you prepare your own) and let you be.

NANCY'S HIDEAWAY B&B $$
☎ 325-3132, 866-325-3132; www.nancyshideaway .com; 73-1530 Uanani Pl; studios/cottages incl breakfast $125/145; 💻

For a peaceful retreat, go upland 6 miles to either a freestanding studio or one-bedroom cottage, each clean and contemporary, with kitchenette. No young kids.

1ST CLASS B&B B&B $$$
☎ 329-8778, 888-769-1110; www.dolbandb .com; 77-6504 Kilohana St; studios incl breakfast $165-175; 💻

It's rather like staying at grandma's, if she had two airy kitchenette studios overlooking panoramic Kailua Bay. The units are well furnished and sparkling clean, but rather pricey. Longtime resident Dolores does cook a hot breakfast, from Belgian waffles to frittatas. No children.

Hotels

Book online to save big-time.

UNCLE BILLY'S
KONA BAY HOTEL Independent Hotel $$
☎ 329-1393, 800-367-5102; www.unclebilly .com; 75-5744 Ali'i Dr; r $100-144; Ⓟ per day $5; 🅿 💻 📺

Although not oceanfront, the 143-room Kona branch of Uncle Billy's family-run hotels is conveniently located downtown. Nicely renovated rooms at this casual low-rise are comfortably furnished with desks, extra chairs, TV and minifridge.

KING KAMEHAMEHA'S
KONA BEACH HOTEL Hotel $$
☎ 329-2911, 800-367-2111; www.konabeachhotel .com; 75-5660 Palani Rd; r $119-179; Ⓟ per day $7; 🅿 📺

The 460-room King Kam has the worn look of an aging glamour gal. But what an enviable location at the head of Ali'i Dr, perfect for watching the Ironman Triathlon or just strolling along the waterfront. Rooms include two double beds, lanai, refrigerator, TV and phone. Bought by a Californian company in 2007, renovations are slated for late 2008.

ROYAL KONA RESORT Hotel $$$
☎ 329-3111, 800-774-5662; www.royalkona .com; 75-5852 Ali'i Dr; r $130-285; Ⓟ per day $10; 🅿 💻 📺

Spread over three striking towers, the Royal Kona has a breezy, open-air feel. Surrounded by a tropical theme and Don's Mai Tai Bar, you'll know you're in Hawaii. Rooms in the remodeled Ali'i and Lagoon Towers are nicer (and pricier) than those in the Bay Tower; all are rather small (350 sq ft). A protected, saltwater lagoon is perfect for kids.

Condos

Condos can save you money if you're staying for a week or more (to justify the non-refundable cleaning fee charged by most places). Remember, however, that individual units will vary in quality and style. Most condos provide free parking. Ask whether wi-fi applies to units or only common areas.

To snag the best deals, check a variety of sources, including www.vrbo.com (search by condo name) and Google.

KONA TIKI HOTEL　　　　　　Condo $

ourpick Map p72; ☎ 329-1425; www.konatiki .com; 75-5968 Ali'i Dr; r incl continental breakfast $69-82, with kitchenette $92; 🐾

On a budget? You can still afford oceanfront units at the cozy Kona Tiki, a well-kept 15-unit complex. Rooms are basic (sans TV, phone and air-con) but clean, with fridge, lanai and fantastic oceanfront view. Seven-night minimum; no credit cards.

HALE KONA KAI　　　　　　Condo $$

ourpick Map p72; ☎ 329-2155, 800-421-3696; hkk.kona@verizon.net; 75-5870 Kahakai Rd; 1br $90-160; 🐾 💻 🐾

All rooms overlook crashing surf at this well-managed, oceanfront complex. The rentable 22 units vary in style, but all are renovated and include separate living room, full kitchen and lanai overlooking the water. Rates range between $160 and $175 during the high season. Ideally located off Ali'i Dr's main commercial stretch.

KONA MAGIC SANDS RESORT　　Condo $$

Map p72; ☎ 329-3333; 77-6452 Ali'i Dr; r $115-150; 🐾 🐾

Large studios all offer oceanfront lanai, but 2nd- and especially 3rd-floor units are best. With White Sands Beach adjacent to the south, the location is perfect for beachgoers. The all-concrete building keeps out noise and heat. Hawaii Resort Management manages about 15 of 37 total units.

ROYAL SEA-CLIFF RESORT　　Condo $$$

Map p72; ☎ 329-8021, 800-688-7444; www .outrigger.com; 75-6040 Ali'i Dr; studios $150-180, 1br $175-315, 2br $225-400; 🐾 💻 🐾

Enter the spacious atrium with giant sago palms and gurgling (albeit artificial) stream and – aaah! – you know you picked a winner. Professionally run by the Outrigger company, the 63 rentable units at this airy 142-unit resort are large, with stylish furnishings, full kitchen and washer-dryer. Added pluses include freshwater and saltwater pools, sauna, covered parking and free hula workshops. Good value if you book online or off-season.

Hula dancers at the King Kamehameha's Kona Beach Hotel luau　　　　　GREG ELMS

KONA REEF Condo $$$$

Map p72; ☎ 329-2959, 800-367-5004; www
.castleresorts.com; 75-5888 Ali'i Dr; 1br $180-260,
2br from $350; ✂ ▣ ▣

A 130-unit complex, the Reef is comfortable if rather generic. Almost half of the units are managed by Castle Resorts, which provides some hotel services (eg for lockouts and plumbing disasters). A decent-sized pool abuts the rocky coastline; no swimming beach. Wi-fi only around pool and lobby.

**RESORTQUEST
KONA BY THE SEA** Condo $$$$

Map p72; ☎ 327-2300, 877-997-6667,
866-774-2924; www.resortquesthawaii.com;
75-6106 Ali'i Dr; 1br $224-395, 2br $279-460;
✂ ▣ ▣

An attractive home away from home, this well-managed complex boasts a sandy beach (albeit artificial). ResortQuest manages most of the 186 large units (about 920 sq ft to 1260 sq ft), which are consistent in quality and all include two bathrooms. Amenities include spa, daily cleaning service and in-suite washer-dryer. Avoid rack rates.

Some condos retain a primary management firm for bookings, but many have no central agency. Thus you must check with various rental agencies, including the following, which operate mainly by phone and internet:

ATR Properties (☎ 329-6020, 888-311-6020; www
.konacondo.com)

Hawaii Resort Management (☎ 329-3333,
800-244-4752; www.konahawaii.com)

Knutson & Associates (☎ 329-6311, 800-800-6202;
www.konahawaiirentals.com)

Property Network (☎ 329-7977, 800-358-7977;
www.hawaii-kona.com)

**SunQuest Vacations & Property Management
Hawaii** (☎ 329-6438, 800-367-5168; www.sunquest
-hawaii.com)

West Hawaii Properties (☎ 334-1199, 800-799-5662;
www.konarentals.com)

GETTING THERE & AWAY
Air

If arriving at **Kona International Airport at Keahole** (KOA; ☎ 329-3423; www.hawaii.gov/dot/airports

/hawaii/koa; Queen Ka'ahumanu Hwy), 7 miles north of Kailua-Kona, try to avoid late-afternoon arrivals on weekdays, when the highway is jammed with commuters.

Bus

The free Hele-On Bus (see p290) runs from Kailua-Kona to Captain Cook (five daily on weekdays, one hour 20 minutes) from 6:30am to 4:15pm. It runs to Hilo (3½ hours) once daily from Monday to Saturday, departing Kailua-Kona at 6:30am. Runs to Oceanview Estates (one hour), Kapa'au (2½ to four hours), Pahala (two hours) and South Kohala (two hours 30 minutes) are very limited. Check the website for current schedules (www.hawaii-county.com /mass_transit/heleonbus.html).

Between Kailua and Keauhou, another option is the **Ali'i Shuttle** (☎ 938-1112; one way $2), which runs Monday through Saturday. On weekdays, five southbound runs start (from 7am) from Ali'i Dr near Kailua Pier. Five northbound runs start from the Keauhou Shopping Center at 6:25am. There's only one run in either direction on Saturdays. Call to confirm times and locations.

Car & Motorcycle

The drive from Kailua-Kona to Hilo (via Waimea) is 92 miles and takes 2½ hours; for other driving times and distances, see p291. Around Kailua-Kona, the Queen Ka'ahumanu Hwy and Mamalahoa Hwy are jammed in the early morning and late afternoon. See p290 for car rental information.

Motorcycle rentals are steep but, hey, the cachet of circling steamy Kilauea Caldera on a Harley might well be worth it. **Kona Harley-Davidson** (☎ 326-9887; www.konaharleydavid son.com; 74-5615 E Luhia St; per day $100-125) rents a fleet of 22 Big Twin/V-Rod and Sportster models.

GETTING AROUND
To/From the Airport

A car is almost necessary on Hawai'i, but if you're not renting one, taxis (see below) are available at the airport from dawn to dusk; late pickups can be booked in advance. The fare averages $25 to Kailua-Kona and $50 to Waikoloa. Speedi Shuttle (☎ 329-5433, 877-242-5777; www.speedishuttle .com) charges about the same, but might be economical for large groups. Book in advance.

Bicycle

A bicycle is feasible for in-town transportation. Hawaiian Pedals (☎ 329-2294; www .hawaiianpedals.com; Kona Inn Shopping Village, 75-5744 Ali'i Dr; per day $20; ☺ 9am-9pm) rents mountain and hybrid bikes. Affiliated HP Bike Works (☎ 326-2453; www.hpbikeworks.com; 74-5599 Luhia St; per day $35-50; ☺ 9am-6pm Mon-Sat) rents higher-end bikes. Rentals include helmet, lock, pump and patch kit.

Bus

The Hele-On Bus (p290) and Ali'i Shuttle (p70) make stops within Kailua-Kona.

Car & Motorcycle

Ali'i Dr in downtown Kailua-Kona is bumper-to-bumper in the late afternoon and evening. Free public parking is available in a lot between Likana Lane and Kuakini Hwy. Many of the shopping centers along Ali'i Dr have free parking lots.

Taxi

Call ahead for pickup. Try D&E Taxi (☎ 329-4279) or Ilima's Taxi (☎ 989-5211).

AROUND KAILUA-KONA

To the south, Kailua-Kona flows into Keauhou, a condo-heavy resort area. Upland on the slopes of Hualalai, the tiny art community of Holualoa marks the north end of Kona coffee country.

KEAUHOU RESORT AREA

With wide thoroughfares and well-groomed landscapes, Keauhou feels like an upscale suburb: easy, pleasant and bland. Once the site of a major Hawaiian settlement, the area is now staunchly modern, with a planned community of hotels and condos, a shopping center and a 27-hole golf course. The major natural attraction is Kahalu'u Beach Park.

Information

The following shops and other essentials are at the Keauhou Shopping Center (☎ 322-3000; www.keauhou-resort.com/shopping.asp; cnr Ali'i Dr & Kamehameha III Rd):

Bank of Hawaii (☎ 322-3380; ☺ 9am-6pm Mon-Fri, to 2pm Sat & Sun) With 24-hour ATM.

Keoki's Surfin' Ass Café (☎ 322-9792; per hr $8; ☺ 6:30am-8pm Mon-Fri, to 6:30pm Sat & Sun) Offers internet access and fax services.

KTA Super Store (☎ 322-2311; ☺ store 7am-10pm, pharmacy 8am-6pm Mon-Fri, 9am-5pm Sat) Locally owned supermarket that includes pharmacy.

Longs Drugs (☎ 322-5122; ☺ store 8am-9pm Mon-

Sat, to 6pm Sun, pharmacy 9am-6pm Mon-Fri, 9am-1pm Sat) General store with pharmacy.

Post office (☎ 322-7070; ☺ 9am-4pm Mon-Fri, 10am-3pm Sat)

Beaches

KAHALU'U BEACH PARK

Whether young or old, extreme athlete or couch potato, everyone appreciates Kahalu'u, the island's best easy-access snorkeling spot that also boasts offshore surf breaks. Protected by an ancient breakwater called Paokamenehune (which, according to legend, was built by the *menehune,* or 'little people'), the bay is pleasantly calm and shallow. You're guaranteed to see tropical fish and *honu* without even trying.

That said, Kahalu'u is too popular for its own good. Snorkelers can literally bump into one another. The salt-and-pepper beach (composed of lava and coral sand) is a mass of humanity, which some will find convivial and others will want to escape. First-time visitors will probably overlook the annoyances, but longtime residents lament the daily crowds and ocean degradation.

When the surf's up, local surfers challenge the offshore waves, but they're too much for beginners. Kahalu'u can harbor strong rip currents that pull in the northward direction off the rocks near St Peter's

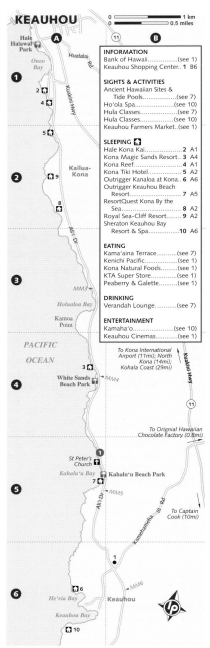

KEAUHOU

0 — 1 km
0 — 0.5 miles

To Kona International
Airport (11mi); North
Kona (14mi);
Kohala Coast (29mi)

To Original Hawaiian
Chocolate Factory (0.8mi)

To Captain
Cook (10mi)

PACIFIC
OCEAN

Church. The lifeguard-staffed park is well
equipped with showers, restrooms, picnic
tables and grills.

Sights & Activities

🌺 ANCIENT HAWAIIAN SITES & TIDE POOLS

Outrigger Keauhou Beach Resort, 78-6740 Ali'i Dr
On the resort grounds just south of Kahalu'u
Beach Park, ancient Hawaiian sites and tide
pools still remain along an easy path. Ask at
the front desk for a site map.

At the north end are the ruins of Ka-
puanoni, a fishing heiau, and the recon-
structed summer beach house of King Kalakaua
next to a spring-fed pond that served as a
royal bath. To the south are other heiau
sites, including the remains of the Ke'eku
Heiau, a probable *luakini* heiau (temple of
human sacrifice).

A *pahoehoe* (smooth lava) rock shelf in
front of the Outrigger contains scads of
tide pools. Here you'll see sea urchins, small
tropical fish and, at high tide, green sea
turtles.

Just south of the Outrigger is the now-
defunct Kona Lagoon Hotel. At very low
tide petroglyphs are revealed on a flat lava
tongue in front of the closed hotel's northern side, most being about 25ft from the
shore.

🌺 ORIGINAL HAWAIIAN CHOCOLATE FACTORY

☎ 322-2626, 888-447-2626; www.originalhawaiian
chocolatefactory.com; 78-6772 Makenawai St;
👁 tours by appointment
A must for chocolate fans: the *only* chocolate
grown, harvested, processed and packaged
in Hawaii. Bob and Pam Cooper moved
to Kona in 1997 to grow coffee but now
specialize in their uniquely 100% Hawaiian
chocolate. They are pushing for legislation
that requires 'Hawaiian chocolate' to be
made only with Hawaii-grown beans. Call
ahead for free tours.

🌺 KEAUHOU FARMERS MARKET

our pick www.keauhoufarmersmarket.com;
Keauhou Shopping Center, cnr Ali'i Dr & Kamehameha III Rd; 👁 8am-noon Sat
Buy fresh! Buy local! That's the apt slogan
for this farmers market where the produce
is all Big Island grown. Find seasonal fruits

Original Hawaiian Chocolate Factory   GREG ELMS

and veggies, coffee, homemade preserves and baked goods, potted orchids, free-range eggs and more. Free samples and live music. Unlike the touristy Kailua-Kona farmers markets selling knickknacks from who-knows-where, this neighborly event focuses on small-scale farmers and their fantastic bounty.

HULA REHEARSALS & CLASSES

Watch real hula when the Halau Kala'akeakauikawekiu hula school holds public rehearsals at the Sheraton Keauhou Bay Resort & Spa (☎ 930-4900; 78-128 Ehukai St; ⏲ 2:30-5pm & 5:30-6:30pm Wed, 8am-1pm Sat). Here, you can see the close relationship between *kumu* (teachers) and their adult and *keiki* students.

On Mondays at the Outrigger Keauhou Beach Resort (☎ 322-3441; 78-6740 Ali'i Dr; ⏲ hula 4-5:30pm, chanting 5:30-7pm, Hawaiian language 7-8:30pm Mon), anyone can join the hula and other classes led by Kumu Keala Ching, a well-known Native Hawaiian teacher. Watch respectfully or join in.

Also, the Keauhou Shopping Center offers daily ukulele lessons (⏲ advanced 10am, beginner 11am), a lei-making class (⏲ noon) and a Polynesian dance show (⏲ 6pm). All are free, but you must bring your own ukulele.

HO'OLA SPA

☎ 930-4848; Sheraton Keauhou Bay Resort & Spa, 78-128 Ehukai St; 50min massage $110, 50min facial $115; ⏲ 8am-8pm
Although there are ritzier spas in South Kohala and North Kona, the Sheraton's 3200-sq-ft facility offers the best resort-spa experience in the Kailua-Kona vicinity. The menu of massages, facials and body

wraps is rather predictable, but treatments are all well done and relatively affordable. The stunning setting, overlooking crashing waves and lava rock, never lets you forget where you are.

KEAUHOU BAY & PIER

Many tour cruises (see p58) launch from the small pier at this protected bay. It's more of a launching point than a destination in itself, but locals do use the small beach, picnic tables and sand volleyball pits. A local outrigger canoe club is headquartered here, and you can watch them practicing in the late afternoon.

Against the hillside, just south of the dive shacks, a stone marks the site where Kamehameha III was born in 1814. The young prince was said to have been stillborn and brought back to life by a visiting kahuna (priest).

To get here, turn *makai* (seaward) off Ali'i Dr onto Kamehameha III Rd. Restrooms and showers are available.

ST PETER'S CHURCH

An ever-popular setting for weddings, the picturesque 'Little Blue Church' practically sits on the water. Made of clapboard and a

St Peter's Church   GREG ELMS

corrugated-tin roof in the 1880s, the church was moved from White Sands Beach to its current site in 1912. This site was once an ancient Hawaiian temple, Ku'emanu Heiau. Hawaiian royalty, who surfed at the northern end of Kahalu'u Bay, paid their respects here before hitting the waves.

To get here, stop on the *makai* side of Ali'i Dr, just north of the 5-mile marker.

Festivals & Events

Indulge your sweet tooth at the Kona Chocolate Festival (☎ 987-8722; www.konachocolatefestival .com; Sheraton Keauhou Bay Resort & Spa, 78-128 Ehukai St; admission advance booking/day of event $40/50), a three-day, late-March event that culminates in a gala evening of chocolate masterpieces by top Big Island chefs. Proceeds go to non-profits such as Na'alehu Theater, an arts and education organization for kids.

Eating

PEABERRY & GALETTE   Café $

☎ 322-6020; Keauhou Shopping Center, cnr Ali'i Dr & Kamehameha III Rd; crepes $7.50-13; 9:30am-8pm Mon-Thu, to 10pm Fri & Sat, to 6pm Sun

With its Illy espresso, sleek decor and Euro-techno tunes, this café strives hard for uber-coolness. Never you mind. The kitchen serves delectable sweet and savory gourmet crepes, plus satisfying salads. The only flaw? Throwaway cups and utensils.

KENICHI PACIFIC   Pacific Rim/Sushi $$$$

our pick ☎ 322-6400; Keauhou Shopping Center, cnr Ali'i Dr & Kamehameha III Rd; sushi $7-15, mains $20-30; lunch Tue-Fri, dinner daily

Ignore the mall setting. Just savor the impeccable Pacific Rim fusion cuisine, finally done right. Memorable mains include subtly smoky bamboo salmon, miso pan-seared mahimahi, and macadamia-crusted lamb with taro risotto. Sushi cuts are fresh and generous, while the molten chocolate cake is worth the splurge.

KAMA'AINA TERRACE   Hawaii Regional $$$$

☎ 322-3441; Outrigger Keauhou Beach Resort, 78-6740 Ali'i Dr; adult/child 6-12yr Friday buffets $35/17.50; breakfast & dinner daily, 9:30am-1pm Sun brunch

Oceanfront hotel restaurants are commonplace throughout Hawaii, but this open-air

eatery offers decent food at decent prices. Satisfy large appetites with the seafood and prime-rib buffet dinner on Fridays or the lavish Sunday brunch buffet ($28.95). From Sunday to Thursday, join the oldsters from 5:30pm to 6:30pm for early-bird dinner specials ($24.95).

For groceries and deli takeout, head to KTA Super Store (☎ 322-2311; Keauhou Shopping Center, cnr Ali'i Dr & Kamehameha III Rd; 7am-10pm) or Kona Natural Foods (☎ 322-1800; Keauhou Shopping Center; 9am-7pm Mon-Sat, 10am-5pm Sun, deli 9am-4:30pm Mon-Sat). Keauhou's farmers market (p72) is the Kona Coast's best.

Drinking & Entertainment

VERANDAH LOUNGE

☎ 322-3441; Outrigger Keauhou Beach Resort, 78-6740 Ali'i Dr; 4-10:30pm

Chill out at the wraparound bar, drink in hand, waves crashing. The scene is sedate and mature (in other words, the crowd is middle-aged and older). Live jazz on Tuesday nights and Hawaiian music on all other nights.

KAMAHA'O

☎ 930-4828; www.sheratonkeauhou.com/kamahao .htm; Sheraton Keauhou Bay Resort & Spa, 78-128 Ehukai St; adult/child 6-15yr $80/40; Mon & Fri

Focusing on Hawaiian myths and legends, the Sheraton's luau is neither a must nor a don't. But for those seeking a luau show, this won't disappoint. The polished dancers are acrobatic and impressive, while the buffet (including 'ahi poke, Waimea mixed greens, seared mahimahi and roasted suckling pig) is surprisingly good.

For first-run movies, Keauhou Cinemas (☎ 324-0172; Keauhou Shopping Center, cnr Ali'i Dr &

Kamehameha III Rd) offers seven screens at a mall with ample parking.

Sleeping

The first two hotels listed following are decent deals only if you book online to avoid rack rates.

OUTRIGGER KEAUHOU
BEACH RESORT   Hotel $$$

☎ 322-3441, reservations 800-688-7444; www .outrigger.com; 78-6740 Ali'i Dr; r $145-235; P per day $7; [icons]

Location, location, location. This airy hotel is surrounded by Kahalu'u Beach to the north and tide pools all around. Oceanfront rooms literally overlook the water, where green sea turtles often appear. While not posh, the hotel was renovated in 2008 and has a pleasant, open-air design amid historically significant grounds (see p72).

SHERATON KEAUHOU BAY
RESORT & SPA   Hotel $$$$

☎ 930-4900, 877-716-8109; www.sheratonkeauhou .com; 78-128 Ehukai St; r $189-289; P per day $6; [icons]

The only true 'resort' in the Kailua-Kona area, the Sheraton boasts a sleekly modern

Drying Kona coffee beans   PRODUCE TO PRODUCT INC

design, upscale spa, massive pool with spiral slide, fine dining and over 500 rooms, but unfortunately no beach. Despite the grand atmosphere, the resort caters to kids, with a *keiki* center including foosball, Play-Station, basketball, ping pong and a movie theater. Internet rates are surprisingly affordable.

OUTRIGGER KANALOA
AT KONA   Condo $$$$

☎ 322-9625, 800-688-7444; www.outrigger.com; 78-261 Manukai St; 1br $195-280, 2br $220-345; P per day $15; [icons]

This gated, townhouse-style condo feels exclusive, safe and private, sitting on an oceanfront lava ledge. Units are huge (one-bedrooms average 1200 sq ft to 1300 sq ft); two-bedroom units include two full bathrooms. With three pools, night-lit tennis courts and an adjacent golf course, you can practically stay put. Of the 166 units, Outrigger manages 84.

Getting Around

A free shuttle (☎ 322-0088) runs between the Outrigger Keauhou Beach Resort and the Sheraton Keauhou Bay Resort & Spa from about 8am to 8pm. It also makes three daily trips into downtown Kailua-Kona. For a schedule check the front desk of any Keauhou hotel or www.konagolf.com/kona golf/shuttle.cfm.

HOLUALOA

Everyone should visit Holualoa, a tiny (population 6000) coffee-farming village 1400ft above Kailua-Kona. Here, the retro buildings, old-time families and slow pace preserve old Hawaii alongside the modern shops and art galleries. At the higher elevation, the climate is cooler and wetter, while coastal views are magnificent.

Orientation & Information

From Kailua-Kona, turn *mauka* (inland) on Hualalai Rd. The entire town is lined up along the Mamalahoa Hwy, just north of the Hualalai Rd intersection. Parking is easy, but regrettably the rural highway is increasingly becoming an alternate route for the jammed Queen Ka'ahumanu Hwy.

UPCOUNTRY COFFEE TASTING

Gourmet coffee has long gone mainstream, and many farms have established visitor centers, where they give free tours and samples. See www.konacoffeefest.com/drivingtour for a list.

- **Holualoa Kona Coffee Company** (☎ 877-322-9937, 800-334-0348; www.konalea.com; 77-6261 Mamalahoa Hwy; ☙ 8am-4pm Mon-Fri) The Kona Le'a Plantation, owned by the Twigg-Smith family, grows organic coffee.
- **Kona Blue Sky Coffee** (☎ 877-322-1700; www.konablueskycoffee.com; 76-973A Hualalai Rd; ☙ 9am-3:30pm Mon-Sat) This 400-acre Twigg-Smith estate is huge by Kona standards. Tours include a short video.
- **our pick** **Mountain Thunder Coffee Plantation** (☎ 325-2136, 888-414-5662; www.mountainthunder .com; 73-1944 Hao St; ☙ 9am-5pm Mon-Sat) Established in 1998, this family-owned organic farm is located in lush Kaloko Mauka, about 15 minutes from Kailua-Kona. Free tours (all day but morning is best) include Discovery Channel video, visits to the mill and roaster, samples and farm animals. Recommended are the reasonably priced private tours ($15 plus 20% tip; additional fee for optional lunch delivery), given Monday through Friday. You can even roast your own 5lb of Kona coffee.

Sights & Activities

ART GALLERIES
our pick Mamalahoa Hwy

Holualoa is a tiny village but don't underestimate the quality of its artists. Here you'll find legitimate, internationally known, highly commissioned artists creating art beyond the stereotypical tropical motifs. Most galleries are open from 10am to 4pm, Tuesday to Saturday.

Standouts include the following:

Dovetail (☎ 322-4046) Showcases elegant work by local artist and custom furniture designer Gerald Ben.

Holualoa Ukulele Gallery (☎ 324-4100; www .konaweb.com/ukegallery/index.html; ☙ 10:30am-4:30pm Tue-Sat) Owner and artisan Sam Rosen displays his own and others' beautifully handcrafted ukulele (which average $450 to $950). Rosen also teaches 10-day and 10-week ukulele-making workshops. Stop by to listen to a *kanikapila* (jam session) on Wednesday evenings (6pm to 9pm).

Ipu Hale Gallery (☎ 322-9096) Rare collection of *ipu* (gourds) decoratively carved and dyed by an ancient Hawaiian method unique to Ni'ihau island. Owner Michael Harburg learned the technique in 1997 and today is perhaps the only remaining practitioner.

Hawaiian gourds at Ipu Hale Gallery

GREG ELMS

Kimura Lauhala Shop GREG ELMS

L Capell Fine Art (☎ 937-8893; Hwy 180) Vivid acrylic paintings and woodblock prints show contemporary interpretations of the island.

Studio 7 Gallery (☎ 324-1335) Serene, museum-like gallery features prominent artist and owner Hiroki Morinoue's watercolor, oil, woodblock and sculpture pieces. Setsuko, his wife, is an accomplished potter and the gallery director.

DONKEY MILL ART CENTER
☎ 322-3362; www.donkeymillartcenter.org; 78-6670 Mamalahoa Hwy; admission free; ☷ 10am-4pm Tue-Sat

The Holualoa Foundation for Arts & Culture created this community-minded art center in 2002. Open to visitors are free exhibits, plus lectures and workshops taught by recognized national and international artists. The center's building, built in 1953, was once a coffee mill with a donkey painted on its roof, hence the name. It's 3 miles south of the village center.

MALAMA I KA OLA HOLISTIC HEALTH CENTER
☎ 324-6644; 76-5914 Mamalahoa Hwy

This health center offers yoga classes, massage, meditation and alternative healthcare treatments.

Eating & Sleeping

HOLUAKOA CAFÉ   Café $
☎ 322-2233; Mamalahoa Hwy; lunch mains $6.50-8; ☷ 6:30am-3pm Mon-Fri

Holualoa's only eatery serves the standard café fare: sandwiches, soups, salads and espresso. Note: the name is not misspelled.

KONA HOTEL   Hostel $
☎ 324-1155; 76-5908 Mamalahoa Hwy; s with shared bathroom $30, d with shared bathroom $35-40

Built in 1926, the Inaba family's pink hotel is more historical icon than commercial hotel. The seemingly unchanged decor and photographs downstairs are worth viewing, whether or not you stay in one of the 11 spartan rooms. Mrs Inaba prefers to check out potential guests in person so don't bother calling.

LEAVES OF HALA

Hawaiians wove the dried *lau* (leaves) of the *hala* (pandanus) tree into floor mats, hats, baskets, fans and other household items. Strong and flexible, *lauhala* is surprisingly hardy and long-lasting. Today, most *lauhala* items sold in Hawaii are actually mass-produced in the Philippines and sold cheaply to unwitting tourists. But in Holualoa, **Kimura Lauhala Shop** (☎ 324-0053; cnr Hualalai Rd & Mamalahoa Hwy; ☷ 9am-5pm Mon-Fri, to 4pm Sat), now run by the Kimura family's fourth generation, sells high-quality, genuine Hawaiian *lauhala* crafts. Originally, they purchased *lauhala* items from Hawaiian weavers to sell at the family's general store. During the Great Depression, a family member learned the craft. Today local weavers supply the shop with a variety of handmade souvenir or gift items, from traditional hats to zipper purses and signature lined totes.

KAILUA-KONA

THE ORCHID INN
B&B $$$

☎ 324-0252; www.theorchidinn.com; 76-5893A Old Government Rd; d $190-225; 💻

Upscale style plus gracious B&B equals the Orchid Inn, with two uniquely decorated rooms. The Zanzibar room is African-exotic, with a handsome bed angled for a stupendous ocean view. The Garden room, airier and laze-around comfier, offers more privacy (downstairs of the main house). Stroll the surrounding garden and enjoy home-cooked breakfasts. No kids under 16.

HOLUALOA INN
Inn $$$$

☎ 324-1121, 800-392-1812; www.holualoainn .com; 76-5932 Mamalahoa Hwy; r incl breakfast $260-340, ste $280-350; 💻 📱

If money is no issue, this luxury inn is a worthy splurge. The contemporary mansion features gleaming hardwoods, original artwork, fine linens and six uniquely decorated rooms (not all with ocean view). The location, smack in the heart of Holualoa village, allows easy access to shops and galleries. Kids over 12 only, please.

ISLAND VOICES

NAME: RENEE KIMURA
OCCUPATION: FOURTH-GENERATION SHOP OWNER, KIMURA LAUHALA SHOP
RESIDENCE: HOLUALOA

Did your store always feature lauhala? My great-grandfather originally sold general merchandise, including food, clothes, lanterns and kerosene. The Hawaiians in the community would sometimes weave *lauhala* (pandanus leaf) items to barter for groceries. Selling the *lauhala* hats and baskets helped our family survive during the Depression.

Is Hawaiian lauhala different from foreign imports? We harvest the *hala* leaves when they are already dried, so the finished product has a different color: more brown than green.

Is lauhala weaving a dying art form? It has declined, but we still have a handful of top *lauhala kumu* (teachers). Today we find retired people taking an interest. Maybe they have more time or feel nostalgic. But it must come from the heart. *Lauhala* weaving was traditionally done at home out of economic necessity; it was not a leisure pastime but part of daily life.

Is each creation unique? When she taught me to weave hats, my *kumu* said that I'd *know* when to add more *hala*. The *hala* tells you. She meant that I must notice and feel it. Customers might want to specify exactly how to design a hat – longer here, shorter there – but it's a piece of art, determined by the *hala* itself.

Describe your childhood in Holualoa. Like many families here, we owned a small coffee plantation. Our school year was based on the coffee harvest: from August to November, we'd pick coffee beans all day, from sunrise until dark, with a break for a *bento* (Japanese-style box lunch). The immigrant experience was very different from today's new coffee farmers. They can afford to clear the land smooth. And they can hire immigrant labor to work the fields.

KONA COAST

From ancient Hawaiian royalty to royally ancient tourists, the Kona Coast was, is and probably always shall be the island's most popular playground. Air and water temperatures are deliciously warm year-round and the crystal blue ocean combined with continual sunshine are undeniably addictive. Kayaking and snorkeling one day, lazing on a white- or black-sand beach the next, exploring sacred Hawaiian sights and visiting an organic coffee farm are just some of the options around here. So alluring is this part of Hawai'i, it's not surprising the vast majority of visitors base themselves in and around Kailua-Kona.

KONA COAST
ITINERARIES

IN TWO DAYS *This leg: 40 miles*

NORTH OR SOUTH? (p95 or p82) Before day one dawns, choose between northern beaches or southern adventures and culture – avoid bridging both in a day or you'll be stuck in traffic in the middle.

❶ KEALAKEKUA BAY (p86) Begin your first day early, paddling your kayak across this clear blue bay (careful! dolphins resting here) to the Captain Cook Monument (p86), where you'll don the mask for some of the island's best snorkeling.

❷ PU'UHONUA O HONAUNAU NATIONAL HISTORICAL PARK (p91) Explore the sacred, slightly spooky Place of Refuge, a site deeply rooted in Native Hawaiian legends. Have your snorkel gear handy for jumping in at Two-Step (p93).

❸ FINE DINING AROUND CAPTAIN COOK (p89) Day one will leave you famished. Try homemade pastas at Mi's (p84) or melt-in-your-mouth sashimi at Teshima Restaurant (p82).

❹ MAKALAWENA BEACH (p99) Dedicate day two to exploring this magnificent beach – but you'll have to hike to get here. If it's winter, the bodyboarding will be decent and you can snorkel with turtles any time.

❺ MANINI'OWALI BEACH (KUA BAY) (p99) Catch the sunset and your last waves at the coast's most easily accessed white-sand beach. The crowds should be thinner by the time you arrive.

IN FOUR DAYS *This leg: 55 miles*

❻ HAWAII GATEWAY ENERGY CENTER (p98) After following the two-day itinerary, check out one of the country's 'greenest' buildings. You can learn about the future of energy here, or just ogle the structure on your way to OTEC Beach (p98) or surfing at Pine Trees (p98).

❼ HONOKOHAU BEACH (p95) Tide pools, gorgeous sunsets and ancient culture are hallmarks here. Walk in royal footsteps along the Ala Hele Kahakai trail, exploring the sacred sites of the Kaloko-Honokohau National Historical Park (p97)

before hooking up with your manta dive (p60) in the harbor.

❽ KIHOLO BAY (p101) Get to this marine wonderland early on your last day for watching wildlife, chilling on black-sand beaches and swimming in lava tubes.

❾ KUKIO BAY (p100) Take some afternoon sun at this small, serene beach good for swimming – even for the little ones – before catching the sunset at the Four Seasons' Beach Tree Bar & Grill (p101).

The Kona Coast offers some of the island's best snorkeling

GREG ELMS

FOR WATER BABIES

❶ **KEALAKEKUA BAY (p86)** Start your water adventures kayaking across this brilliant, well-conserved bay to Ka'awaloa Cove with spectacular snorkeling.

❷ **TWO-STEP (p93)** Another fabulous snorkeling spot awaits near **Pu'uhonua o Honaunau (p91)**. Beat the crowds by going at sunset, a powerful time of day to imagine ancient Hawaiian ne'er-do-wells fighting their way to safety.

❸ **MANTA RAY DIVE (p60)** True, there's not much Big Island nightlife, but what there is will knock your socks off, such as an after-dark dive with the manta rays.

❹ **MANINI'OWALI BEACH (KUA BAY) (p99)** If you're looking for some reliable

bodyboarding waves, this is the beach. It can get crowded due to the easy-on, easy-off access, but paddle out to the rocks at the northern end to escape the hordes.

❺ **KIHOLO BAY (p101)** Dig your toes into super soft black sand while watching for whales or turtles. When you get bored, check out the innumerable tide pools and the freshwater lava tube. Sea kayakers will have fun at this beach.

❻ **MAKALAWENA (p99)** Locals grumble about these beautiful sandy coves becoming crowded over the years, but where else can you bodyboard, swim, snorkel, fish and kayak all in one day? Plus these beaches absorb 'crowds' well.

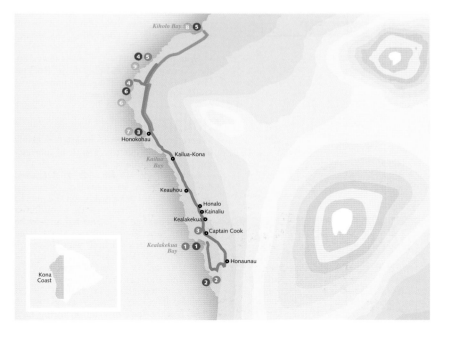

KONA COAST

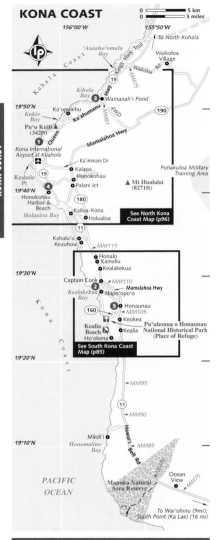

KONA COAST

0 — 5 km
0 — 3 miles

156°00'W   155°50'W

SOUTH KONA COAST

The dozen or so miles between Kailua-Kona and Captain Cook are among the most historically action-packed on Hawai'i. Along this stretch of the Kuakini Hwy (Hwy 11), Hawaiian kings, queens and commoners mingled with the circumnavigator Captain James Cook and his rabble-rousing crew before massive bloodshed ensued; the great god Lono slid from the heavens for the Makahiki harvest festival; and taboo breakers braved shark-infested waters to reach the 'Place of Refuge.' Or not. Upcountry is the 'Kona Coffee Belt,' where the history of coastal agriculture continues to unfold on organic coffee farms and struggling macadamia nut plantations. Take time to poke around charming villages, talk story with a shopkeeper or detour on a side road and you'll discover the Hawai'i people long for – where trees blossom wildly, ukulele are crafted, first-edition books lurk and aloha thrives.

With light traffic (can we get an amen?), you can drive from Kailua to Kealakekua Bay in about 30 minutes, but plan on an hour or more during the morning or evening rush. The South Kona Coast is short on sandy beaches (for that, head north; p95), but long on snorkeling and diving spots.

Note that when Hwy 11 meets Hwy 180, its common name switches from Kuakini Hwy to Mamalahoa Hwy, the name most South Kona addresses take.

HONALO

Where Hwy 11 bends to meet Hwy 180 is little Honalo, home to a couple of interesting Japanese heritage sites.

Daifukuji Soto Mission (☎ 322-3524; www. daifukuji.com; 79-7241 Mamalahoa Hwy; ☯ 8am-4pm Mon-Sat, no admission during services), on the *mauka* (inland) side of Hwy 11, is a Buddhist temple housed in a quirky red-and-white Hawaiian farmhouse with two altars, large drums and other spiritual gear. If you're lucky, the *taiko* (Japanese drum) group will be practicing. As in all Buddhist temples, leave your shoes at the door.

Teshima Restaurant (☎ 322-9140; 79-7251 Mamalahoa Hwy; mains $12-16; ☯ 6:30am-1:45pm & 5-9pm) has the look of a union hiring hall,

Island Insights

The northern section (from Keauhou to Kealakekua) of the long-awaited, badly needed and highly controversial **Mamalahoa/Hokulia Bypass** was opened on a trial basis in summer 2008.

HIGHLIGHTS

❶ **BEST BEACH:** Makalawena (p99)
❷ **BEST VIEW:** From inside your mask at Ka'awaloa Cove (p87)
❸ **BEST ACTIVITY:** Beachcombing at Kiholo Bay (p101)
❹ **BEST CUP O' JOE:** 100% Kona Peaberry at Kona Coffee & Tea Company (p97)
❺ **BEST COUNTRY ROAD MEANDER:** Painted Church Rd to Middle Ke'ei Rd (p90)

Highlights are numbered on the map on p82.

but the warmth of home. For almost 70 years this family-run place has been serving up *'ono* (delicious) Japanese food to hungry locals and wanderers. The fresh catch sashimi plate is divine and the *bento* boxes ($7.50) are handy for picnics. Kids will be happy with a cheeseburger ($6). Request the back booth and get a sliver of ocean view. Cash only.

KAINALIU

Packed with odd and quaint shops, plus good places to eat, Kainaliu is a prime lunch and linger spot – which is handy if you get caught in the 'Kainaliu Krawl' traffic nightmare. Check out fine Hawaiian fabrics at the long-standing **Kimura Store** (☎ 322-3771; 9am-6pm Mon-Sat, 10:30am-4:30pm Sun) and then pop in to **Just Ukes** (☎ 323-8003; 9am-5pm Mon-Sat) for some instruments, plus photos by the talented Kim Taylor Reece. A treasure trove of books awaits at **Island Books** (☎ 322-2006; 79-7360 Mamalahoa Hwy). Owner Marc Medler's brain is another gold mine – pick it for the best local titles and hot-button issues.

For a night on the town, grab a toothsome meal (or *liliko'i* mojito) at the **Aloha Angel Café** (☎ 322-3383; 79-7384 Mamalahoa Hwy; breakfast & lunch $6-14, dinner $14-22; 8am-2:30pm Mon & Tue, 8am-2:30pm & 5-9pm Wed-Sun) and seats at the handsome **Aloha Theatre** (☎ 322-2323; www.alohatheatre.com; 79-7384 Mamalahoa Hwy; tickets $10-25). Quality theater, indie film and live music are the program here. Budget tip: buy

in advance to save $5 (for advance sales, phone ☎ 322-2122).

ourpick Roadhouse Café (sandwiches $5; 11am-5pm Mon-Fri) is one of the island's best-value places, with bodacious submarine sandwiches and inventive phyllo parcels, plus many tasty baked goods (except the vegan cookies, blech).

KEALAKEKUA

A sacred place meaning 'pathway of the gods,' Kealakekua is bound by the 600ft-high Pali Kapu o Keoua cliffs, where the powerful deity Lono slid from the heavens to earth. The *ali'i* (chiefs) were buried high up on those same cliffs centuries ago, and at their base the Hiki'au Heiau religious center hosted sacrifices to honor Ku. You won't find a better snorkeling/kayaking combination than this pristine bay anywhere on the island.

Orientation & Information

Kealakekua is the commercial center of Kona's upland towns, with a **post office** (☎ 322-1656; cnr Hwy 11 & Haleki'i Rd; 9am-4:30pm Mon-Fri, 9:30am-12:30pm Sat) and **First Hawaiian Bank** (☎ 322-3484; 81-6626 Mamalahoa Hwy). The main hospital serving the entire Kona Coast, **Kona Community Hospital** (☎ 322-9311; www.kch.hhsc.org; 79-1019 Haukapila St), is here.

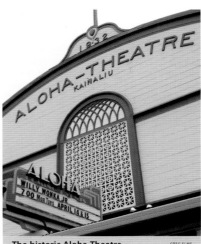

The historic Aloha Theatre   GREG ELMS

Sights

GREENWELL FARMS
☎ 888-592-5662; www.greenwellfarms.com; Mamalahoa Hwy; ☺ 8am-4pm Mon-Fri, to 3pm Sat
If you've learnt everything you know about coffee at Starbucks, head to this 150-acre family farm established in 1850. Run by fourth-generation Greenwells, this is one of Kona's oldest and best-known **coffee plantations**, roasting coffee cherry from over 200 local growers. Take a **free tour** and sample coffee and fruit at a shady picnic table. The farm is between the 110- and 111-mile markers.

HN GREENWELL STORE MUSEUM
☎ 323-2275; 81-6581 Mamalahoa Hwy; adult/child $7/3; ☺ 10am-2pm Mon-Fri
Housed in one of Kona's oldest buildings, this museum between the 111- and 112-mile markers is a taste of turn-of-the-century Kona. Dating from 1875 and meticulously restored in 2006, the costumed interpreters (think Colonial Williamsburg Hawaiian-style) bring the multicultural, agricultural history of the area to life as they wield period dry goods and talk story. You'll smell coffee roasting and sweet bread baking in the traditional **Portuguese Bread Oven** (☺ 11am-2pm Thu) outside.

These folks also have the **Kona Coffee Living History Farm** (☎ 323-2006; www.konahistorical.org/tours-farm.html; adult/child $20/7.50; ☺ tours on the hour 9am-2pm Mon-Fri), if historical tours led by costumed docents are your thing.

❀ AMY BH GREENWELL ETHNOBOTANICAL GARDEN
our pick ☎ 323-3318; www.bishopmuseum.org /exhibits/greenwell/greenwell.html; suggested donation $4, guided tours 1pm Wed & Fri $5, free guided tours 10am 2nd Sat of month; ☺ 8:30am-5pm Mon-Fri
The Big Island's only ethnobotanical garden, this fascinating 15-acre living museum is arranged as an *ahupua'a* (triangular land division beginning upland and narrowing toward the coast) displaying the flora of Hawai'i before Western contact. Walk yourself through landscaped paths thick with endemic, indigenous and introduced plants or go deeper on the **guided tour**. They also cultivate the **Kamehameha butterfly** here, one of only two butterflies native to the Big Island.

Activities

BIG ISLAND YOGA CENTER
☎ 329-9642; www.bigislandyoga.com; 81-6623 Mamalahoa Hwy; 90min/2hr drop-in class $14/16
Strike a pose alongside limber locals in the airy, wooden studios of this yoga center. The center's experienced staff has offered Iyengar-method classes since 1989; mats and props provided.

MAMALAHOA HOT TUBS & MASSAGE
our pick ☎ 323-2288; www.mamalahoa-hottubs .com; 1/2 people 1hr $25/40; ☺ by appointment noon-9pm Thu-Sat, to 8pm Sun
While not quite 'Hawaii's answer to Esalen' as the press clips boast, the wooden hot tubs here are well designed, allowing for both privacy and **stargazing**. For deeper relaxation, throw in a massage ($75 for a 30-minute soak and one-hour massage).

AKALANI MASSAGE SCHOOL
☎ 323-3800; www.hawaiianmassageschool.com; 81-6587 Mamalahoa Hwy; ☺ 6:15pm & 7:45pm Mon & Wed, 9am & 10:30am Thu
Kealakekua is a hotbed of healing and wellness, with great services at great prices. For a taste, try a one-hour massage ($30) at this popular massage school.

Eating

MI'S ITALIAN BISTRO   Italian $$
☎ 323-3880; 103 Mamalahoa Hwy; appetizers & pizzas $5-12, mains $14-21; ☺ 11:30am-8:30pm Tue-Sun
This intimate eatery run by husband-and-wife team Morgan Starr and Ingrid Chan features homemade pasta, organic veggies and a laid-back, classy vibe. Combine a wickedly good seafood corn chowder with a thin-crust pizza or Italian sausage *rigate*. The lasagna is lackluster, however, and the wine a short pour, so bring your own ($15 corkage). Budget tip: the two-course lunch special is just $11.50.

KE'EI CAFÉ   Bistro $$
☎ 322-9992; mains $15-23; ☺ 10:30am-2pm Mon-Fri, dinner Tue-Sat
For fine dining, look no further than this romantic café upstairs in a generic minimall on the *mauka* side of Hwy 11 just south of

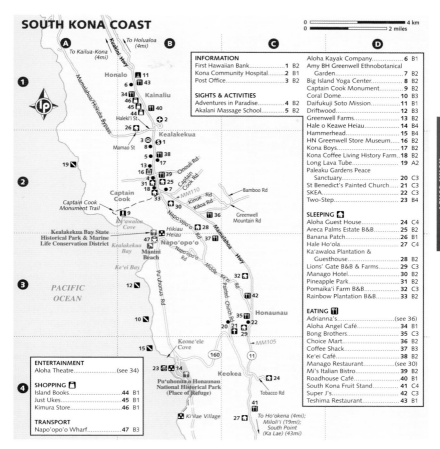

SOUTH KONA COAST

0 —————— 4 km
0 —————— 2 miles

INFORMATION
First Hawaiian Bank....................1 B2
Kona Community Hospital........2 B1
Post Office...............................3 B2

SIGHTS & ACTIVITIES
Adventures in Paradise..............4 B2
Akalani Massage School............5 B2

Aloha Kayak Company................6 B1
Amy BH Greenwell Ethnobotanical
  Garden..................................7 B2
Big Island Yoga Center..............8 B2
Captain Cook Monument..........9 B3
Coral Dome.............................10 B3
Daifukuji Soto Mission.............11 B1
Driftwood................................12 B3
Greenwell Farms.....................13 B2
Hale o Keawe Heiau.................14 B4
Hammerhead...........................15 B4
HN Greenwell Store Museum...16 B2
Kona Boys...............................17 B2
Kona Coffee Living History Farm..18 B2
Long Lava Tube.......................19 A2
Paleaku Gardens Peace
  Sanctuary.............................20 C3
St Benedict's Painted Church...21 C3
SKEA......................................22 B2
Two-Step.................................23 B4

SLEEPING
Aloha Guest House...................24 C4
Areca Palms Estate B&B...........25 B2
Banana Patch...........................26 B1
Hale Ho'ola.............................27 C4
Ka'awaloa Plantation &
  Guesthouse..........................28 B2
Lions' Gate B&B & Farms..........29 C3
Manago Hotel..........................30 B2
Pineapple Park........................31 B2
Pomaika'i Farm B&B.................32 C3
Rainbow Plantation B&B...........33 B2

EATING
Adrianna's...........................(see 36)
Aloha Angel Café.....................34 B1
Bong Brothers.........................35 C3
Choice Mart............................36 B2
Coffee Shack...........................37 B3
Ke'ei Café...............................38 B2
Manago Restaurant................(see 30)
Mi's Italian Bistro....................39 B2
Roadhouse Café.......................40 B1
South Kona Fruit Stand.............41 C4
Super J's.................................42 B2
Teshima Restaurant..................43 B1

ENTERTAINMENT
Aloha Theatre.......................(see 34)

SHOPPING
Island Books............................44 B1
Just Ukes................................45 B1
Kimura Store...........................46 B1

TRANSPORT
Napo'opo'o Wharf....................47 B3

KONA COAST

the 113-mile marker. It does a nice fresh catch (market price), but spare your wallet by going for lunch, when the gazpacho ($9) is sublime. Request one of the terrace tables for terrific ocean views.

Sleeping

BANANA PATCH   Cottage $$
☎ 322-8888, 800-988-2246; www.bananabanana
.com; Mamao St; studio $115, 1-/2br cottages
$125/150; 🖳
One day, in some way, Hawai'i will make you want to shed your clothes, which is perfectly OK in these comfortable, clothing-optional cottages secluded amid tropical foliage. Clean and tasteful, these units are

terrific for independent, private souls, with full kitchen, lanai, gardens and Jacuzzi.

ARECA PALMS ESTATE B&B   B&B $$
☎ 323-2276, 800-545-4390; www.konabedand
breakfast.com; Mamalahoa Hwy; r incl breakfast
$115-145; 🖳
Country comfort and the aloha spirit combine seamlessly in the spotless, wooden home of Janice and Steve Glass. The airy rooms are meticulously outfitted (lots of pillows and closet space, lush robes) and your hosts share their local knowledge freely. Kick back in the family room or watch the sun set in the Jacuzzi. You'll eat like a queen here, with fresh, unique breakfasts daily. It's between the 110- and 111-mile markers.

Pods of spinner dolphins frequent Kealakekua Bay

GREG ELMS

Other possibilities include the following:
Pineapple Park (☎ 323-2224, 877-800-3800; www
.pineapple-park.com; 81-6363 Mamalahoa Hwy; dm $25, r
without/with bathroom $75/85; 💻) Dorm beds are cheek-
by-jowl berths in a windowless room (request the Staff or
Tide unit for a slight upgrade); shared kitchen, laundry and
an interesting international guest list are draws.
Rainbow Plantation B&B (☎ 323-2393,
800-494-2829; www.rainbowplantation.com; 81-6327B
Mamalahoa Hwy; r incl breakfast $88-109) A variety of
rooms in a lush setting, including a dry-docked cabin
cruiser.

CAPTAIN COOK

Captain Cook is a small town with big,
brilliant views. Named after the ill-fated
circumnavigator who landed and perished
in the waters below, Captain Cook is peppered with homey B&Bs, free roadside cof-
fee-tasting rooms and places renting kayaks
for the paddle-snorkel combination across
Kealakekua Bay to Ka'awaloa Cove. You
can also hike in to the cove (see p88).

Sights

KEALAKEKUA BAY STATE
HISTORICAL PARK & MARINE LIFE
CONSERVATION DISTRICT

Beautiful, historical 🌺 **Kealakekua Bay** is the
big draw on the south coast. Local organizations and businesses are working hard to
keep it that way, as more people communing with the wildlife could threaten this
marine-life conservation district. It seems
to be working: we didn't see one scrap of
litter at this heavily visited site. For tips on
adventuring responsibly here, see the boxed
text on p87.

To reach the park, take Napo'opo'o Rd,
off Hwy 11, for 4½ miles, passing a couple
of **ice cream shops** and **cafés** en route. At
the bottom of the road you'll turn right
for **Hiki'au Heiau**, a broad stone platform
temple dedicated to bad-ass god Ku that
was Kealakekua's religious center, or left
for the **wharf** and kayak launch. There are
bathrooms and showers near the heiau.

From Napo'opo'o Beach, the white, phal-
lic **Captain Cook Monument** is visible a mile
away at Ka'awaloa Cove. The Hawaiians
killed Cook and four of his men here in
1779 in a bloody tit-for-tat retaliation; 17
Hawaiians also died. The **ruins** of the ancient village of Ka'awaloa sit on the land
behind the 27ft monument, erected in 1878
by Cook's countrymen.

Nearby Beaches & Bays

South of Kealakekua Bay, **Manini Beach** is a
small, remote beach without an easy entry
point thanks to a rocky shoreline. Swimming is difficult (the best ocean access is to
your right, just after entering the beach),
but when calm, the **snorkeling** is respectable. The point just south of here gets regular northwest swells, so **surfing** is another
possibility.

Island Insights

It is illegal to harass or feed (not to mention hunt, capture or kill) Hawai'i's wild **dolphins** *(nai'a)*. By law, people must remain 50yd from dolphins. If you see someone violating this law, put that cell phone to good use by notifying the **NOAA** (National Oceanic & Atmospheric Administration; ☎ 800-853-1964).

Further south is **Ke'ei Bay**, a local spot worth visiting to escape the crowds at Ka'awaloa Cove. There's a beach and small canoe launch, but no facilities – respect residents' privacy here. Surfers and paddlers test the waters, but swimming is poor. To get here, take the unpaved road just past Manini Beach (if you hit Ke'ei Transfer Station, you've gone too far).

From Ke'ei Bay, you can follow paved Pu'uhonua Rd for 2.25 miles to Pu'uhonua o Honaunau (p91).

Activities

SNORKELING

We were skeptical, but the snorkeling at wildly popular **Ka'awaloa Cove**, in Kealakekua Bay in a shallow bend adjacent to the Captain Cook Monument, is stellar. The coral gardens, tropical fish and an underwater cliff just 50yd from shore are electrifying.

If you're visiting in winter, you may want a wetsuit top.

Of course, everyone is gaga to see the spinner dolphins that come into this bay to rest. Unfortunately, where wildlife and the masses meet, controversy can ensue. The popularity of this spot for **wild dolphin** encounters has alarm bells ringing in environmental and animal rights' circles, since human contact can disturb habitat, and eating, sleeping or mating habits (see the boxed text below).

If you don't want to paddle or hike into the cove, you can catch a **snorkeling cruise** (for tour operators, see p58). Most go to Kealakekua Bay, but some visit less trafficked coves nearby. Tours cost from $95/60 for adults/children aboard either catamarans or rafts; catamarans allow about an hour more snorkeling in the bay.

DIVING

There are many good dive sites clustered around Kealakekua Bay, including Ka'awaloa Cove, with its exceptional diversity of coral and fish in depths from about 5ft to 120ft. Other sites near here include **Hammerhead** (deep dive with pelagic action), **Coral Dome** (a big, teeming cave with a giant skylight) and **Driftwood** (featuring lava tubes and white-tip reef sharks).

In the aptly named **Long Lava Tube**, an intermediate site just north of Kealakekua Bay, lava 'skylights' shoot light through the ceiling of the 70ft tube, and you may see

KONA COAST

HO'OKULEANA IN KEALAKEKUA BAY

Ho'okuleana, the Hawaiian concept of personal responsibility, is key to sustainability in pristine natural areas such as Kealakekua Bay. Since this bay is also dolphin and sea turtle territory, visitors are asked to observe the following guidelines:

- Prevent sunblock slicks: apply sunscreen at least 20 minutes before entering the water so it has time to soak in. Better yet, wear a shirt and skip the block.
- Avoid a coral crash: wearing a life jacket while snorkeling maintains buoyancy and prevents touching down on sensitive organisms.
- Leave nothing but bubbles: take all your garbage and other litter you find.
- Use the facilities: there are no bathrooms across the bay and the woods there are sacred ground, so use the facilities next to Hiki'au Heiau instead.
- Maintain a safe distance: legally, you must remain 10yd from turtles and 50yd from dolphins and whales. Under no circumstances should you chase or pursue wildlife.
- Lift, don't drag: avoid dragging your kayak over the rocks when pulling out and relaunching at Ka'awaloa Cove. The plastic bits left behind are toxic to marine life.
- No maverick launches and landings: follow outfitter instructions about permissible launch and landing sites. It's *kapu* (taboo) to launch kayaks around the heiau.

KONA COAST

Top Picks

KONA COAST FOR KIDS

- **Butterflies at Amy BH Greenwell Ethnobotanical Garden** (p84)
- **Turtle Spotting at Makalawena** (p99)
- **Swimming and beachcombing at Kiholo Bay** (p101)
- **Snorkeling in Ka'awaloa Cove** (p87)
- **More snorkeling, plus swimming and turtles at Kikaua Beach** (p100)

crustaceans, morays – even Spanish dancers. Outside are countless lava formations sheltering conger eels, triton's trumpet shells and schooling squirrelfish.

See p60 for a list of recommended dive shops in Kailua-Kona.

KAYAKING

Most snorkelers rent kayaks along Hwy 11, launch at Napo'opo'o Wharf and paddle 30 to 45 minutes across the bay to Ka'awaloa Cove. The prevailing wind is from the northwest, so returning is usually faster and easier. Launching is a bit tricky because there's a several-foot drop from the concrete landing into the water. With rubbery arms after a day of paddling and snorkeling, the pullout can be even more difficult. Luckily, a clutch of locals are there to help, for which they'll expect a $5 tip.

There are a couple of Hawaiian-owned outfits renting kayaks beyond the wharf on Pu'uhonua Rd; the best deal is US$50 for the day. Guided kayaking tours are prohibited in Kealakekua Bay proper, but you can join a tour to other, similarly spectacular coves along the coast; we like Plenty Pupule Adventure Sports (p120) in Kawaihae.

Tours and rentals are also available along Hwy 11 at the following places:

Adventures in Paradise (☎ 323-3005, 888-371-6035; www.bigislandkayak.com; 81-6367 Mamalahoa Hwy; 1-/2-person kayaks per day $35/60; ⏰ 8am-5pm) Good customer service and gear including Rx masks.

Aloha Kayak Company (☎ 322-2868, 877-322-1444; www.alohakayak.com; Mamalahoa Hwy; 1-/2-person kayaks $35/60; ⏰ 8am-5pm) Check out the tours (including in glass-bottomed kayaks) led by this Hawaiian-owned outfit. Opposite Teshima Restaurant.

☀ **ourpick** **Kona Boys** (☎ 328-1234; www.kona boys.com; 79-7539 Mamalahoa Hwy; 1-/2-person kayaks

$47/67; ⏰ 7:30am-5pm) This (pricier) outfit sets the standard with proactive support of environmental and sustainability initiatives. Learning to surf is another option with these good fellows – group lessons run $75/125 for one/two hours (somewhat more for one-on-one instruction).

HIKING

While not a particularly interesting hike, the steep **Captain Cook Monument Trail** to Ka'awaloa Cove gives a different perspective onto the bay and saves you on kayak rental (though the paddle over, especially when the dolphins are around, is far more thrilling). Go early to avoid the heat, and pack plenty of water and snorkel gear.

To get to the trailhead, turn *makai* (seaward) off Hwy 11, onto Napo'opo'o Rd, and drive to the third telephone pole, where there's an orange arrow indicating a dirt road toward the sea – look for cars parked near here. Take the dirt road (not the chained asphalt road); when it forks after 200yd, stay to the left. The route is fairly simple, and in most places runs between two rock fences on an old 4WD road. When in doubt, stay to the left. After about an hour, the trail flattens out; head left as the trail nears the water to reach the monument.

Queen's Bath, a little lava pool with brackish spring-fed water, lies a few minutes' walk from the monument toward the cliffs. The cool water is a refreshing way to wash off the salt before hiking back.

Kayaking on Kealakekua Bay

A few minutes beyond Queen's Bath, the path ends at **Pali Kapu o Keoua**, the 'sacred cliffs of Keoua,' a chief and rival of Kamehameha. Hawaiian royalty were buried in the caves pocking the cliffs, and it's speculated that some of Captain Cook's bones were placed here as well. A few lower caves are accessible, but filled with old beer cans. The harder-to-access caves higher up probably still contain bones, but these sacred sites should not be disturbed.

Going down is a relatively easy hour-long hike, but plan on 1¼ hours (strong hikers) to three hours for the uphill return. Don't miss the trail's right-hand turn back up onto the lava ledge, as another 4WD road continues straight from the intersection north along the coast – for miles. There are no facilities at the bottom of the trail.

Eating

MANAGO RESTAURANT   Comfort Food $
☎ 323-2642; www.managohotel.com; Manago Hotel, Mamalahoa Hwy; mains $8-14; ☺ breakfast, lunch & dinner Tue-Sun

Don't be put off by the bingo parlor atmosphere at this historic traveler's stopover where locals and visitors devour Manago's famous pork chops. The liver and onions is a house specialty, or try the fried whole *opelu* (mackerel scad). For breakfast, there's a complete egg, meat, toast, juice and coffee combo for $5.50 – one of South Kona's best deals.

COFFEE SHACK   Café $
☎ 328-9555; www.coffeeshack.com; 83-5799 Mamalahoa Hwy; meals $9-14; ☺ 7:30am-3pm

When you see the parking crisis between the 108- and 109-mile markers, you'll know you've arrived at this longtime favorite where the bread is fresh, the patio views are priceless and the meals feed two, easy. The salads (Caesar, Greek, Cobb) are huge, just like the sandwiches. A bit misleading, that espresso-bar sign (there's no coffee to go), but lingering here is fun anyway, listening to local gossip.

Other places around here worth a stop include **Super J's** (Mamalahoa Hwy; mains $7; ☺ 10am-6pm Mon-Sat), serving authentic, tasty Hawaiian *kalua* pig (cooked in an underground pit) for takeout, and **Choice Mart** (☎ 323-3994; Kealakekua Ranch Center; ☺ 6am-9pm Mon-Sat, to 8:30pm Sun), the only proper grocery store for miles. Down below in the same shopping center, **Adrianna's** (☎ 936-8553; ☺ 11am-8pm) serves solid Mexican food with typical upbeat Latino flair.

Sleeping

MANAGO HOTEL   Independent Hotel $
☎ 323-2642; www.managohotel.com; Mamalahoa Hwy; s $56-61, d $59-64, tatami r $78, s/d with shared bathroom $33/36

A great budget option, this no-frills, historical hotel has been hosting travelers since 1917. Now run by the family's third generation,

GREG ELMS

the Manago Hotel has clean, spare rooms; the best have private bathroom, balcony and ocean views. The tatami rooms include a *furo* (Japanese bathtub). The koi pond and gardens provide nice atmosphere, as do the locals who hang out here. It's between the 109- and 110-mile markers. Book *early*.

POMAIKA'I FARM B&B
B&B $$
☎ 328-2112, 800-325-6427; www.luckyfarm.com; Mamalahoa Hwy; r incl breakfast $85-90, s/d coffee barn $90/95

Bought by new owners in late 2007, the 4 acres at Lucky Farm (*pomaika'i* means lucky) are receiving overdue TLC. The two greenhouse rooms are rustic in a good way, with wooden interiors, screens for windows, plus a shared lanai overlooking the orchards. For sweethearts, there's the intimate and private coffee barn with refreshing outdoor shower tucked among the trees. Skip the cheaper farmhouse room ($70) in the cluttered main house. All rooms share an awkward kitchen area. It's between the 106- and 107-mile markers.

KA'AWALOA PLANTATION & GUESTHOUSE
B&B $$
our pick ☎ 323-2686; www.kaawaloaplantation .com; Napo'opo'o Rd; r incl breakfast $125, ste $175; 🖳

Sigh. There are some places too beautiful for words – like this guesthouse with wraparound lanai and unparalleled coastal views. Maybe it's the fine linens, the exquisitely decorated rooms with ocean views or the organic produce growing everywhere. The aloha of the hosts and their attention to detail have something to do with it, surely, as does the privileged location on Napo'opo'o Rd. Sitting in the outdoor hot tub here and watching the sunset might be Hawai'i's most romantic interlude.

HONAUNAU

Growing by leaps and bounds amid thick coffee and macadamia nut groves, Honaunau is a fun place to explore without a guidebook – if only because there will be much more to discover here by the time you read this. Of course, nearby Pu'uhonua o Honaunau National Historical Park, the 'Place of Refuge,' remains the star attraction, but meander down Painted Church Rd,

stopping at fruit stands and coffee shacks with sea views for another type of refuge.

Sights & Activities

ST BENEDICT'S PAINTED CHURCH
☎ 328-2227; 85-5140 Painted Church Rd; donations suggested; 🕑 mass at 7am Tue, Thu & Fri, 4pm Sat, 7:15am Sun

A pulpit with a view, gravestones bursting with tropical blooms, and a little chapel with floor-to-ceiling 'outsider art' make this church a picturesque side trip. A self-taught artist and Catholic priest, John Berchmans Velghe came to Hawai'i from Belgium in 1899 and founded a church near the Place of Refuge before moving it 2 miles upslope, snagging one of the coast's prettiest vistas.

Determined to convert the illiterate natives, Father John painted the walls with a series of biblical scenes ('Hell,' 'The Temptation of Jesus') as visual aids. He modeled the wall behind the altar on the Gothic cathedral in Burgos, Spain. The trompe l'oeil here is delightful, in that naïf art kind of way. Come early or late, when the light is softer and the birds most vocal. For a unique experience, catch **services in Hawaiian** (🕑 7:15am 2nd Sun of the month). Everything is accessible to people in wheelchairs.

PALEAKU GARDENS PEACE SANCTUARY
☎ 328-8084; www.paleaku.com; 83-5401 Painted Church Rd; admission $5; 🕑 9am-4pm Tue-Thu, 7am-9pm Sat

Nine acres of shrines, meditation nooks and even a mini Milky Way await at this tranquil garden sanctuary tucked along Painted Church Rd. The innovative **galaxy garden** is the first accurate representation of our universe rendered in plants. A self-guided tour makes a great introduction to this unique, peaceful place; if you like what you see, try a drop-in **yoga class** ($12) or **stargazing** (admission free, reservations required; 🕑 7-9pm Sat).

Courses

The Society for Kona's Education & Art, or 🌺 SKEA (☎ 328-9392; www.skea.org; 84-5191 Mamalahoa Hwy), is a hotbed of activity, with pilates, Polynesian dance and Japanese ink painting classes, plus pidgin poetry readings and concerts on the lawn. Look for it between the 105- and 106-mile markers.

Eating

Should hunger strike, there are a couple of simple roadside places, including **Bong Brothers** (☎ 328-9289; www.bongbrothers.com; 84-5227 Mamalahoa Hwy; soups and sandwiches $5; ☼ 9am-6pm Mon-Fri, 10am-6pm Sun) with veggie sandwiches and other healthy fare. The coffee served from this landmark building (1929) is from beans grown, pulped, dried and milled on the coffee farm here.

An attraction in its own right, the **South Kona Fruit Stand** (☎ 328-8547; 84-4770 Hwy 11; ☼ 9am-6pm Mon-Sat) has everything from tart cashew apples to filling breadfruit, goopy *abiu* (yellow sapote) and purple jaboticaba. Look for the pineapple flags lining the road.

Sleeping

HALE HO'OLA   B&B $$
☎ 328-9117, 877-628-9117; www.hale-hoola .com; 85-4577 Mamalahoa Hwy; r incl breakfast $110-150; 💻
With only three rooms, staying with Mary and Bob assures personal service. The rooms are comfortable, if small, but extras such as private lanai with distant ocean views, robust breakfasts and great mattresses compensate. The view from the Palm Suite shower is sublime. Couples note: thin walls here make intimacy audible.

ALOHA GUEST HOUSE   B&B $$$$
☎ 328-8955, 800-897-3188; www.alohaguest house.com; 84-4780 Hwy 11; r incl breakfast $180-350; 💻
Start saving now, because if you're coming all the way to Hawai'i, you should have the finest digs, damn the cost. Heady views from the lanai, guest living room and king-sized bed will make you swoon, guaranteed. The views are complemented by the luxurious amenities, including organic bath products, deliciously customized bathrooms and a hot tub. The Honu room is accessible to people in wheelchairs.

Also recommended:
Hawaiian Style Cabin (☎ 328-0717; www.vrbo .com/158038; cabins $75) New, studio-style house located

1 mile inland from Captain Cook is the deal of the island. Get it while it lasts.
Lions' Gate B&B & Farms (☎ 328-2335, 800-955-2332; www.konabnb.com; Hwy 11; r incl breakfast $110, ste $175-180; 💻) Privacy, comfort and gorgeous views recommend this working mac nut and coffee farm.

PU'UHONUA O HONAUNAU NATIONAL HISTORICAL PARK

Visiting this unique **national park** (☎ 328-2326; www.nps.gov/puho; 1-week pass adult/car $3/5, Tri-park Annual Pass $25; ☼ 7am-8pm, visitor center 8am-5pm) fronting Honaunau Bay is a memorable experience. You'll almost always hear this park referred to as the **Place of Refuge**, since the name, meaning 'place of refuge at Honaunau,' is such a tongue twister. In 2008, the park acquired 238 acres of adjacent land, more than doubling its extent. If you're on-island the weekend closest to July 1, pop down for the **cultural festival**, an extravaganza of traditional food, hula and crafts, plus *hukilau* (net fishing) demonstrations and a 'royal court.'

Pu'uhonua o Honaunau temple   GREG ELMS

Ki'i (wooden statues) welcomed *kapu* (taboo) breakers to Pu'uhonua o Honaunau   GREG ELMS

Early morning or late afternoon is the optimum time to visit the park to avoid the midday heat and crowds. For an especially powerful (if eerie) atmosphere, visit on the full moon. Twenty-minute orientation talks are given at 10am, 10:30am, 11am, 2:30pm, 3pm and 3:30pm. Beach wheelchairs (like SUVs for the mobility challenged) are available free at the visitors center.

History

In ancient Hawai'i the *kapu* (taboo) system regulated every waking moment. A commoner could not look at the *ali'i* or walk in his footsteps. Women couldn't cook for men, nor eat with them. Fishing, hunting and gathering timber was restricted to certain seasons. And on and on.

The penalty for breaking *kapu* was death. After all, violating *kapu* infuriated the gods, according to the Hawaiian belief system. And gods wrought volcanic eruptions, tidal waves, famine and earthquakes. To appease ticked-off gods, violators were hunted down and killed.

There was one loophole, however; one chance to save your hide. Commoners who broke a *kapu* could be spared if they reached the sacred ground of a *pu'uhonua* (place of refuge). A *pu'uhonua* also gave sanctuary to defeated warriors and wartime 'noncombatants' (men who were too old, too young or unable to fight).

To reach the *pu'uhonua* was no small feat. Since royals and their warriors lived on the grounds surrounding the refuge, *kapu* breakers had to swim through violent, open ocean, braving currents and sharks, to safety. Once inside the sanctuary, priests performed ceremonies of absolution to placate the gods. *Kapu* breakers could then return home to start fresh.

Sights

While most of the half-mile, sandy **walking tour** trail is accessible with standard and beach wheelchairs, visiting sights near the water requires walking across rough lava.

Pu'uhonua o Honaunau comprises two sections: the royal grounds and the place of refuge. First is the royal grounds, where Kona *ali'i* and their warriors lived. **Hale o Keawe Heiau**, the temple on the cove's outcropping, was built around 1650 and contains the bones of 23 chiefs. It was believed the chiefs' mana (spiritual essence) remained in their bones and bestowed sanctity on those entering the grounds. A fishpond, lava tree molds, hand-carved koa canoe and a few thatched shelters are also in this section. Sea turtles nibble and rest around **Keone'ele Cove**, which was once the royal canoe landing.

Ohia trees carved into *ki'i* (statues) standing up to 15ft high front an authentic-looking heiau reconstruction. Leading up to the heiau is the **Great Wall** separating the royal grounds from the *pu'uhonua*. Built around 1550, this stone wall is more than 1000ft long and 10ft high. Inside the wall are two older heiau.

An oceanfront **picnic area** with tables and barbecues in a palm-tree grove lies just south of the park center. It's a pretty sweet spot. Here **tide pools** in *pahoehoe* (smooth lava) rock contain *pipipi* (tiny black mollusks), coral, sea hares and sea urchins.

Activities

After wandering the self-guided trail, you might try some **wildlife watching**: humpback whales are offshore in winter, plus turtles

and dolphins and even hoary bats can be seen here (after sunset is best).

SNORKELING

Just north of the Place of Refuge is **Two-Step**, second only to Kealakekua Bay for its visibility and variety. It's also a popular **kayak** put-in, so you can paddle here, too. Grab your gear and hang a left outside the park entrance.

Snorkelers step off two naturally formed lava steps (hence the name) immediately north of the boat ramp into about 10ft of water. It then drops off to about 25ft. Look for, but by no means touch, the predatory, razor-sharp 'crown of thorns' starfish feasting on live coral polyps here.

A rising tide means better snorkeling, since the water's deeper and the tide brings in fish. Unfortunately, high winter surf can create rough waters. Sunbathing is discouraged by park rangers and locals, and visitors cannot leave towels or mats on the ground.

While you're strongly discouraged from snorkeling in the park itself, green sea turtles frequent shallow Keone'ele Cove inside the Place of Refuge.

HIKING

The 2-mile round-trip **1871 Trail to Ki'ilae Village** is a mellow way to walk off lunch. The trailhead is off the road toward the picnic grounds.

You'll pass a collapsed lava tube, temple ruins and a *holua* (sled course), before reaching the steep **Alahaka Ramp**, which allowed riders on horseback to travel between villages. Halfway up the ramp is Waiu-O-Hina lava tube, which opens to the sea.

At the top of the ramp, incredible vistas of scalloped ocean coves spread out below. Keep going to the spot where Ki'ilae Village once stood, heading back where the trail ends at a fence. Ask rangers for an information booklet about the site.

HO'OKENA

It's probably a blessing most tourists just zip by the turnoff for this **beach** between the 101- and 102-mile markers. But meander a couple of miles down to this fishing community and you'll discover a dark sandy beach locals will wish you didn't. Err on

KONA COAST

Outrigger canoes at Miloli'i Beach   GREG ELMS

the side of respectful caution as you explore here and let the fun unfold.

Ho'okena was once a bustling village with two churches, a school, a courthouse and a post office. King Kalakaua sent Robert Louis Stevenson here in 1889 to show him a typical Hawaiian village. Stevenson stayed a week (this could happen to you!) and wrote about Ho'okena in *Travels in Hawaii*.

In the 1890s, Chinese immigrants began to colonize Ho'okena. Shops, restaurants, a tavern and a hotel opened, and the town got rougher and rowdier. In those days, Big Island cattle were shipped from the Ho'okena landing to market in Honolulu. When the circle-island road was built, the steamers stopped coming and people moved away. By the 1920s, this was more ghost town than boom town.

Today Ho'okena is a small fishing village with a little mellow beach lapped by sparkling tranquil waters. The vibe is local here (some drug activity, too) and tourists of a type usually don't stick around long. When the winter surf is up, young spongers hit the waves. When it's calm, **kayakers** paddle around, and the **snorkeling** is good straight out from the landing. It drops off pretty quickly, and there's lots of coral, but there are strong currents further out, so again, respect. Dolphins have been known to rest in Kauhako Bay. There is no drinking water.

Camping is allowed with a county permit (see p273), but campers have been harassed here in the past.

MILOLI'I

Even more remote and standoffish than neighboring Ho'okena, Miloli'i is a **fishing village** fighting to maintain its traditional ways and this includes keeping development out. Needless to say, privacy is paramount in these parts and curious tourists are tolerated – barely.

Miloli'i ('fine twist') was named for its skilled sennit twisters, who used bark from the *olona* (a native shrub) to make fine cord and highly valued fishnets. Villagers still live close to the sea, and many continue to make a living from it, including Miloli'i *kupuna* (elders) who participate in the Community Conservation Network's **Traditional Knowledge Project** (www.conservationpractice.org), passing on customs and knowledge to local youth.

The turnoff is just south of the 89-mile marker on Hwy 11, 5 miles down a steep, winding, paved single-lane road that cuts across a 1926 lava flow. At the end of the road, you'll reach a natty beach park pocked with **tide pools**. Explore the coastal area past the church for nice surprises. Camping along the rocky shore is allowed with a county permit (see p273).

NORTH KONA COAST

Dropping from the lush Kohala Mountains down to the sere North Kona Coast, it's hard to believe you're on the same island, let alone just 20 minutes from upcountry ranchland where cows graze on tall green grass.

If you're coming from Kailua-Kona, you're probably bored already by the lava fields covered in coral graffiti extending to the sparkling sea. Penetrate those fields, however, and you'll be snorkeling with turtles, walking on powdery black sand and waiting for the famously elusive and spectacular green flash as the sun disappears beyond the horizon. Turn inland and you'll see Mauna Kea, Mauna Loa (both snowcapped in winter) and, between the two, Mt Hualalai. North Kona technically runs 33 miles along Queen Ka'ahumanu Hwy (Hwy 19), from Kailua-Kona up the Kona Coast to Kawaihae, where South Kohala begins.

HONOKOHAU HARBOR

Almost all of Kona's catch comes in at this harbor 2 miles north of Kailua-Kona, including the 'granders' – fish weighing over 1000lb. The majority of snorkeling/diving tours (p58) and whale-watching tours (p61) also leave from here. To reach the harbor, turn *makai* on Kealakehe Rd, just north of the 98-mile marker.

Beaches

HONOKOHAU BEACH

Just minutes from the bustle of Kailua-Kona is this beautiful hook-shaped beach with a mix of black lava, white coral and wave-tossed shell fragments. Bring your reef shoes – you'll need them for the rocky bottom here. The water is usually too cloudy for snorkeling, but just standing on shore you'll see green turtles. Look for more feeding around the 'Ai'opio fishtrap, bordered by an ancient heiau at the south end of the beach.

To get here, turn right into the first harbor parking lot (look for the small public coastal access sign). Near the end of the road is the signposted trailhead; a five-minute walk on a well-beaten path leads to the beach. You can also reach Honokohau Beach along the easy Ala Hele Ike Trail starting from **Kaloko-Honokohau National Historical Park** (p97) – a beautiful way to end the day.

Continue past the first parking lot to the second and you'll see an **altar** on the shoreline to the south and 'Alula Beach, a sandy grotto lapped by aqua-green water just steps away. If you walk north through the lot you'll enter a peaceful, grassy coconut grove with lawn chairs for kicking back and watching the water traffic.

Activities

SNORKELING

From Honokohau Harbor south to Kailua Bay is a marine-life conservation district, but the snorkeling is mediocre. For the good stuff, there are many tours sailing out of Honokohau Harbor for snorkeling at Kealakekua Bay and with the **manta rays** (p60) at night.

DIVING

This stretch of coast is littered with dive sites, accessed by boats leaving from Honokohau Harbor. **Turtle Pinnacle** is a premier turtle-spotting site, with great photo opportunities.

Another good spot is off **Kaiwi Point**, south of Honokohau Harbor, where sea turtles, large fish and huge eagle rays swim around respectable drop-offs. Northbound is **Suck 'Em Up**, a couple of lava tubes you swim into, letting the swell pull you through. Other nearby sites include **Eel Cove**, **Golden Arches** and **High Rock**.

Ocean Eco Tours (☎ 324-7873; www.oceanecotours .com; 74-425 Kealakehe Pkwy), in Honokohau Harbor opposite Harbor House, has tours to all the popular diving spots in these parts. It also offers surfing lessons.

See p60 for a list of other recommended diving operators.

FISHING

Scads of fishing charters leave from Honokohau Harbor; for information on bookings, see p61. If you're just after the money

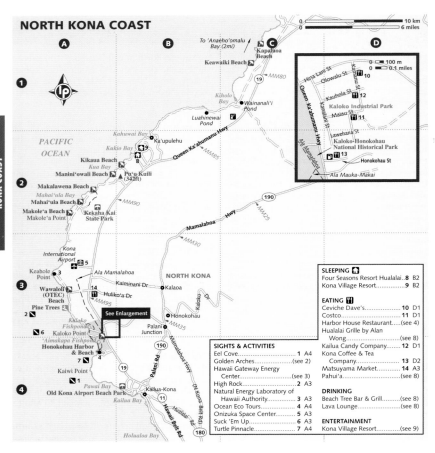

NORTH KONA COAST

SLEEPING 🛏️
Four Seasons Resort Hualalai..**8** B2
Kona Village Resort..............**9** B2

EATING 🍴
Ceviche Dave's....................**10** D1
Costco.................................**11** D1
Harbor House Restaurant.....(see 4)
Hualalai Grille by Alan
 Wong...............................(see 8)
Kailua Candy Company.......**12** D1
Kona Coffee & Tea
 Company..........................**13** D2
Matsuyama Market............**14** A3
Pahui'a.............................(see 8)

DRINKING
Beach Tree Bar & Grill.........(see 8)
Lava Lounge......................(see 8)

ENTERTAINMENT
Kona Village Resort............(see 9)

SIGHTS & ACTIVITIES
Eel Cove.............................**1** A4
Golden Arches.................(see 2)
Hawaii Gateway Energy
 Center.............................(see 3)
High Rock..........................**2** A3
Natural Energy Laboratory of
 Hawaii Authority.............**3** A3
Ocean Eco Tours.................**4** A4
Onizuka Space Center.........**5** A3
Suck 'Em Up......................**6** A3
Turtle Pinnacle...................**7** A4

shot, you can catch the boats as they pull up and weigh their haul of marlin and *'ahi* (yellowfin tuna) around 11:30am and 3:30pm. Drive straight in, park near the gas station and walk to the dock behind the adjacent building.

HIKING
Winner of the 2007 Keep it Hawai'i award and chosen Ecotour Operator of the Year (2006) by the Hawaii Ecotourism Association, **ourpick** **Hawai'i Forest & Trail** (☎ 331-8505, 800-464-1993; www.hawaii-forest.com; 74-5035B Queen Ka'ahumanu Hwy) is the outfit for those wishing to delve into the island's greenest depths. From its super popular Mauna Kea summit and stargazing tour to

its exclusive hikes into the Hakalau Forest Wildlife Refuge, you won't regret an adventure with these experts.

Eating

🍴 CEVICHE DAVE'S   Ceviche $
☎ 326-4737; Suite 100, 73-4976 Kamanu St; ceviche $7; ⏱ 10:30am-6pm Tue-Sun
Dave is a surfer, world traveler, eco-conscious business guy, master wood carver and ceviche phenom. Pull up one of the four stools for the island-inspired 'Kohanaiki' (cilantro, mac nuts, bell pepper and *liliko'i* juice) or the Tahitian-style 'Ta'apuna' featuring coconut milk. Everything is made with fish 'caught yesterday

at South Point' or equally fresh. Thatched lanai, sparkling conversation and loads of aloha give Dave's the warmth of a true beach-shack *cevicheria*.

HARBOR HOUSE RESTAURANT
Seafood $$

☎ 326-4166; harbor complex; mains $7-18; ⏰ 11am-7pm Mon-Sat, to 5:30pm Sun

The beer and gossip are flowing at this perennially popular place with reliable food, harbor views and fair prices. Make like the locals and duck out of traffic for happy-hour schooners (18oz beer for $2.50; 4pm to 6pm Monday to Saturday, to 5:15pm Sunday) and flaky fish and chips at one of the terrific harbor-view tables.

Several places are along the highway across from the harbor and in the Kaloko Industrial Park, including the following:

Costco (☎ 334-0770; www.costco.com; 73-5600 Maiau St; annual membership $50; ⏰ 10am-8:30pm Mon-Fri, 9:30am-6pm Sat, 10am-6pm Sun) Cheesy pizza, cheap gas and volume discounts on everything; members only.

Kailua Candy Company (☎ 329-2522, 800-622-2462; www.kailua-candy.com; cnr Kauhola & Kamanu Sts; ⏰ 8am-6pm Mon-Sat, 10am-4pm Sun) Outrageously good chocolates are made at this family factory. Free samples!

Kona Coffee & Tea Company (☎ 329-6577, 888-873-2035; www.konacoffeeandtea.com; Suite 5A, 73-5053 Hwy 19; ⏰ 7am-5pm Mon-Fri, 9am-5pm Sat, 1-5pm Sun) Life is too short for bad coffee: head here for award-winning 100% Kona. Free tastings include Peaberry.

Matsuyama Market (cnr Hwy 19 & Huliko'a Dr; ⏰ 8am-7pm Mon-Sat, 9am-5pm Sun) The closest beer, wine and groceries to the resorts and harbor.

KALOKO-HONOKOHAU NATIONAL HISTORICAL PARK

Kaloko-Honokohau (☎ 329-6881; www.nps.gov /kaho; admission free; ⏰ 8am-5pm) should be obligatory for new arrivals. Hidden in those ominous-looking lava fields are the innovations that allowed the ancient Hawaiians to thrive in this hostile landscape: fish traps, lava planters used to grow taro and other staples, plus the very *ahupua'a* (Kaloko and Honokohau) that give the park its name. These traditional land divisions cut a wedge from mountain to sea, ensuring each community had equal slice of the bounty. Pure

genius. There are also **heiau, burial caves** and **petroglyphs**. The 1160-acre park is sacred Hawaiian ground and it's said the bones of Kamehameha were secretly buried near Kaloko Fishpond.

Yet this national historical park is virtually unknown, even by locals, who associate Kaloko with Costco, located in the Kaloko Industrial Park across the highway. Sad, but true. Despite the seemingly endless expanse of lava rock and unbearable midday heat, this is a good place to explore. Go in the early morning, in the late afternoon or when it's overcast, so you can enjoy it without fainting.

The entrance is between the 96- and 97-mile markers, where there's a small but informative visitors center. From here there are several trailheads, including the coastal **Ala Hele Kahakai** – a 1-mile restored segment of the ancient King's Trail – leading to Kaloko and the three-quarter-mile **Ala Hele Ike Trail** to lovely Honokohau Beach.

Sights & Activities

At the north corner of the park is **Kaloko Fishpond**, where some 200 archaeological sites have been discovered. Its sister property, **'Aimakapa Fishpond**, is the biggest on the Kona Coast – you can't miss it toward the southern end of the park. The **bird-watching** is notable here, with *'alae ke'oke'o* (Hawaiian coot; looks like a fat, black pheasant) and *ae'o* (Hawaiian black-necked stilt; tall, long-beaked bird dressed like a penguin) frequenting the fishpond. Both are endangered native birds making a comeback. There's a *holua* (stone slide) near here, too.

Inland from the northern end of Honokohau Beach are **anchialine ponds** – pools of brackish water that provided drinking water to the ancients. Today they're a unique habitat for marine and plant life.

KEAHOLE POINT

Funny place, Keahole Point. Just offshore, the seafloor drops abruptly, providing a continuous supply of both cold water from 3000ft depths and warm surface water. These are ideal conditions for ocean thermal-energy conversion (OTEC), deep sea water extraction and aquaculture. All of this

KONA COAST

DETOUR ➡

KONA COAST BACKCOUNTRY

Walking across fields of 'a'a (rough, jagged lava) under a hot, beating sun is like stumbling over sharp Cap'n Crunch in an oven. But once you plunge into the clear, turquoise depths of the Kona Coast's remote beaches, you'll see all that ankle-wrenching was worth it. Not up for a grueling hike? Take the shorter route between the 78- and 79-mile markers off Hwy 11.

One section of coast highly worth the effort is the trail from 'Anaeho'omalu Bay south to **Keawaiki Beach**. Hugging the coastline, the trail is relatively well marked, crossing varying beaches and lava fields. Start by heading south from the beach at the Waikaloa Beach Marriott. Adding continued solitude with each forward step, the protected coves and outer reefs at **Kapalaoa Beach** provide good possibilities for swimming, snorkeling and surfing. Look for the Pu'uanahulu Homesteads after the first point and, a mile beyond, a lone palm at Akahu Kaimu. Tucked just behind the beach here is probably the most pristine **brackish pool** on the island. A few fish, eels and other sea life have made their way in through subsurface caves, so snorkel in this large pool when the tide is high.

Continue for another 2 miles over rugged 'a'a flows, and past swimming holes and hidden snorkeling gems when the water is calm. The trail is occasionally marked by white coral, but mainly follows the coast until the beach at Keawaiki. You'll know you've arrived when you reach the former estate of Francis I'i Brown, an influential and loved 20th-century Hawaiian businessman. Passing the house, look for the lava trail through a grove of mesquite trees. This leads 1.5 miles back to the highway.

Bring at least 2L of water per person and ample food for this long day hike. The sun is intense from reflection off the lava and sea, and there is almost no shade so make sure to bring a wide-brimmed hat, sunglasses and lots of sunscreen.

is happening here, plus there's a beach and one of the island's best breaks.

Beaches & Sights

WAWALOLI (OTEC) BEACH

Nicknamed OTEC, since it's at the end of the Nelha (see below) access road, Wawaloli Beach has some interesting tide pools, tempered by the jets flying overhead. Swimming isn't good here, except at high tide when the protected tide pools and other pockets in the lava-rock coastline are brimming.

NATURAL ENERGY LABORATORY OF HAWAII AUTHORITY

Nelha; ☎ 329-8073; www.nelha.org; ⏱ 9am-1pm

That funny-looking building with the gigantic solar panels on Hwy 19 is Nelha's visitors center and crown jewel: the ❀ **Hawaii Gateway Energy Center**. This 'zero-net energy facility' was voted one of the 10 greenest buildings in the country by the American Institute of Architects in 2007. Learn about Nelha's research and technologies at its **public lectures** (☎ 329-8073; www.keaholepoint.org; adult/child/senior & student $8/free/5; ⏱ 10-11:30am Tue-Thu). Reservations are recommended.

Almost 40 businesses call this 'ocean science and technology park' home, including **Kona Blue** (www.kona-blue.com), the aquaculture gurus responsible for the Kona Kampachi (a type of yellowtail tuna) you see on menus from the Four Seasons (p100) to Merriman's (p133), and **Kona Deep** (www.dswihawaii.com), one of the brands of 100% Hawaii Deep Sea Water desalinated and bottled here. At $5 a liter, that has to be super 'ono drinking water. Curiously, this water is one of the state's leading exports. You can also tour and taste offerings from the **abalone farm** (tour $25; ⏱ 10am Mon, Wed & Thu) here.

The turnoff is 1 mile south of Kona airport, between the 94- and 95-mile markers.

Activities

SURFING

From OTEC beach, you can also reach **Pine Trees** (⏱ 6am-8pm), one of the Big Island's best surfing breaks. This is a local spot where the waves fill up on weekends when everyone's out surfing several breaks depending on the tide and swell (an incoming midtide is favorable in general, but these breaks often close out in higher winter swells). Get friendly with the regulars if you want in on the action. Take the Nelha road until it veers right, then look leftward for a well-worn 4WD road leading south. It's about 2 miles further on to Pine Trees. It's called Pine Trees because, way back, some local surfers saw mangroves near the break and (failing plant ID) thought they were pines.

ONIZUKA SPACE CENTER

In addition to beef and orchids, Hawai'i also raises astronauts. The **Astronaut Ellison S Onizuka Space Center** (☎ 329-3441; adult/child $3/1; ⏰ 8:30am-4:30pm), between the departure and arrival huts at Kona Airport, pays tribute to the Big Island native who perished in the 1986 *Challenger* disaster.

The little **museum** features exhibits and educational films about space, and proudly displays a piece of moon rock, a NASA space suit and scale models of spacecraft.

KEKAHA KAI STATE PARK

For a memorable beach experience, take a day to explore 1600-acre **Kekaha Kai** (⏰ 9am-7pm Thu-Tue), formerly known as Kona Coast State Park. Accessible by 4WD or foot, the several beaches comprising the park have remote coves full of turtles, picturesque sand dunes and calm pools for swimming. Use the facilities at the main beach before setting out – the rest is wonderfully undeveloped.

Beaches

MAHAI'ULA BEACH

The easiest beach to reach is Mahai'ula, with salt-and-pepper sand, lots of shade, tide pools, picnic tables and room to roam. **Snorkeling** and **swimming** are usually good here, but during big winter swells, **surfing** happens on the bay's north side. Winter also brings **whales**, which you'll see breaching in the distance.

For a softer, whiter beach, walk north along the coast across a short lava flow to **Magoon's** (so-called for the local family that used to own these parts – the abandoned house near the coconut grove was theirs). Snorkeling is lackluster here, but **swimming**

and **kayaking** shine in this protected scoop of sand with lots of shade. You can hook up with the path to Makalawena Beach (below) here, beyond the coconut grove at the northern end.

Access to these beaches is via a chunky lava road between the 90- and 91-mile markers. Unless you have a 4WD, the best way to traverse the 1.5 miles is on foot. Park at the improvised lot a quarter-mile in from the highway and use your thumb – drivers going your way will take pity on your sun-beaten head and give you a lift.

MAKALAWENA BEACH

our pick This 4WD/hike combination leads to several coves of progressively softer white sand and turquoise waters that, though popular, absorb crowds so well you may have a minibeach to yourself.

The first cove after clearing the dunes has a protected **baby pool** on the south end and brackish **Opaeula Pond** inland for washing off the salt; keep walking north to the second cove for more protected swimming and good **bodyboarding** waves, especially in winter. At the third cove, the sands are even softer and **snorkeling** is a possibility; give the many sea turtles a wide berth.

Practice aloha during a visit here by packing out your trash and respecting the privacy of others. This is a local camping and fishing getaway and the growing popularity of these beaches is contentious for some.

There are several ways to get here. With a 4WD, the Kekaha Kai access road between the 90- and 91-mile markers is yours for the taking. After 1.25 miles (before reaching the Kekaha Kai facilities), turn right onto the lava road. Park in the lot there and walk across the lava flow and dunes to the beach. The walk is under 30 minutes on a well-beaten path over bitchy '*a*'a.

No 4WD? No problem. Take the Kekaha Kai access road as far as you dare and hike the remainder, accessing the trail heading north after 1.25 miles of walking along Mahai'ula Beach.

MANINI'OWALI BEACH (KUA BAY)

Definitely one of Kona's most user-friendly beaches, crescent-shaped Manini'owali, also called Kua Bay, boasts powdery white sand and clear blue waters good for **swimming** and **bodyboarding**. Even without shade, this is a top beach for fun in the sun – try paddling your board to the loaf-shaped rock to the north for a 5ft cliff jump. Unfortunately, the new paved access road means this beach (and the waves, especially) is often crowded. It's a good place for kids to meet other kids.

To get here, turn onto the Kekaha Kai State Park access road between the 88- and 89-mile markers.

MAKOLE'A BEACH
Amazingly, there's a secluded **black-sand beach** near Kekaha Kai's main parking lot. To reach this small, dark treasure on foot, head south along Mahai'ula Beach to the easy-to-navigate 'path' crosscutting the lava fields along the coast. With a 4WD, turn left at the parking lot, drive for about 1000yd until you reach a path marked by coral, then get out and hoof it when the lava becomes too rough. Let's hope some coconuts wash up here to provide future shade – for now, bring the high-SPF sunscreen.

KA'UPULEHU
Once a thriving fishing village in a string of them dotting this length of coast, Ka'upulehu was wiped out by the 1946 tsunami and abandoned until the Kona Village Resort opened here in 1965. The luxurious Four Seasons Hualalai followed in 1996. These are the island's poshest resorts, which by law have to provide public coastal access – meaning you can sun yourself like a turtle after a seaweed buffet here. What you can't do is hit the links at the PGA-tour **Four Seasons Hualalai Course** (☎ 325-8000; www .fourseasons.com/hualalai/golf.html), designed by golfing legend Jack Nicklaus: it's for members and guests only (including those from Kona Village).

Beaches
KIKAUA BEACH
🕑 **dawn to 30min after dusk**
Obviously artificial (the thin layer of sand laid over concrete is hard on the feet), this beach created by the private club it fronts has some things going for it. There's lots of shade and a completely protected cove is perfect for teaching little kids to **swim** and even **snorkel**. Around the kiawe-covered point are gaggles

of turtles, some quite large. Plus, access is limited to 25 cars, so it's never that crowded. Access is via Kuki'o Nui Rd near the 87-mile marker; go to the gate and request a pass.

KUKIO BAY
🕑 **dawn-dusk**
Get the five-star resort beach without the price by visiting the scalloped, palm-fringed coves of Kukio Bay. The sand is soft, the **swimming** is good (even for kids) and there are beach trails leading north to the Four Seasons and south to more stretches of pristine sand. To get here, turn at Ka'upulehu Rd, between the 87- and 86-mile markers; tell the gatekeeper you're headed to the beach.

Eating
HUALALAI GRILLE BY ALAN WONG
Hawaii Regional $$$$

our pick ☎ 325-8525; Golf Clubhouse, Four Seasons Resort Hualalai, 72-100 Ka'upulehu Dr; appetizers $11-19, mains $37-54; 🕑 dinner
'One of the best meals I've eaten, ever,' declared a die-hard foodie after devouring the five-course tasting menu developed by celebrity chef Alan Wong ($70/100 without/with wine pairing). The soy-braised short ribs are so good they should be illegal, and the diver scallop is sublime. Wong's signature soup and sandwich is the weak link, surprisingly, but the desserts compensate. The mahimahi in wasabi butter entrée is heaven on a plate. Come hungry.

Also at the Four Seasons is the elegant oceanfront **Pahui'a** (☎ 325-8000; mains $32-48; 🕑 6:30-11:30am & 5:30-9:30pm), serving an elaborate breakfast buffet ($32) by day and upscale regional Hawaiian cuisine by night.

Drinking & Entertainment

KONA VILLAGE RESORT
☎ 325-5555, 800-367-5290; 1 Kahuwai Bay Dr;
adult/child 3-5yr/6-12yr $98/40/67; 🕑 5:30pm
Wed & Fri

The island's oldest commercial luau
achieves authenticity with pig cooked in
an *imu* (traditional earthen oven), its old
Hawaii setting and talented fire-eaters.
Wednesday is Polynesian-style; Friday is
Hawaiian. Reservations are required.

BEACH TREE BAR & GRILL
☎ 325-8000; Four Seasons Resort Hualalai, 72-100
Ka'upulehu Dr; 🕑 11:30am-8:30pm

You don't have to be a guest to have the best
sunset seat – just come on down, have some
cocktails and enjoy the nightly **hula and live
music** (🕑 6pm).

Also at the Four Seasons is the **Lava Lounge**
(🕑 5:30-10pm), with award-winning musicians and sushi nightly.

Sleeping

KONA VILLAGE RESORT   Resort $$$$
☎ 325-5555, 800-367-5290; www.konavillage
.com; 1 Kahuwai Bay Dr; 1br hale $660-975; 💻 🛰

If you really want to get away, unique Kona
Village (no phones, clocks, radios or TV)
is for you. The trade-off is an intimate,
culturally rich experience connecting with

nature at this 82-acre beach resort tucked
among lava flows, fishponds and petroglyphs. Accommodations are in individual
thatched-roof *hale* (houses), and rates include meals and activities (luau, outrigger
canoeing), plus 100% Kona coffee (something even the Four Seasons doesn't offer).
Kona Village has an award-winning kids'
program, too. Recently acquired by the Four
Seasons, upgrades are happening fast here,
with 25 new *hale* under construction.

FOUR SEASONS RESORT
HUALALAI   Resort $$$$
☎ 325-8000, 888-340-5662; www.fourseasons
.com; 72-100 Ka'upulehu Dr; r $725-1035, 1br ste
$1450-2260, 2br ste $2215-3335, incl breakfast;
🅿 🛰 💻 🛰

The Hualalai is not the island's only five
diamond resort by accident. Those acco-
lades are earned through lavish attention to
detail (fresh orchids in every room, crayons
and kids' robes, multimedia lending library)
and top-flight service. The golf course, spa
and lap pool are world class, plus there's a
big, well-stocked snorkel tank, including
manta rays. Downstairs units have wonderful outdoor showers. A hip, rock 'n' roll
clientele adds to the cachet here. The only
drawbacks are the resort's sloping, rocky
beach, which attracts loads of turtles but offers limited swimming, and lanai overlooking public areas, which can lack privacy.

KIHOLO BAY

If you're looking for a beach with a little
something for everyone, head to 2-mile-
wide ⟨ourpick⟩ **Kiholo Bay** (🕑 7am-7pm). Incred-
ibly, this oasis in the lava is not thronged
by visitors, despite the wonderful **black-sand
beaches**, chances for **wildlife viewing** and
swimming in a lava tube. This is a fun destination for explorers, with a tide-dependent
landscape that changes dramatically.

Upon arrival, turn left (south), go to
the end of the beach and take the lava
path toward the coconut grove in the distance, where there's a series of secluded
black beaches. Soft sand, whales breaching
offshore, shells and solitude are all here;
the lower the tide, the bigger the beach.
With calm waters, you can swim. The coconut grove rings **Luahinewai**, a large, cold,
spring-fed pond belonging to that private

Hale at Kona Village Resort   CONNER GORRY

KONA COAST

estate you see. **Sea kayaking** around this point to the south will delight experienced paddlers.

Back on the main beach, you can explore far to the north, especially when the tide's out. The seaweed-covered tide pools host lots of *honu* (turtles), and you're almost certain to see some. Once the gravel path ends, look inland for **Keanalele**, a lava tube filled with the clearest freshwater you're likely to lay eyes on. Swimming the 40ft tube, between the two sky holes, is a rush. The amazing wooden abode near here with exquisitely carved details is known as the **Bali house**: you'll know it when you see it.

To get here, turn *makai* on the gravel road between the 82- and 83-mile markers. Follow the road for a mile, taking the left-hand fork and parking at the abandoned round house.

ISLAND VOICES

NAME: KASSIE MAKANA KOMETANI
OCCUPATION: STUDENT, OPEN OCEAN SWIMMER, FUTURE WORLD TRAVELER
RESIDENCE: HAWI

What is open ocean swimming exactly? In some races, like Cinco de Mayo at 'A Bay,' you swim around buoys. In others you swim from one beach to another. That's what I did at Kukio Bay, where I had to swim for a mile.

Did you win? I don't really do it to win. I do it for the experience and exercise.

Don't you get creeped out by things in the water? Not really, you get used to it. You know all that marine life is there, but you're just concentrating on finishing. Sometimes I get bitten by micro jelly fish, but they don't really hurt. It's like something's nibbling on you. I saw a turtle once. That was distracting!

So I guess you want to be an Ironman triathlete? I'm not a runner. I mean, I like to run, but I'm not sure I want to do the triathlon. Maybe. I want to learn like four or five different languages and travel. I have a list of places and sometimes I get out my map and magnifying glass and build on the list…Europe, South America, Asia. I don't think Antarctica's on the list.

What's your favorite thing to do on the Big Island? I like to go camping. Makalawena Beach is one of my favorite spots. It's cool how there are several beaches that you can walk to and discover.

What's the best thing about living here? It's not like the city with tall buildings and traffic and stuff. Here you can actually see the stars. They're so beautiful! Then there's the marine life and ocean.

What haven't you done here that you'd like to? I've never seen the lava. And Mauna Kea. I can't go up there yet.

Do you have any advice for kids coming to the Big Island? Bring sunscreen. And never turn your back on the ocean. And with the big waves – you have to dive under them. It kind of feels cool on your back and then you just pop back up.

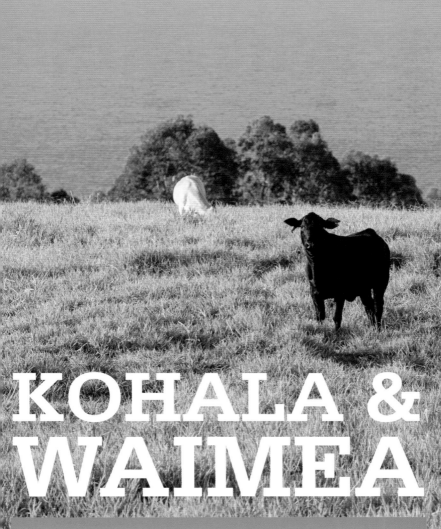

KOHALA &
WAIMEA

Kohala is a study in contrasts. South Kohala is the archetypal sun-and-sea resort mecca, while North Kohala proudly remains rural with nary a high-rise in sight. Waimea, a long-standing ranch town in between, is a central stop for cross-island travelers. From Waikoloa to Kawaihae, Hawaiian history is evident in ancient trails, heiau (temples), fishponds and petroglyphs. Since the 1960s, however, swanky resorts and golf courses have been the main attraction. In counterpoint to the south's artificial oases, North Kohala is a stunning natural wonder, with magnificent pastureland blanketing the Kohala Mountains, quaint plantation towns, and Pololu Valley's rugged cliffs and valleys.

KOHALA & WAIMEA
ITINERARIES

IN TWO DAYS *This leg: 25 miles*

❶ V BEACH STATE RECREATION AREA (p117) Any of South Kohala's renowned beaches are best enjoyed first thing in the morning. Hapuna Beach is convenient for most, as it accommodates the whole range of water sports (although not all at once).

❷ PUAKO PETROGLYPH PRESERVE (p112) Pack a picnic and kick back at Holoholokai Beach Park (p111), a whole different shore, all lava and coral stones. Afterward, take a mini hike to a fascinating concentration of petroglyphs.

❸ SPA SPLURGE (p113) For the ultimate in pampering, Spa Without Walls and the Mauna Lani Spa will not disappoint.

❹ PU'UKOHOLA HEIAU NATIONAL HISTORIC SITE (p119) On day two, head north. King Kamehameha I built this heiau

during his fight for supremacy over the Hawaiian Kingdom – and while it's in ruins, it still inspires awe.

❺ HAMAKUA MACADAMIA NUT COMPANY (p119) Stop at the tidy visitors center for a free tour and ample samples!

❻ POLOLU VALLEY (p127) The view from the lookout will only whet your appetite for deeper exploration into this mysterious valley. Hike down the short but steep (and slippery) trail to the beach.

❼ HAWI (p124) End your day at historic Hawi, a former plantation village that boasts a variety of pleasing eateries. Sushi Rock (p124) and Bamboo (p125) are definitely on the map, so reserve a table if possible.

IN FOUR DAYS *This leg: 35 miles*

❽ KOHALA MOUNTAIN ROAD (p124) On your third day, head to Waimea (p129) on this bucolic, two-lane highway; with such stunning views of the vast island, it's almost a traffic hazard.

❾ ISAACS ART CENTER (p130) Kick back in misty, *paniolo* (cowboy) Waimea town. At first glance, you'll see only strip malls along the highway, but among its charms are many fine-art galleries, such as Isaacs.

❿ HORSEBACK RIDING (p131) See the ranchland from the back of a horse with Dahana Ranch Roughriders.

⓫ KOHALA FOREST RESERVE TRAIL (p135) End the day hiking the 'White Road' trail through magical forestland, with green gulches, moss-covered bridges, countless waterfalls and other natural wonders.

⓬ MAUNA KEA GOLF COURSE (p117) Golfers, don't miss your chance to play this legendary course (or its humbler sister course, the Hapuna Golf Course). Also worthy are the Waikoloa Beach Course (p109) and its sister Kings' Course, and the Francis I'i Brown North & South Courses (p113). If you're on a budget, snag twilight rates in the afternoon.

⓭ SNORKELING CRUISE (p108) Nongolfers, go underwater. South Kohala waters are pristine, full of interesting marine life and much-less trafficked than Kailua-Kona's.

⓮ BROWN'S BEACH HOUSE (p114) This oceanfront icon is among the best venues for Hawaii Regional Cuisine and memorable sunsets.

FOR HISTORY

❶ KALAHUIPUA'A FISHPONDS & HISTORIC TRAIL (p111) On the grounds of the Mauna Lani Bay Hotel & Bungalows, these ancient Hawaiian sites are beautifully preserved.

❷ PUAKO PETROGLYPH PRESERVE (p112) A short walk from Holoholokai Beach Park leads to a large, well-preserved collection of petroglyphs carved in smooth lava fields.

❸ ALA KAHAKAI TRAIL (p119) From Kawaihae to Puako, this trail follows the footsteps of ancient Hawaiians along the coast, passing undeveloped shoreline, anchialine ponds, rugged lava rock, sandy beaches and today's chichi resorts. Sunscreen is a must.

❹ LAPAKAHI STATE HISTORICAL PARK (p121) Use your imagination when walking the site of an ancient Hawaiian village.

❺ MO'OKINI LUAKINI HEIAU (p122) Standing alone on the remote North Kohala Coast, this heiau is testament to the island's mana (spiritual essence). Also see **Pu'ukohola Heiau (p119)**, built by Kamehameha the Great.

❻ KOHALA'S HISTORICAL ARCHITECTURE (p124 and p125) North Kohala's two towns, Hawi and Kapa'au, charm 'em all with dapper restored buildings surrounded by rural farming land. Worth a stop is **Kenji's House (p125)**, a café, minimuseum and art co-op on a long-standing homestead.

❼ PARKER RANCH MUSEUM & HISTORIC HOMES (p129) This modest little museum offers a glimpse of the lifestyle and legacy of Hawaii's biggest ranching family.

KOHALA & WAIMEA

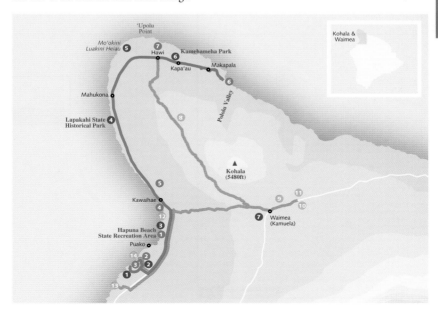

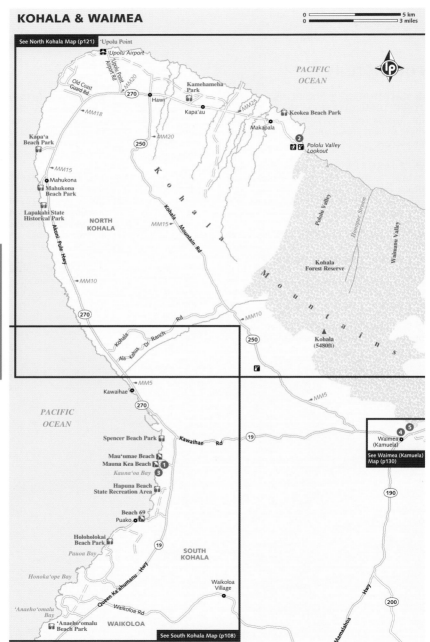

KOHALA & WAIMEA

0 ————————— 5 km
0 ————————— 3 miles

See North Kohala Map (p121)

Upolu Point

Upolu Airport

PACIFIC
OCEAN

Upolu Point
Airport Rd

270

Old Coast
Guard Rd

MM20

Kamehameha
Park

Hawi

MM25

Kapa'au

Keokea Beach Park

MM18

Makapala

Kapa'a
Beach Park

250

MM20

Pololu Valley
Lookout

K
o
h
a
l
a

MM15

Mahukona

Mahukona
Beach Park

Kohala Mountain Rd

Lapakahi State
Historical Park

NORTH
KOHALA

MM15

Pololu Valley

Honopue Stream

Waimanu Valley

Akoni Pule Hwy

MM10

Kohala
Forest Reserve

M
o
u
n
t
a
i
n
s

270

Kohala   Rd

MM10

250

Kohala
(5480ft)

Kohala   Dr Ranch

Ala Kahua

MM5

Kawaihae

270

MM5

PACIFIC
OCEAN

Spencer Beach Park

Kawaihae   Rd

19

Waimea
(Kamuela)

Mau'umae Beach

Mauna Kea Beach

Kauna'oa Bay

See Waimea (Kamuela)
Map (p130)

Hapuna Beach
State Recreation Area

Beach 69

Puako

190

Holoholokai
Beach Park

Pauoa Bay

19

SOUTH
KOHALA

Honoka'ope Bay

Waikoloa
Village

200

'Anaeho'omalu
Bay

Queen Ka'ahumanu Hwy

Waikoloa Rd

Mamalahoa Hwy

'Anaeho'omalu
Beach Park

WAIKOLOA

See South Kohala Map (p108)

HIGHLIGHTS

❶ **BEST BEACH:** Mauna Kea Beach at Kauna'oa Bay (p116)
❷ **BEST VIEW:** Pololu Valley Lookout (p128)
❸ **BEST ACTIVITY:** Sampling *poke* at the Aloha Festivals Poke Contest (p117)
❹ **BEST LOCAL GATHERING:** Waimea Farmers Market (p133)
❺ **BEST WAY TO SPEND $20:** Sunday brunch at Daniel Thiebaut (p133)

Highlights are numbered on the map on p106.

SOUTH KOHALA

Along the Queen Ka'ahumanu Hwy (Hwy 19), all you see are stark fields of lava. But veer onto the resort-area roads toward the ocean and you'll reach the Big Island's world-renowned Gold Coast.

'Anaeho'omalu Beach Park   GREG ELMS

WAIKOLOA RESORT AREA

Although the Waikoloa name is most famous, its two mega hotels and golf course, while impressive, are not necessarily South Kohala's finest. But this resort area does offer two upscale shopping malls and the lion's share of events.

Orientation & Information

A *makai* (seaward) turnoff just south of the 76-mile marker leads to the Waikoloa Resort Area, containing the hotels, golf courses and shopping malls. For general services, such as a post office, go to Waikoloa Village, an inland residential community, by turning *mauka* (inland) onto Waikoloa Rd north of the 75-mile marker.

The Big Island Visitors Bureau (☎ 886-1655, 800-648-2441; www.bigisland.org; Suite B15, Kings' Shops; 250 Waikoloa Beach Dr) is better than nothing, but don't expect a strong opinion.

Beaches

'ANAEHO'OMALU BEACH PARK
Waikoloa Beach Dr; ⏳ parking 6am-8pm
Although 'A Bay' is less famous than other Big Island beaches, it does offer benefits: easy access, salt-and-pepper sand, and calm waters (the only place suited to windsurfing on Hawai'i). The Waikoloa Beach Marriott fronts the beach's north end but ancient fishponds add a buffer zone between the two. In that area, there's decent snorkeling directly in front of the sluice gate, where you'll find coral formations, a fair variety of fish and possibly sea turtles. Drinking water, showers and restrooms are available.

'Anaeho'omalu was once the site of royal fishponds, and archaeologists have found evidence of human habitation here dating back more than 1000 years. A short footpath with interpretive plaques starts near the showers and passes fishponds, caves, ancient house platforms and a shrine.

To get here, turn left off Waikoloa Beach Dr opposite the Kings' Shops.

Sights & Activities

Ocean Sports' Ocean Activity Center at 'Anaeho'omalu Beach Park is a one-stop

KOHALA & WAIMEA

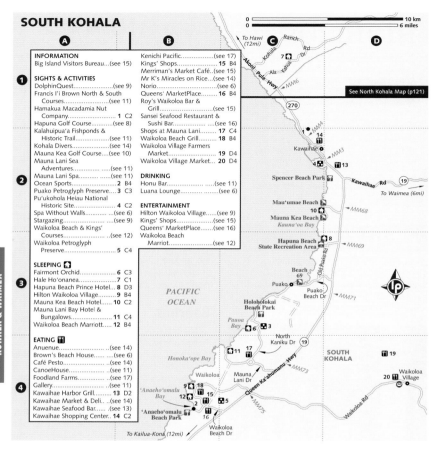

SOUTH KOHALA

INFORMATION
Big Island Visitors Bureau....(see 15)

SIGHTS & ACTIVITIES
DolphinQuest.......................(see 9)
Francis I'i Brown North & South
    Courses.......................(see 11)
Hamakua Macadamia Nut
    Company........................... **1** C2
Hapuna Golf Course.............(see 8)
Kalahuipua'a Fishponds &
    Historic Trail................(see 11)
Kohala Divers....................(see 14)
Mauna Kea Golf Course....(see 10)
Mauna Lani Sea
    Adventures..................(see 11)
Mauna Lani Spa...............(see 11)
Ocean Sports...................... **2** B4
Puako Petroglyph Preserve.. **3** C3
Pu'ukohola Heiau National
    Historic Site...................... **4** C2
Spa Without Walls........... ..(see 6)
Stargazing........................(see 9)
Waikoloa Beach & Kings'
    Courses.......................(see 12)
Waikoloa Petroglyph
    Preserve...................... **5** C4

SLEEPING
Fairmont Orchid.................. **6** C3
Hale Ho'onanea.................. **7** C1
Hapuna Beach Prince Hotel.. **8** D3
Hilton Waikoloa Village........ **9** B4
Mauna Kea Beach Hotel...... **10** C2
Mauna Lani Bay Hotel &
    Bungalows.................. **11** C4
Waikoloa Beach Marriott...... **12** B4

EATING
Anuenue.........................(see 14)
Brown's Beach House...... ..(see 6)
Café Pesto........................(see 14)
CanoeHouse......................(see 11)
Foodland Farms.................(see 17)
Gallery.............................(see 11)
Kawaihae Harbor Grill........ **13** D2
Kawaihae Market & Deli....(see 14)
Kawaihae Seafood Bar...... (see 13)
Kawaihae Shopping Center.. **14** C2

Kenichi Pacific...................(see 17)
Kings' Shops..................... **15** B4
Merriman's Market Café..(see 15)
Mr K's Miracles on Rice...(see 14)
Norio...............................(see 6)
Queens' MarketPlace...... **16** B4
Roy's Waikoloa Bar &
    Grill............................(see 15)
Sansei Seafood Restaurant &
    Sushi Bar.....................(see 16)
Shops at Mauna Lani...... **17** C4
Waikoloa Beach Grill......... **18** B4
Waikoloa Village Farmers
    Market....................... **19** D4
Waikoloa Village Market... **20** D4

DRINKING
Honu Bar..........................(see 11)
Luana Lounge....................(see 6)

ENTERTAINMENT
Hilton Waikoloa Village......(see 9)
Kings' Shops....................(see 15)
Queens' MarketPlace....(see 16)
Waikoloa Beach
    Marriott......................(see 12)

See North Kohala Map (p121)

PACIFIC
OCEAN

---

shop for rentals such as bodyboards ($5 per hour), kayaks ($12 per 30 minutes) and wacky hydrobikes ($25 per 30 minutes).

WAIKOLOA PETROGLYPH PRESERVE
Waikoloa Beach Dr, near Kings' Shops; admission free
This collection of petroglyphs carved in lava rock is so easy-access that it merits a stop, although it's not South Kohala's finest petroglyph preserve (see p112). Many of the petroglyphs date back to the 16th century; some are graphic (humans, birds, canoes) and others cryptic (dots, lines). Western influences appear in the form of horses and English initials.

To get here, park at the Kings' Shops mall and walk for five minutes on the signposted

path. Never touch or walk on the petroglyphs. Kings' Shops offers a free, one-hour **petroglyph tour** at 10:30am daily.

OCEAN SPORTS
☎ 886-6666; www.hawaiioceansports.com; 69-275 Waikoloa Beach Dr
Ocean Sports, established in 1981, monopolizes the ocean-activity market in South Kohala. Fortunately the company is well run, if slightly steep in its pricing. Cruises include **whale watching** ($74) aboard a 49-passenger catamaran and **snorkeling tours** by Zodiac raft ($129) or cat ($99). The company also offers **glass-bottom boat rides** ($21) and **sunset dinner sails** ($90). Kids between six and 12 pay half price. Cruises depart from

either 'Anaeho'omalu Bay or Kawaihae Harbor (p118).

WAIKOLOA BEACH & KINGS' COURSES

☎ 877-924-5656; www.waikoloabeachresort.com /golf.php; Waikoloa Beach Marriott, 69-275 Waikoloa Beach Dr; guest/nonguest $130/195

The Waikoloa Beach Marriott boasts two top golf courses: the coastal Beach course is known for its par-five 12th hole; the Kings' course is more challenging and offers Scottish-style links. Wait until mid-afternoon to tee off for a 50% discount. Carts are mandatory.

DOLPHIN QUEST

☎ 800-248-3316; www.dolphinquest.org; Hilton Waikoloa Village, 425 Waikoloa Beach Dr; per person from $200, family up to 6 $1300; ☯ 9am-4pm

Minds differ on whether 'dolphin encounters' are good or bad. (Same with zoos.) Judging by the popularity of this program, however, many willingly pay big bucks to meet this adored sea creature face to face. No matter that $200 buys you but 20 minutes of dolphin time. Dolphin Quest's location at the showy, Disney-esque Hilton Waikoloa Village is somehow appropriate. In any case, the dolphins seem to accept being cooped up in tanks, and they're carefully supervised during guest programs.

STARGAZING

☎ 886-1234, ext 2760; www.stargazehawaii.com; Hilton Waikoloa Village, 425 Waikoloa Beach Dr; adult/child 5-11yr $25/15; ☯ 8pm Tue

Take advantage of Kohala's consistently clear night skies and join professional astronomers in identifying stars using a high-powered telescope.

Festivals & Events

Great Waikoloa Food, Wine & Music Festival (☎ 886-1234; www.dolphindays.com; Hilton Waikoloa Village; admission $100) Sample the creations of two-dozen prominent Hawaii chefs, plus fine wines and boutique brews, accompanied by world-class jazz artists. Held on the third weekend in June, this festival is part of the three-day Dolphin Days Summer Fest, established in 1994 to celebrate the first birthday of the first dolphin born at the resort.

A Taste of the Hawaiian Range (☎ 322-4892; www .ctahr.hawaii.edu/taste; Hilton Waikoloa Village; admission $35) Celebrated Big Island chefs work magic with local range-fed meats (including beef, lamb, pork, mutton, sau-

sages, poultry and goat) and local produce in late September or early October. Save room for gourmet desserts and drinks. Portions are generous and the price is right.

our pick Moku O Keawe (☎ 936-4853; www.mokuo keawe.org; Waikoloa Resort Area; hula competition admission per night $15) Established in 2006, this early November hula competition includes *kahiko* (ancient), *'auana* (modern) and *kupuna* (elder) categories. The three-night event is logistically easy compared with the iconic, sell-out Merrie Monarch Festival (p182). It might lack the big-name cachet but it does showcase serious hula.

Eating

As a rule, the resort restaurants are mediocre and overpriced. For better options, head to the two malls, Kings' Shops (www.waikoloa beachresort.com/shops.php; 250 Waikoloa Beach Dr) and Queens' MarketPlace (www.waikoloabeachresort.com /marketplace.php; 201 Waikoloa Beach Dr), with food-court fare (including Starbucks, Dairy Queen and Arby's) and big-name outposts.

WAIKOLOA BEACH GRILL   American $$

☎ 886-6131; www.wbgrill.com; 69-1022 Keana Pl; mains $10-18; ☯ 11am-9pm, bar to midnight

With neither a resort nor a mall location, this eatery overlooking the golf course is pleasantly uncrowded. The two award-winning, internationally trained chefs serve island-inspired American classics, such as Big Island–beef hamburgers, ribs with wasabi potato salad and phyllo crab cakes. The dinner menu is all tapas style (appetizer portions), so the affordable prices might be misleading.

Top Picks

KOHALA & WAIMEA FOR KIDS

- **Horseback riding** (p131 and p126)
- **Waimea Park playground** (p129)
- **Spencer Beach Park** (p118)
- **Parker Ranch petting zoo** (p131)
- **Mauna Kea Beach at Kauna'oa Bay** (p116)
- **Snorkeling and whale-watching cruises** (p108 and p113)
- **Waimea Farmers Market** (p133)
- **Imagination Toys** (p134)
- **Glass-bottom boat rides** (p108)
- **Puako tide pools** (p116)

MERRIMAN'S
MARKET CAFÉ   Mediterranean $$$
☎ 886-1700; www.merrimanshawaii.com; Kings'
Shops; dinner mains $17-27; ⏰ 11:30am-9:30pm
Don't confuse Peter Merriman's Waikoloa
outpost with his flagship (p133) in Waimea.
This alfresco café is casual, less expensive
and more touristy. Foodies from sophisticated cities might find the Mediterranean-
inspired fare unremarkable, but the kitchen
does feature organic island-grown produce
and fresh local fish. It's not a must-try, but
it easily trumps the resort offerings.

SANSEI SEAFOOD
RESTAURANT & SUSHI BAR   Japanese $$$
our pick ☎ 886-6286; www.sanseihawaii.com;
Queens' MarketPlace; mains $20-40, sushi $4-22;
⏰ dinner
Local celebrity chef DK Kodama will surprise you with innovative, fusion Japanese
cuisine, from Dungeness-crab ramen in truf-
fle broth to *panko*-crusted (with Japanese
breadcrumbs) *'ahi* (yellowfin tuna) sushi.
His succulent dry-aged beef ups the ante for
a great steak. Extensive wine list, compli-
ments of master sommelier Chuck Furuya.

ROY'S WAIKOLOA
BAR & GRILL   Hawaii Regional $$$
☎ 886-4321; www.roysrestaurant.com; Kings'
Shops; mains $26-30; ⏰ 5:30-10pm
Always ridiculously bustling and noisy,
Roy's will either delight or disappoint. We
suggest that you focus on the food and not
the atmosphere or sketchy service. The still-
creative main courses, such as rack of lamb
in a *liliko'i* (passion fruit) cabernet sauce or
blackened *'ahi* with pickled ginger, won't
disappoint.

For groceries, Waikoloa Village Market (☎ 883-
1088; Waikoloa Highlands Center, 68-3916 Paniolo Ave;
⏰ 6am-9pm) in Waikoloa Village is a full-
service grocery store with deli, bakery and
ATM. On Saturdays, try the Waikoloa Village
Farmers Market (Waikoloa Community Church, Paniolo
Ave; ⏰ 7-10am).

Entertainment
Find free daily entertainment at the two
shopping malls. Kings' Shops (www.waikoloa-
beachresort.com/shops.php; ⏰ shows 6pm Mon-Fri, 4pm
Sat & Sun) presents Hawaiian music, hula and

jazz. The best gig to catch is slack key guitarist John Keawe on Tuesdays. The lineup
for Queens' MarketPlace (www.waikoloabeachresort
.com/marketplace.php; ⏰ shows 5-6pm Mon-Wed, 4-6pm
Thu & Fri, 2-4pm Sat & Sun) is hula and Hawaiian
music, featuring the award-winning classic
vocalist Darlene Ahuna on Thursdays.

If you can afford the Kona Village luau
(p101), go for it. Otherwise, try the follow-
ing standard luau shows in Waikoloa:
Hilton Waikoloa Village (☎ 886-1234; 425 Waikoloa
Beach Dr; adult/child 5-12yr $82/41; ⏰ 6pm Tue & Fri)
The 'Legends of the Pacific' luau show features various
South Pacific dances and includes a dinner buffet and one
cocktail. Note that seniors (65 and above) and teens (13 to
18) pay $65.
Waikoloa Beach Marriott (☎ 886-6789,
888-924-5656; www.waikoloabeachmarriott.com; 69-275
Waikoloa Beach Dr; adult/child $75/36; ⏰ 5:30pm Sun
& Wed) This poolside luau is the typical commercial show
with Hawaiian-style dinner buffet, open bar and Polyne-
sian dances. The setting by 'Anaeho'omalu Bay is a plus.

Sleeping
HILTON WAIKOLOA VILLAGE   Hotel $$$$
☎ 886-1234, 800-221-2424; www.hiltonwaikoloa
village.com; 425 Waikoloa Beach Dr; garden-view r
$200-570, ocean-view r $240-690; 🅿 per day $9;
⌨ 🖥 🏊
You'll either love or hate the showy, theme-
park features of this 62-acre, 1240-room
mega-hotel. A monorail and covered boats
let you navigate the sprawling grounds without scuffing your flip-flops, while kids splash
aboard kayaks in waveless artificial water-
ways. There's visual interest everywhere,
from a giant Buddha sculpture near the lobby
to interesting collections of Polynesian and
Asian art pieces or replicas along sidewalks.
Rooms are comfy enough but they're standard business class, not luxury – and *nothing*
(internet access, gym, kitchen appliances) is
included in the nightly rate. This fantasyland
might suit families with low-attention-span
kids and bargain hunters seeking an affordable Gold Coast resort.

WAIKOLOA BEACH
MARRIOTT   Hotel $$$$
☎ 886-6789, 888-924-5656; www.waikoloabeach
marriott.com; 69-275 Waikoloa Beach Dr; r $280-400;
🅿 per day $7; ⌨ 🖥 🏊
The Hilton might be Waikoloa's glamour gal,
but the Marriott is the solid girl next door.

This airy, 555-room hotel is rather standard in design, but it fronts 'Anaeho'omalu Bay and thus boasts an awesome beach setting, plus three oceanfront pools. Renovated around 2006, rooms feature quality beds (down comforters and 300-count linens), tastefully muted decor and the expected amenities, from cable TV to refrigerator. Internet access is wi-fi in public areas and wired in rooms.

MAUNA LANI RESORT AREA

Constructed in 1983 by a Japanese company, the Mauna Lani Resort Area resembles its neighbors, with high-end hotels, condos and golf courses. But it deserves special attention for its significant historical sites and for the Mauna Lani Bay Hotel & Bungalows' refreshingly open attitude toward nonguests who come to explore its trails and fishponds.

Beaches

The best beaches for swimming or snorkeling are small and located around the two large hotels. The beach fronting the Mauna Lani Bay Hotel & Bungalows (p114) is protected and relatively calm, but the water is shallow. Just 10 minutes south of the hotel by foot, in Makaiwa Bay, there's a small, calm lagoon fronting the Mauna Lani Beach Club condo. To get here, park at the hotel and walk south along the path past the fishponds.

One mile south of the hotel (at the boundary of the overall resort area), there's a small salt-and-pepper beach at Honoka'ope Bay. When seas are calm, swimming and snorkeling are fine but not fantastic. Walk here by an old coastal trail or drive toward the golf courses and turn left at Honoka'ope Pl.

Located at the Fairmont Orchid (p115), Pauoa Bay is an excellent, little-known snorkeling spot, but nonguest access is frowned upon by the hotel.

HOLOHOLOKAI BEACH PARK

Forget about sand and gentle waves here. Instead enjoy picnicking and strolling at this pleasantly uncrowded beach, blanketed by chunks of white coral and black lava. On the calmest days, the waters are fine for snorkeling. Facilities include restrooms, showers, drinking water, picnic tables and grills.

YOUR RESORT MATCH

Choosing among the Gold Coast resorts is no easy trick, so here's a quick primer to distinguish the three overall resort areas. Lively and less exclusive, the relatively affordable **Waikoloa Resort Area** has one major beach and two shopping malls. More upscale and expensive, the **Mauna Lani Resort Area** offers the finest restaurants and spas, plus unique natural and historical attractions, from tide pools to petroglyphs. And the **Mauna Kea Resort Area**, where it all began, falls between the other two in cost and boasts the best beaches and golf courses.

Here's a cheat sheet:

- **Waikoloa Beach Marriott** (p110) Pleasant, if bland, design but prime beachside location.
- **Hilton Waikoloa Village** (p110) Extravagantly man-made theme-park of a resort, entertaining for kids.
- **Mauna Lani Bay Hotel & Bungalows** (p114) Airy architecture and lush landscaping amid ancient Hawaiian sites.
- **Fairmont Orchid** (p115) Luxurious and elegant, with outstanding restaurants and spa.
- **Mauna Kea Beach Hotel** (p118) *The* best golf course and *the* perfect beach.
- **Hapuna Beach Prince Hotel** (p118) Bulky structure of pillars and circles, flanking the world-renowned Hapuna Beach.

Also consider the two ultraexclusive resorts in North Kona: the impeccable **Four Seasons Resort Hualalai** (p101) and the 'unplugged' **Kona Village Resort** (p101).

To get here, take Mauna Lani Dr and veer right at the circle; turn right on the marked road immediately before the Fairmont Orchid. The Puako petroglyphs are accessed from the park.

Sights

KALAHUIPUA'A FISHPONDS

Mauna Lani Bay Hotel & Bungalows, 68-1400 Mauna Lani Dr; admission free
These ancient fishponds are among the island's few remaining working fishponds and, as in ancient times, they're stocked

Ancient lava carvings at Puako Petroglyph Preserve   GREG ELMS

with *awa* (Hawaiian milk fish). Water circulates from the ocean through traditional *makaha* (sluice gates), which allow small fish to enter but keep mature, fattened catch from leaving. The fishponds lie along the beach just south of the hotel, partly under a shady grove of coconut palms and *milo* (native hardwood) trees.

KALAHUIPUA'A HISTORIC TRAIL
Mauna Lani Bay Hotel & Bungalows, 68-1400 Mauna Lani Dr; admission free
This easy trail starts on the hotel's inland side, at a marked parking lot opposite the resort's little grocery store. Get a free, self-guided trail map from the concierge desk.

The first part of the historic trail meanders through a former Hawaiian settlement that dates from the 16th century, passing lava tubes once used as cave shelters and a few other archaeological and geological sites marked by interpretive plaques. Keep a watchful eye out for quail, northern and red-crested cardinals, saffron finches and Japanese white-eyes.

The trail then skirts fishponds lined with coconut palms and continues out to the beach, where you'll find a thatched shelter with an outrigger canoe and a historic cottage with a few Hawaiian artifacts on display. If you continue southwest past the cottage, you can loop around the fishpond and back to your starting point (for a round-trip of about 1.5 miles).

🐾 PUAKO PETROGLYPH PRESERVE
ourpick Access from Holoholokai Beach Park
With more than 3000 petroglyphs, this preserve is among the largest collections of ancient lava carvings in Hawaii. The simple pictures might not make sense to you, but viewed altogether, they are fascinating and worth a visit.

The 1300yd walk from Holoholokai Beach Park to the preserve adds to the experience: take the well-marked trail at the *mauka* side of the park. The walk is easy, but wear sturdy footwear and expect blazing sun (the path is only partly shaded).

Activities
MAUNA LANI SEA ADVENTURES
☎ 885-7883; www.hawaiiseaadventures.com;
Mauna Lani Bay Hotel & Bungalows, 68-1400 Mauna Lani Dr
This outfit offers three-hour morning snorkeling cruises ($65) five mornings per week; the fee applies to all, but kids (ages three to 12) pay half price on Sundays and Wednes-

ANCIENT HAWAIIAN ART

Ancient Hawaiians carved *ki'i pohaku* (stone images), or **petroglyphs**, into *pahoehoe* (smooth lava). These mysterious carvings are most common on the Big Island, perhaps because it is the youngest island, with the most extensive fields of *pahoehoe*. The simple images include human figures, animals and important objects such as canoes and sails. No one can prove why the Hawaiians made *ki'i pohaku* or placed them where they did. Many petroglyph fields are found along major trails or on the boundaries of *ahupua'a* (land divisions).

In addition to the Puako petroglyphs, others remain in **Waikoloa** (p108) and at **Hawai'i Volcanoes National Park** (p216).

Touching the petroglyphs will damage them, so never step on or make rubbings of them. Photography is fine and best done in the early morning or late afternoon, when the sun is low.

days. From mid-December to mid-April, 1½-hour whale-watching cruises (adult/child 3-12yr $65/40) run five afternoons per week.

Although Kailua-Kona is the Big Island's hub for scuba diving, the waters off Mauna Lani are perhaps even better (and also much less crowded). Mauna Lani Sea Adventures is also the main dive operator (two-tank dive $144) here. Divemasters are competent, friendly and flexible. The dive sites are close to shore, so the boat docks between dives, allowing for a snack or bathroom break. Well-regarded certification courses also offered.

FRANCIS I'I BROWN NORTH & SOUTH GOLF COURSES

☎ 885-6655; Mauna Lani Bay Hotel & Bungalows, 68-1400 Mauna Lani Dr; guest/nonguest $145/210

The two Mauna Lani courses are among the island's top world-class golf courses. The South Course is more scenic and popular, with its signature 15th hole featuring a tee shot over crashing surf. The North Course is more challenging and interesting, however, with a par-three 17th hole within an amphitheater of black lava rock. The

twilight rate drops to $100 for both guests and nonguests.

SPAS
MAUNA LANI SPA

☎ 881-7922; Mauna Lani Bay Hotel & Bungalows, 68-1400 Mauna Lani Dr; massages from $145, facials from $155; ☷ treatments 9am-5pm

This top-ranked spa's visual appeal is undeniable, with 40,000 sq ft of indoor/outdoor space extravagantly landscaped with fragrant tropical flora, a lava-rock sauna and calm pools for water therapy. It would be over-the-top if it weren't so darned *classy*. Treatments are elaborate and done with the spa's signature body oil, clay mud and other natural concoctions. When booking, ask about your therapist's experience level, however.

SPA WITHOUT WALLS

our pick ☎ 887-7540; www.fairmont.com/orchid; Fairmont Orchid, 1 North Kaniku Dr; indoor/outdoor massages from $159/169, facials from $145; ☷ treatments 8am-7pm

Walls aren't bad per se, but you won't miss 'em here. Instead, lie back for a facial or massage in alfresco *hale* (houses), hidden

KOHALA & WAIMEA

THE MAN BEHIND THE NAME

Who is this **Francis I'i Brown**, for whom golf courses and restaurants are named? Born in 1892, Brown was a prominent Native Hawaiian statesman and athlete, recognized in golf, swimming, diving, surfing, fishing and polo. As Hawaii's first prominent golfer, Brown in the 1920s and '30s won important US amateur tournaments and the Japan Open. During a practice round for the British Open, he set a course record at the Old Course at St Andrews.

Brown was a landowner in South Kohala and he regarded Kalahuipua'a, now known as Mauna Lani, as a special retreat where he could 'be Hawaiian,' and tend the natural fishponds, raise animals, fish and entertain with *ho'okipa* (hospitality). His native roots go deep, as he was the grandson of John Papa I'i, the son of a Kona chief and a trusted childhood friend of the future Kamehameha II.

...coconut palms, waterfalls,
...y ponds. The head therapist
...l and dedicated to Hawaiian
...... she maintains a steady, well-
train... .ff. Choose from varied massage,
facial and body treatments featuring local
botanicals, such as the 'Kona coffee–Ka'u
orange' exfoliation.

Eating & Drinking

GALLERY — Chinese $$
☎ 885-7777; Mauna Lani Bay Hotel & Bungalows, 68-1400 Mauna Lani Dr; dinner mains $12-30; ☺ lunch daily, dinner Tue-Sat

For a change from the pricey resort restaurants, your best bet is this Cantonese-style Chinese eatery at the Mauna Lani Bay Hotel's golf clubhouse. Dishes include salt-and-pepper calamari, and Peking duck served in steamed buns.

KENICHI PACIFIC — Pacific Rim/Sushi $$$
☎ 881-1515; Shops at Mauna Lani; sushi $7-15, mains $20-30; ☺ 5-10pm

With a stellar reputation in **Keauhou** (see p74), this nouveau Japanese restaurant opened a Mauna Lani branch in early 2008. The menu was not set at the time of research, but sources promised that it would include favorites such as *ono tataki* (seared wahoo) and spicy tuna tempura rolls.

🌿 NORIO — Japanese $$$$
☎ 887-7320; Fairmont Orchid, 1 North Kaniku Dr; sushi rolls $12-24, mains $30-50; ☺ dinner

Chef Norio Yamamoto specializes in classic Japanese cuisine, especially sushi and sashimi featuring the freshest local seafood. In addition to *'ahi* and other deep-sea fish, he uses abalone and lobster that are farm-raised at North Kona's **Natural Energy Lab of Hawaii** (p98). Cooked entrées include grilled Kobe-style beef, seared foie gras sushi and steamed clams with Hamakua mushrooms.

🌿 CANOEHOUSE — Hawaii Regional $$$$
☎ 885-6622; Mauna Lani Bay Hotel & Bungalows, 68-1400 Mauna Lani Dr; mains $30-45; ☺ dinner

The Mauna Lani's fanciest restaurant is lovely all round, with an oceanfront setting and a menu that highlights seafood and local ingredients. Locally raised lobster shines in a tempura appetizer or with other

Kona shellfish in kaffir-lime broth, while the Ahualoa goat cheese and potato ravioli (with Hilo corn and Hamakua mushrooms) is a satisfying veg option.

🌿 BROWN'S BEACH HOUSE — Hawaii Regional $$$$
☎ 885-2000; Fairmont Orchid, 1 North Kaniku Dr; mains $40-68; ☺ lunch & dinner

The prices might deter you, but besides the money issue, this oceanfront gem has no faults. The service is gracious and the menu is practically a circle-island tour of the best Big Island ingredients. Standouts include the Waimea heirloom tomato salad, crispy Kona *kampachi* (locally farm-raised yellowtail) and Big Island goat cheese cheesecake with Asian pear. It's the classiest act in the Mauna Lani Resort Area – but be prepared to swallow the tab.

For groceries, **Foodland Farms** (☎ 887-6101; ☺ 5am-11pm) is a full-service gourmet supermarket with an impressive deli selection at the **Shops at Mauna Lani** (☎ 885-9501; 68-1330 Mauna Lani Dr). The mall also has a Starbucks and a handful of sit-down restaurants.

For evening drinks (and a more affordable dinner), try an oceanfront bar:

Honu Bar (☎ 885-6622; Mauna Lani Bay Hotel & Bungalows, 68-1400 Mauna Lani Dr; appetizers $12-18, mains $16-44; ☺ 5:30-11pm) Awesome bar menu (served till 9pm) ranges from roast chicken and Hamakua-mushroom pizza to Keahole lobster tail. Or just unwind with premium wines, cocktails and liqueurs.

Luana Lounge (☎ 885-2000; Fairmont Orchid, 1 North Kaniku Dr; ☺ 4-11pm) This casual indoor/outdoor space lets you enjoy the sunset, drinks and *pupu* (appetizers), and special exhibits of top local artists' work.

Sleeping

🌿 MAUNA LANI BAY HOTEL & BUNGALOWS — Hotel $$$$
our pick ☎ 885-6622, 800-367-2323; www.maunalani.com; 68-1400 Mauna Lani Dr; r $355-875; Ⓟ ⊠ ▣ ⊠

Among the top South Kohala resorts, the Mauna Lani offers a wonderfully Hawaiian atmosphere. The parklike grounds feature landscaped tropical gardens, hundreds of towering coconut palms and precious historic sites, and the staff is exceptionally courteous and committed to Hawaiian culture. Renovated in the mid-1990s, the

The very Hawaiian and very green Mauna Lani Bay Hotel & Bungalows

GREG ELMS

342 rooms are modern in amenities and decor; 90% are oceanfront or ocean-view. Rates include basic services (eg parking, phone, high-speed internet access), so there are no extra charges. This eco-conscious resort uses solar power for its daytime water-pumping needs, drought-resistant grass for the golf greens and recycled water for irrigation. It even raises endangered *honu* (sea turtles) on site. In case you're wondering, the five 'bungalows' are each 2500 sq ft, with 24-hour butler service; each one starts at $5500 per night.

FAIRMONT ORCHID   Hotel $$$$

☎ 885-2000, 800-845-9905; www.fairmont.com /orchid; 1 North Kaniku Dr; r $400-850; P per day $15; 💻

Elegant and almost formal (for Hawai'i), the Orchid never lets you forget that you're at an exclusive, luxury hotel. The architecture feels more continental than overtly Hawaiian, but the meticulously maintained grounds are buoyantly tropical. The 540 rooms are quite posh, but less so than the post-renovation Mauna Lani counterparts. The Orchid's spa and restaurants are first-rate, adding to the pampering quality. Amenities, such as in-room internet access ($14 per day), are rather pricey.

PUAKO

Puako is just a mile-long row of beach homes, where the single road through 'town' is marked with numerous 'shoreline access' points. To get here, turn *makai* down Puako Beach Dr between the 70- and 71-mile markers.

Beaches, Sights & Activities

The clear waters and shallow reef of Puako Bay are great for kayaking, snorkeling and diving. Rent kayaks from Plenty Pupule Adventure Sports (p120).

BEACH 69

Waialea Bay; ⏲ 7am-8pm

This beautiful white-sand beach boasts a small, calm bay for **swimming** and **snorkeling**. Around the boundary, shady trees offer a few private spots. Restrooms and showers are available. From Puako Beach Dr, take the first right turn onto Old Puako Rd. Find telephone pole No 71 to the left and park. Follow the 'road' to its end, and then tramp along the footpath that runs parallel to a wooden fence. In case you're wondering, telephone pole No 71 was once numbered No 69, which gave the beach its nickname.

Mauna Kea Beach and Kauna'oa Bay

CONNER GORRY

PUAKO TIDE POOLS

Puako is known for giant tide pools, set in the swirls and dips of the *pahoehoe* (smooth lava) coastline. Some pools are deep enough to shelter live coral and other marine life. There's no sandy beach, but a narrow strip of pulverized coral and lava covers the shore.

For the easiest beach access, go to the south end of the village, stopping just before the 'Road Closed 500 Feet' sign. Take the short dirt road toward a small cove that's used for **snorkeling** and **shore diving**; note that the surf is generally too rough in winter. A couple of minutes' walk north brings you to a few **petroglyphs**, a board for **konane** (a game similar to checkers) chinked into the lava, and tide pools deep enough to cool off in.

MAUNA KEA RESORT AREA

Beaches, beaches, beaches. This resort area trumps Waikoloa and Mauna Lani in its proximity to great beaches. The development began in the early 1960s when the late Laurance Rockefeller obtained a 99-year lease on the land around Kauna'oa Bay from his friend Richard Smart, owner of

Parker Ranch. Five years later, Rockefeller opened Mauna Kea Beach Hotel, the first luxury hotel on the Neighbor Islands. Since then, other ritzy hotels have burst onto the scene, but the Mauna Kea Beach Hotel will remain the granddaddy of them all.

Beaches & Activities

KAUNA'OA BAY

our pick Of all the Big Island's beaches, Kauna'oa Bay (called **Mauna Kea Beach** where it flanks the hotel) is arguably the most visually perfect. The crescent-shaped bay is blanketed in powdery white sand, while the clear waters are calm and shallow (generally less than 10ft). **Snorkeling** is only average near the shore; go to the north end along the rocky ledge.

Best of all, the beach is never crowded. It is open to the public, but the hotel sets aside only 30 parking spaces daily for nonguests. Arrive by 9am. You can also dine at the hotel (when it reopens in late 2008) to gain access.

MAU'UMAE BEACH

This beautiful beach boasts white sand, shady trees and protected waters – and feels even more private and local than Kauna'oa Bay. Locals are proprietary about this gem (for good reason) so don't overstep your welcome.

To get here, go toward the Mauna Kea Beach Hotel, turn right on Kamahoi and cross two wooden bridges. Look for telephone pole No 22 on the left and park (you'll probably see a bunch of cars parked). Walk down the trail to the Ala Kahakai sign and turn left toward the beach. You can also get here from nearby Spencer Beach by walking 10 minutes on the Ala Kahakai Trail (p119), a shady coastal path.

HAPUNA BEACH STATE RECREATION AREA

Hapuna is world-famous for its magnificent half-mile sweep of white powder sand and crystal clear waters. Water conditions vary depending on the season. In summer, when waves are flat, Hapuna affords good swimming, snorkeling and diving. (Bear in mind, the fish population has woefully declined since the 1980s.) When the surf's up in winter, the bodyboarding is awesome. In general, Hapuna waters are too choppy for tots or nonswimmers. Remember that waves over 3ft should be left for the experts; drownings are not uncommon here.

Due to its drive-up access and popularity (and the lack of state funds), the restrooms

Hapuna Beach   GREG ELMS

and picnic area can be rather grungy. Still, at least there *are* facilities, including pay phones, drinking water, showers, restrooms and a picnic area. Lifeguards are on duty.

For a happy beach day, arrive early to snag a parking space and stake out a good spot. Bring industrial-strength sunscreen because there's little shade.

No-frills backpacker types should spend a couple of nights in one of the six state-owned A-frame cabins (per night $20) near the beach. The awesome location is perfect for sunset and moonrise watching. While rather run-down and makeshift, the cabins are decently livable and each sleeps four people on wooden platforms (bring your own beddings). There are restrooms, showers and a cooking pavilion with a stove and fridge. If you're game, see p273 for reservation information.

MAUNA KEA & HAPUNA GOLF COURSES

☎ 882-5400, 880-3000; Mauna Kea Beach Hotel, Hapuna Beach Prince Hotel; Hapuna course guest/nonguest $125/165

Golfers dream about playing the combined 36 holes of these two premier courses: the first is a 72-par championship course that consistently ranks among the top 10 courses in the world, while the second has a 700ft elevation gain and was designed by Arnold Palmer and Ed Seay. The Mauna Kea course is closed for renovation until late 2008.

Festivals & Events

Poke (cubed, marinated raw fish) is Hawaii's comfort food and locals indulge their *poke* cravings at the annual Aloha Festivals Poke Contest (☎ 880-3424; www.pokecontest.com; Hapuna Beach Prince Hotel, 62-100 Kauna'oa Dr; admission $5) in September. Over 55 professional and amateur chefs compete and offer samples of their creations, which range from the traditional to the wacky. The Aloha Festivals $5 ribbon is your ticket to dozens of festival attractions, but major events require additional admission fees.

Eating & Sleeping

Backpackers can rent A-frame cabins at Hapuna Beach (see p117).

KOHALA & WAIMEA

SACRED SITES

Ancient Hawaiians built a variety of heiau (temples) for different gods and different purposes: healing the sick, sharing the harvest, changing the weather, offering human sacrifice and succeeding in warfare. Some heiau were modest thatched structures, but others were enormous stone ones.

Today, the eroded ruins of heiau, found across the Islands, often only hint at their original grandeur. After Kamehameha II (Liholiho) abolished the *kapu* (taboo) system in 1819 (see p248), many were destroyed or abandoned. But on the Big Island, two of the largest and best-preserved heiau remain: **Pu'ukohola Heiau** (a war temple; p119) and **Mo'okini Luakini Heiau** (a sacrificial temple; p122).

The war temples were typically massive platforms built with boulders, plus covered shelters for kahuna (priests), ceremonial drums and idols of the temple's patron god. The larger the heiau, the more threatening it appeared to enemies. Indeed, the sheer magnitude of Pu'ukohola Heiau, built during Kamehameha the Great's rise to power, foreshadowed his ultimate conquest of the Hawaiian Islands.

Luakini heiau (temples of human sacrifice) were always dedicated to Ku, the war god. Only Ku deserved the greatest gift, a human life, and only the highest chiefs could order it. But human sacrifice was not taken lightly. Typically, people gave offerings of food to Ku. The actual act of killing was not a necessary ritual; an enemy slain in battle was acceptable. But the victim had to be a healthy man, never a woman, a child or an aged or deformed man.

MAUNA KEA BEACH HOTEL   Hotel $$$$
☎ 882-7222, 888-977-4623; www.maunakeabeach hotel.com; 62-100 Mauna Kea Beach Dr

After suffering major earthquake damage in October 2006, the hotel closed for renovation and will reopen in late 2008. Prior to its closure, the classily understated hotel was notable mainly for its beach, golf course and status as the pioneering Gold Coast resort. Rooms were rather small and plain compared with the lavish accommodations at other top resorts. A post-renovation review is much anticipated.

HAPUNA BEACH PRINCE HOTEL   Hotel $$$$
☎ 880-1111, 866-774-6236; www.hapuna beachprincehotel.com; 62-100 Kauna'oa Dr; r $350-1350; 🖳

The Mauna Kea Beach Hotel's 'sister' resort, open since 1994, boasts an ideal location on Hapuna Beach. Some find the imposing architecture, manicured lawns, golf course and restaurants all top-notch but somewhat aloof, but TripAdvisor ranked it among the Top 10 Best Hotels for Romance. With 350 rooms, it largely gears its services to Japanese tourists and even has a bilingual concierge desk. Rooms are standard business class but the bathrooms are large (and oceanfront suites have both a full and a half bathroom). The hotel shares amenities with the Mauna Kea, and buses transport guests between the two.

KAWAIHAE

Kawaihae is a nondescript port town, where fuel tanks and cargo containers give it an industrial vibe. It's mainly a convenient food stop, with a family beach and historic heiau toward the south. But its deepwater commercial harbor, which is the island's second-largest, will become the Big Island's Superferry terminal in 2009, thus big changes await this little town. Offshore, Kawaihae is a relatively untrafficked spot for diving and snorkeling.

Beaches & Sights

SPENCER BEACH PARK

Shallow, sandy and gentle, this beach has a plain-Jane reputation but it's ideal for kids (and popular with local families). Come to swim rather than to snorkel; the waters are slightly silty due to Kawaihae Harbor to the north.

Located off the Akoni Pule Hwy just north of the 2-mile marker, the park has a lifeguard, picnic tables, barbecue grills, restrooms, showers, drinking water and campsites. A footpath leads south to Mau'umae Beach.

The **campsites** are exposed and crowded together, but it's still the best camping beach north of Kona. See p273 for information on obtaining a county permit.

PU'UKOHOLA HEIAU NATIONAL HISTORIC SITE

By 1790 Kamehameha the Great had conquered Maui, Lana'i and Moloka'i. But power over his home island of Hawai'i proved to be a challenge. When told by a prophet that he'd rule all the Islands if he built a heiau dedicated to his war god Kuka'ilimoku atop Pu'ukohola (Whale Hill) in Kawaihae, Kamehameha built **Pu'ukohola Heiau** (☎ 882-7218; admission free; ⏱ 7:30am-4pm).

It is believed that Kamehameha and his men formed a human chain 20 miles long, transporting rocks hand to hand from Pololu Valley in North Kohala. After finishing the heiau by summer 1791, Kamehameha held a dedication ceremony and invited his rival and cousin, Keoua, the chief of Ka'u. When Keoua came ashore, he was killed and taken to the *luakini* heiau (temple of human sacrifice) as the first offering to the gods. With Keoua's death, Kamehameha took sole control of the Big Island, eventually ruling all the Islands by 1810.

Back then Pu'ukohola Heiau was adorned with wooden *ki'i* (statues) and thatched structures, including an oracle tower, altar, drum house and shelter for the high priest. After Kamehameha's death in 1819, his son Liholiho and powerful widow Ka'ahumanu destroyed the deity images and the heiau was abandoned.

Today, only the basic rock foundation remains, but it's still a massive 224ft by 100ft, with 16ft to 20ft walls. To get here, turn *makai* off the Akoni Pule Hwy halfway between the 2- and 3-mile markers.

🥥 HAMAKUA MACADAMIA NUT COMPANY

☎ 882-1690; www.hawnnut.com; Maluokalani St; admission free; ⏱ 8am-5pm

Compared with the Hershey-owned Mauna Loa mac-nut headquarters near Hilo, this locally owned company is tiny. But the spanking-clean factory and gift shop is staffed by multigeneration locals who give tours, answer questions and otherwise emanate much aloha spirit. An eco-conscious company, it uses ground mac-nut shells (not fossil fuels) to steam-dry its nuts. Generous **free samples**. To get here, turn *mauka* just north of the 4-mile marker, less than a mile from Kawaihae.

Activities

DIVING & SNORKELING

Most visitors make a beeline to Kailua-Kona and the Kona Coast for diving and snorkeling. But the waters off the Kohala Coast are just as pristine and teeming with marine life – and they're much less crowded. The reef here drops off more gradually than along the Kona Coast, so you'll probably see **reef sharks**, **spinner dolphins**, **turtles** and **manta rays**, but not large schools of tuna and other deepwater fish. Kohala is the oldest area of the Big Island, so coral growth is lush, with lots of lava tubes, arches and pinnacles.

The best dive and snorkel outfit, **Kohala Divers** (☎ 882-7774; www.kohaladivers.com; Kawaihae Shopping Center, Akoni Pule Hwy; dives $89-119, snorkeling $69; ⏱ departures 7:45am & sunset) is conveniently located near Kawaihae Harbor and also offers intro to advanced diving courses and whale watching. Staff are knowledgeable and friendly and keep dive groups small (maximum of six).

KOHALA & WAIMEA

ALA KAHAKAI TRAIL FROM KAWAIHAE TO PUAKO

For a different perspective on South Kohala's signature beaches and resorts, view them by foot along a 6-mile stretch of the 175-mile Ala Kahakai **historic trail** from North Kohala to Hawai'i Volcanoes National Park. You'll view pristine shoreline and natural anchialine ponds impossible to see from the highway. Start at the southern end of Spencer Beach Park, where you'll pass thick kiawe groves until you reach Mau'umae Beach and eventually the Mauna Kea Resort Area, including the renowned golf course. After you navigate the Hapuna Beach Prince Hotel and then the beach, the trail continues down to Beach 69. The whole hike, especially the last leg, is scorching. Of course, you can turn back at any point. Wear strong sun protection and expect to sweat.

KAYAKING

Like diving and snorkeling, kayaking is another activity that's awesome and relatively uncrowded in Kawaihae. A morning paddle to Mau'umae Beach is an invigorating way to wake up! Rent kayaks from **Plenty Pupule Adventure Sports** (☎ 880-1400; www.plenty pupule.com; single or tandem for 1/4/7 days $55/160/250; ⏱ 7am-7pm), the only outfit that rents the 'tri-yak' (kayak built for three), ideal for two parents with a kid. Call for location.

Eating & Sleeping

KAWAIHAE HARBOR GRILL   Seafood $$$
☎ 882-1368; Akoni Pule Hwy; dinner mains $20-32; ⏱ breakfast, lunch & dinner Wed-Sun, lunch & dinner Mon & Tue
This grill attracts a huge local following (especially Waimea residents) due to the reliable seafood, kid-friendly service and lively upstairs **Kawaihae Seafood Bar** (☎ 880-9393; mains $12-24; ⏱ 11am-10:30pm), with a thatched-hut bar and yummy *poke* burgers and ginger steamed clams.

HALE HO'ONANEA   B&B $$
☎ 882-1653, 877-882-1653; www.houseofrelax ation.com; Ala Kahua Dr; ste $100-130; 💻
About 5 miles north of Kawaihae, the price

is right for these three B&B units, set on peaceful grassy knolls 900ft above sea level. The Bamboo Suite is priciest, but the high ceiling, hardwood floor and stunning 180-degree horizon view are worth it. The other two get smaller and more makeshift as the price drops, but all are clean and homey, with kitchenette, lanai, satellite TV and wi-fi.

Across the harbor, **Kawaihae Shopping Center** (Akoni Pule Hwy) is a minimall with decent eateries, including the following:
Anuenue (cones from $2.50, fast food $3.50) Wide selection of Big Island Ice Cream Company's premium stuff, including classic Kona coffee, unique chunky white-chocolate ginger and much more. Hot dogs, veg burgers and chili bowls hit the spot after a beach day.
Café Pesto (☎ 882-1071; lunch/dinner mains $11/25; ⏱ 11am-9pm Sun-Thu, to 10pm Fri & Sat) This casual sit-down restaurant (a branch of Hilo's original) never misses with a range of salads, pastas, meats and seafood, all featuring fresh island ingredients.
Kawaihae Market & Deli (☎ 880-1611; ⏱ 4:30am-9pm Mon-Fri, 5:30am-8pm Sat & Sun) For sundries or deli takeout; you'll find standard convenience items plus locally made pasta and tofu salads.
Mr K's Miracles on Rice (☎ 882-1511; sushi rolls $4-5, mains $5-6.50; ⏱ lunch & dinner) For budget Japanese, this hole-in-the-wall serves generous *donburi* (bowl of rice and main dish, such as teriyaki beef or shrimp tempura). Ideal for takeout.

NORTH KOHALA

While big development has transformed most of Hawai'i, the island's northwestern tip remains rural, slow-paced and loyal to its local roots. North Kohala was sugar country until the Kohala Sugar Company closed down in 1975. Since then, its historic towns, Hawi and Kapa'au, have established just enough art galleries, boutiques and prominent restaurants to survive as minor tourist attractions.

Geologically the oldest part of the island, North Kohala is home to significant ancient-Hawaiian historical sites and windswept, rugged beaches. Rather than the stark lava of South Kohala, you'll see the Kohala Mountains covered with grassy pastureland; toward the eastern coast, the land grows more verdant and ends at stunning Pololu Valley.

To get here, there's a mountain road (Kohala Mountain Rd; Hwy 250) and a coastal

road (Akoni Pule Hwy; Hwy 270), which intersect in Hawi.

AKONI PULE HIGHWAY (HIGHWAY 270)

The Akoni Pule Hwy is straight and easy, with unobstructed views of the horizon. The sights following are listed in order from south to north.

PUA MAU PLACE
☎ 882-0888; www.puamau.org; Ala Kahua Dr; adult/child to 16yr/student & senior $10/6/8; ⏱ 9am-4pm
Pua mau means 'always flowering,' which is the goal for 45 acres of native and exotic plants on the otherwise-arid western side of North Kohala. The colorful **hibiscus maze**, **aviary** and larger-than-life **bronze sculptures**

KOHALA & WAIMEA

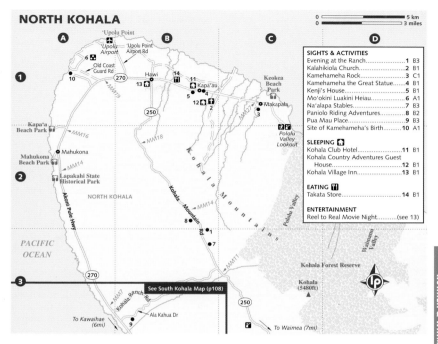

(giant insects, for example) are nice, but overall the flora looks immature, with not enough of the lushness you would expect. Indeed, the area receives only 3in of annual precipitation. To their credit, the nonprofit organizers are trying to raise $500,000 to install a solar-power system for its extensive irrigation needs.

To get here, turn inland onto Ala Kahua Dr just north of the 6-mile marker.

LAPAKAHI STATE HISTORICAL PARK

☎ 882-6207; admission free; ⏱ 8am-4pm, closed state holidays

This coastal park was a remote fishing village 600 years ago. Eventually some of the villagers moved to the wetter uplands and became farmers, trading their crops for fish. In the process, Lapakahi grew into an *ahupua'a,* a wedge-shaped division of land radiating from the mountains to the sea. When the freshwater table dropped in the 19th century, the village was abandoned.

An unshaded, 1-mile loop trail traverses the 262-acre grounds, passing the remains of stone walls, house sites, canoe sheds and fishing shrines. Visitors can try their hand at Hawaiian games, with game pieces and instructions laid out for 'o'o ihe (spear throwing), konane (checkers) and 'ulu maika (stone bowling). Nothing is elaborately presented – so visitors need wild imaginations to appreciate the modest remains.

Lapakahi's clear waters are loaded with tropical fish and belong to a marine-life conservation district. But this is a historical, not recreational, park, with historically sacred waters. Park staff may grant permission for snorkeling, but they generally discourage it.

The park is located just south of the 14-mile marker.

MAHUKONA BEACH PARK

Without a sandy beach or swimmable waters, Mahukona warrants only a brief poking around. After you turn off the Akoni Pule Hwy, the right-hand lane leads to a small pier. Once a key port for the Kohala Sugar Company, today it's a low-key fishing spot for locals.

Beyond the landing, there are **snorkeling** and **diving** spots that can be explored during calm waters. Entry, via a ladder, is in about 5ft of water. Heading north, it's possible to follow an anchor chain out to a submerged boiler and the remains of a ship 25ft down. Overall, however, the setting is not very inviting.

If you veer left after the turnoff, you'll reach the county park, where a ratty cluster of picnic tables and restrooms overlooks a scenic, if formidable, beach. The **camping** area is barely maintained and campers should bring plenty of drinking water and insect repellent. For information on camping permits, see p273.

KAPA'A BEACH PARK

Barely a 'park,' Kapa'a Beach is definitely not for swimming. Rough waves pound the rocky shore, creating obvious hazards. You can find solitude here or use the picnic tables for a scenic rest stop. But the park can be deserted and unkempt, without decent restrooms. Camping is allowed, but you can find better spots.

To get here, turn *makai* just north of the 16-mile marker on the Akoni Pule Hwy.

MO'OKINI LUAKINI HEIAU

☎ on O'ahu 808-373-8000; admission free

It takes advance planning or a muddy hike to see this temple, among the oldest and most significant in all of Hawaii. While the stone structure is much diminished since ancient times, its remains still measure 250ft by 125ft, with walls 6ft high.

Mo'okini Luakini Heiau was a 'closed' heiau, reserved for *ali'i nui* (kings and chiefs) for fasting, praying and offering human sacrifices to the gods. Dedicated to the god Ku, the heiau was built around AD 480 by up to 18,000 'little people' passing water-worn basalt stones in complete silence from Pololu under the supervision of Kuamo'o Mo'okini. Five hundred years later Pa'ao, a priest from Samoa, raised the walls to 30ft and introduced human sacrifices to stem dilution of the royal bloodlines and to enforce stricter moral codes of conduct.

In 1963 the National Park Service designated Mo'okini Luakini Heiau as Hawaii's first registered National Historic Landmark and, 15 years later, deeded it to the state. The current kahuna *nui* (high priestess), Leimomi Mo'okini Lum, is the seventh high priestess of the Mo'okini bloodline serving the temple. In 1978 Lum lifted the *kapu* (taboo) that restricted access to the temple, thereby opening it to visitors.

The heiau suffered damage from the October 2006 earthquake but Lum has decided against repairing it, and the state will honor her decision. At the time, she said: 'It has been here 1500 years. I'm not going

Mo'okini Luakini Heiau, one of the state's oldest and most significant

LUCI YAMAMOTO

ISLAND VOICES

NAME: SHIRO TAKATA
OCCUPATION: BUSINESSMAN AND PROPRIETOR OF TAKATA STORE
RESIDENCE: HAWI

When was Takata Store established? My father started a dry goods and grocery store in 1923, before I was born in 1929. Do you know the restaurant Bamboo (p125)? That was our location from 1926 to 1991. During WWII, my father was interned for four years. My mother had to take care of the store and seven kids.

Did you always work at the store? I was the fourth son, so I got to play sports [at Kohala High School] instead of working at the store. But when I graduated, there was no choice but to help. I worked 60 or more hours a week. Family labor was considered free, not an expense. Back then, we delivered goods to plantation camps, house to house; none of the workers had cars.

How has North Kohala changed since your childhood? Kohala was once an isolated, contained community – mostly Japanese and Hawaiians, some Filipinos. There was no Akoni Pule Hwy. The roads were rough. Only once a year, at Christmas, we'd drive to Hilo to shop.

Are you surprised that both of your sons are now running the business? I sent them away to Hawaii Preparatory Academy [a private school in Waimea] for high school. I wanted them to better themselves, to have better options than I did. When my older son, a computer programmer, returned from many years on the mainland to help with the store, we had to expand.

How do you feel about the newcomers to North Kohala? If North Kohala hadn't changed since plantation days, I would be the same plantation boy. I've adjusted my style because of the new people. Now I might compliment a customer: 'nice dress!' The mainland haole, not the locals, taught me to say things like that. Hawi and Kapa'au wouldn't be so beautiful and well-preserved without the newcomers; they're the ones restoring the historic buildings. No way would a local have created Kenji's House (p125).

Is North Kohala getting too gentrified? If there are only wealthy or retired people living here, the community will decline. I try to rally residents to put the community first. People from the mainland find it clean and quiet here, so they come and build a house. But they don't feel obligated to the community. If they come for the friendly environment, they must participate and be friendly themselves.

to change it. I'm 80. I don't look that good, but I looked good when I was 20.'

About 1000yd down a dirt road below the heiau is the legendary **site of Kamehameha's birth**. Legend says that when Kamehameha was born on a stormy winter night in 1758, his mother was told by a kahuna that her son would be a powerful ruler and conquer all the Islands. Upon hearing this, the ruling high chief of Hawai'i ordered all male newborns killed. Thus, after Kamehameha was taken to the Mo'okini Luakini Heiau for his birth rituals, he was spirited away into hiding in the mountains.

HAWI

Hawi (hah-*vee*) can fit all of its businesses within two blocks, but it looms large in picturesque charm and notable restaurants. It was once a major plantation town for the Kohala Sugar Company, and many local residents are descendants of sugar workers. Mainland transplants are bringing big money to little Hawi (still only 1000 strong) and leading its transformation from rustic boondocks to tourist destination.

The town offers only basic services, such as a post office, grocery store and gas station. The movie house went under in 2001, but if you're hankering for a movie, join the locals for **Reel to Real Movie Night** (reelto realkohala@gmail.com; The Barn, behind Kohala Village Inn; suggested donation $3; ☾ 7:30pm Fri). Popcorn and bottled water free with donation!

Don't miss driving down **Kohala Mountain Road** (Hwy 250), which starts in the heart of town and gently zigzags down to Waimea. The 3500ft elevation might seem paltry compared with the lofty Mauna Kea, but it still affords stupendous views of the Kohala Coast. Try it both ways: drive down for lunch in foodie-mecca Waimea and then up for a completely different perspective.

Eating & Drinking

KOHALA COFFEE MILL
Café $
☎ 889-5577; Akoni Pule Hwy; snacks $3-5;
☾ 6am-6pm Mon-Fri, to 5:30pm Sat & Sun
A comfy place to hang out and treat yourself to muffins, fresh-brewed Kona coffee and heavenly Tropical Dreams ice cream. Also check out the shave ice and fudge at adjoining **Upstairs at the Mill** (☎ 889-5015), where you can also find internet access ($5 per 30 minutes) and art displays.

KAVA KAFÉ
Café $
☎ 889-0505; Kohala Trade Center, Akoni Pule Hwy; drinks under $5; ☾ 4:20-9pm
Sidle up to the counter and give it a go: order either traditional kava (the mildly relaxing juice of the 'awa plant) or a flavored version, such as Maya Chocolate, made with coconut milk, ginger, chocolate, cayenne and cinnamon. Get two-for-one drinks during the daily happy hour (from 4:20pm). *Wahine* (women) drink *free* on Ladies Night Tuesdays.

SHORT N SWEET
Bakery/Café $
☎ 889-1444; www.shortnsweet.biz; Kohala Trade Center, Akoni Pule Hwy; sandwiches $6-9; ☾ 9am-3pm, closed Tue
Pastry chef Maria Short turns out an impressive array of pastries, breads and specialty cakes (including showstopping wedding masterpieces) at her cheery two-table eatery. In addition to baked goods, find gourmet focaccia sandwiches and fresh salads. Save room for a sweet treat such as Maria's popular Kohala Crunch Bar, which tops mac-nut brittle with bittersweet chocolate ganache and a dusting of cocoa powder.

HULA LA'S MEXICAN KITCHEN
Mexican $
☎ 889-5668; Kohala Trade Center, Akoni Pule Hwy; mains $7-9.50; ☾ 11am-8pm Mon-Thu, to 4pm Fri-Sun
This little Mexican eatery is ideal for takeout (seating is limited), vegetarians or anyone with salsa cravings. Standouts include the filling burritos, grilled fish atop organic greens and homemade papaya salsa.

SUSHI ROCK
Sushi $$
our pick ☎ 889-5900; Akoni Pule Hwy; nigiri $4-6, sushi rolls $9-17; ☾ noon-3pm & 5:30-8pm Sun-Tue & Thu, to 9pm Fri & Sat
Who'd expect first-rate sushi from a non-Japanese chef in rural Hawi? Nobody, until local boy Rio Miceli started rolling his unique (if rather offbeat), island-influenced specialties, such as the Kohala ('*ahi poke*, fresh papaya and cucumber, rolled in mac nuts). Purists might balk at goat cheese, caramelized Maui onion or melted Parmesan in their sushi – until they encounter Miceli's inspired creations.

A Sushi Rock creation   GREG ELMS

Retro-style Bamboo restaurant   LUCI YAMAMOTO

BAMBOO   Hawaii Regional $$
☎ 889-5555; Kohala Trade Center, Akoni Pule Hwy; lunch $9-14, dinner $12-30; ☷ 11:30am-2:30pm & 6-8pm Tue-Sat, 11:30am-2:30pm Sun
In a cozy retro building, lit with festive twinkling lights and lively with Hawaiian music, Bamboo feels like old Hawaii. It's fine dining, yet local-style casual, with T-shirt-clad waiters and reasonable prices. Entrées are island influenced but without much innovation, eg coconut grilled chicken and sesame-nori-crusted tiger shrimp.

LUKE'S PLACE   American $$
☎ 889-1155; 55-510 Hawi Rd; mains $14-25; ☷ noon-10pm Sun, Mon, Wed & Thu, to 11pm Fri & Sat
New in 2007, this not-yet-established restaurant has good potential, especially due to its dining room, which is large yet cozy, with solid wooden furnishings that recall a country lodge. The menu is predictable, with standard salads, spaghetti or lasagna, and one option for each meat type. The Tiki Lounge bar, within the restaurant, is convivial and a rare North Kohala drinking spot. In the foyer, the intriguing display of fine art and Asian collectibles is also for sale.

For groceries, Takata Store (☎ 889-5413; Akoni Pule Hwy; ☷ 8am-7pm Mon-Sat, to 1pm Sun), between Hawi and Kapaʻau, is a well-stocked, family-run market.

Sleeping
KOHALA VILLAGE INN   Independent Hotel $
our pick ☎ 889-0404; www.kohalavillageinn.com; 55-514 Hawi Rd; r $65-75, ste $100-120
Styled like a one-story motel, this retro inn offers tidy rooms with hardwood floors, tasteful furnishings, TV, ceiling fan and lots of character. Located in the heart of Hawi, every destination in town is within walking distance. Granted, the motel-level quality includes unreliable wi-fi, thin walls, no view and minimal continental breakfast, but it's an overall best-value option. And if you gripe about supermarket bagels and English muffins, remember, hey, they're *free*.

KAPAʻAU
Like Hawi, Kapaʻau has become a tiny tourist destination with art galleries and boutiques. The two-block main drag lacks Hawi's selection of restaurants, but does include a courthouse, police station, library and bank. North Kohala was King Kamehameha's childhood home, so the King Kamehameha Day festivities on June 11 have extra significance here.

Sights & Activities
KENJI'S HOUSE
our pick ☎ 884-5556; Akoni Pule Hwy; admission free; ☷ 11am-5pm
Nobody famous, Kapaʻau native Kenji Yokoyama (1931–2004) is now known for his seashell 'art.' An avid free diver and constant recycler and repairer, he collected all the rocks, driftwood and shells that he glued together into little sculptures. While not fine art, when viewed en masse in his lifetime abode, they're original, fanciful, earnest and quite memorable. The exhibit,

Island Insights
When James Luke opened the original **Luke's Place** in 1950, it was Hawi's liveliest night spot. Luke was the grandson of Chinese immigrants who arrived in the 1880s for sugar plantation work. North Kohala's last plantation closed in 1975 and business slowed, but Luke's Place stuck around till 1987. No restaurant has succeeded in that spot since then. Today's owner, Jim Sargent, has restored both the historic building and the original name, hoping that Luke's Place will again become Hawi's gathering place.

THE RANCH LIFE

Windswept pastureland. Grazing cattle. Cloud-dappled skies. North Kohala makes folks yearn to be a *paniolo* (cowboy), at least for a day. So head to a working ranch along the breathtaking Kohala Mountain Rd. Riders must be at least eight years old and 4ft tall.

- **Evening at the Ranch** (☎ 987-2108; www.eveningatkahua.com; Kohala Ranch Rd; adult/child $104/55; ❧ dinner Tue & Thu) Hosted by the Richards family, who own Kahua Ranch, this evening event includes a sunset barbecue dinner, open beer and wine bar, guitar jam session, games such as roping and horseshoe pitching, telescope stargazing and a campfire. The group averages 100 guests, but guests can mingle with real ranchers. A compelling alternative to a comparably priced luau.
- **Naʻalapa Stables** (☎ 889-0022; www.naalapastables.com; Kohala Ranch Rd; rides $68-88, adult/child wagon tour $36/18) Naʻalapa Stables organizes rides across the pastures of the 8500-acre Kahua Ranch, affording fine views of the coast from its 3200ft elevation. Also offered is a narrated historical tour of the ranch aboard an 1860s-style farm wagon.
- **Paniolo Riding Adventures** (☎ 889-5354; www.panioloadventures.com; Hwy 250; rides $69-159) Offers short, long, picnic and sunset rides over 11,000-acre Ponoholo Ranch, a working cattle ranch. Horses are all riding horses, and they're selected for the rider's experience. Boots, hats, chaps and jackets are provided free of charge.

KOHALA & WAIMEA

called **Kenji's Room: A Mini Museum**, is part of the overall Kenji's House site, which includes a **restaurant** (see Pico's Bistro, p127) and the **North Kohala Artists Cooperative Gallery**.

KAMEHAMEHA THE GREAT STATUE

The statue on the front lawn of the North Kohala Civic Center has a famous twin in Honolulu, standing across from Iolani Palace. The Kapaʻau one was the original, constructed in 1880 in Florence, Italy, by American sculptor Thomas Gould. When the ship delivering it sank off the Falkland Islands, a second statue was then cast from the original mold. The duplicate statue arrived at the Islands in 1883 and took its place in downtown Honolulu. Later the sunken statue was recovered from the ocean floor and sent here, to Kamehameha's childhood home.

KALAHIKIOLA CHURCH

In 1855 Protestant missionaries Elias and Ellen Bond built this church on their vast estate (obviously, missionary life wasn't one of total deprivation). It's not a mustsee, but towering banyan trees and peaceful macadamia-nut orchards surrounding the church make it a scenic detour. Large portions of three of the church's walls crumbled in the 2006 earthquake, and the congregation immediately began fundraising to rebuild.

The church is 900yd up ʻIole Rd, which is on the *mauka* side of the highway between the 23- and 24-mile markers.

KAMEHAMEHA ROCK

According to legend, Kamehameha carried this rock uphill from the beach to demonstrate his prodigious strength. Much later, when a road crew attempted to move it to a different location, the rock stubbornly fell off the wagon – a sign that it wanted to stay put. Not wanting to upset Kamehameha's mana, the workers left it in place. Don't blink or you'll miss it, sitting on the inland roadside about 2 miles east of Kapaʻau, on a curve just past a small bridge. Also keep your eyes peeled for the facade of the **Tong Building**, a colorful old Chinese hall secluded in the trees above the rock.

KEOKEA BEACH PARK

off Akoni Pule Hwy; ❧ gate 7am-11pm
About 3.5 miles from Kapaʻau, this beach park isn't a big draw because there's no sandy beach. But it is striking, with tall, reddish cliffs rising above a boulder bay. The surf really surges with a west swell, attracting a motley crew of experienced local surfers. Swimming is sketchy due to dangerous shore breaks and strong currents. The facilities are shoddy, but there are barbecue grills, showers, drinking water and portable toilets. The marked turnoff is about 1.5 miles before the Pololu Valley

Lookout. On the way down to the beach, you'll pass an old **Japanese cemetery** with gravestones inscribed in *kanji* (Japanese script).

Kamehameha Park (Map p106), located on Kamehameha Park Rd off the Akoni Pule Hwy on the *makai* side, offers a modern gymnasium, ballpark, swimming pool, picnic tables and kiddie playground, all free for the public. For yoga, the only studio around is the **North Kohala Community Center** (☎ 889-0583; Sakamoto Bldg, 55-3877 Akoni Pule Hwy; drop-in class $15), a quiet, low-key place.

Eating

SAMMY D'S   Diner $
☎ 889-5288; 54-3854 Akoni Pule Hwy; meals $6-8; ⏰ 11am-8pm Tue-Thu, 11am-4pm & 6-8pm Fri & Sat
This is the local-style version of Kohala Rainbow Café. Fill up on burgers, sandwiches and plate lunches including mahimahi, Korean chicken and the house specialty, roast pork.

KOHALA RAINBOW CAFÉ   Café $
☎ 889-0099; Akoni Pule Hwy; sandwiches & salads $8; ⏰ 11am-5pm
Also known as Jen's, this comfy hangout spot offers ample indoor seating and wholesome eats, such as chicken Caesar salads, hearty chili, sandwich wraps with organic greens and fresh-fruit smoothies.

Don't Miss

- **Kava Kafé's spicy chili-cinnamon-chocolate kava drinks** (p124)
- **The mysterious ancient drawings at Puako Petroglyph Preserve** (p112)
- **Spa Without Walls** (p113)
- **Aloha Festivals Poke Contest** (a *poke* smorgasbord!) (p117)
- **Hiking down Pololu Valley** (p128)
- **Hawi's Friday movie night** (p124)
- **The eccentrically appetizing sushi rolls at Sushi Rock** (p124)
- **Gallery hopping at Isaacs Art Center** (p130)
- **The scenic drive down (or up) Kohala Mountain Road** (p124)

PICO'S BISTRO   Café $
☎ 884-5555; Kenji's House, Akoni Pule Hwy; mains $8-11; ⏰ 11:30am-3:30pm & 5-7pm
With umbrella-shaded patio seating and a teeny kitchen, Pico's resembles a beachside food stand. But the menu is all gourmet, featuring homemade pastas, quiches, chicken and lamb kebabs, and classic salads – made with local, organic produce. Fresh-fruit smoothies ($5) include the eye-opening Lime Malia (homemade lime sorbet, seltzer and fresh lime juice). Biodegradable cutlery and containers.

Shopping

For new and used books, **Kohala Book Shop** (☎ 889-6400; Akoni Pule Hwy; ⏰ 11am-5pm Mon-Sat) is a well-stocked indie shop. Nearby, women who love jewelry will find **Elements** (☎ 889-0760; Akoni Pule Hwy; ⏰ 10am-6pm Mon-Fri, to 5pm Sat) irresistible, with its eclectic collection of locally made finery.

Sleeping

KOHALA CLUB HOTEL   Inn $
☎ 889-6793; www.kohalaclubhotel.com; 54-3793 Akoni Pule Hwy; r $56, cottages $90
Just a quarter-mile from town, this tiny inn offers clean rooms with private bathrooms for an unbelievable price. The main house contains four small, no-frills rooms with either a queen bed or two twins, plus a TV. With two bedrooms, the cottage is perfect for families.

KOHALA COUNTRY ADVENTURES GUEST HOUSE   Inn $$
☎ 889-5663, 866-892-2484; www.kcadventures .com; off Akoni Pule Hwy; r $85-160
If 'rustic' and 'country' appeal to you, try this relaxed, lived-in house on 10 acres of ungroomed tropical gardens, with fruit trees, livestock and coastal views. The Sundeck Suite is comfy for families, with kitchenette, three beds and an open loft layout. It's a comfy, not fancy, place and host Bobi Moreno, a longtime resident, puts everyone at ease.

POLOLU VALLEY

our pick With a stunning row of steep, mystical cliffs, this ancient valley is utterly memorable – and proves the diversity of

KOHALA & WAIMEA

Pololu Valley from the lookout

© ROGER FLETCHER / ALAMY

the Big Island landscape. If Waipi'o Valley highlights the island's green lushness, Pololu Valley reveals its contemplative side, in twilight shades and thick mists. The Akoni Pule Hwy ends at the **Pololu Valley Lookout**, which is the endpoint for those who cannot hike down the trail.

Pololu Valley was once abundant with wetland taro, when Pololu Stream carried water from the deep, wet interior to the valley floor. When the Kohala Ditch was built in 1906, however, it diverted much of the water and ended taro production. The valley's last residents left in the 1940s, and the area is now forest-reserve land.

For 100 years, the privately owned ditch has been a lifeline for Kohala ranches and farms, but it stopped flowing after major damage from the 2006 earthquake. The $3.5 million repairs were in progress at the time of research.

Sights & Activities

Shaded by a tree canopy, the trail from the lookout to the valley floor is steep and rocky, but switchbacks keep it from being overly strenuous. On average, walking time is 30 minutes. Think twice about trekking down after rainfall, as the mud-slicked rocks will be precarious. Walking sticks are often left at the trailhead. There are no facilities.

A compact **black-sand beach** at the valley's mouth is scenic for strolling but too rough for swimming. You might see local surfers testing the waves, however. In the past, intrepid hikers could continue to the next valley, **Honokane Nui**, but it's been impassable due to landslides ever since the 2006 earthquake. The trail is treacherously slippery and traverses private property managed in part by **Surety Kohala** (☎ 889-6257; Hawi), which you can call to inquire about the trail's current status. Avoid venturing beyond Pololu Valley while the trail remains closed, and never hike near the ocean, where pounding waves can sweep you away.

Tours

Hawaii Forest & Trail (☎ 331-8505, 800-464-1993; www.hawaii-forest.com; adult/child under 12yr waterfall tour $114/89; adult/child 6-12yr 4WD tour $99/79) offers two tours in the Kohala area. One traverses the Kohala Ditch Trail to waterfalls; transportation from the Waikoloa Resort Area is included. The other goes through Pololu Valley in a six-wheel off-road vehicle and on foot.

WAIMEA (KAMUELA)

Tucked between the Kohala Mountains and Mauna Kea's northern flank, Waimea is a conflicted place. Weatherwise, it's split into the 'dry side' and the 'wet side,' and strangely, it's a town with two names. Then there are all the transplants – organic farmers, astronomers, artists – plus new money and upscale restaurants, making it feel more like suburban Marin County than Hawaiian cowboy country. Yet a *paniolo* town it shall probably always remain, since Waimea is essentially owned and operated by Parker Ranch – Hawai'i's biggest cattle ranch (see the boxed text on p132).

Waimea makes a good base to explore Kohala, Mauna Kea and the Hamakua Coast, since all are easily accessible. If you enjoy fine food and theater, *mo bettah*, since some of the island's best is here in cow town. Waimea has wacky weather, going from sun to rain in the swish of a horse's tail, so jeans and sweaters are definitely needed up here at 2670ft.

ORIENTATION

You'll know when you pass from Waimea's dry side to the wet side, around the intersection of Kawaihae Rd (Hwy 19) and Mamalahoa Hwy (Hwy 190).

Note that Hwy 190 is usually called Mamalahoa Hwy. From Hilo, Hwy 19 is also called Mamalahoa Hwy, but once it intersects with Hwy 190, it's called Kawaihae Rd. Further east, there's Old Mamalahoa Hwy, which intersects Hwy 19 at both ends.

Don't Miss

- **Views from Kohala Mountain Road** (p124)
- **Waimea Farmers Market's $1-a-minute massages** (p133)
- **Hawaiian shirts, board shorts, 25¢ novels and $2 resort robes at the Salvation Army Thrift Store** (☎ 885-2155; 64-1013 Mamalahoa Hwy)
- **Bathroom at Tako Taco** (p133)
- **Kamuela Liquor Store** (☎ 885-4674; 64-1010 Mamalahoa Hwy; 🕑 8am-7:30pm Mon-Sat, 9am-5pm Sun) Everything from single malts to *reposados*; decent prices, too.

INFORMATION

Emma's Washerette (Mamalahoa Hwy; 🕑 4:45am-9pm Sun-Thu, 4:15am-11pm Fri & Sat) Across from Tako Taco.

North Hawaii Community Hospital (☎ 885-4444; www.northhawaiicommunityhospital.org; 67-1125 Mamalahoa Hwy; 🕑 24hr) Emergency services available.

Post office (☎ 885-6239; 67-1197 Mamalahoa Hwy) Located southwest of Parker Ranch Center. Waimea mail should be addressed Kamuela.

SIGHTS

If you've got the kids in tow, don't miss the all-wooden playground in **Waimea Park**. With time for only one Parker Ranch site, make it the historic homes.

PARKER RANCH MUSEUM & VISITOR CENTER

☎ 885-7655; www.parkerranch.com; Parker Ranch Center, 67-1185 Mamalahoa Hwy; adult/child/senior $8/6/7; 🕑 10am-5pm Mon-Sat, last entry 4pm

You can unravel the Parker legacy with a visit to this small museum displaying family memorabilia, rodeo action shots, traditional Hawaiian quilts and cowboy gear. There's a 25-minute documentary on Parker Ranch, which, while interesting, doesn't justify the steep admission price (welcome to Waimea). By purchasing dual admission to the museum and historic homes you save a dollar (whoopee!).

PARKER RANCH HISTORIC HOMES

☎ 885-5433; www.parkerranch.com; Parker Historical Houses Rd; adult/child/senior $9/8/8.50; 🕑 10am-5pm Mon-Sat, last entry 4pm

These two 19th-century homes at the end of a wooded drive are a study in contrasts. Big boss man John Palmer Parker lived in the ultramodest **Mana Hale**, an 1840s home built of Hawaiian koa wood in the Cape Cod architectural style common to Parker's native Massachusetts. The original interior was dismantled board by beautiful board and rebuilt here. It's now decorated with period furnishings and historic photos of the hardy Parker clan.

KOHALA & WAIMEA

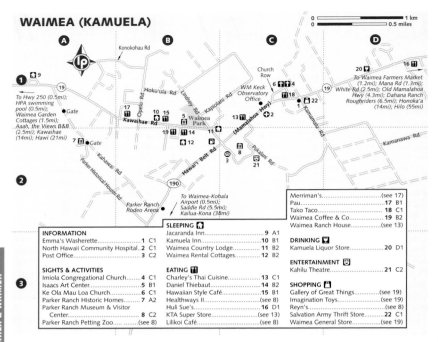

WAIMEA (KAMUELA)

INFORMATION	
Emma's Washerette	**1** C1
North Hawaii Community Hospital	**2** C1
Post Office	**3** C2

SIGHTS & ACTIVITIES	
Imiola Congregational Church	**4** C1
Isaacs Art Center	**5** B1
Ke Ola Mau Loa Church	**6** C1
Parker Ranch Historic Homes	**7** A2
Parker Ranch Museum & Visitor Center	**8** C2
Parker Ranch Petting Zoo	(see 8)

SLEEPING	
Jacaranda Inn	**9** A1
Kamuela Inn	**10** B1
Waimea Country Lodge	**11** B2
Waimea Rental Cottages	**12** B2

EATING	
Charley's Thai Cuisine	**13** C1
Daniel Thiebaut	**14** B2
Hawaiian Style Café	**15** B1
Healthways II	(see 8)
Huli Sue's	**16** D1
KTA Super Store	(see 13)
Lilikoi Café	(see 8)
Merriman's	(see 17)
Pau	**17** B1
Tako Taco	**18** C1
Waimea Coffee & Co	**19** B2
Waimea Ranch House	(see 13)

DRINKING	
Kamuela Liquor Store	**20** D1

ENTERTAINMENT	
Kahilu Theatre	**21** C2

SHOPPING	
Gallery of Great Things	(see 19)
Imagination Toys	(see 19)
Reyn's	(see 8)
Salvation Army Thrift Store	**22** C1
Waimea General Store	(see 19)

On a small *pu'u* (hillock) nearby is **Pu'uopelu**, the estate's sprawling 7000-sq-ft grand manor, built in 1862 and occupied by successive waves of Parkers. The home's last resident, Richard Palmer Smart, was quite the character. A cabaret and Broadway performer, dandy and world traveler, Smart amassed one hell of a Chinese and European **art collection**, now adorning the opulent home. Smart's theater career is recounted in the 'Broadway Room,' plastered with playbills and sultry photos. Local gossips say this theatrical eccentric liked to greet tourists in his bathrobe before his death in 1992. His **gardens** here are fabulous.

ISAACS ART CENTER

`our pick` ☎ 885-5884; www.isaacsartcenter.org; 61-1268 Kawaihae Rd; ☺ 10am-5pm Tue-Sat

Sometimes *where* art is shown is as moving as the art itself (Bilbao, NYC Guggenheim), and that's the case at this art center. When Building N from the Waimea school was slated for demolition, George and Shirley Isaacs and friends snapped into action to save the 1915 schoolhouse, moving it

piece by piece (even the blackboards) to its present location. The result is a series of bright, spacious galleries displaying an excellent collection of local and international artwork.

As you tread the original Douglas fir floorboards, the smell of oil paint and exotic woods mingles with dreams of owning that gorgeous koa rocker ($8000) or the exquisite *milo*, tiger and *kahili* koa wood breakfront ($15,000). Some items are not for sale, including Herb Kawainui Kane's classic *The Arrival of Captain Cook at Kealakekua Bay in January 1779,* in the entryway.

Proving that art appreciation need not be a snooty, alienating experience, Director Bernard Nougés often greets visitors

Island Insights

Funny word, *paniolo*. Its origin is a tickler too: it comes from 'españoles,' the name Hawaiians gave to the Mexican cowboys who taught the islanders to rope and ride.

Experience Waimea *paniolo*-style
GREG ELMS

personally, explaining the craftsmanship behind a particular piece or the relevance of a painting's symbolism – even to trail-worn backpackers. A portion of proceeds from the center's sales goes to the Hawai'i Preparatory Academy.

CHURCH ROW
In 1830 it was a grass hut. In 1838 it grew into a wooden building adorned with coral stones, carried on the backs of the parishioners. In this way, Imiola Congregational Church (www.imiolachurch.com; admission free; services 9:30am), Waimea's first Christian church, communed with Hawaii.

The current church, built entirely of koa, was constructed in 1857 and restored in 1976. In the churchyard is the grave of missionary Lorenzo Lyons, who arrived in 1832 and spent 54 years in Waimea. Lyons translated and wrote many hymns in Hawaiian, including the popular 'Hawai'i Aloha,' still sung here in Hawaiian the first Sunday of the month.

The green-steepled church next door is the much-photographed, all-Hawaiian Ke Ola Mau Loa Church. Buddhists, Baptists and Mormons also have places of worship along this curved row.

ACTIVITIES
DAHANA RANCH ROUGHRIDERS
our pick ☎ 885-0057, 888-399-0057; www.dahana ranch.com; adult/child 90min ride $70/60; rides 9am, 11am, 1pm & 3pm, reservations essential
Hitting the trail is easy here in horse country. Located in the magnificent foothills of

Mauna Kea, Dahana Ranch Roughriders is owned and operated by a Native Hawaiian family. With Hawai'i's most established horse outfit, you'll be riding American quarter horses bred, raised and trained by third- and fourth-generation *paniolo*. These are open-range rides, available to kids as young as three. More advanced rides are also on offer. The ranch is 7.5 miles east of Waimea, off Old Mamalahoa Hwy.

PARKER RANCH PETTING ZOO
☎ 885-7655, 877-885-7999; www.parkerranch .com; Parker Ranch Center, 67-1185 Mamalahoa Hwy; admission incl pony ride $25; pony rides 9am, 10am, 1pm & 2pm
If the kids are up for a pony rather than a horse, head to this zoo, where children even a year old can ride a pony, and pet and feed a variety of farm animals.

Swimmers will swoon at HPA's big, clean outdoor swimming pool (☎ 885-7321; 65-1692 Kohala Mountain Rd; admission $3; 12:30-1:30pm Mon-Fri, 1-4pm Sun), administered with aloha.

TOURS
Maverick chef Peter Merriman was mixing mango and goat cheese before the term Hawaii Regional Cuisine was even coined. Learn about how he brings his signature dishes to your table on Hawai'i Forest & Trail's Merriman's Culinary & Farm Adventure Tour (☎ 331-8505, 800-464-1993; www.hawaii-forest .com; per person $155; 2:30pm Mon-Thu). The five-hour tour leaving from Merriman's visits local farms supplying the free-range lamb

COW POWER

Parker Ranch is like the giant koa trees lining the pastures along Mana Rd: big and old as dirt. Founded in 1847, it was until recently the nation's largest privately owned ranch, peaking at 250,000 acres. To make ends meet in today's withering market, however, the ranch has had to sell off parcels (24,000 acres to the US military in 2006 alone), so that it currently has over 30,000 cattle on 150,000 acres. Still, that's almost 7% of the entire Big Island, producing 15 million pounds of beef annually.

In 1793 King Kamehameha the Great was gifted a herd of long-horned cattle by British Captain George Vancouver. So the herd would grow, prescient Kamehameha made the cows *kapu* (taboo). The conservation measure was a little *too* effective, however, and by 1815 the wild herd was threatening the land and its people.

Enter Massachusetts mariner John Palmer Parker, who arrived on the Big Island in 1809 at the tender age of 19. Parker was so deft with a rifle, Kamehameha contracted him to control the cattle problem. With the typical pluck and determination of pioneering New Englanders, Parker cut the herd down to size, demanding elite specimens as payment.

Kamehameha was delighted with the results and granted Parker the quality cows, plus the hand of one of his granddaughters. With the princess and cattle came the royal chattel: a chunk of land that led to control over the entire Waikoloa *ahupua'a*, a traditional land division running from the mountains to the sea. A few domesticated cows later and the Parker Ranch legacy was born.

And what a legacy: in 1908 three Hawaiian *paniolo* (cowboys), trained by Mexican-Spanish cowboys brought over for the purpose, traveled to compete in the Cheyenne Frontier Days World Championship Rodeo. And *braddah* Ikua Purdy won! Purdy's big win put Hawaiian cowboys on the map, and cowboys have since become a rich part of Waimea tradition. Indeed, Hawaiians still win rodeos both here and on the mainland. The centennial was celebrated as 'Year of the Paniolo.' Learn more at the **Paniolo Preservation Society** (www.paniolopreservation.org).

and organic goodies that wind up in your four-course meal that ends the tour. No children under eight.

FESTIVALS & EVENTS

Waimea Cherry Blossom Festival (☎ 961-8706; Parker Ranch Center & Church Row Park; admission free) Dark pink blossoms are greeted with *taiko* drumming, *mochi* (sticky rice cake) pounding and other Japanese cultural events on the first Saturday in February.

Fourth of July Rodeo (☎ 885-2303; Parker Ranch Rodeo Arena, 67-1435 Mamalahoa Hwy; admission $6) This event celebrating over 45 years of ranching has cattle roping, bull riding and other hoopla.

Old Hawaii on Horseback Traditional *pa'u* riding, with lei-bedecked women in flowing dresses, is not to be missed, nor is the post-ride concert. Held biennially in August.

Round-Up Rodeo (☎ 885-5669; www.parkerranch .com; Parker Ranch Rodeo Arena, 67-1435 Mamalahoa Hwy; admission $5) On the first Monday in September after the Labor Day weekend, this is another whip-cracking event.

Aloha Festivals Ho'olaule'a (☎ 885-7786; http:// alohafestivals.com/v3/pages/events/hawaii.jsp; admission free) Statewide Aloha festivals bring free concerts, craft

fairs and the Paniolo Parade to Waimea in the third week of September.

Waimea Ukulele & Slack Key Guitar Institute Concert (☎ 885-6017; www.kahilutheatre.org; admission from $5) This is the go-to event at the Kahilu Theatre in early November, with concerts, evening *kanikapila* (open-mike jam sessions) and workshops by the giants of uke and slack key guitar, including Cyril Pahinui and Dennis Kamakahi. Private lessons are also available ($65).

Christmas parade In early December, the town gets into the Kalikimaka spirit with a block party.

EATING

With all its variety and high-quality eats, Waimea is a good place to stuff yourself silly.

PAU   Eclectic $

our pick ☎ 885-6325; http://paupizza.com; Opelo Plaza, 65-1227 Opelo Rd; salads & sandwiches $4-9; ⊙ 11am-4pm Mon-Fri

Fresh, quick and sassy are the keywords for this Waimea newcomer. Delicious should be appended to the list, with daily offerings such as local greens with spiced pecans, apples and blue cheese, and homemade chicken pot pie. It also makes some fine, thin-crust pizzas ($17 to $22 for a 16in pie). The laid-back dining space will be open for dinner by the time you read this.

LILIKOI CAFÉ   Café $
☎ 887-1400; Parker Ranch Center, 67-1185 Mamalahoa Hwy; mains $5-11.50; ☷ 7:30am-4pm Mon-Sat

You want bangers and mash, but your sweetie craves quiche. Odd pairing, but it works at this sunny café serving healthy, innovative food such as avocado stuffed with tuna, apples, raisins and pine nuts, and beautiful artichoke and pasta salad. The fresh carrot, apple, beet and ginger juice is the bomb ($4.75). No Styrofoam is used at this healthful stop. Hurrah!

TAKO TACO   Mexican $
☎ 887-1717; 64-1066 Mamalahoa Hwy; mains $5-12; ☷ 11am-8:30pm Mon-Sat, noon-8pm Sun

Attempting to re-create a Mexican *taqueria*, this small, colorful place serves big portions of tacos, nachos and burritos (including fish and veggie). Wash it all down with a stiff mango margarita ($6). The *'ono* (delicious) quesadilla with mushrooms, cheese and caramelized onions lives up to its name, but the chicken taco is blah. With lots of Day of the Dead decorations to ogle and a *na keiki* (children's) menu, this is a great place for kids.

CHARLEY'S THAI CUISINE   Thai $$
our pick ☎ 885-5591; Waimea Center, 65-1144 Mamalahoa Hwy; appetizers & salads $7-11.95, mains $9.50-14; ☷ 11am-3pm & 5-9pm

Great value and killer taste are a winning combination at this local hot spot. The atmosphere is Thai tourist bureau, but who cares when you're supping on a perfectly spiced dried curry with shrimp? The other curries are equally tasty and the *tom kha gai* (coconut milk, lemongrass and chicken soup) is heavenly. It's almost all good – the *pad talay* (stir-fried shrimp) with mushroom is uninspiring.

MERRIMAN'S   Hawaii Regional $$$$
☎ 885-6822; Opelo Plaza, 65-1227 Opelo Rd; lunch $7-12, dinner $17-33; ☷ lunch Mon-Fri, dinner daily

Peter Merriman, one of the chefs who spearheaded the Hawaii Regional Cuisine craze, still serves inventive fare at his flagship restaurant. Local, chemical-free ingredients go into signature dishes such as wok-charred *'ahi* and Kahua Ranch garlic striploin with melted goat cheese ($36). Can't decide? There are handy samplers (appetizers and desserts for $29, mains $45). Lunch is a more affordable affair. Reservations are highly recommended for this tourist magnet.

DANIEL THIEBAUT   Asian/Seafood $$$$
☎ 887-2200; www.danielthiebaut.com; 65-1259 Kawaihae Rd; appetizers $8.50-15, mains $25-45; ☷ 3:30-9pm Mon-Sat, 10am-1:30pm & 3:30-9pm Sun

Even chef Daniel isn't sure what to call his menu these days ('he's not feeling the French-Asian thing right now,' according to staff). But forget the semantics – the local and organic (whenever possible) meals, such as lobster bouillabaisse, bacon-wrapped tenderloin or Hilo corn crabcake, are delicious at this top foodie destination. The classy our pick Sunday brunch buffet ($18.50) is unbelievable value and the food and wine pairing (per person $100, minimum 6 people) at the chef's table makes for a very special dinner.

You can save big in tony Waimea by cooking for yourself or fixing a picnic with supplies from ✿ KTA Super Stores (☎ 885-8866; Waimea Center, 65-1144 Mamalahoa Hwy; ☷ 6am-11pm) or Healthways II (☎ 885-6775; Parker Ranch Center, 67-1185 Mamalahoa Hwy; ☷ 9am-7pm Mon-Sat, to 5pm Sun). The ✿ Waimea Farmers Market (☎ 885-9808; ☷ 7am-noon Sat), near the 55-mile marker, is not to be missed. In addition to buying organic fruits and veggies directly from the farmers, you can gorge on sweet or savory crepes ($6 to $9), teriyaki chicken ($7), even brick-oven pizza ($12).

Other good Waimea eats abound, including the following:

Hawaiian Style Café (☎ 885-4295; 64-1290 Kawaihae Rd; mains $6.50-10; ☷ 7am-1:30pm Mon-Sat, to noon Sun) Take a number for a stool at this classic local place serving huge plates of biscuits and gravy, *loco moco* (rice, fried egg and hamburger patty topped with gravy) and other giant cowboy fillers.

Huli Sue's (☎ 885-6268; www.hulisues.com; 64-957 Mamalahoa Hwy; mains $12-24, barbecue $15-19; ☷ 11:30am-8:30pm Mon-Sat) Excellent kiawe-smoked barbecue, burgers, organic salad bar and toothsome sweets brought to you by chef Mark Vann of Fujimamas (p65) fame.

Waimea Coffee & Co (☎ 885-2100; Parker Sq, 65-1279 Kawaihae Rd; ☷ 7am-4pm Mon-Fri, 8am-3pm

KOHALA & WAIMEA

Sat, 9am-2pm Sun) Cool atmosphere goes well with 100% pure Kona coffee here; good lunch selection, too.

Waimea Ranch House (☎ 885-2088; Waimea Center, 65-1144 Mamalahoa Hwy; mains $15-33; ✆ lunch Wed-Sun, dinner Wed-Mon) Perfectly grilled rib eye, or filet with Gorgonzola. Come here with an appetite and expense account. Budget travelers can eat lighter fare at the bar.

ENTERTAINMENT
KAHILU THEATRE
☎ 885-6017, box office 885-6868; www.kahilu theatre.org; Parker Ranch Center, 67-1185 Mamalahoa Hwy; admission $15-45; ✆ box office 9am-3pm Mon-Fri, show times vary

Big Islanders come from far and wide to see musicians such as Badi Assad and Hugh Masekela, plus top-flight drama (eg Elton John's *Aida*) and dance (the Paul Taylor Dance Company) at this theater. The annual **Waimea Ukulele & Slack Key Guitar Institute Concert** (p132) is another big draw. Come early to browse the lobby **art gallery**.

SHOPPING
Waimea shopping is unique, with many artists, designers and jewelry makers represented in local stores. Save your souvenir shopping for here and you'll snag some quality, original goods. Places to stop and shop include the following:

Gallery of Great Things (☎ 885-7706; Parker Sq, 65-1279 Kawaihae Rd; ✆ 9am-5:30pm Mon-Sat, 10am-4pm Sun) The name says it all. Browse the several rooms of Hawaiian, Polynesian and Asian art, furnishings and photographs and you'll agree.

Imagination Toys (☎ 885-0430; Parker Sq, 65-1279 Kawaihae Rd) Learning is fun here, for kids of all ages.

Reyn's (☎ 885-4493; Parker Ranch Center, 67-1185 Mamalahoa Hwy; ✆ 9:30am-5:30pm Mon-Sat, to 4pm Sun) This is the place to get a classy, muted, reverse-aloha shirt – after all, it was invented here!

Island Insights

If the name **Jake Shimabukuro** pops up on a Kahilu Theatre concert schedule while you're in Waimea, run, don't walk, to the box office. Experiencing the 'Jimi Hendrix of the ukulele' (and O'ahu native) live is unforgettable.

Waimea General Store (☎ 885-4479; Parker Sq, 65-1279 Kawaihae Rd) The super eclectic mix here is fun to peruse, from Le Creuset and Arabic compasses to soap and vintage hula-girl cards.

SLEEPING
Waimea isn't cheap, but the rural scenery and good sleeping weather make for a welcome change from the hot Kohala Coast, just 20 minutes downhill.

KAMUELA INN   Independent Hotel $
☎ 885-4243, 800-555-8968; www.hawaii-bnb.com /kamuela.html; 1600 Kawaihae Rd; r $60-85, ste $90-100, incl breakfast; 💻

This is Waimea's affordable place to stay. Clean and simple (if a little musty), the standard rooms have TV and private bathroom, while the deluxe rooms are group-friendly (request one with private lanai). Suites have two bedrooms, full kitchen and dining room – the penthouses are super value. The priciest Executive Suites ($185) are spacious. Digs in the newer Mauna Kea wing are brighter and fresher.

AAAH, THE VIEWS B&B   B&B $$
☎ 885-3455; www.aaahtheviews.com; 66-1773 Alaneo St; r with shared bathroom $110-125, ste $195-210, incl breakfast; 💻

This B&B epitomizes both aloha and 'ohana (family), two terms constantly heard on Hawai'i. It's not only the lovely yard and shared lanai along a babbling stream, but the hospitality, too – from hiking tips to star charts. The name is apt since the rooms have ample windows (12 different kinds in the dreamy Dream Room!) with gorgeous mountain views. All rooms have cable TV, DVD, phone, fridge, microwave and coffee maker. The cheapest rooms share a bathroom, which dents their value.

WAIMEA GARDEN COTTAGES Cottages $$
☎ 885-8550; www.waimeagardens.com; studios $140, cottages $150-160, incl breakfast; 💻

If you're looking for independent, comfortable digs where you can soak in a hot tub, cook your own dinner and take morning coffee in a private garden, the Kohala Cottage here is for you. The smaller Waimea Cottage is cozy and romantic, with fireplace, kitchenette and private garden. There's also a spacious studio near a seasonal stream. This nonsmoking property is 2 miles west of town (near the intersection of Kawaihae Rd and Hwy 250); three-day minimum stay.

JACARANDA INN   Inn $$$
☎ 885-8813; www.jacarandainn.com; 65-1444 Kawaihae Rd; r $149-159, ste $169-199, cottages $450; 💻

Tucked among charming gardens behind the mansion that once hosted Kissinger and Jackie O (not at the same time, presumably), each of the eight rooms here is unique and lovely, especially the bathrooms, some with deep whirlpool tubs overlooking the inn's 11 acres. Luxurious details include canopy beds, lanai, Hawaiian quilts, leather club chairs and dehumidifiers. One room is ADA-compliant. Get some friends together and splurge on the three-bedroom, three-bathroom private cottage, with full kitchen, fireplace and hot tub.

Some other ideas for Waimea accommodations include the following:

Waimea Country Lodge (☎ 885-4100, 800-367- 5004; www.castleresorts.com; 65-1210 Lindsey Rd; r $120-130,

with kitchenette $140) Motel is more like it: plywood doors, cheesy art and tight bathrooms. This is a last resort.

Waimea Rental Cottages (☎ 885-8533; www .waimearentalcottages.com; PO Box 2245, Kamuela, HI 96743; studio per day/week/month $125/850/2600, 1br $135/925/2800; P 💻) Two small, comfortable (and pricey) cottages are conveniently located in town. The studio has a kitchen, the one-bedroom just a kitchenette.

GETTING THERE & AROUND
The one-runway Waimea-Kohala Airport (MUE) is serviced by Pacific Wings (☎ 888-575-4546; www.pacificwings.com), with flights between Honolulu, Kahului, Maui, Kailua-Kona and Waimea.

The free Hele-On Bus (☎ 961-8744; www .co.hawaii.hi.us/mass_transit/heleonbus.html; ☾ Mon-Sat) goes from Waimea to Kailua-Kona on its No 16 Kailua-Kona route (1½ hours), and to Hilo on its No 7 Downtown Hilo route (1¾ hours).

The drive from Kailua-Kona is 40 miles along Hwy 190, which becomes Old Mamalahoa Hwy in town. From Hilo the drive is 55 miles along Hwy 19 around the Hamakua Coast.

AROUND WAIMEA

KOHALA FOREST RESERVE
One of the island's best day hikes starts just 3 miles out of town. Unfortunately, the wonderful Kohala Forest Reserve Trail (Map p106), which traverses verdant native forest and meanders beside the aqueous Upper Hamakua Ditch before plopping you atop the back of Waipi'o Valley for unparalleled views, could not be hiked at the time of writing. At least you had to be very determined (and determined to trespass) to hike this fragile trail at that time. The 2006 earthquake and subsequent flooding caused landslides, making the trail slightly dangerous (but not impassable). A call to the Department of Land & Natural Resources (DLNR) confirmed the land was unstable, but worse, they've been unable to secure the short, but legally necessary, easement for this hike. As if the nine padlocks on the first gate left any doubt. Locals urge hikers to keep the pressure on by calling DLNR (☎ 974-4221) to check on the status of this trail.

Thinking positively for when it reopens… To do this hike, turn left on White Rd (after the 54-mile marker on Mamalahoa Hwy) and go 1 mile to the end of the road. Enter the gate (close it behind you!), round 1.5 miles past Waimea Reservoir to another gate and you'll reach the official entrance to the Kohala Forest Reserve.

Almost immediately, you dive into a lush forest of large ohia trees, giving a taste of what these hills felt like before ranching took over. The wide gravel path here narrows as it follows the moss-covered ditch and the forest becomes choked over with beautiful but invasive bamboo and ginger. The trail here is a bit rocky, converging with and leaving the ditch at various points. Keep an eye out for a giant uprooted (but still living) tree on your right; the steep trail there is an interesting short side jaunt to the ditch sluice.

After another 15 minutes of hiking through pretty hardwood forest, you emerge at the first magnificent viewpoint.

KOHALA & WAIMEA

The Kohala Forest Reserve Trail ends at the back of verdant Waipi'o Valley KARL LEHMANN

Below are the upper streams of Waipi'o Valley drainage and, beyond, a glorious view to the ocean. Just after the viewpoint, keep vigilant for a deep **lava tube cave** good for exploring, up on your left. From here, the trail is a fine thread along the valley ridge and a misstep could easily be fatal, so take care. Another 2 miles of trail dips into green gulches and across mossy bridges, with incomparable valley views, until you come to a mountain slide, from where you'll have to turn back. If the trail has been reestablished by the time you read this, you can follow it as long as you're able, before turning back (there is no loop trail here). Even if the entire valley is fogged in, this is still a lovely and miraculous hike. It isn't appropriate for children, however, and it helps to have a little goat in you.

WAIMEA BACK ROADS

For a peaceful, scented back road meander, turn right off Hwy 19 onto the **Old Mamalahoa Hwy**, just west of the 52-mile marker. (Coming from Hilo, turn left at the 43-mile marker opposite Tex Drive-In and then take the next immediate right.) This 10-mile detour winds through hill country, with small roadside ranches, old wooden fences and grazing horses. Take it slow, snap some pictures and get a taste of what Waimea used to be like. This makes a picturesque **cycling** route, but take care on the narrow, winding road, especially once you enter the forested curves of Ahualoa.

Diehards may want to explore the old miner's **quarry cave**, along the roadside 4 miles from the turnoff coming from Waimea. The entrance is at the bend in the road hemmed in by root-encrusted escarpments. Beyond the dying ferns of the most easterly cave, there's litter, beer bottles and a labyrinth of tunnels dug by early miners. Another set of caves just west looks like two eye sockets and requires an uphill scramble to enter.

Another back road drive is a long, hard 44 miles southeast along **Mana Rd**, wending around Mauna Kea. The landscapes are even more spectacular here, with expansive mountain vistas and green as far as the eye can see, but after 1.7 miles you are violating your rental car contract *in flagrante* when the road turns to dirt. You'll need a good 4WD to go the whole way, but you'll definitely be on the road less traveled. This is a great **mountain biking** excursion. Mana Rd is at the Mamalahoa Hwy 55-mile marker.

MAUNA KEA & SADDLE ROAD

Caution: you're entering hallowed ground. According to the Hawaiian creation myth, every palm tree, grain of sand, volcano and valley in the Hawaiian Islands was created at Mauna Kea. This sacrosanct 'Mount of Wakea' is home to the gods, the place between heaven and earth where *na kanaka maoli,* the Native Hawaiians, were born. Not surprisingly, it's considered the most sacred place in all the Islands. At 13,796ft, Mauna Kea – more precisely, its true summit, Pu'u Wekiu – is also Hawaii's highest peak, with some of the world's clearest stargazing and most powerful telescopes. The only access to Mauna Kea is via Saddle Rd Hwy.

MAUNA KEA & SADDLE ROAD
ITINERARIES

IN ONE DAY *This leg: 22 miles*

❶ PU'U HULUHULU (p150) Take the short walk up *'Shaggy Hill'* to get the lay of the land before heading to see the sunset. The contrast between the lava flows and green shrubbery of the *kipuka* (oasis) is wild.

❷ ONIZUKA VISITOR INFORMATION STATION (p142) You'll probably be feeling the altitude when you reach the visitors center at 9200ft. Spend some time here acclimatizing and picking the rangers' brains for fascinating facts about the mountain, astronomy and Hawaiian culture.

❸ MAUNA KEA SUNSET (p142) This is our top spot for sunset views, best appreciated from the summit or *Pu'u Kalepeamoa*, a short walk from the visitor station.

❹ STARGAZING ON MAUNA KEA (p145) Want your mind blown? Get some hot chocolate, bust out the mittens (aka socks) and peer through powerful telescopes at distant corners of the universe.

IN THREE DAYS *This leg: 54 miles*

❺ MAUNA KEA SUMMIT (p146) After day one's fun, earn another notch on your hip belt summiting Hawaii's tallest mountain. Don't miss the short detour to *Lake Wai'au* (p143).

❻ SUNSET ON MAUNA KEA (p142) You probably won't be up for stargazing after summiting, but stick around for another sunset at Pu'u Kalepeamoa near the visitor station. Every day's end is different atop Mauna Kea!

❼ PU'U 'O'O TRAIL (p150) Begin day three with this 7-mile hike combining cool, native forest with lava flows and birdsong. Even experienced island hikers like this one for its profound solitude.

❽ MAUNA LOA OBSERVATORY ROAD (p150) This one-lane, windy road ending at the Mauna Loa Weather Observatory (forecast: *cold*) at 11,150ft is a bit tricky to drive, but you may be rewarded with the mystical *'Mauna Kea shadow'* as you watch the sun go down.

Mauna Kea summit observatories at sunset

ABBOT LOW MOFFAT III

FOR NA KEIKI

❶ PU'U 'O'O TRAIL (p150) This not-too-strenuous hike with lots of lava, native trees and birds can be tailored longer or shorter depending on stamina and attention span. Plus, kids just love to say *Pu'u 'O'o.* The meadow in the middle is perfect for a picnic lunch.

❷ STARGAZING ATOP MAUNA KEA (p145) Beholding the Crab Nebula and distant planets makes for lifetime memories. With a pocketful of cookies and some piping hot chocolate sold on site, this becomes a multi-sensory memory. Engage the really little ones with the Subaru

Telescope's astronomy page for kids: www .naoj.org/Kids/index_e.html.

❸ SUMMITING MAUNA KEA (p148) What kid can say they've climbed the world's tallest mountain? Not many, especially because it isn't advisable for those under 16. Unless you go with the professionals: **Mauna Kea Summit Adventures** takes kids 13 and over.

❹ PU'U HULUHULU (p150) Almost more fun to say than *Pu'u 'O'o,* **'Shaggy Hill'** is an easy 20-minute hike that ends with great views of the mighty mountains. Follow it up with sunset on Mauna Kea.

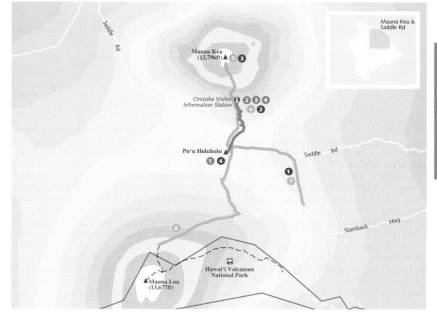

MAUNA KEA & SADDLE ROAD

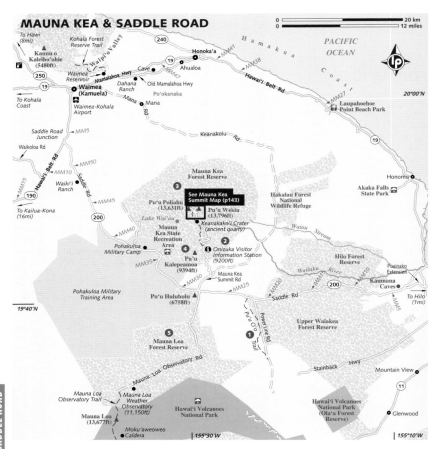

MAUNA KEA & SADDLE ROAD

Mauna Kea or 'White Mountain,' is called 'Mauna O Wakea' by native cultural practitioners. Wakea (Sky Father) and Papahanaumoku (Earth Mother) met atop the mountain, did their thing, and made the kahuna (priests) and *ali'i* (royalty), effectively becoming the progenitors of all Hawaiians. They created the Islands and taro, too. This is where it all began.

HISTORY

Mauna Kea, or 'White Mountain,' is called 'Mauna O Wakea' by native cultural practitioners. Wakea (Sky Father) and Papahanaumoku (Earth Mother) met atop the mountain, did their thing, and made the kahuna (priests) and *ali'i* (royalty), effectively becoming the progenitors of all Hawaiians. They created the Islands and taro, too. This is where it all began.

For the scientific world, it all began in 1968 when scientists from the University of Hawai'i (UH) began observing the universe from atop the mountain. Smart folks: the summit here is so high, dry, dark and pollution free, it permits investigation of the furthest reaches of the observable universe. Today, astronomers from 11 countries staff 13 observatories atop Mauna Kea's summit – the largest conglomeration of high-powered telescopes anywhere. They huddle in a small area of the Mauna Kea Science Reserve, a chunk of land leased by UH through 2033, comprising everything above 12,000ft.

Many Native Hawaiians are opposed to the 'golf balls' – the white observatories – dotting the summit. While not anti-science, they believe unchecked growth on the mountain threatens the *wahi pana* (important or sacred places) there, including *heiau* (temples), Lake Wai'au and burial sites. In one dramatic episode in 2006, an

HIGHLIGHTS

❶ **BEST DAY HIKE:** Pu'u 'O'o Trail (p150)
❷ **BEST VIEW:** Saturn through a telescope (p145)
❸ **BEST ACTIVITY:** Watching the sunset followed by stargazing atop Mauna Kea (p145)
❹ **BEST THRILL:** Snowboarding Hawaii's tallest mountain (p147)
❺ **BEST BRAGGING RIGHTS:** Summiting Mauna Kea one day and Mauna Loa the next (p146 and p150)

Highlights are numbered on the map on p140.

ahu lele (sacred altar) built for ceremonies on the mountain was desecrated. Mercury spills from some observatories using the volatile element to float the mirrors in their telescopes have also occurred. Threats to fragile alpine ecosystems are another arrow in the activists' quiver. Their cause isn't to yell 'fore!' and swipe the golf balls from Mauna Kea, but rather to prevent more from being built.

In 2006 a judge revoked a permit for NASA to build six new telescopes on the summit. In 2007 the same judge ruled that a cultural and natural management plan had to be in place before the construction of two other major telescopes could proceed.

ORIENTATION & INFORMATION

To get to the Onizuka Visitor Information Station and the summit beyond, take the Mauna Kea Access Rd, off Saddle Rd, just before the 28-mile marker coming from Hilo. It takes an hour to Onizuka from Hilo, Waimea or Waikoloa, and two hours from Kailua-Kona. The summit is 8 miles beyond the visitor station.

There are no restaurants, gas stations or emergency services anywhere on Mauna Kea or Saddle Rd. It's strongly recommended that 4WD vehicles are used beyond the Onizuka Visitor Information Station. For more information, see p149. Hiking is another possibility; see p146.

Be prepared for rapidly changing (and possibly severe) weather conditions, with daytime temperatures anywhere from the 60s (°F) to below freezing and possible high winds. In winter, several feet of snow can fall in a single storm. Call the **recorded hotline** (☎ 935-6268) for info on weather and road conditions. Even if the fog's as thick as pea soup on Saddle Rd, it's crystal clear at the mountaintop 325 days a year.

For a pleasant visit, come prepared with a full tank of gas, warm clothing, sunglasses and sunscreen. Drink plenty of water and throw some in the trunk just in case, along with some snacks.

DANGERS & ANNOYANCES

At altitudes above the Onizuka Visitor Information Station (9200ft), your body might not adjust properly to the low atmospheric pressure – there's 40% less oxygen and atmospheric pressure at the summit than at sea level. Altitude sickness and respiratory conditions are common. The risk increases with faster ascents, higher altitudes and greater exertion; being physically fit offers no protection. Symptoms include nausea, headaches, drowsiness, loss of balance, breathlessness, dehydration and impaired reason (oh, it's the altitude!). If you feel ill at the summit, descending is your only remedy. Kids under 16, expectant moms and those with high blood pressure or circulatory conditions should not go to the summit.

All travelers to the summit should stop first at the Onizuka center for at least 30 minutes to acclimatize. Even that is no guarantee you won't get sick further up.

Island Insights

Welcome to Hawai'i's heavyweight bout of the century. In this corner, we have the scientific community pushing for more observatories atop Mauna Kea. And in the other corner, we have Native Hawaiian activists fighting for a moratorium. To see where the two contenders stand, check out the **Mauna Kea Science Reserve Master Plan** (www.hawaii.edu/maunakea) and **Kahea's Protect Mauna Kea program** (www.kahea.org/maunakea). Ding, ding, ding.

SIGHTS

ONIZUKA VISITOR INFORMATION STATION

Map p140; ☎ 961-2180; www.ifa.hawaii.edu/info /vis; admission free; ⊙ 9am-10pm

Officially the Onizuka Center for International Astronomy, this station was named for Big Island native Ellison Onizuka, one of the astronauts who perished in the 1986 *Challenger* space shuttle disaster.

The drive from the Saddle Rd intersection to the information station is just over 6 miles (and 2500ft in elevation). As you climb, you break through the cloud cover until it spreads out like a soft feather bed below you. Mauna Kea doesn't appear as a single peak but rather a jumble of lava-rock peaks, some black, some red-brown, some seasonally snowcapped.

Before pushing on to the summit, it's essential to spend 30 minutes acclimatizing at the Onizuka Visitor Information Station. One of the best ways to pass the time is talking to the rangers, interpretive guides and volunteers – they're extremely knowledgeable on all aspects of Mauna Kea, including hiking, historical and cultural significance, road access and astronomy.

The center is modest: a room with photos of the observatories, information on discoveries made from the summit, computer-driven astronomy programs, and exhibits on the mountain's history, ecology and geology. You can watch a video about Mauna

Island Insights

What an odd coincidence: when a telescope is opened for the very first time, it's called its 'first light,' and Mauna Kea is the first spot in all the Hawaiian Islands to receive the first light of day.

Kea's observatories or peruse astronomy magazines while having a cup of coffee or soup, sold here. There's a gift shop, of course. At night, the popular stargazing program (p145) kicks in.

Across from the visitors center, a 15-minute uphill hike crests Pu'u Kalepeamoa, a cinder cone offering glorious sunset views. The mountain you're looking at is Hualalai (Map p82; 8271ft).

SUMMIT ROAD

Map p143

Driving to the summit requires a few special considerations: you should have a 4WD, be acclimatized and do it during the daytime – vehicle headlights are prohibited between sunset and sunrise because they interfere with astronomical observation. You must descend 30 minutes after sunset. See p149 for important information on driving to the summit.

About 4½ miles up from the visitor information station, just before the gravel road turns paved, on the east side of the road,

Mauna Kea volcano viewed from the approach road

GREG ELMS

is 'moon valley.' This is where the *Apollo* astronauts test drove their lunar rover before their real space odyssey to the moon.

There are a couple of sights worth a detour en route to the summit. Just after the 6-mile marker, there's a parking area; below here is the trailhead to `our pick` Lake Wai'au and Keanakako'i, the old adze quarry. Fed by permafrost, the shallow lake is the third-highest in the USA and a sacred place for Native Hawaiians: this alpine lake is the *piko* (umbilical cord) connecting heaven and earth. To ensure a baby has the strength of the mountain, real umbilical stumps are placed in the lake, even today. Ancient Hawaiians made and traded adzes made from the hard basalt at the fragile quarry – entering it is highly discouraged. It'll take an hour or so to see both, depending on your level of fitness and acclimatization.

SUMMIT OBSERVATORIES

At the summit, massive round observatories rise up white and silver from the vast, stark terrain. It's a striking juxtaposition and it may feel like you've discovered a fu-

Mauna Kea summit observatory   GREG ELMS

turistic human colony on another planet. In a way, you have: these observatories staffed by scientists from around the world constitute the greatest collection of state-of-the-art optical, infrared and millimeter/submillimeter telescopes on Earth. At almost 14,000ft, the summit is above 40% of the Earth's atmosphere, and over 90% of its water vapor. Only the Andes match Mauna

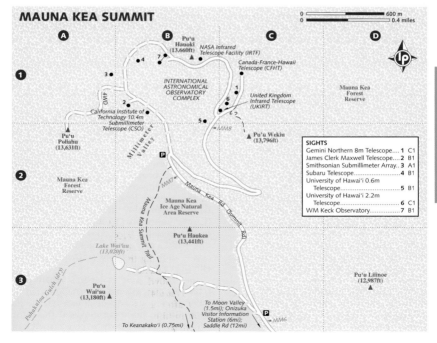

MAUNA KEA SUMMIT

0 — 600 m
0 — 0.4 miles

SIGHTS

Gemini Northern 8m Telescope	**1** C1
James Clerk Maxwell Telescope	**2** B1
Smithsonian Submillimeter Array	**3** A1
Subaru Telescope	**4** B1
University of Hawai'i 0.6m Telescope	**5** B1
University of Hawai'i 2.2m Telescope	**6** C1
WM Keck Observatory	**7** B1

MAUNA KEA & SADDLE ROAD

ISLAND VOICES

NAME: CHAD KALEPA BAYBAYAN
OCCUPATION: EDUCATIONAL SPECIALIST AND NAVIGATOR-IN-RESIDENCE, 'IMILOA ASTRONOMY CENTER
RESIDENCE: KAILUA-KONA

Hawaiian voyaging was almost a lost tradition. How did it re-emerge? In 1976 master navigator Mau Piailug and crew sailed *Hokule'a*, a traditional voyaging canoe, from Hawaii to Tahiti. The idea was to re-create and test an artifact and use it as the basis for extended research; it was an archaeological experiment. Since then there has been a voyaging explosion; it's a process of rediscovery where we're honoring and exploring the culture of our ancestors.

What is wayfinding? Wayfinding is a system using all available natural clues to guide the canoe. By the height of the stars we can tell our latitude, by the flotsam and jetsam and the birds, we know how close we are to land. But, we're sailing in the wake of our ancestors. They were *so* observant. We probably only capture 1% or 2% of their skill set.

How does Mauna Kea play into wayfinding? It's really hard to navigate without any instruments. On a clear day, you can see Mauna Kea from 60 miles to 100 miles out. Usually it's covered in clouds, but that's a sign of land. Or we'll see the glow of the volcano.

What would you say to visitors to Mauna Kea? To Hawaiians, it is very, very sacred. It's hard for us to come to terms with development of the mountain, but it's the best place on the planet to explore the universe – that's our responsibility and burden. In my mind, the future and salvation of humankind depend on exploration, on finding new islands in space.

Kea for cloudless nights, but air turbulence there makes viewing more difficult.

It's a veritable United Nations on the mountaintop, with a bevy of countries administering different telescopes – Taiwan and the USA collaborate on the **Smithsonian Submillimeter Array**; the UK, Netherlands and Canada run the **James Clerk Maxwell Telescope**; and a consortium of seven nations uses the **Gemini Northern 8m Telescope**. The **University of Hawai'i 0.6m Telescope** was the first on Mauna Kea in 1969; it's now used mostly for training undergraduates from the university.

Meanwhile, the world's largest and most powerful optical-infrared telescope is housed in the **WM Keck Observatory** (Map p143; www.keckobservatory.org), a joint project of the California Institute of Technology (Caltech), the University of California and NASA. Keck made a breakthrough in telescope design with a unique honeycomb feature comprised of 36 hexagonal mirror segments (each 6ft across) that function as a single piece of glass. In January 1996, the 390in **Keck I** telescope discovered the most distant galaxy ever observed, at 14 billion light-years away. The discovery of this 'new galaxy,' in the constellation Virgo, has brought into question the very age of the universe itself, because the stars in this galaxy seemingly predate the big bang. A replica of the first telescope, **Keck II** went online in October 1996. The two interchangeable telescopes can function as one – 'like a pair of binoculars searching the sky' – allowing them to study the cores of elliptical galaxies.

Just 150yd west is Japan's **Subaru Telescope** (Map p143; www.naoj.org). Inaugurated in 1999 after a decade of construction, its $300-million price tag makes it the most expensive observatory ever constructed,

Sunset from the Mauna Kea summit

GREG ELMS

and its 22-ton mirror, reaching 27ft in diameter, is the largest optical mirror in existence. For the curious, Subaru is the Japanese word for the Pleiades constellation.

Since you can't peer through the telescopes, the observatories are almost more interesting from outside than in. There are only two that you can enter unguided: the WM Keck Observatory visitor gallery (admission free; 10am-4pm Mon-Fri), which includes a display, 12-minute video, public bathrooms and a viewing area inside the Keck I dome; and the University of Hawai'i 2.2m Telescope (Map p143; admission free; 9:30am-3:30pm Mon-Thu). The Subaru Telescope and Onizuka Visitor Information Station offer guided summit tours (see p147).

our pick Sunsets and moonrises near the summit are phenomenal. Look toward the east at sunset and you may see the 'Mauna Kea shadow' – a gigantic silhouette of Mauna Kea looming over Hilo. Moonrises at this high altitude cause unusual sights, depending on the clouds and weather: the moon might appear squashed and misshapen, or ablaze like a brushfire.

The short, 200yd trail to Mauna Kea's true summit begins opposite the University of Hawai'i 2.2m Telescope; it's harder than it looks, and doesn't necessarily make for a better sunset. The summit is marked by a US Geological Survey (USGS) summit benchmark. It's wicked cold up here, with bracing winds and permafrost.

ACTIVITIES
Stargazing

For a truly unique Big Island experience, check out the Onizuka Visitor Information Station's free our pick stargazing program (Map p143; ☎ 961-2180; admission free; 6-10pm). The skies upon which the telescopes here are trained are among the clearest, driest and darkest on the planet. In fact, at the station you're above the elevation of most major telescopes worldwide. Specialists focus the scopes on the most interesting phenomena available that day; they try to handle special requests, and wheelchair-bound gazers have use of special attachments. This is the only place you can use telescopes on Mauna Kea; there are no public telescopes

Island Insights

Have you noticed the weird orange and pink streetlights all around the Big Island? In order to provide Mauna Kea astronomers with the best viewing conditions possible, streetlights on the island have been converted to these low-impact sodium tubes. Rather than using the full iridescent spectrum, these use only a few wavelengths, which the telescopes can be adjusted to remove.

MAUNA KEA & SADDLE ROAD

at the summit. You can show up anytime for the stargazing (though combining it with the sunset is best) and stay for as long as you like.

In addition to the regular nightly program, there are interesting Saturday night programs (admission free; ☽ 6pm), including 'The Universe Tonight' (first Saturday of the month), where an astronomer discusses recent discoveries made at the observatories, and 'Malalo I Ka Lani Po' (third Saturday), where a community member discusses a cultural aspect of Mauna O Wakea. Regular evening stargazing follows.

Hiking

To get a better taste of the sacred mountain, you can do the 15-minute uphill hike to Pu'u Kalepeamoa. The trailhead to this cinder cone offering the best sunset views is across the street from the visitor station. Beyond the parking lot is another short trail leading to an area protecting the weird (and endangered) silversword. Driving toward the summit, you can also hike to Lake Wai'au (p143) in under an hour.

MAUNA KEA SUMMIT TRAIL
Map p143

For a hardcore experience, there's the daunting 6-mile Mauna Kea Summit Trail, starting at 9200ft and climbing almost 4600ft to the summit. Thin air, steep grades and biting weather make this a strenuous hike; plan on eight hours for the round-trip and bring a gallon of water per person – dehydration is a real danger at these altitudes. This hike is not recommended in inclement weather. Get a near-predawn start to give yourself the maximum hours of daylight. Before heading out, go to the Onizuka Visitor Information Station to sign in, get a hiking map and consult with rangers about weather and other conditions.

Park at the Onizuka Visitor Information Station and walk up the road to the Kilohana picnic area, from where you'll follow signs for the Humu'ula Trail. This uphill climb is well signposted for the first mile as it continues doggedly upward, occasionally jogging around cinder cones; avoid the false spurs leading back to the access road. The already thin vegetation starts to disappear altogether as you make your way higher

and the trail is marked with red poles and reflectors.

After about an hour, the summit road comes back into full view, about 100yd to your right. Remember to take your time acclimatizing, with frequent rest and water breaks if necessary. After the two-hour point, the ascent becomes more gradual, weaving among giant cinder cones. After a leveling off through basalt flows and glacial till, the trail rises through white boulders and the summit of Mauna Kea looms far ahead.

This part of the hike passes through the Mauna Kea Ice Age Natural Area Reserve. A Pleistocene glacier once moved down this slope, carrying earth and stones that carved grooves, which are still visible in the rocks. After about three hours you enter a broad valley, followed by a sharp, short ascent on crumbly soil over a rise. Keanakako'i, an ancient adze quarry, comes into view; look for large piles of bluish-black chips. From this spot, extremely dense and hard basalt was quarried by ancient Hawaiians to make tools and weapons that were traded throughout the Islands. Please do not disturb anything in this protected area.

After a steep mile-long ascent, the trail connects with a road and a four-way junction beyond. From the junction, find the trailhead for the 10-minute detour to Lake Wai'au. Hawaii's only alpine lake sits at 13,020ft, making it the third-highest lake in the country. The lake is only 10ft deep,

The snow-covered peak of Mauna Kea

yet it's never dry. It's fed by permafrost (left over from the last Ice Age) and meltwater from winter snows, which quickly evaporate elsewhere on Mauna Kea.

Back at the four-way junction, make your way north (uphill yet again) for the final upward push to the Mauna Kea Access Rd. Suddenly the observatories pop into view and straight ahead is Millimeter Valley, nicknamed for the three submillimeter observatories on the summit. The trail ends here at the access road's 7-mile marker, just below the hairpin turn, but don't start congratulating yourself just yet: the summit is still a long 1½ miles up and away.

To summit or not to summit? If you just can't take any more and are willing to relinquish bragging rights, you can turn back and descend the way you came or along the road. Though two miles longer, the latter is faster and easier.

You've come this far, so suck it up for the last 1½ miles to the summit if you can. To reach it, follow the main road up to the right (not the spur road into Millimeter Valley) for over 1 mile. Past the 8-mile marker, where the road forks, veer right and look for a 'trail' opposite the University of Hawai'i 2.2m Telescope observatory. This 200yd trail-of-use descends steeply east, crosses a saddle and scrambles up Pu'u Wekiu to Mauna Kea's true summit.

Walking back down the way you came is an option, of course, but the trail's steep grade and crumbling cinders make for a tricky, unnerving descent, especially as daylight fades and afternoon clouds roll in. It's faster to take the paved road instead and hiker aloha means someone will probably give you a ride.

Skiing & Snowboarding

Hitting the slopes in Hawai'i is strictly DIY – there are no outfitters, tours, gear or lifts. No matter for snow-loco locals who slide down the mountain (or try to) on surfboards, bodyboards, even inner tubes. But the Big Island draws an active crowd and some folks have gear stashed in the closet for when the white stuff starts to fall on Mauna Kea's upper slopes. Some winters it's more than others, but there's usually snow for the carving for a couple of months beginning in January or February.

Skiing Mauna Kea, with its high altitude, corn snow and crud, is a notch on your novelty belt. The slopes can be very steep and there are vertical drops of 5000ft. Commercial ski tours on Mauna Kea are prohibited and equipment rentals aren't available, so once the snow starts to fall, start to make friends who can trick you out. Tip: those who surf like to snowboard.

TOURS

The Onizuka Visitor Information Station offers summit tours (admission free; ⊙ 1pm Sat & Sun). You must provide your own 4WD

GREG ELMS

Get above the clouds on the way up Mauna Kea

ABBOT LOW MOFFAT III

transportation. The tour begins at the visitors center, where you spend the first hour acclimatizing and watching Mauna Kea astronomy videos. After the orientation, you caravan up to the summit, where a docent talks about the telescopes, their history, ownership and what they're typically looking at. Tours visit at least one telescope, usually the University of Hawai'i 2.2m Telescope and/or WM Keck's 10m telescope. Tours depart from the summit at about 4:30pm and are subject to cancellation at any time depending on the weather, so call ahead. You cannot have been scuba diving in the 24 hours prior to the summit visit.

You can visit the world's largest single-piece mirror telescope, the Subaru Telescope (www.naoj.org/Information/Tour/Summit; admission free; ⊙ 10:30am, 11:30am & 1:30pm), on 30-minute summit tours offered up to 15 days per month, in English and Japanese. You must make advance reservations (online only) and you need your own transportation to the summit.

If you prefer not to drive, you can jump on a summit sunset tour (see following listings). These usually last eight hours and take in the sunset and stargazing. Tours providing dinner always have a vegetarian option.

🌸 HAWAI'I FOREST & TRAIL
☎ 331-8505, 800-464-1993; www.hawaii-forest .com; tours $176; ⊙ 2:30pm
This outfit hosts an elaborate sunset/stargazing tour with parkas, gloves and gour-

met picnic dinner (minestrone soup, fish in a mac-nut–pesto crust, wild rice, veggies and dessert). It's super popular, so book early. Pick-up locations are across from Honokohau Harbor, Kings' Shops (in the Waikoloa Resort Area), and the junction of Hwys 190 and 200, 6 miles south of Waimea. Children 16 and over.

MAUNA KEA SUMMIT ADVENTURES
our pick ☎ 322-2366, 888-322-2366; www.mauna kea.com; tours $197; ⊙ 2pm
This granddaddy of Mauna Kea tours has been taking folks to the summit for over 20 years. Distinguishing this outfit are vans with panoramic windows and an 11in Celestron telescope – if you're into the stars, this is the tour for you. A hearty hot dinner and warm weather gear are included in the price. Advance online bookings receive a 15% discount. Pick-up locations are Kailua-Kona, Kings' Shops, and the junction of Hwys 190 and 200. Children 13 and over.

ARNOTT'S LODGE
☎ 969-7097; www.arnottslodge.com; 98 Apanane Rd, Hilo; guests/nonguests $75/110; ⊙ Mon, Wed & Fri
This bare-bones tour for the budget set offers short hiking opportunities around the visitors center and to the summit. You must provide your own warm clothing, food and drinks. Instead of a telescope, guides use a 'high-powered visible laser' – this is not the tour for astronomy geeks. Tours depart from the Hilo Bay Hostel (p188) and the nearby Hilo Hawaiian Hotel (p188).

FESTIVALS & EVENTS

For one (hopefully) fine day each summer in mid-June, Waiki'i Ranch on the slopes of Mauna Kea hosts the kicking annual Waiki'i Music Festival (☎ 883-2077), a big concert showcasing Hawaii's top talent. Waiki'i Ranch is off Saddle Rd on the Waimea side. Have fun *and* support a good cause: the festival benefits North Hawaii Community Hospital and North Hawaii Hospice.

SLEEPING

It bears repeating: there are no services along Saddle Rd. The closest accommodations besides camping are in Waimea (p134) and Hilo (p188).

At the 35-mile marker is the Mauna Kea State Recreation Area (Map p140), with campground and cabins. The site is sometimes closed during droughts; get an update by calling the Division of State Parks (☎ 974-6200; www.hawaii.gov/dlnr/dsp; PO Box 936, Hilo, HI 96721; ⏰ 8am-noon Mon-Fri). There is no water at this site used mainly as a way station for local hunters, but the cabins have basic kitchens and bathrooms, and space for up to six people. Nearby maneuvers at the Pohakuloa

Training Area (see the boxed text below) can be noisy.

With an elevation of 6500ft, the area commonly experiences cool days and cold nights and is a good base for Mauna Kea or Mauna Loa hikes, plus it has unbelievable views of the two mountains. For permit information, see p273.

GETTING THERE & AROUND

From Kona and Waimea, Saddle Rd (Hwy 200) starts just south of the 6-mile marker on Hwy 190. From Hilo, you can take either Kaumana Dr or the Puainako Extension (Hwy 2000) – both become Saddle Rd. The latter feeds into Hwy 11 and is the best bet coming from Volcano. Start with a full tank of gas – Saddle Rd is gas station free. Look for the turnoff to Mauna Kea near the 28-mile marker heading east.

Driving to the summit is suitable only for 4WD vehicles. Once you pass Hale Pohaku, the residential complex for scientists just above the Onizuka center, the 8 miles to the summit are unpaved gravel for the first 5 miles and pavement for the remainder. The uphill drive takes about 25 minutes. You should drive in low gear and loosen the gas

---

TRAINING TROOPS ON HAWAI'I

Around the 45-mile marker on Saddle Rd, things turn a little strange – the tarmac devolves into a potholed hell reminiscent of Havana's worst inner-city streets, signs in ominously official language warn off trespassers, and you may even have to pull over to let a tank or 10 pass. Welcome to the **Pohakuloa Training Area** (PTA), the largest military training area in the state, where specialized Stryker brigades are trained for Iraq combat and, according to Army documents dating from 2007, depleted uranium (DU) has been used.

Given that the 133,000-acre training area sits on the high plateau where Hualalai, Mauna Loa and Mauna Kea (the sacrosanct mount where all of Hawaii and its people were born) converge, and 21 endangered species live, it's not surprising the military presence has raised the hackles of environmental and cultural activists. But on a tourism-dependent island such as Hawai'i, the presence of depleted uranium – a radioactive element banned under the Geneva Convention and listed as a weapon of indiscriminate destruction by the UN – took the issue to a different level.

Enter House Bill 1452, introduced by representative Josh Green (District 6 Kailua-Kona). Green, a leader on all sorts of progressive issues, from recycling to rural health care, introduced the bill recommending testing for DU around military bases in the interest of public health. In 2007 the bill passed the state house and senate, but died for lack of funding. A more economical version of the bill, requiring air-sampling stations to test for radiation and contaminated dust near Hawaiian bases, was reintroduced as House Bill 2076 in February 2008.

Read a local newspaper in your Hawaiian travels and you're likely to learn a whole lot more about Pohakuloa. If you want to know before you go, see www.afschawaii.org/dmz/index .html.

cap to prevent vapor lock. The upper road can be covered with ice, and loose cinder is always a problem. Be particularly careful on the way down, especially if you're showing any signs of altitude sickness. Driving when the angle of the sun is low – in the hour after sunrise or before sunset – can create extremely hazardous, blinding conditions.

AROUND MAUNA KEA

MAUNA LOA'S NORTHERN FLANK

Mauna Loa is somewhat of an enigma for visitors – it looms large all around, but how do you actually get on the Long Mountain? The answer is simple: drive up Mauna Loa Observatory Rd. This unsigned road takes you close to the top and delivers kicking views. To actually summit Mauna Loa, however, you'll have to rely on your own two feet via either the Mauna Loa Observatory Trail (the 'easy' way), the Mauna Loa Summit Trail (the 'OK, so you can hike' way) or the 'Ainapo Trail (the 'where do we send the medal?' way). For detailed descriptions of these hikes, see the boxed text on p220.

If you want to drive almost all the way up the mountain, Mauna Loa Observatory Road (Map p140) starts near the 28-mile marker on Saddle Rd, almost opposite the Mauna Kea Access Rd and next to Pu'u Huluhulu (opposite). When summit conditions are just right, you can glimpse the 'Mauna Kea shadow' at sunset – a curious phenomenon whereby Mauna Kea casts a blue-purple shadow behind itself and over Hilo.

The single-lane, 17.5-mile asphalt road ends at a parking area just below the weather observatory (11,150ft). There are no facilities. The narrow road is passable in a standard car, but it's in terrible condition and bedeviled by blind curves. Allow an hour. This road is sometimes closed during winter months.

SADDLE ROAD HIKES

The section of Saddle Rd heading east between Mauna Loa and Hilo is sprinkled with interesting short hikes.

The easy trail up the cinder cone Pu'u Huluhulu (Shaggy Hill; Map p140), an ancient *kipuka* (oasis) created more than 10,000 years ago, makes a piquant appetizer before going up Mauna Kea. The 20-minute hike climbs through secondary growth to the top of the hill, from where there are panoramic views of Mauna Kea, Mauna Loa and Hualalai. The *pahoehoe* (smooth lava) and *'a'a* (jagged lava) surrounding the *kipuka* are between 1500 and 3000 years old, courtesy of Mauna Kea. They provide striking contrast to the verdant hill. The trailhead is very near the turnoff to Mauna Kea, just past the 28-mile marker heading west.

Head further east and a more substantial hike traversing forest, meadows, old lava flows and *kipuka* is a treat for birders. Among the koa and ohia, you can see (or at least hear) honeycreepers such as the *'apapane* and *'i'iwi* on the old Pu'u 'O'o Trail; note this is not the same trail as the active Pu'u 'O'o cinder cone in Hawai'i Volcanoes National Park (described on p222). This 7-mile loop hike, marked by *ahu* (cairns) and trail tags, is fairly easy to follow. If it turns vague, turn back, but you should be able to follow it to eventually connect with the 4WD road known as Power Line Rd (marked with a PLR sign) that loops back to the highway. Note that you'll be about 0.5 miles from where you left your car. There's a gate at the end of Power Line Rd, but this is a legal, hikeable trail. Coming from Hilo, the turnoff for the trailhead is on the left side almost exactly halfway between the 22- and 23-mile markers.

The endemic silversword © CORBIS PREMIUM RF / ALAMY

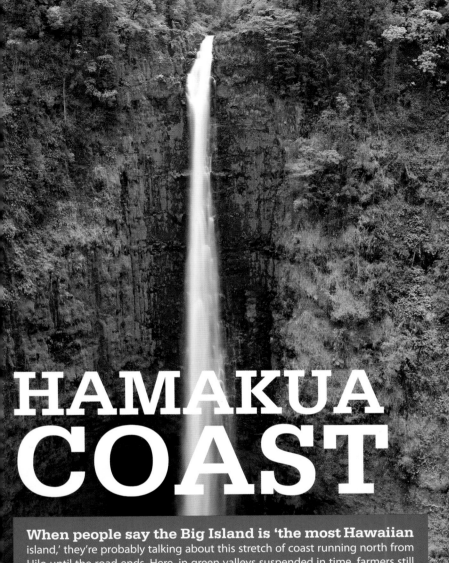

HAMAKUA COAST

When people say the Big Island is 'the most Hawaiian island,' they're probably talking about this stretch of coast running north from Hilo until the road ends. Here, in green valleys suspended in time, farmers still grow taro and pound it into poi, while the melodious notes of a ukulele drift toward dusk, inviting the night marchers. The Hamakua Coast is wildly fertile and beautiful, where thunderous waterfalls shoot mist and rainbows across mossy chasms, and green sugarcane grows wild on bluffs between deep-blue sky and still bluer sea. Go slow here, discovering lonely trails, back roads and new friends. Have time only for the highlights? Don't worry, you'll return.

HAMAKUA COAST
ITINERARIES

IN TWO DAYS *This leg: 61 miles*

❶ **HOTEL HONOKA'A CLUB (p157)** Get into the local swing of things on day one by checking into this modest hotel. Granted, it ain't the Ritz, but you'll make instant friends and learn what's doing.

❷ **WAIPI'O VALLEY (p158)** This is it, the one. At the ranger shack, take time to talk story with Rocky – he'll steer you to *da kine* spots. Walk the insanely steep road down to the valley. Play on the beach, frolic in the river.

❸ **CAFÉ IL MONDO (p155)** Dinner and a movie end day one. Bring your own vino to accompany your pizza at this casual place

owned by a guitar-strumming Brazilian. Afterwards, catch a flick at the **Honoka'a People's Theatre (p156)**.

❹ **KALOPA STATE RECREATION AREA (p163)** Don't tell, but this is one of the Big Island's fabulous unsung day trips. Hike the trails through native forest, play Frisbee on the lawn, and have a picnic to start day two.

❺ **WORLD BOTANICAL GARDENS & UMAUMA FALLS (p166)** Finish day two at this botanical garden with over 5000 species of plants, from florid to funky. Meander the trails here to the triple-decker cascades.

IN FOUR DAYS *This leg: 56 miles*

❻ **AKAKA FALLS (p165)** Follow the two-day itinerary, then get here early on day three or the sun will futz with your light for photographing these beautiful 'drive-up' falls. Lunch in Honomu (p165).

❼ **PEPE'EKEO 4-MILE SCENIC DRIVE (p165)** Wild fruit litters the roadway, rock

walls weep with waterfall ribbons and secret trails abound. Spend the rest of day three exploring this lovely back road.

❽ **WAIPI'O ON HORSEBACK (p163)** You didn't get enough, did you? Go deeper into Waipi'o Valley the old-fashioned (and low-impact) way – on horseback.

Blossoms in the World Botanical Gardens   LAWRENCE WORCESTER

FOR HIKERS

❶ KALOPA STATE RECREATION AREA (p163) Warm up the camping juices and get in a few short hikes in the beautiful woods of this secluded park. Take your pick between a tent site and a cabin.

❷ WAIKAUMALO COMMUNITY PARK (p166) Continue your conditioning regimen rockhopping at this little-visited park along Old Mamalahoa Hwy. This back road is prime turf for earning your explorer's badge.

❸ WAIPI'O TO WAIMANU VALLEY (p162) You can't camp in Waipi'o anymore, so you'll have to push straight through to Waimanu. Get an early start – those switchbacks are killer. Spend at least two nights in this exquisite amphitheater valley.

❹ HI'ILAWE FALLS (p161) Bring determination, waterproof gear and lots of aloha to hike 1.75 miles back into the valley to these thunderous falls. You'll need good weather, too, since the adventure requires repeatedly crossing a stream prone to flash flooding.

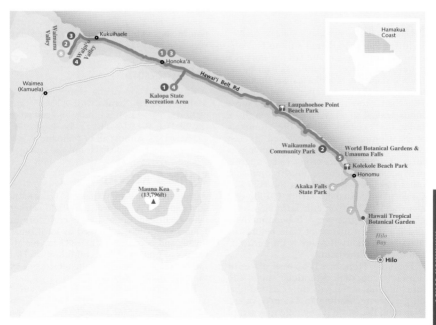

HAMAKUA COAST

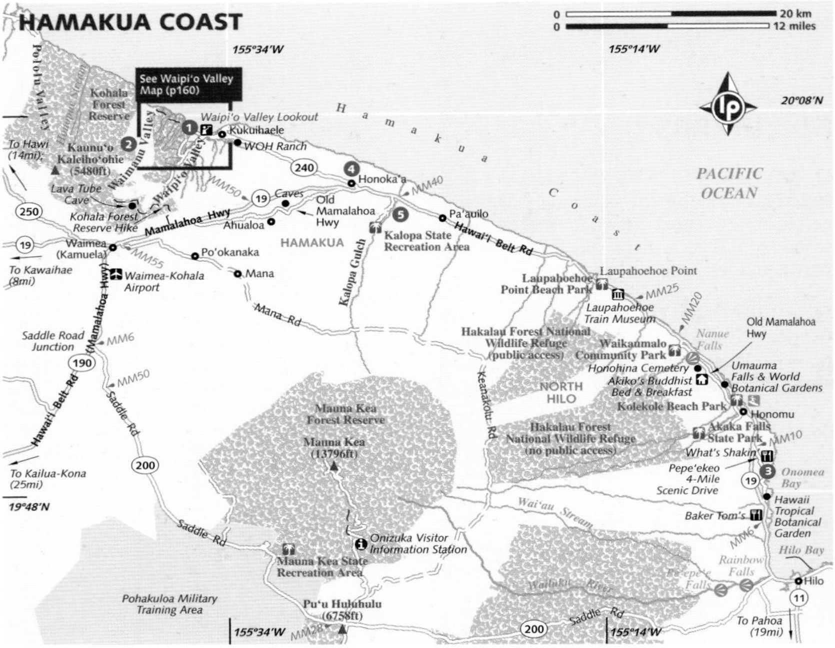

HONOKA'A

In little Honoka'a, there's still no bar, off-the-grid is de rigueur and talking story is a major-league sport. That doesn't mean the town is stagnant: Honoka'a, once the third-largest Hawaiian city after Honolulu and Hilo thanks to its powerful cattle and sugar industry, had to reinvent itself when those industries crashed. When the Honoka'a Sugar Company mill processed its last harvest in 1993, the agricultural town was forced to diversify its crops; today's farms produce the tomatoes, mushrooms and other goodies whipped up at the Hilo Bay Café (p184), Hualalai Grille (p100) and elsewhere. Indeed, organic farming – from goat cheese to green tea – is booming here and it's only a matter of time before the town reinvents itself again as the agritourism capital of the island.

For now, Honoka'a is a sweet place for browsing chockablock antique stores and lunching on a tempeh or grass-fed-beef burger before heading to Waipi'o Valley. Watching the world go by here may tempt you to stay awhile. Luckily there are some very fine places to lay your head.

Information

All the basics are strung along or just off Mamane St: two banks with ATMs, a gas station, grocery store, laundry and **post office** (☎ 935-3311; 45-490 Lehua Rd; ⌚ 9am-4pm Mon-Fri, 8:15-9:45am Sat). Almost all of Mamane St is a wi-fi hot spot (try near Honoka'a Video).

Sights & Activities

Beside the library on Mamane St is the **Katsu Goto Memorial**. A Japanese cane-field worker who eventually opened a general store in Honoka'a, Goto was hanged by local sugar bosses and accomplices in 1889 for his attempts to improve labor conditions on Hamakua plantations. He's considered one of the first union activists.

Do you possess the coveted purple aura? You can find out at **Starseed Beads & Gems** (☎ 775-9344; 45-3551A2 Mamane St; ⌚ 10am-5pm

HIGHLIGHTS

❶ **BEST BEACH:** Waipi'o Beach (p161)
❷ **BEST VIEW:** Waimanu Valley from Muliwai Trail (p162)
❸ **BEST ACTIVITY:** Poking around Pepe'ekeo 4-Mile Scenic Drive (p165)
❹ **BEST PLACE TO MEET LOCALS:** Ecstatic Dance at Honoka'a People's Theatre (below)
❺ **BEST PLACE TO LOSE YOURSELF:** Kalopa State Recreation Area (p163)

Highlights are numbered on the map on p154.

Mon-Fri, to 4pm Sat), where aura photographs cost around $20.

Shh. The first rule of Ecstatic Dance is you do not talk at **ourpick Ecstatic Dance** (Honoka'a People's Theatre; donation $5-10; ⊗ 6:30pm 3rd Thu of month). Beyond that, there are no rules: just show up, shut up and get your body moving to whatever the DJ is spinning (usually a techno/house mix).

Festivals & Events

Hamakua Music Festival (☎ 775-3378; www .hamakuamusicfestival.org; Honoka'a People's Theatre, Mamane St; admission $20-30) Top-notch Hawaiian, jazz and blues bands jam at this event that awards scholarships to Big Island music students and funds public-school music teachers. Held mid-May and early October.
Honoka'a Western Weekend (☎ 933-9772; Mamane St; admission free) Sleepy Mamane St startles awake with a barbecue, parade, country dance and rodeo in late May.
Annual Taro Festival This one-day affair in November is a poi-fect way to see everything that can be done with taro (and some things that probably shouldn't!).

Eating

JOLENE'S KAU KAU KORNER   Diner $
☎ 775-9498; 45-3625 Mamane St; sandwiches & burgers $3-7.25, mains $8-12; ⊗ 10:30am-8pm Mon, Wed & Fri, to 3pm Tue & Thu
For a meat fix, try this spot, where a little bit of everything (shrimp, chicken, spareribs) is served in what feels like your neighbor's dining room – locals dishing on tourists, the proposed paper mill and traffic nightmares included.

TEX DRIVE-IN   Drive-In $
☎ 775-0598; www.texdrivein.com; 45-690 Pakalana Rd; sandwiches & plate lunches $5-9; ⊗ 6am-8:30pm
Tex sells more than 60,000 of its famous *malasadas* (a sugary delight like a hole-less doughnut) a month. At 96¢ for plain, and just a quarter more for fillings such as papaya-pineapple or Bavarian crème, this is a classic Big Island deal. Breakfast, fresh fish burgers and plate lunches are also served. This joint is also a Big Island trailblazer in the use of sustainable packaging, recycling and other green-friendly initiatives.

SIMPLY NATURAL   Comfort Food $
☎ 775-0119; 34-3625 Mamane St; dishes $5-9; ⊗ 8am-4pm Mon-Sat, 9am-1pm Sun
The bright, chipper surroundings and staff here complement the healthy food, including the yummy weekend waffles with fresh fruit. At lunchtime, try the feta, asparagus and tomato melt. Games (Scrabble, mancala) and **open-mike nights** (⊗ 6:30-9:30pm last Fri of month) make this a fun, family outing.

CAFÉ IL MONDO   Italian $$
☎ 775-7711; www.cafeilmondo.com; 45-3626A Mamane St; sandwiches $6, pizzas $12-14.50; ⊗ 11am-8pm Mon-Sat
Intimate and Italian is a killer combination at this place specializing in pizzas and pastas. The calzone are huge pillows bursting with flavorful vegetables; bring your own wine to wash it down and swoon when owner Sergio starts his guitar serenade.

To load up on supplies, try the following:
Farmers market (Mamane St; ⊗ 7:30am-noon Sat) Fresh produce, directly from the farmers.
Hamakua Natural Foods (☎ 775-7266; 45-3221 Mamane St; ⊗ 10am-6pm Mon-Fri, to 5pm Sat) The name says it all.
TKS Supermarket (cnr Mamane St & Plumeria Rd) The only grocery in town.

Island Insights

The only Native Hawaiian governor in the history of the USA, **John D Waihee III** (1986–94), hails from Honoka'a.

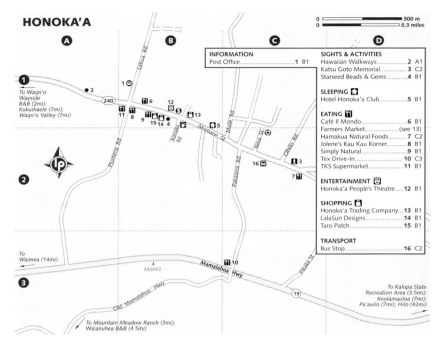

Entertainment

HONOKA'A PEOPLE'S THEATRE
☎ 775-0000; Mamane St; movie tickets adult/child/senior $6/3/4
In a historic building dating from 1930, this theater shows movies and is HQ for **Ecstatic Dance** (p155) and the **Hamakua Music Festival** (p155). The café here jumps with locals socializing before events.

Shopping

HONOKA'A TRADING COMPANY
☎ 775-0808; Mamane St; ⏰ 10:30am-5pm
If a couple of Honoka'a aunties emptied their attics, basements and garages, it would look like this hangar-sized store. Weave between vintage aloha wear, antiques, used books (great Hawaiiana selection), rattan and koa furniture, and hand-selected Hawaiian artifacts.

TARO PATCH
☎ 775-7228; Mamane St; ⏰ 9am-5pm
With a little of everything, this superlative shop is the place for souvenirs – from beautiful ceramic dishes and funky, feathery *slippahs* (flip-flops) to Waipi'o Valley mouse pads and organic soaps. The amazing selection of jewelry and other accessories, plus hula girl everything, will part you from your cash here.

LALASUN DESIGNS
☎ 775-1818; www.lalasun.com; 45-3577 Mamane St; ⏰ 11am-5pm
Psychedelia was never as chic as it is here, where artist/owner Leilea Satori is on hand to explain how she creates wearable art. Her fashionable batik dresses, miniskirts, pants and shirts (for *kane* and *wahine*) of silky soft rayon are super hip(pie). Don't miss the unique guitar pick earrings ($10 to $20) made by her little sister.

Sleeping

To really get away from it all, consider one of the lovely B&Bs in upcountry Ahualoa. Budget travelers have to either camp or stay at the good-value hotel in town.

HOTEL HONOKA'A CLUB
Independent Hotel $

☎ 775-0678, 800-808-0678; www.hotelhonokaa.com; Mamane St; dm/r with shared bathroom $20/30, r $65-90, ste $130; 💻

Caveat emptor: this place is slightly ragged around the edges, with thin walls, industrial carpet and dark shower stalls. But if you're looking for local color, look no further. The best rooms are on the top floor, with queen bed facing a wall of windows enjoying sea views. The 2nd-floor rooms have versatile bed configurations and some adjoin into a family-friendly suite. Look at several options as every room is different. Dorm beds have linens, but no blankets.

KEOLAMAULOA
Vacation Rental $$

☎ 776-1294; http://keolamauloa.com; 2br house 2/3/4 people $100/125/150; 💻

Want your revelatory traveler sense restored? Check out Pa'auilo, a historic country town hiding 7 miles south of Honoka'a. This fully equipped house is on delightful grounds with gurgling waterfalls, a koi pond, native trees and distant ocean views. The view from the tub is more sultry still. Kick off your shoes and figure out how to extend your stay (discounts available). Nonsmoking property.

🌺 WAIANUHEA B&B
B&B $$$$

our pick ☎ 775-1118, 888-775-2577; www.waianuhea.com; 45-3505 Kahana Dr, Ahualoa; r $195-310, ste $400, all incl breakfast; 💻

If you've got the money, honey, head straight to this exquisite place in peaceful upcountry Hamakua. Waves of relaxation will wash over you as you weigh your options from the king-sized bed: jump-start the fireplace or hit the Jacuzzi? With fine art, Tiffany lamps, fun Philippe Starck chairs, bright skylights and gleaming hardwood floors, impeccable and wonderfully unpretentious taste oozes from every cranny.

Many other places are tucked around Honoka'a, including the following:
Mountain Meadow Ranch (☎ 775-9376; www.mountainmeadowranch.com; 46-3895 Kapuna Rd, Ahualoa; ste/cottages incl breakfast $95/135; 🅿 💻) The two-bedroom cottage here is delightful and private, with full kitchen, wood stove and laundry.
Waipi'o Wayside B&B (☎ 775-0275, 800-833-8849; www.waipiowayside.com; Hwy 240; r incl breakfast

Top Picks

HAMAKUA COAST FOR KIDS

- Malasadas at Tex Drive-In (p155)
- Discovering Waipi'o Valley (p158)
- Camping at Kalopa State Recreation Area (p163)
- Beholding Akaka Falls (p165)
- Exploring the Pepe'ekeo 4-Mile Scenic Drive (p165)

$100-190; 🅿 💻) Country comfort is exemplified in the five rooms here; good choice if you have to work while on vacation.

Getting There & Away

The free **Hele-On Bus** (☎ 961-8744; www.co.hawaii.hi.us/mass_transit/heleonbus.html) travels between downtown Hilo and Honoka'a (one hour) 18 times on weekdays and three times on Saturday. There are several departures a day for the South Kohala resorts (40 minutes to an hour) and one a day for Kona (1½ hours).

KUKUIHAELE

About 7 miles north of Honoka'a, a loop road off Hwy 240 leads to sleepy Kukuihaele. Its name means 'traveling light' in Hawaiian, referring to the 'night marchers,' torch-bearing ghosts of Hawaiian warriors who pass through here to Waipi'o. As the legend goes, if you look at the night marchers *(huaka'ipo)* or get in their way, you die. Survival is only possible if one of your ancestors is a marcher – or if you lie face down on the ground.

Kukuihaele consists of some houses and a 'commercial center' – the **Last Chance Store** (Map p160; ☎ 775-9222; ⏰ 9am-3:30pm Mon-Sat) and **Waipi'o Valley Artworks** (Map p160; ☎ 775-0958, 775-7157, 800-492-4746; www.waipiovalleyartworks.com; ⏰ 8am-5pm), from where tours into Waipi'o Valley start.

Eating & Shopping

If you want snacks, canned chili, beer, water or wine, don't miss the Last Chance Store.

HAMAKUA COAST

Waipi'o Valley Artworks sells ice cream, muffins, sandwiches and coffee (plus fine koa wood furniture and bowls, and ceramic art). Overnight parking for campers headed to Waimanu is available here (per day $15; call first in July and August).

Sleeping

HALE KUKUI ORCHARD RETREAT
Vacation Rental $$$

☎ 775-7130, 800-444-7130; www.halekukui.com; 48-5460 Kukuihaele Rd; studios $145, 2br cottages $180-195; Ⓟ

The contrast between Waipi'o's green cliffs and the vast blue Pacific Ocean is captured beautifully from these rentals, where you can stuff yourself silly on papaya, banana, star fruit and more. Even the studio here is well equipped (full kitchen, dining area) and tranquil, unless the other guests are rowdy – thin walls are a downer. Individual private decks and Jacuzzis compensate, however.

CLIFF HOUSE HAWAII
Vacation Rental $$$

☎ 775-0005, 800-492-4746; www.cliffhouse hawaii.com; Hwy 240; 2br house $200, each additional person $35; 💻

Skip the helicopter ride and stay in the aptly named Cliff House, perched on 40 gorgeous acres above the awe-inspiring Waipi'o Valley *pali* (cliff). The wraparound lanai could be the best private sunrise/whale-watching spot on Hawai'i. The beds are queen-sized and house extras include a barbecue, telescope, satellite TV, and washer and dryer. Back on the same 40-acre parcel is the less dramatic but still beautifully situated **Hawaii Oceanview House** (2br house $155).

For a genuine splash out, spend a few nights at the **Hamakua Hideaway Cliff House** (☎ 866-775-7467; www.hawaiicliffhouse.com; d $195; 💻), an ultraprivate and lovely bungalow with those killer coastal vistas.

WAIPI'O VALLEY

There's something tantalizing about the end of the road. It's where adventure meets the unknown and 'what do we do now?' becomes a wonderfully enticing prospect. You'll feel it when Hwy 240 dead-ends on the cliffs overlooking Waipi'o Valley, the largest of seven spectacular amphitheater valleys on the windward side of the Kohala Mountains. Waipi'o (Curving Water) is an emerald patchwork of forest, lotus and *lo'i* (taro patches) 6 miles deep, where waterfalls plunge earthward from 2000ft vertical *pali*. Completing this natural tableau of divine proportions is the river cleaving the valley floor toward the surf-fringed, boulder-strewn, black-sand beach. Few sites in Hawaii rival sacred Waipi'o for dramatic beauty.

Waipi'o Valley and coast from the Waipi'o lookout   GREG ELMS

ISLAND VOICES

NAME: LEILEA SATORI
OCCUPATION: ARTIST/OWNER, LALASUN DESIGNS
RESIDENCE: PA'AUILO

You're from Maui. What brought you to the Big Island? Maui will always be my home, my heart is there, but in Maui they're farming development while here they're farming food. The potential for sustainability, the fertility, living off the land – it all drew me to the Big Island. And I wanted to connect more with Hawaiian culture, which is so strong here. There's so much aloha. You can feel it.

Why Honoka'a? I loved the whole coastline and the historical appeal, the look of the town. It's super cute and local. It's also very diverse. It's not Kona. And there's so much to discover here – I've been here two and a half years and I'm still exploring.

What have you discovered lately? Skiing Mauna Kea was amazing to me. Being able to go up there and ski is epic. It felt pretty close to god. And it's surreal – to go skiing and then come down to the ocean.

What inspired you to make clothes? I wanted to wear my art. I think it's an expression of inner spirit and it makes me happy wearing colorful, fun clothing. I took a batik class in high school and started my first studio with a friend dip-dyeing T-shirts. That was in 1994. Then I bought a Circle Pacific ticket and studied batik in a small family studio in Bali and traveled around Asia learning different textile arts.

Your designs are beautiful. What's the process? It's hand-painted batik. I ink the master designs on white fabric and then apply the wax with a canting tool. The wax acts as a barrier to the color that's applied by hand afterwards using water-soluble dye. Once the dye is fixed, the piece is boiled to get the wax out.

What's next for you? My store has opened a direct doorway into the community and I love that. I'm moving into making more art and supporting the material design here on Hawai'i.

History

Known as the Valley of the Kings, Waipi'o was the ancient breadbasket of the Big Island. Not coincidentally, it was also Hawai'i's political and religious center and home to the highest *ali'i* (chiefs or royalty). 'Umi, the Big Island's ruling chief and spiritual leader in the early 16th century, was a farmer and fisherman who propagated many of Waipi'o's original *lo'i*. Some of these are still cultivated today and you may see farmers knee-deep in their patches.

Waipi'o is also where Kamehameha the Great received the statue of his fearsome war god, Kukailimoku.

According to oral histories, several thousand people lived in this fertile valley before Westerners showed up. Important heiau (temples) scattered throughout Waipi'o are evidence of its status. The most sacred, Paka'alana, was a *luakini* heiau (temple of human sacrifice) and one of the island's two major *pu'uhonua* (places of refuge; the other is a national historical park – see p91).

HAMAKUA COAST

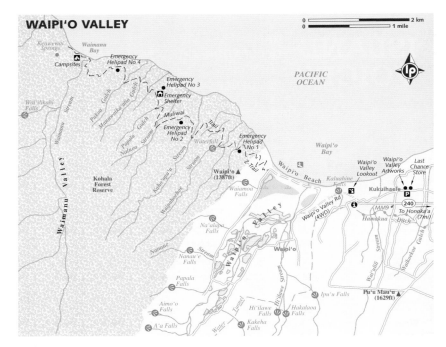

You won't see Paka'alana: it was destroyed in a war between Ka'eokulani of Kaua'i and Kamehameha I.

In 1823 William Ellis, the first missionary to descend into Waipi'o, guessed the population to be around 1300. In the 1880s immigrants, mainly Chinese, began to settle in the valley's green folds and taro cultivation gave way to rice, though the traditional staple was never eliminated and, over time, Waipi'o couldn't compete with cheaper rice being mass produced in California. Eventually taro rebounded, with valley factories producing labor-intensive poi.

In 1946 Hawai'i's most devastating tsunami slammed waves far back into the valley. Interestingly, no one in this sacred place perished during this natural disaster or the great 1979 flood. Once the waters receded, however, most people resettled 'topside,' and Waipi'o has been sparsely populated ever since.

Taro cultivation and poi production are building blocks of the Hawaiian identity that continue today in the jealously guarded valley. The cultural resurgence of the '60s and '70s, combined with younger generations trying to retain their roots, assured the crop's future. At the time of writing, Hawai'i's taro farmers were awaiting passage of State Senate Bill 958, calling for a 10-year moratorium on the testing, cultivating and patenting of genetically engineered taro. Already, of the 300 varieties that once existed, just one represents 90% of all taro produced today. 'No to GMO taro' is a very hot topic here.

Other goodies produced in Waipi'o include lotus root, avocados, citrus and *pakalolo* (marijuana).

Orientation & Information

Like most people, your seat mate from Flight 148 will admire the valley from the **scenic lookout** and drive away. But if you're after more, stop to talk with the ranger at the **information booth** (8am-dusk) to discover your options. Hikers could also consider doing the top of Waipi'o hike, accessed from Waimea (see Kohala Forest Reserve, p135).

For a day at the beach, you can hike the short, steep road down in 45 minutes (see Waipi'o Valley Hike, opposite) or 4WD it in 15 (the ranger won't let you try in a regular car). There are bathrooms at the bottom, but no potable water. Strong, prepared hikers can venture the 1.75 miles (1½ hours) back into the valley to experience the powerful beauty of Hi'ilawe Falls – swollen streams and weather permitting. Before setting off, read the boxed text below.

Dangers & Annoyances

Hiking in and beyond the valley requires fording streams that can swell instantly during the winter rainy season. It's dangerous to attempt to cross streams if the water is above your knees. Such rising waters should be considered life-threatening obstacles, as flash floods are possible. Be patient – the water should subside in a few hours.

If you decide you must cross (eg it's getting dark), look for a wide, relatively shallow stretch of stream rather than a bend. Before braving the current, unclip your backpack's chest strap and belt buckle so you can slip out easily and swim to safety if you lose your balance. Use a walking pole, grasped in both hands, on the upstream side (as a third leg), or go arm in arm with a companion, clasping at the wrist, and cross side-on to the flow, taking short steps.

Don't drink from *any* creeks or streams without first boiling or treating the water. Feral animals roam the area and leptospirosis is present.

Activities

Once the sun begins setting, locals start **surfing** Waipi'o's daunting break. Read the water and talk to locals before paddling out – the rip currents and treacherous undertow aren't for hodads (poser surfers). This isn't a swimming beach, so mostly you'll be hiking or just rambling around the valley. There are many **tours** (p163) too.

Plan on at least two nights' backcountry camping in 🌿 **Waimanu Valley**. Good weather is essential for a positive experience, and don't underestimate the difficulty of this short but tough hike. You can park your car at Waipi'o Valley Artworks (p157) for a steep $15.

WAIPI'O VALLEY HIKE
1 mile, 30-45min

The point of this hike is the destination, not the journey. It's slow-going on the 25%-grade road, but nothing too strenuous. There's no shade, so carry plenty of water for the short, precipitous descent beginning from the **scenic lookout**.

At the bottom, the road left leads to where wild Waipi'o horses are usually grazing lazily along the stream; keep walking and you'll have distant views of **Hi'ilawe Falls**, which, at over 1400ft, are the state's tallest falls, with over 1000ft of free-fall, another state record. Hiking to the falls is possible but challenging – consider yourself forewarned. No trail exists for this nearly 2-mile, four-hour round-trip hike and you'll have to crisscross the stream half a dozen times, request passage from residents and bushwhack *a lot*. This adventure is not recommended for children or during heavy rains. If you attempt this hike, please respect the privacy of valley residents.

Turn right at the bottom of the hill and after 10 minutes you'll reach **Waipi'o Beach**. This black beach is lined with graceful ironwood trees and big dark boulders. Most of the time even wading in these rough waters isn't advisable, but when it's calm, Waipi'o Beach is sublime. Look for spinner dolphins and whales offshore.

Walk toward the stream mouth for a good view of **Kaluahine Falls**, cascading down the cliffs to the east. Getting to the falls is

R-E-S-P-E-C-T IN THE Y-P-O

Sensitivity and respect are prerequisites for following the 25%-grade road down into Waipi'o Valley. In this sacred valley peppered with *wahi pana* (important places), you are guests of the residents and their ancestors. For everyone's benefit, here are some simple guidelines:
- Pack out your trash.
- Use only the port-o-potty for your business.
- Explore with aloha.
- Don't enter or cross private lands unless invited.
- Respect *kapu* (taboo) signs.
- Do not disturb heiau (temples).

Waipi'o Valley by horseback

© DOUGLAS PEEBLES PHOTOGRAPHY / ALAMY

more challenging than it looks. High surf breaking over the uppermost rocks can be dangerous. Local lore holds that **night marchers** (see p157) periodically descend from the upper valley to the beach and march to **Lua o Milu**, a hidden entrance to the netherworld.

If you have the strength and time, follow the **Muliwai Trail** to the third sweeping switchback for amazing Waipi'o views.

MULIWAI TRAIL TO WAIMANU VALLEY
8.5 miles, 6½-8hr

To connect with the Muliwai trailhead, ford the stream where calmest and walk toward the far end of the beach; there's a shaded path just inland that deposits you at the base of the cliffs. From here, the path turns left, then veers right and ascends under thick forest cover. This ancient Hawaiian footpath rises over 1200ft in a mile of hard laboring up the steep northwest cliff face (it's nicknamed Z-Trail for the killer switchbacks). Hunters still use this trail to track feral pigs.

The hike is exposed and hot, so try to cover this stretch early. Eventually the trail moves into ironwood and Norfolk pine forest, and tops a little knoll before gently descending and becoming muddy and mosquito-ridden. The view of the ocean gives way to the sounds of a rushing stream.

The trail crosses a gulch and ascends past a sign for Emergency Helipad No 1. For the next few hours the trail finds a steady rhythm of gulch crossings and forest ascents. A waterfall at the third gulch is a source of fresh water; treat it before drinking. For a landmark, look for Emergency Helipad No 2 at about the halfway point from Waipi'o Beach. Beyond that, there's an open-sided emergency shelter with pit toilets and Emergency Helipad No 3.

Rest here before making the final difficult descent. Leaving the shelter, hop across three more gulches and pass Emergency Helipad No 4, from where it's less than a mile to **Waimanu Valley**. Over a descent of 1200ft, this final section of switchbacks starts out innocently enough, with some artificial and natural stone steps, but the trail is poorly maintained and extremely hazardous later. A glimpse of **Wai'ilikahi Falls** on the far side of the valley might inspire hikers to press onward. The trail is narrow and washed out in parts, with sheer drop-offs into the ocean, and no hand holds apart from mossy rocks and spiny plants. If the descent is impossible, head back to the trail shelter for the night.

Waimanu Valley is a mini Waipi'o, minus the tourists. On any given day you'll bask alone amid a stunning deep valley framed by cliffs, waterfalls and a black-sand beach. From the bottom of the switchbacks, the boulder-strewn beach is 10 minutes past the camping regulations signboard. When safe, ford the stream to reach the **campsites** on its western side.

Waimanu Valley once had a sizable settlement and contains many ruins, including house and heiau terraces, stone enclosures and old *lo'i*. In the early 19th century an estimated 200 people inhabited Waimanu, but the valley was abandoned by the remaining three families after the 1946 tsunami.

On the return trip, be careful to take the correct trail. Walking inland from Waimanu Beach, don't veer left on a false trail-of-use that attempts to climb a rocky streambed. Instead keep heading straight inland past the camping regulations sign to the trail to the switchbacks. It takes about two hours to get to the trail shelter, and another two to reach the waterfall gulch: refill your water here. Exiting the ironwood forest soon after, the trail descends back to the floor of Waipi'o Valley.

Tours

If you're up for a hiking adventure, **Hawaiian Walkways** (Map p156; ☎ 775-0372, 800-457-7759; www.hawaiianwalkways.com; adult/child guided hikes $95/75), in Honoka'a, takes you to waterfalls and swimming holes via a private trail.

If hiking isn't for you, there are other options, including the following:
Na'alapa Stables (Map p121; ☎ 775-0419; www
.naalapastables.com; rides $88; ☼ 9am & 12:30pm) Visit the valley on a 2½-hour horseback ride; children eight and over are welcome. Tours leave from Waipi'o Valley Artworks (p157).
Waipi'o Ridge Stables (☎ 775-1007, 877-757-1414; www.waipioridgestables.com; rides $85-165; ☼ 9am) Tour around the valley rim to the top of Hi'ilawe Falls (2½ hours) or combine with a forest trail ride (five hours), ending with a picnic and swim at a hidden waterfall. Departs Waipi'o Valley Artworks (p157).
Waipi'o Valley Wagon Tours (☎ 775-9518; www
.waipiovalleywagontours.com; adult/child $55/25;
☼ 10:30am, 12:30pm & 2:30pm Mon-Sat) This 1½-hour jaunt in a mule-drawn wagon carts visitors around the valley floor. Tours leave from WOH Ranch, 0.5 miles beyond the 7-mile marker.

Sleeping

Backcountry camping in Waimanu Valley requires a state permit (free, maximum six nights). Facilities include fire pits and composting outhouses. Reservations are taken no more than 30 days in advance by the **Division of Forestry & Wildlife** (☎ 974-4221; 19 E Kawili St, PO Box 4849, Hilo, HI 96720; ☼ 8am-4:30pm Mon-Fri). With two weeks' notice they'll mail you the permit.

KALOPA STATE RECREATION AREA

A favorite local hideaway is this 100-acre **ourpick** state park (Map p154), with trails, camping and cabins in a quiet native forest at a cool 2000ft. This is a great place to explore forests as they (almost) were when the Polynesians first arrived. There's a nature loop and hiking trail, plus large grassy expanses fringed by ironwood trees to let the kids run around on while you prep the picnic.

Camping is delightful in a grassy area surrounded by tall trees. Group cabins (eight people maximum) have bunk beds, linens and blankets, plus hot showers and a fully equipped kitchen. Permits are required. For details, see p273.

To get here, turn *mauka* (inland) off the Hawai'i Belt Rd at the Kalopa Dr sign; follow park signs for 3 miles.

Hiking

An easy 1320yd **nature trail** loop begins near the cabins and passes through old ohia forest, where some of the trees measure over 3ft in diameter. You may hear the *'elepaio*, an easily spotted brown-and-white native forest bird with a loud whistle.

A longer **hiking trail** leads into the adjoining forest reserve with old-growth forest and tremendous tree ferns. Begin along Robusta Lane, on the left between the caretaker's house and the campground. It's about 600yd to the edge of Kalopa Gulch, through a thick eucalyptus forest. The trail continues along the gulch rim for another mile, while several side trails along the way branch off and head west back into the recreation area. You can loop together over 4 miles on the spottily maintained trails.

LAUPAHOEHOE

Laupahoehoe, meaning 'leaf of *pahoehoe* (smooth-flowing lava),' is appropriate for the landmark **Laupahoehoe Point** (Map p154), a flat lava peninsula formed by a late-stage Mauna Kea eruption. It's located midway

THE HARROWING TALE OF THE HORNET

When Hollywood is ready to make the next blockbuster action epic, they should come to little Laupahoehoe to tell the tale of the clipper ship *Hornet* and its heroic crew. Here's the basic script.

On January 15, 1866, the *Hornet* sailed from New York, bound for San Francisco, with Captain Josiah A Mitchell at the helm. On May 3, a bungling officer caused the ship to catch fire. From two longboats adrift, the crew of 31 watched their ship burn through the night, finally slipping below the Pacific without a trace.

With four hams, 28lb of salt pork, some raisins, bread and water, the despondent men floated in the ocean, facing typhoons, sharks and thirst. Eventually the two boats got separated, the men resorted to gnawing on wood and leather, valiant Captain Mitchell had to suppress a mutiny, and everyone was thinking cannibalism (but no one did it). For 43 days and 4300 miles the men drifted, struggling to see one more sunrise. On June 15, the 15 survivors sighted land at Laupahoehoe. One fainted with joy. Others were too weak to rise from the floorboards. Trouble was, they couldn't land because the breakers were so rough, and they were too weak. They drifted hopelessly, about to be dashed against the rocks, when two Hawaiians dove into the violent surf, swam to the boat and rowed it to shore. Bananas, taro, melon and more were heaped upon the men. There was great rejoicing and a little-known journalist broke the story to the world. Read Mark Twain's telling of the tale at www.twainquotes.com/18660719u.html.

between Honoka'a and Hilo via a steep, 1.5-mile **scenic drive** down to the coast, with spectacular cliffs in the distance and dense foliage all around.

On April 1, 1946, tragedy hit the small plantation town when a tsunami 30ft high wiped out the schoolhouse on the point, killing 20 children and four adults. Today a **monument** listing the victims stands at Laupahoehoe Point. After the tsunami the whole town moved uphill. Every April there's a **community festival** with food, music and old-timers talking story.

In February, the **Laupahoehoe Music Festival** (admission $10; ☺ 9am-5pm) comes to the beach park to raise scholarship money for local students, with good eating, quality hula and tunes by the likes of Sugah Daddy and Bruddah Smitty.

Beaches & Sights

Only real crazy *buggahs* would swim at windy, rugged Laupahoehoe, where the fierce surf sometimes crashes up over the rocks and into the parking lot. Many of the immigrant plantation laborers first set foot on the Big Island at Laupahoehoe.

The county beach park on the point has full facilities, making it a popular **camping** spot for locals and visitors alike. For permit information, see p273.

LAUPAHOEHOE TRAIN MUSEUM

☎ 962-6300; www.thetrainmuseum.com; adult/child $3/2; ☺ 9am-4:30pm Mon-Fri, 10am-2pm Sat & Sun

Celebrating the Hilo Railroad – one of the most expensive railroads ever built – this small museum houses ephemera and photographs from Hawai'i's bygone railroad era. Knowledgeable docents burst with pride explaining the restored length of track and ol' Rusty the switch engine. The museum is between the 25- and 26-mile markers.

Laupahoehoe Train Museum　　　GREG ELMS

KOLEKOLE BEACH PARK

Beneath a highway bridge, this park (Map p154) sits at the side of Kolekole Stream. The river-mouth break is a local **surfing** and **bodyboarding** hot spot, but ocean swimming is dangerous. There are small **waterfalls** and full facilities. **Camping** is allowed with a county permit (see p273), but the narrow area can get crowded and boisterous with picnicking local families.

To get here, turn inland off the Hawai'i Belt Rd at the southern end of the Kolekole Bridge, about 1300yd south of the 15-mile marker.

HONOMU

Honomu (Map p154) is a quaint old sugar town that might be forgotten today if it weren't for its proximity to Akaka Falls. Life here remains rural and slow paced. 'Main St' is lined with old wooden buildings housing shops, eateries and an all-volunteer internet café. Another Honomu attraction is the two mammoth banyan trees across the street, just south of the junction for Akaka Falls.

Eating & Sleeping

WOODSHOP GALLERY & CAFÉ   Café $
☎ 963-6363; www.woodshopgallery.com; Hwy 220; lunch dishes $6-9; ☺ 11am-5:30pm
There are several places to chow down in Honomu, including a pizza parlor and bakery, but this place is the best. Try a burger and lemonade or homemade ice cream and espresso – it's all good and served with aloha. Following lunch, go on a shopping spree among the extraordinary collection of handcrafted bowls, photos and blown glass.

AKIKO'S BUDDHIST BED & BREAKFAST   Hostel $
ourpick ☎ 963-6422; www.alternative-hawaii .com/akiko; s/d with shared bathroom $65/75, per week $350/420, cottages $85, studio per 2 weeks $602
You need not be Buddhist to stay at this popular place, but it helps to be modest. Rooms are simple – a futon on the floor in the main house or twin beds in a separate house nearby. Two off-the-grid cottages in

the garden are teeny but nice and there's an artist's studio for longer retreats (two-week minimum). Longtime local Akiko coordinates the end-of-year **mochi pounding festival**, leads **tai chi classes** and hosts some of the most interesting **cultural events** around (see http://alternative-hawaii.com/akiko/ calendar.htm). The B&B is in Wailea, just over 2 miles north of Honomu, on a marked turnoff from the Hawai'i Belt Rd.

TARA YOGA CENTER   Yoga Retreat $$
☎ 333-2080; www.tarayogacenter.com; near Kolekole Beach Park; per night $120-160, per retreat $1750-2000
If you're seeking peace and healing, this secluded, 40-acre retreat center is sure to soothe. The youthful married owners teach a spiritual form of yoga that emphasizes breath and meditation training. Facilities are elegant, surrounded by storybook countryside; the vibe is serene, family-oriented and pure (no drugs or alcohol). This off-the-grid center composts and recycles, and uses solar power, rainwater and alternative-fuel vehicles.

AKAKA FALLS STATE PARK

The Big Island's 'drive-up' waterfall is hugely impressive. Join the tourists walking single-file along a half-mile rain-forest loop thick with massive philodendrons, fragrant ginger, dangling heliconia and gigantic bamboo. Only a tiny fraction of the park's 65 acres is open to the public.

At the time of writing the path to 100ft **Kahuna Falls** was closed, which is no great loss: it's pretty and all, but kind of lame when compared with **Akaka Falls**, which plummets 420ft down a fern-draped cliff. Its mood depends on the weather – sometimes it rushes with a mighty roar, creating a violent froth in the pool below, or it may be gently cascading.

To get here, turn onto Hwy 220 between the 13- and 14-mile markers.

PEPE'EKEO 4-MILE SCENIC DRIVE

Once again, Old Mamalahoa Hwy delivers the kicking tropical scenery Hawaii is famous for. This time it's a 4-mile scenic loop off the Hawai'i Belt Rd between the 7- and 8-mile markers (see below for another 4-mile scenic drive). At the north end of the drive, **What's Shakin'** (Map p154; ☎ 964-3080; 10am-5pm) serves luscious smoothies and fresh, *'ono* (delicious) food. At the south end, back on Hwy 11, don't miss **Baker Tom's** (Map p154; ☎ 964-8444; 27-2111 Mamalahoa Hwy; 6:30am-6:30pm), where the cookies are divine and the *malasadas* rival Tex's.

Cruising the narrow road, you cross a series of one-lane bridges spanning little streams hemmed in by lush jungle. In places the sun is almost blocked out by *liliko'i* (passion fruit), guava and tall mango and African tulip trees, which drop their orange flowers on the road. There are also many **small paths** leading to babbling rivers or the coast.

Flora buffs should check out **Hawaii Tropical Botanical Garden** (Map p154; ☎ 964-5233; www .hawaiigarden.com; adult/child $15/5; 9am-5pm) for the self-guided trails among 2000 species of tropical plants situated amid streams and waterfalls. Buy your ticket at the yellow building on the *mauka* side of the road. The flowers and scenery are gorgeous, rain or shine (bumbershoots provided).

For a quick, pretty hike down to **Onomea Bay**, take the Na Ala Hele trailhead on the *makai* (seaward) side of the road, just north of the botanical garden. After a 10-minute hike down a slippery jungle path, you'll come to a finger of lava jutting into the sea. A spur to the right leads to a couple of small waterfalls and a cove. Continuing straight brings you to the diminutive bluffs overlooking the batik blues of Onomea Bay. Look for a rope tied to an almond tree for low-tide beach access. Hawaiian monk seals have been sighted here.

DETOUR ➡

OLD MAMALAHOA HIGHWAY

When you're ready for another off-the-tourist-track **scenic road** loaded with exploration opportunities, detour to this 4-mile portion of the bypassed Old Mamalahoa Hwy (Map p154). Before you do, however, don't miss the bridge over **Nanue Falls** on Hwy 19 between the 18- and 19-mile markers; park south of the bridge and walk back for vertiginous views of the steep gulch.

At the 19-mile marker, look for the sign for **Waikaumalo Community Park** (the turnoff is easy to miss coming from Hilo). Here, a grassy slope (with picnic area) leads to a pretty stream – don the reef shoes and rock-hop upstream, if you like getting muddy.

Driving on, Old Mam Hwy becomes a one-lane road, dipping among a series of stream gulches overhung with thick foliage; various pullouts near the bridges invite you to park and explore. A little less than halfway along, keep an eye peeled for **Honohina Cemetery**, a historic Japanese graveyard full of flowers pushing through the crumbling, *kanji*-covered headstones.

The south end of the road is anchored by the **World Botanical Gardens** (☎ 963-5427; www.wbgi.com; adult/child 6-12yr/13-17yr $13/3/6; 9am-5:30pm), near the 16-mile marker. The fee is a bit steep for the modest gardens, but they get you in by providing the only easy access to the beautiful, three-tiered **Umauma Falls**.

Umauma Falls   GREG ELMS

HILO

Hilo should have an inferiority complex. It gets less than half of Kailua-Kona's tourists. But the townsfolk know better. Sure, it's rainy. But 130in of annual precipitation guarantees a leafy landscape, where waterfalls gush and every homeowner has a green thumb. Sure, it seems ordinary and familiar (despite its tropical splendor). But Hilo has enough critical mass to be a *real* community. This ain't no tourist town! Locals will outnumber you wherever you go. Since the 1990s, moneyed outsiders have discovered this livable place, boosting real-estate values and somewhat changing its boondocks reputation. But Hilo remains staunch to its plantation-era roots and unpretentious vibe.

HILO ITINERARIES

IN TWO DAYS *12 miles*

❶ LYMAN HOUSE MEMORIAL MUSEUM & MISSION HOUSE (p176) Start by strolling through Hilo's old town, where the neat retro buildings, indie shops and scenic bay setting will surely charm you.

❷ PACIFIC TSUNAMI MUSEUM (p177) To appreciate Hilo's true grit (behind its modest demeanor), learn about its survival after two catastrophic 20th-century tsunami.

❸ EAST HAWAI'I CULTURAL CENTER (p176) Just southwest, find Hilo's best venue for visual art by local artists. Check the schedule for myriad events, from evening concerts by big names to hands-on workshops, Hawaiian music, crafts and more.

❹ TWO LADIES KITCHEN (p186) Silky-soft, sweet and oh-so-pretty. Buy a box of traditional Japanese *mochi* (sticky rice dessert), made by two local ladies.

❺ LILI'UOKALANI PARK (p174) Wind down with a sunset picnic at this scenic park by the bay. Go early to stroll, jog or walk the pedestrian bridge to Mokuola (Coconut Island; p175).

❻ BEACHES (p173) Wake early for a beach day, Hilo-style. Surfers, check out Hilo's go-to break at Honoli'i Beach, while families should head to Richardson Ocean Park or to Onekahakaha Beach for the littlest ones.

❼ ITSU'S (p184) Follow with a rainbow ice shave from Hilo's favorite mom-and-pop shop.

❽ 'IMILOA ASTRONOMY CENTER OF HAWAI'I (p176) In the afternoon, visit this engaging museum on ancient Hawaiian voyaging and modern astronomy on Mauna Kea. Get the background here before ascending the real summit.

❾ RAINBOW FALLS (p177) Afterward, pay your respects to Hilo's 100-plus inches of annual rain by visiting Rainbow Falls, Pe'epe'e Falls & Boiling Pots (p177) and, for the more intrepid, Wai'ale Falls (p177).

'Imiloa Astronomy Center

GREG ELMS

FOR FOODIES

❶ **HILO FARMERS MARKET (p175)** On Wednesday or Saturday, arrive early at this eye-popping farmers market, where a dollar will buy you four succulent papayas.

❷ **CAFÉ 100 (p182)** No trip to Hilo is complete without a *loco moco* from this iconic drive-in. Head here after a morning at one of Hilo's rugged but pretty beaches.

❸ **MEHANA BREWING COMPANY (p178)** Hilo's only craft brewery produces excellent ales and lagers, which you can taste-test here. Expect a tasting room but no pub.

❹ **MAUNA LOA MACADAMIA-NUT VISITOR CENTER (p178)** Drive past rows of macadamia trees to this touristy yet intriguing look at the Big Island's savored nut.

❺ **SEASIDE RESTAURANT (p185)** This family-run restaurant and fishery was producing delicious mullet in Hawaiian-style ponds long before that fish hit the gourmet radar. Bring an appetite to this no-frills icon.

❻ **HILO BAY CAFÉ (p184)** For a contrast, try this foodie favorite, with a sophisticated menu featuring the best Big Island produce, fish and meat.

❼ **BIG ISLAND CANDIES (p186)** Crowded (and definitely on the tour-bus circuit) but irresistible, this local business phenom will hook you with its signature chocolate-dipped macadamia shortbread.

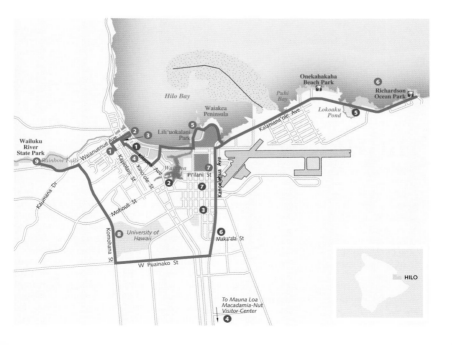

HILO

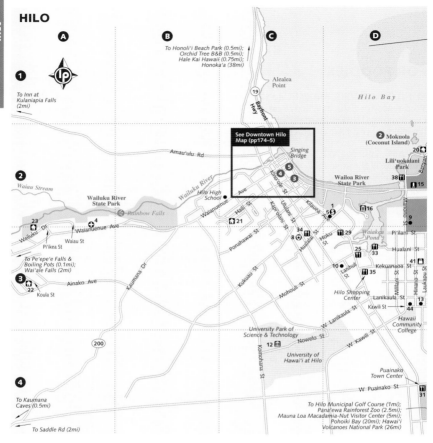

HILO

To Inn at
Kulaniapia Falls
(2mi)

To Honoli'i Beach Park (0.5mi);
Orchid Tree B&B (0.5mi);
Hale Kai Hawaii (0.75mi);
Honoka'a (38mi)

Alealea
Point

Hilo Bay

Bayfront Hwy

See Downtown Hilo
Map (pp174–5)

Amau'ulu Rd

Singing
Bridge

Mokuola
(Coconut Island)

Lili'uokalani
Park

Wailuku River

Waiau Stream

Wailuku River
State Park

Wailoa River
State Park

Rainbow Falls

Hilo High
School

Waianuenue Ave

Haili St

Kino'ole St

Ululani St

Keawe St

Kilauea Ave

Kamehameha Ave

Waiakea
Pond

Pi'ilani St

Wailuku Dr

Waiau St

Pi'ikea St

To Pe'epe'e Falls &
Boiling Pots (0.1mi);
Wai'ale Falls (2mi)

Ainako Ave

Koula St

Kaumana Dr

Ponahawai St

Huala̅la̅i St

Mōku St

Hualani St

Kekuanaoa St

Kūkūau St

Mohouli St

Lanihuli St

Manono St

Kīna'u St

Hilo Shopping
Center

Lanikaula St

Kawili St

Hawaii
Community
College

University Park of
Science & Technology

Komohana St

Nowelo St

University of
Hawai'i at Hilo

W Lanikaula St

W Kawili St

Puainako
Town Center

To Kaumana
Caves (0.5mi)

W Puainako St

To Saddle Rd (2mi)

To Hilo Municipal Golf Course (1mi);
Pana'ewa Rainforest Zoo (2.5mi);
Mauna Loa Macadamia-Nut Visitor Center (5mi);
Pohoiki Bay (20mi); Hawai'i
Volcanoes National Park (26mi)

HIGHLIGHTS

❶ **BEST BEACH:** Richardson Ocean Park (p173)
❷ **BEST VIEW:** Mokuola (Coconut Island; p175)
❸ **BEST ACTIVITY:** Downtown stroll, rain or shine (p180)
❹ **BEST LOCAL ART:** East Hawai'i Cultural Center (p176)
❺ **BEST SOUVENIR:** Anything by Sig Zane Designs (p187)

Highlights are numbered on the map above.

pop 41,000

HISTORY

Since its first Polynesian settlers farmed and fished along the Wailuku River, Hilo has been a lively port town. In the 20th century, it was the trading hub for sugarcane grown in Puna and Hamakua, connecting in both directions with a sprawling railroad, the Hawaii Consolidated Railway.

Then, on April 1, 1946, a massive tsunami slammed the island, taking 96 lives in Hilo alone and demolishing towns, train trestles and bridges. Hilo rebuilt its waterfront, but in 1960 another tsunami struck, taking 61 lives in Hilo and again obliterat-

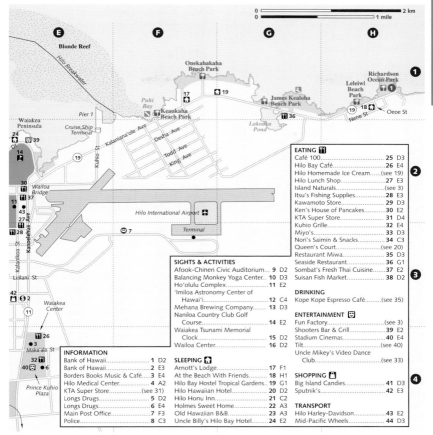

EATING

Café 100	**25**	D3
Hilo Bay Café	**26**	E4
Hilo Homemade Ice Cream	(see 19)	
Hilo Lunch Shop	**27**	E3
Island Naturals	(see 3)	
Itsu's Fishing Supplies	**28**	E3
Kawamoto Store	**29**	D3
Ken's House of Pancakes	**30**	E2
KTA Super Store	**31**	D4
Kuhio Grille	**32**	E4
Miyo's	**33**	D3
Nori's Saimin & Snacks	**34**	C3
Queen's Court	(see 20)	
Restaurant Miwa	**35**	D3
Seaside Restaurant	**36**	G1
Sombat's Fresh Thai Cuisine	**37**	E2
Suisan Fish Market	**38**	D2

DRINKING

Kope Kope Espresso Café	(see 35)	

ENTERTAINMENT

Fun Factory	(see 3)	
Shooters Bar & Grill	**39**	E2
Stadium Cinemas	**40**	E4
Tilt	(see 40)	
Uncle Mikey's Video Dance Club	(see 33)	

SHOPPING

Big Island Candies	**41**	D3
Sputnik's	**42**	E3

TRANSPORT

Hilo Harley-Davidson	**43**	E2
Mid-Pacific Wheels	**44**	D3

SIGHTS & ACTIVITIES

Afook-Chinen Civic Auditorium	**9**	D2
Balancing Monkey Yoga Center	**10**	D3
Ho'olulu Complex	**11**	E2
'Imiloa Astronomy Center of Hawai'i	**12**	C4
Mehana Brewing Company	**13**	D3
Naniloa Country Club Golf Course	**14**	E2
Waiakea Tsunami Memorial Clock	**15**	D2
Wailoa Center	**16**	D2

SLEEPING

Arnott's Lodge	**17**	F1
At the Beach With Friends	**18**	H1
Hilo Bay Hostel Tropical Gardens	**19**	G1
Hilo Hawaiian Hotel	**20**	D2
Hilo Honu Inn	**21**	C2
Holmes Sweet Home	**22**	A3
Old Hawaiian B&B	**23**	A3
Uncle Billy's Hilo Bay Hotel	**24**	E2

INFORMATION

Bank of Hawaii	**1**	D2
Bank of Hawaii	**2**	E3
Borders Books Music & Café	**3**	E4
Hilo Medical Center	**4**	A2
KTA Super Store	(see 31)	
Longs Drugs	**5**	D2
Longs Drugs	**6**	E4
Main Post Office	**7**	F3
Police	**8**	C3

ing all coastal buildings. No one wanted to live downtown anymore. Hilo's bayfront became open space, parks and shops.

Since the 1960s, the new economy has favored tourism – but almost exclusively in sunny West Hawai'i. When the sugar industry left in the 1980s and '90s, Hilo focused its economy on diversified agriculture (especially tropical flora), the university, retail and, of course, tourism. Despite Kailua-Kona's status as the new economic and political powerhouse, Hilo remains the county capital and still wields much control over the financial pie, to the chagrin of some Kona residents. In fact, some are pushing to split the county into East and West Hawai'i.

ORIENTATION

The two major roads into Hilo are the Hawai'i Belt Rd (Hwy 19) from the Hamakua Coast and Kanoelehua Ave (which becomes Volcano Hwy, or Hwy 11) from the airport, Puna, Hawai'i Volcanoes National Park and Ka'u. Note that Hwy 19 is called Bayfront Hwy in and around Hilo.

Within Hilo, most attractions are located downtown, between Kamehameha Ave and Kino'ole St (both parallel to the bay), and between Waianuenue Ave and Mamo St (both perpendicular to the bay). East of downtown, Banyan Dr is Hilo's modest hotel row, but most B&Bs are located in residential neighborhoods near downtown.

HILO

Hilo's main retail district is the cluster of suburban-style malls (with Wal-Mart and other chain stores) on Kanoelehua Ave, southwest of the airport.

INFORMATION
Bookstores

our pick **Basically Books** (Map p174; ☎ 961-0144, 800-903-6277; 160 Kamehameha Ave; ⏱ 9am-5pm Mon-Sat, 10am-4pm Sun) Longtime indie bookseller specializing in maps, travel guides and locally published titles.

Book Gallery (Map p174; ☎ 935-4943; 259 Keawe St; ⏱ 9:30am-5pm Mon-Fri, to 3pm Sat) Indie with wide selection of locally published history, cookbook and children's titles.

Borders Books Music & Café (Map p170; ☎ 933-1410; Waiakea Center, 301 Maka'ala St; ⏱ 9am-9pm Sun-Thu, to 11pm Fri & Sat) Full-service chain with in-store Starbucks. Greatest selection of books, CDs and periodicals.

Emergency & Medical Services

Hilo Medical Center (Map p170; ☎ 974-4700, emergency room 974-6800; 1190 Waianuenue Ave; ⏱ 24hr emergency) Near Rainbow Falls.

KTA Super Store (Map p170; ☎ 959-9111, pharmacy 959-8700; Puainako Town Center, 50 E Puainako St; ⏱ pharmacy 8am-7pm Mon-Fri, from 9am Sat) Large supermarket with pharmacy. Store hours run much longer than pharmacy hours.

Longs Drugs Kilauea Ave (Map p170; ☎ 935-3357, pharmacy 935-9075; 555 Kilauea Ave; ⏱ pharmacy 7am-7pm Mon-Fri, to 6pm Sat, 8am-5pm Sun); Prince Kuhio Plaza (Map p170; ☎ 959-5881, pharmacy 959-4508; 111 E Puainako St; ⏱ pharmacy 8am-8pm Mon-Fri, to 7pm Sat, to 5pm Sun) General drugstore; store hours much longer than pharmacy hours.

Police (Map p170; ☎ 935-3311; 349 Kapi'olani St) For nonemergencies.

Internet Access

Bytes & Bites (Map p174; ☎ 935-3520; www.bytes andbites.net; 164 Kilauea Ave; internet per 15min/hr $2.50/8; ⏱ 10am-10pm) Small business center with eight computer carrels in the heart of downtown Hilo. Wi-fi costs only $3 per day.

Library

Hilo Public Library (Map p174; ☎ 933-8888; www .librarieshawaii.org; 300 Waianuenue Ave; ⏱ 11am-7pm Tue & Wed, 9am-5pm Thu & Sat, 10am-5pm Fri) If you buy a three-month nonresident library card ($10), you can use free internet terminals and check out books.

Media

The *Hawaii Tribune-Herald* (www.hawaii tribune-herald.com) is Hilo's daily newspaper of record. Also pick up the two left-leaning weeklies: *Big Island Weekly* (www .bigislandweekly.com) and *Hawai'i Island Journal* (www.hawaiiislandjournal.com).

The lion's share of radio stations is based in Hilo. These stations can be heard only in East Hawai'i, due to the island's geography. Check out http://archive.hawaii radiotv.com/HIRATV/BigIsleRadio.html for a complete listing.

KANO 91.1FM (www.hawaiipublicradio.org) Hawaii Public Radio featuring classical music and news.

KAPA 100.3FM (www.kaparadio.com) Traditional and contemporary island music.

KHBC 1060AM (www.khbcradio.com) Quintessential local lineup, including news and interviews, Hawaiian and country music, and lots of 'talk story.' Don't miss longtime DJ Mel 'Mynah Bird' Medeiros from 6am to 10am Monday to Friday.

KHLO 850AM ESPN sports.

KKBG 97.9FM (http://kbigfm.com) Classic rock.

KPUA 670AM (www.kpua.net) News, sports and talk radio.

KPVS 106.3FM (www.dabeatfm.com) Hawaii hits.

KWXX 94.7FM (www.kwxx.com) Island and pop hits.

Money

All banks in Hilo have 24-hour ATMs.

Bank of Hawaii (Map p170) Kawili St (☎ 961-0681; 417 E Kawili St); Pauahi St (☎ 935-9701; 120 Pauahi St)

First Hawaiian Bank (Map p174; ☎ 969-2222; 120 Waianuenue Ave)

Post

Both post offices hold general-delivery mail, but require you to complete an application in person. See p284 for details.

Downtown post office (Map p174; ☎ 933-3014; 154 Waianuenue Ave; ⏱ 9am-4pm Mon-Fri, 12:30-2pm Sat) Located in the Federal Building.

Main post office (Map p170; ☎ 933-3019; 1299 Kekuanaoa St; ⏱ 8am-4:30pm Mon-Fri, 9am-12:30pm Sat) Located near Hilo airport.

Tourist Information

Big Island Visitors Bureau (Map p174; ☎ 961-5797, 800-648-2441; www.bigisland.org; 250 Keawe St) Basic info and business brochures available. See website for events calendar.

BEACHES

Hilo isn't known for its beaches: too rocky, too rough and too rainy. Waitaminute! There are decently sandy and swimmable spots along Kalaniana'ole Ave, a 4-mile coastal road east of downtown.

ONEKAHAKAHA BEACH PARK
Map p170
Popular with local families, this beach has a broad, shallow, sandy-bottomed pool, protected by a boulder breakwater. The water is only 1ft to 2ft deep in spots, so toddlers can splash safely. An unprotected cove north of the protected pool is deeper but can be hazardous due to pokey *wana* (sea urchins) and rough surf; it's best to stay inside the breakwater. There are lifeguards on weekends and holidays, restrooms, showers, grassy lawns and covered pavilions.

JAMES KEALOHA BEACH PARK
Map p170
Further along the road, this county park is best for older kids and snorkelers. Locals call it 'Four Miles' (the distance between the park and the downtown post office). For swimming and snorkeling, head to the eastern side, which contains a deep, protected basin with generally calm, clear water and pockets of white sand. The park's western side is open ocean and much rougher. Locals surf here in winter or net fish. There are weekend lifeguards, restrooms, showers and covered pavilions.

LELEIWI BEACH PARK
Map p170
Rocky and ruggedly pretty, this beach is Hilo's best shore-dive site. You might see turtles, interesting coral growth and a variety of butterfly fish. The water is freezing until you go past the reef, and the entrance is tricky; ask for advice at Nautilus Dive Center (p179).

RICHARDSON OCEAN PARK
Map p170
Near the end of Kalaniana'ole Ave, this pocket of black sand is Hilo's best all-round beach. During calm surf, swimming is fine, while snorkeling is good on the warmer eastern side. (Waters are cooler on the northern side due to subsurface freshwater springs.) Lava rocks create interesting nooks and crannies, and sea turtles often hang out here. High surf attracts bodyboarders. There are restrooms, showers, picnic tables and a lifeguard.

HONOLI'I BEACH PARK
Map p170
Less than 2 miles north of downtown Hilo, this protected cove is Hilo's best surfing and bodyboarding spot. Don't come here to swim, as the adjacent river tends to muddy

Honoli'i Beach Park

GREG ELMS

HILO

DOWNTOWN HILO

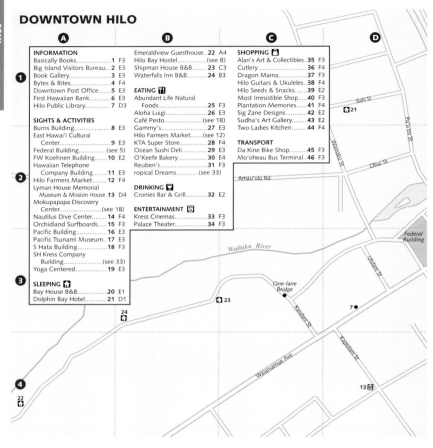

INFORMATION
Basically Books..................1 F3
Big Island Visitors Bureau...2 E3
Book Gallery........................3 E3
Bytes & Bites.....................4 F4
Downtown Post Office......5 E3
First Hawaiian Bank............6 E3
Hilo Public Library............. 7 D3

SIGHTS & ACTIVITIES
Burns Building....................8 E3
East Hawai'i Cultural
    Center............................9 E3
Federal Building..............(see 5)
FW Koehnen Building......10 E2
Hawaiian Telephone
    Company Building........11 E3
Hilo Farmers Market.........12 F4
Lyman House Memorial
    Museum & Mission House.13 D4
Mokupapapa Discovery
    Center......................(see 18)
Nautilus Dive Center........14 F4
Orchidland Surfboards.....15 F3
Pacific Building................16 E3
Pacific Tsunami Museum...17 E3
S Hata Building................18 F3
SH Kress Company
    Building...................(see 33)
Yoga Centered.................19 E3

SLEEPING 🏠
Bay House B&B.................20 E1
Dolphin Bay Hotel...........21 D1

Emeraldview Guesthouse..22 A4
Hilo Bay Hostel..............(see 8)
Shipman House B&B.........23 C3
Waterfalls Inn B&B..........24 B3

EATING 🍴
Abundant Life Natural
    Foods..........................25 F3
Aloha Luigi......................26 E3
Café Pesto.....................(see 18)
Gammy's..........................27 E3
Hilo Farmers Market.......(see 12)
KTA Super Store..............28 F4
Ocean Sushi Deli..............29 E3
O'Keefe Bakery...............30 E4
Reuben's.........................31 F3
Tropical Dreams...........(see 33)

DRINKING 🍹
Cronies Bar & Grill...........32 E2

ENTERTAINMENT 🎭
Kress Cinemas..................33 F3
Palace Theater.................34 F3

SHOPPING 🛍
Alan's Art & Collectibles...35 F3
Cutlery............................36 F4
Dragon Mama...................37 F3
Hilo Guitars & Ukuleles....38 F4
Hilo Seeds & Snacks.........39 E2
Most Irresistible Shop.....40 F3
Plantation Memories........41 F4
Sig Zane Designs.............42 E2
Sudha's Art Gallery..........43 E2
Two Ladies Kitchen.........44 F4

TRANSPORT
Da Kine Bike Shop...........45 F3
Mo'oheau Bus Terminal...46 F3

Iliahi St
Kinoole St

Ohai St

Amau'ulu Rd

Federal Building

Wailuku River

Ululani St

One-lane Bridge

Kalanikoa St

Kapiolani St

🏛 23

7 ●

Wailuku River

Waianuenue Ave

24 🏠

22 🏠

13 🏛

---

the waters. There's a pleasant grassy picnic area, restrooms, showers and a lifeguard. From Hilo, take the Bayfront Hwy north; after the 4-mile marker, turn right onto Nahala St and then left onto Kahoa St. Park on the roadside and walk down to the park.

SIGHTS

In downtown Hilo, charming early-20th-century architecture remains, and many buildings on the National Register of Historic Places now house restaurants, stores and galleries. Wander down back alleys to see aging wooden storefronts, old pool halls and barbershops still using hand-pumped

chairs. Locals refer to the coastal stretch along Hilo Bay as 'bayfront.' Outside the downtown area, the main sights are on Banyan Dr, which starts at Hilo's landmark dock, Suisan Fish Market (p185), where fisherfolk haul in their catches by 7am, although there's no action on Sundays.

LILI'UOKALANI PARK & BANYAN DRIVE
our pick Map p170

Savor Hilo's simple pleasures with a picnic lunch amid Japanese gardens overlooking the bay. Named for Hawaii's last queen, the 30-acre county park has manicured lawns, shallow ponds, bamboo groves, arched bridges, pagodas and a teahouse. At sunrise

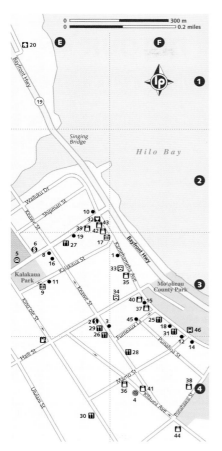

or sunset, join the locals and jog, stroll or just admire the Mauna Kea view.

Adjacent to the park is Banyan Dr, Hilo's mini 'hotel row,' best known for the giant banyan trees lining the road. Royalty and celebrities planted the trees in the 1930s, and, if you look closely, you'll find plaques beneath the trees identifying Babe Ruth, Amelia Earhart and Cecil B DeMille. The road skirts the nine-hole Naniloa Golf Course (p179).

MOKUOLA (COCONUT ISLAND)
Map p170

Tiny Mokuola island, commonly called Coconut Island, connects to land (near Lili'uokalani Park) by a footbridge. The island is a county park with picnic tables and swimming, and it's popular with local fishermen. Definitely stop here for a fun jaunt and a spectacular view of the bay, the town and majestic Mauna Kea in the distance.

HILO FARMERS MARKET
Map p174; cnr Mamo St & Kamehameha Ave;
7am-noon Wed & Sat

Hilo's gathering place is its pioneering farmers market, which opened in 1988 with four farmers selling from trucks. Today, the market is a lively, crowded event, with 125 vendors and a dazzling cornucopia of local produce, flora and fish (plus sneaky imports such as garlic and broccoli). The ready-to-eat fruit is excellent, especially the papayas, apple bananas, star fruit, Ka'u oranges, *liliko'i* (passion fruit) and lychees. Prepared food, including *bento* (Japanese-style box

Lili'uokalani Park

GREG ELMS

lunches with Spam *musubi* – blocks of rice with slices of fried Spam on top, wrapped with black sushi nori), artisan breads and machete-cut coconuts for drinking, can make for a great picnic. On the next block, dozens of craft and clothing stalls entice tourists with sarongs, T-shirts and 'Hawaiian' wood carvings and shell jewelry – occasionally real, often fake.

Currently the vendors' stalls sit on an undeveloped dirt-and-gravel lot, but the owner plans to build a $5 million, three-story structure for the market. Sounds cushy. But do try to catch the makeshift original market with its quasi-developing-world charm.

'IMILOA ASTRONOMY CENTER OF HAWAI'I

our pick Map p170; ☎ 969-9700; www.imiloa hawaii.org; 600 'Imiloa Pl; adult/child 4-12yr $17.50/9.50; ☺ 9am-4pm Tue-Sun, plus Memorial Day & Labor Day

'Imiloa, which means 'exploring new knowledge,' is a $28 million astronomy museum and planetarium complex with a twist: it showcases modern astronomy on Mauna Kea in light of ancient Hawaiian mythology and ocean voyaging.

This juxtaposition might seem incongruous, but there are parallels and continuity between ancient and modern exploration. In the Origins exhibit, attractive displays walk you through the mythical *kumulipo* (Hawaiian creation story) and the scientific big bang theory. The Voyaging exhibit covers ancient Polynesian voyaging and today's advanced telescopes and observatories.

With many hands-on displays, a 3D theater, a restaurant (open from 7am to 4pm) and a 120-seat planetarium, 'Imiloa is a worthwhile family attraction and nicely complements a trip to the actual summit.

When you arrive, a good starting point is the film *Maunakea: Between Earth and Sky*

Island Insights

Hilo's last major tsunami struck at 1:05am on May 23, 1960. The **Waiakea Tsunami Memorial Clock** (Map p170), stuck at that exact time, still stands on Kamehameha Ave near Manono St.

DETOUR ➡

WAI'ALE FALLS

In a beauty contest, Rainbow Falls would be the winner and Pe'epe'e Falls first runner-up. But Wai'ale Falls (off Map p170) will appeal to those who prefer the unconventional. Go further up Waianuenue Ave until you cross a bridge in front of the unmarked falls. No tour buses come here. From the right of the bridge, a quarter-mile hike (expect slippery, mossy, uphill terrain, plus bugs) through the forest leads to the top of the falls, where you can enjoy lava-rock swimming holes and an ocean view. Avoid spur trails that lead to steep drop-offs.

(shown at 11am and 2pm), but also don't miss the eye-popping *Dawn of the Space Age* 3D show.

LYMAN HOUSE MEMORIAL MUSEUM & MISSION HOUSE

Map p174; ☎ 935-5021; www.lymanmuseum.org; 276 Haili St; adult/child $10/3; ☺ 9:30am-4:30pm Mon-Sat

Compact yet comprehensive, this museum covers the basics of Hawaii's natural and cultural history. Downstairs, geologic exhibits explain Hawaii's volcanic origins and include fascinating examples of lava rock, such as 'Pele's tears' (solidified drops of volcanic glass) and 'Pele's hair' (fine strands of volcanic glass), both named after the Hawaiian volcano goddess.

Upstairs, learn about ancient Hawaiian sports, religion and the *kapu* (taboo) system, and see artifacts such as adzes, feather lei and *kapa* (cloth made by pounding paper-mulberry bark). Don't miss the fascinating, perfectly spherical stone. Other exhibits highlight the cultures of Hawaii's ethnic immigrant groups.

Catch an excellent half-hour tour (11am, 1pm and 3pm) of the adjacent Mission House, built by the Reverend David Lyman and his wife, Sarah, in 1839. The minimalist house contains many original furnishings, including Sarah's melodeon, rocking chair, china and quilts, and adds a human element to the historical facts.

HILO

PACIFIC TSUNAMI MUSEUM

Map p174; ☎ 935-0926; www.tsunami.org; 130 Kamehameha Ave; adult/student $7/2; ⏱ 9am-4pm Mon-Sat

Of all the natural disasters, tsunami have killed more Hawaii islanders than all others combined. This neat little museum covers the entire Pacific Ocean but focuses on Hilo's two catastrophic tsunami in 1946 and 1960. Multimedia exhibits, such as chilling computer simulations and filmed oral histories and documentaries, are excellent – especially the heart-wrenching first-person accounts by survivors.

⚘ EAST HAWAI'I CULTURAL CENTER

Map p174; ☎ 961-5711; www.ehcc.org; 141 Kalakaua St; suggested donation $2; ⏱ 10am-4pm Mon-Sat

The best venue for local art is this downtown center, which primarily displays the work of established professionals, but also compelling schoolkids' and other amateurs' masterpieces. Workshops and classes on varied creative forms (eg painting, drawing, ukulele and hula) are ongoing. Check the website for special evening concerts (featuring top artists) and the 'Aloha Sunday' classes (held on the second Sunday monthly) on *lauhala* (pandanus leaf) weaving, lei making and other Hawaiian arts.

WAILOA CENTER & WAILOA RIVER STATE PARK

Map p170; ☎ 933-0416; admission free; ⏱ 8:30am-4:30pm Mon, Tue, Thu & Fri, noon-4:30pm Wed

This eclectic, state-run gallery shows the gamut of exhibits, which change monthly. You might find quilts, bonsai, Chinese watercolors or historical photos, all done by locals.

Surrounding the center is a state park, a quiet spot that's more scenery than scene. The main landmark is a 14ft, Italian-made bronze statue of Kamehameha the Great, erected in 1997 and restored with gold leaf in 2004. The Wailoa River flows through the park, ending at Waiakea Pond, a spring-fed estuarine pond with saltwater and brackish-water fish species (mostly mullet). The park features two memorials: a tsunami memorial dedicated to the 1946 and 1960 victims, and a Vietnam War memorial with an eternal flame.

Rainbow Falls LUCI YAMAMOTO

RAINBOW FALLS

Map p170; Waianuenue Ave

Tour buses might surround you at this rain-forest waterfall, decorated by rainbows if the morning sun and mist cooperate. But you won't regret stopping. Waianuenue (which means 'rainbow seen in water') is the Hawaiian name for the 80ft cascade. If you want to go beyond the lookout, take the short, unpaved path that leads from the left side of the parking lot to the top of the falls. The scenic walk passes a gigantic banyan tree and other storybook scenes, but beware of hungry mosquitoes.

PE'EPE'E FALLS & BOILING POTS

off Map p170; Waianuenue Ave

Go further up Waianuenue Ave past Rainbow Falls to see a dramatic series of waterfalls cascading into swirling, foaming pools (or 'boiling pots'). Swimming is tempting but not advised. Locals trek down on a precarious trail past the 'No Swimming' sign; don't follow them.

⚘ MOKUPAPAPA DISCOVERY CENTER

Map p174; ☎ 933-8184; www.hawaiireef.noaa .gov/center; S Hata Bldg, 308 Kamehameha Ave; admission free; ⏱ 9am-4pm Tue-Sat

The Hawaiian archipelago extends far beyond the eight main islands to the Northwestern Hawaiian Islands. The healthiest coral reefs in the USA are found in this long chain of uninhabited islands and atolls. Learn more about the islands' pristine ecosystems at this modest yet ambitious little center. The 2500-gallon aquarium and lots of interactive displays will catch kids' attention.

KAUMANA CAVES
off Map p170; Kaumana Dr

Unlike the lava tubes in Ka'u (p239) and Puna (p196), this one is 'public' and you need no permission to enter. Formed by an 1881 Mauna Loa eruption, the tube comprising the caves is extensive (enter the left or right opening), but it narrows periodically and lengthy explorations require crawling. Due to years of use (and misuse), this is not a pristine cave. Bring two flashlights minimum. The caves are signposted about 4 miles up Kaumana Dr.

MEHANA BREWING COMPANY
Map p170; ☎ 934-8211; www.mehana.com; 275 E Kawili St; ☺ 9am-5pm Mon-Sat

Hilo's sole craft brewery might be more underground than Kailua-Kona's Kona Brewing Company (with two mega brewpubs; p64), but its six crisp, clean-tasting beers are considered superior. (Celebrated chef Roy

Yamaguchi serves Mehana's 'Roy's Private Reserve,' a mellow, copper-colored ale, at his restaurants, including Roy's Waikoloa Bar & Grill, p110.) Brewmaster Calvin Shindo, whose family established the company in 1995, is a hands-on owner, and the company remains small – the way a microbrewery should be. The tasting room and gift shop are open during business hours.

Check the website of Hilo's fascinating Hawai'i Plantation & Industrial Museum (www .memoriesofhawaiibigisland.com), which was being relocated at the time of research. This personal collection of Hiloan Wayne Subica contains a mishmash of plantation-era relics, household antiques and assorted memorabilia that reveal much about local Hilo folks.

South of Hilo, the following two attractions are worth a quick stop if you're passing by. (Don't bother stopping at Nani Mau Gardens, also along Volcano Hwy south of Hilo; this contrived set of gardens has seen better days and caters primarily to tour groups.)

Mauna Loa Macadamia-Nut Visitor Center (off Map p170; ☎ 966-8618, 888-628-6256; www.maunaloa .com; Macadamia Rd; ☺ 8:30am-5:30pm) While definitely geared to tourists, this center, amid neat groves, would interest any mac-nut fan. Peer through picture windows at the working factory's assembly lines, where nuts are roasted and packaged. In 2004 Hershey acquired the Mauna Loa company, which grows 10,000 acres of nuts. To get here, turn *makai* (seaward) off the Volcano Hwy onto Macadamia Rd, just past the 5-mile marker.

Pana'ewa Rainforest Zoo (off Map p170; ☎ 959-9233; www.hilozoo.com; admission free; ☺ 9am-4pm, petting zoo 1:30-2:30pm Sat) Spread across 12 acres, Hilo's low-key, uncrowded zoo won't wow you, but it's a decent diversion, with free-roaming peacocks meandering past caged monkeys, reptiles, a pygmy hippo and some of Hawaii's endangered birds. The star is a white Bengal tiger named Namaste. To get here, turn *mauka* (inland) off the Volcano Hwy onto W Mamaki St, just past the 4-mile marker.

ACTIVITIES
Swimming

For lap swimming, the Olympic-sized, open-air pool at the Ho'olulu Complex (Map p170; ☎ 961-8698) is generally uncrowded during the day. Call for hours.

Don't Miss

- Live performing arts at the East Hawai'i Cultural Center and Palace Theater (p176 and p187)
- Macadamia shortbread cookies and other sweet-tooth fixes at Big Island Candies (p186)
- Books, maps and nifty gifts at Basically Books (p172)
- Big Island Hawaiian Music Festival (p181)
- Bargain golf at Hilo Municipal Golf Course (p179)
- Miyo's Japanese comfort food (p183)
- Formidable hula at the Merrie Monarch Festival (p182)
- Four papayas for a dollar (!) at the Hilo Farmers Market (p175)
- Hilo Honu Inn's Japanese teahouse room (p189)
- Lyman House Memorial Museum (p176)

HILO

Keaukaha Beach Park

GREG ELMS

Beach swimming is rather limited; see p173 for descriptions of Hilo's beaches.

Diving

The best spot near Hilo is Leleiwi Beach (Map p170), with depths of 10ft to 70ft and sightings of lava arches, coral reefs, turtles and whales in season. Keaukaha Beach Park (Map p170) on Puhi Bay, located about 1.5 miles east of the intersection of Kalaniana'ole and Kanoelehua Aves, is a good beginner dive site. On the east side, there's an interesting dive spot, 'Tetsu's Ledge,' at 30ft. Pohoiki Bay (p202) in Puna is the best dive site in East Hawai'i, with depths of 20ft to 100ft.

Nautilus Dive Center (Map p170; ☎ 935-6939; www.nautilusdivehilo.com; 382 Kamehameha Ave; 2-tank dives $85) is Hilo's trusted, go-to place for dive trips, PADI certification courses and general advice on shore dives.

Surfing

No question: Hilo's best surfing spot is Honoli'i Cove at Honoli'i Beach Park (p173).

For board rentals and surf gear, go to Orchidland Surfboards (Map p174; ☎ 935-1533; www .orchidlandsurf.com; 262 Kamehameha Ave; ☺ 9am-5pm Mon-Sat, 10am-3pm Sun). Owner Stan Lawrence

is an expert surfer, and he opened the Big Island's first surf shop in 1972.

Golf

Hilo is a budget golfer's dream. The best course is the Hilo Municipal Golf Course (off Map p170; ☎ 959-7711; 340 Haihai St; greens fee Mon-Fri $29, Sat & Sun $34), where you'll meet the early-bird local contingent. The nine-hole Naniloa Country Club Golf Course (Map p170; ☎ 935-3000; greens fee Mon-Fri $25, Sat & Sun $35), conveniently located across from Lili'uokalani Park, can feel oddly deserted.

Yoga

Spacious, stylish ✿ Yoga Centered (Map p174; ☎ 934-7233; www.yogacentered.com; 37 Waianuenue Ave; drop-in class $15; ☺ boutique 10am-5pm Mon-Thu, to 4pm Sun) offers challenging *vinyasa* (flowing sequences of poses) classes and a well-stocked boutique carrying only eco-friendly or sweatshop-free fashions and props.

An airy studio within a house, Balancing Monkey Yoga Center (Map p170; ☎ 936-9590; www .balancingmonkey.com; 65 Mohouli St; drop-in class $14; ☺ Sun-Fri) is welcoming and unpretentious, with an indie vibe. Choose from Ashtanga- or Iyengar-based classes, generally small enough for personal attention.

WALKING TOUR
Downtown Hilo Stroll

Enjoy a mid-morning stroll from Hilo's lively old town to Lili'uokalani Park by the bay.

❶ EAST HAWAI'I CULTURAL CENTER (p176) Hilo's art scene isn't stuffy at all, as is evidenced in this airy gallery that features local artists. Next door is the notable **Hawaiian Telephone Company Building**, which was designed in the 1920s by renowned Honolulu architect CW Dickey with Spanish, Italian and Californian mission influences.

❷ KALAKAUA PARK This lovely green space is hardly used as a park, but stop by to see a bronze statue of King David Kalakaua (the 'Merrie Monarch'). The lily-filled pool honors Korean War veterans, and buried under the grass is a **time capsule**, sealed on the last total solar eclipse (July 11, 1991), to be opened on the next one (May 3, 2106).

❸ HISTORIC BUILDINGS The **Federal Building**, built in 1919, houses government

One of Hilo's many historic buildings GREG ELMS

offices and a post office. Across the street, see the traditional **Burns Building** (1911) and the **Pacific Building** (1922) next door. Fronting the bay, the **FW Koehnen Building** (1910) has an eye-catching blue facade with interior koa walls and ohia floors.

❹ PACIFIC TSUNAMI MUSEUM (p177) Amid art galleries and boutiques, this small museum is a crash course on tsunami. It's located in the old First Hawaiian Bank building, another CW Dickey creation, built in 1930.

❺ SH KRESS COMPANY BUILDING This art deco building (1932), a department store until 1980, now houses a **movie theater (p187)**, a charter school and **Tropical Dreams (p184)** ice cream shop. Note the nearby **Palace Theater (p187)**, which, in 1925, was the island's first major playhouse and still offers great shows.

❻ S HATA BUILDING The US government seized this 1912 renaissance-revival building from the original Japanese owner during WWII. After the war, the owner's daughter bought it back for $100,000. Today it houses **Café Pesto (p184)**, among other businesses.

❼ HILO FARMERS MARKET (p175) On Wednesday and Saturday, Hiloans gather at this huge market, with a dazzling array of fresh produce, flowers, fish and more. Bring cash and a bag.

❽ BAYFRONT BEACH PARK Cross Kamehameha Ave to walk along the scenic bay, where canoe paddlers train. The breakwater was built between 1908 and 1929 using 951,273 tons of rock. Before the 1946 and 1960 tsunami, businesses and houses blanketed the grassy fields lined with coconut palms.

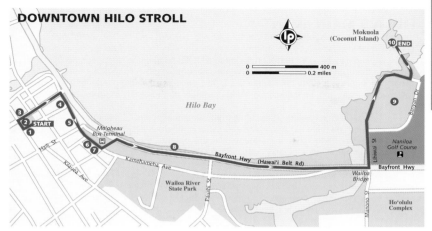

DOWNTOWN HILO STROLL

❾ LILI'UOKALANI PARK (p174) Turn left at Suisan Fish Market (p185) to reach this pretty, Japanese-style park.

❿ MOKUOLA (COCONUT ISLAND) (p175) Cross the footbridge to Mokuola and stroll down Banyan Drive's mini hotel row, shaded by historic banyan trees.

HILO FOR KIDS

Hilo is a family town and kids are welcome everywhere. Any outdoor setting allows kids to romp and parents to relax – and it costs nothing. Picnic at Lili'uokalani Park (p174), cross the footbridge to Mokuola (Coconut Island; p175), visit the zoo (p178) or laze around at Onekahakaha Beach Park (p173). On rainy days, Hilo's numerous museums

are a great standby, especially 'Imiloa Astronomy Center of Hawai'i (p176), Mokupapapa Discovery Center (p177) and Pacific Tsunami Museum (p177).

Another rainy-day option is a video-game arcade, such as the following:

Fun Factory (Map p170; ☎ 969-9137; Waiakea Center, 315 Maka'ala St; tokens 25¢; ☻ 10am-10pm Sun-Thu, to midnight Fri & Sat) Located near Wal-Mart and a food court, this arcade offers marginally better games and prizes than Tilt.

Tilt (Map p170; ☎ 959-3444; Prince Kuhio Plaza, 111 E Puainako St; tokens 25¢; ☻ 10am-8pm Mon-Thu, to 10pm Fri & Sat, to 6pm Sun) Popular with local kids; located in a clean, safe mall with cinemas.

FESTIVALS & EVENTS

For more listings, check www.bigisland .org.

May Day Lei Day Festival (☎ 934-7010; www.hilo palace.com; Palace Theater, 38 Haili St; admission free) Beautiful lei displays, demonstrations, live music and hula on the first Sunday in May.

King Kamehameha Day Celebration (☎ 935-9338; Mokuola; admission free) On June 11, observe the historic reenactment of King Kamehameha's history, plus music and crafts.

Fourth of July Entertainment and food all day at Lili'uokalani Park; fireworks display from Mokuola (Coconut Island).

our pick Big Island Hawaiian Music Festival (☎ 961-5711; www.ehcc.org; Hilo High School, 556 Waianuenue Ave; adult/child $10/free) A mid-July, two-day concert featuring virtuoso musicians in ukulele, steel

---

Top Picks

HILO FOR KIDS
- **Swimming at Onekahakaha Beach** (p173)
- **Locally made ice cream (try Tropical Dreams or Hilo Homemade Ice Cream)** (p184)
- **'Imiloa Astronomy Center of Hawai'i's interactive exhibits** (p176)
- **One-dollar movies at Kress Cinemas** (p187)
- **Picnicking at Lili'uokalani Park** (p174)

HULA'S MAIN EVENT

When the **Merrie Monarch Festival** (☎ 935-9168; www.merriemonarchfestival.org; 2-night admission general/reserved $10/15) comes to town around Easter (late March or early April), forget about booking a last-minute room in Hilo. This three-day hula competition is a phenomenal sellout attraction that turns laid-back Hilo into the most happening place to be. Established in 1964, the festival honors King David Kalakaua (1836–91), who almost single-handedly revived Hawaiian culture and arts, including hula, which had been forbidden by missionaries for almost 70 years.

Top hula troupes from all the Islands vie in *kahiko* (ancient) and *'auana* (modern) categories. *Kahiko* performances are strong and serious, accompanied only by chanting. *'Auana* is closer to the mainstream style, with sinuous arm movements, smiling dancers and melodious accompaniment that includes string instruments. The primal chanting, meticulous choreography and traditional costumes are profoundly moving.

To guarantee a seat, order tickets by mail on December 26 (no earlier postmarks allowed); see the website for seating and payment info. The roughly 2700 tickets sell out within a month. Book your hotel room and car a year in advance. If you prefer, watch the competition on TV (KITV, channel 4) or online (www.kitv.com).

guitar, slack key guitar and falsetto singing. The statewide lineup has included top names such as Cyril Pahinui, Darlene Ahuna, Ozzie Kotani and Brittni Paiva.

International Festival of the Pacific (☎ 934-0177; Japanese Chamber of Commerce, 400 Hualani St; admission free) August celebration of the Japanese in Hawaii, featuring a lantern parade and Japanese tea ceremony at Lili'uokalani Park.

Hawai'i County Fair (Afook-Chinen Civic Auditorium, 799 Pi'ilani St; adult/student $3/2) Pure nostalgia comes to town in September, with carnival rides, games and cotton candy.

EATING

CAFÉ 100
Drive-In $

Map p170; ☎ 935-8683; 969 Kilauea Ave; loco moco $2-5, plate lunches $5-7; ⏱ 6:45am-8:30pm Mon-Sat

Hilo's go-to place for *loco moco* (rice topped with a hamburger patty, fried egg and an obscene dollop of brown gravy) serves 20 rib-sticking varieties. Plate lunches are even heartier and the strawberry 'ice cake' is sweet nostalgia. The open-air patio, with picnic tables seating leisurely diners in T-shirts and *rubbah slippahs* (flip-flops), spells H-I-L-O.

NORI'S SAIMIN & SNACKS
Japanese $

Map p170; ☎ 935-9133; Suite 124, 688 Kino'ole St; noodle soups $4-7; ⏱ 11:30am-3pm Mon, 10:30am-3pm & 4pm-midnight Tue-Sat, 10:30am-11pm Sun

Ignore the strip-mall setting. Focus on the Japanese noodle soups, tasty, filling and perfect for rainy days. Rippled saimin have an irresistibly chewy bite. Beware of spotty service.

ALOHA LUIGI
Mexican/Italian $

Map p174; ☎ 934-9112; 264 Keawe St; mains $5-12; ⏱ 9am-3pm Mon & Tue, to 7pm Wed-Fri

We're always suspicious when a menu offers two cuisines, but the half-Italian owner here serves a tasty Caesar salad (both croutons and dressing are homemade), five-cheese ravioli and mahimahi burritos in a casual, bus-your-own-tray place. Cheerful staffers call your name – 'Aloha Nancy!' or 'Aloha Tom!' – when your order's up. You can't help but smile.

Café 100's legendary *loco moco* GREG ELMS

OCEAN SUSHI DELI   Sushi $$
Map p174; ☎ 961-6625; 239 Keawe St; 6-piece
rolls $3-6, meals $12-14; ⊗ 10am-2pm & 5:30-9pm
Mon-Sat

Think sushi deli, not sushi bar. This means
zero decor, rushed service and cheap eats.
The rolls fall short of excellent but they're
good and creative, featuring fresh fish with
macadamia nuts or tropical fruit, *poke*
(cubed, marinated raw fish) or even chicken
katsu (fried cutlets) tucked inside. Service
and quality can slip during rush hours.

RESTAURANT MIWA   Japanese $$
Map p170; ☎ 961-4454; Hilo Shopping Center,
1261 Kilauea Ave; sushi $5-8, meals $9-17;
⊗ lunch & dinner

Tucked away in a nondescript mall,
Miwa excels in Japanese classics. Generous *teishoku* (full meal) platters include
miso soup, rice, tea and two mains, such
as grilled *saba* (mackerel), teriyaki chicken
and *tonkatsu* (breaded pork cutlets). The
setting is diner casual, but the kimono-clad
servers are a nice touch. Expect no surprises
here, just satisfaction.

KEN'S HOUSE OF PANCAKES   Diner $$
Map p170; ☎ 935-8711; 1730 Kamehameha Ave;
meals $6-12; ⊗ 24hr

The interior resembles any diner anywhere,
but there's something comforting about
a 24-hour diner with a mile-long menu.

Island Insights

The **Hilo Public Library** (p172) is not a
must-see, but if you're in the neighborhood,
examine the two lava stones fronting the
building. The upright **Pinao Stone** once
guarded the entrance of Pinao heiau, an
ancient temple. The reclining **Naha Stone**,
from the same heiau, is estimated at 3.5
tons. According to Hawaiian legend, anyone
who had the strength to budge the stone
would also have the strength to conquer
and unite all the Hawaiian Islands. Kame-
hameha the Great reputedly met the chal-
lenge, overturning the stone in his youth.

Choose from mac-nut pancakes, Spam
omelettes, *kalua* (cooked in an under-
ground pit) pig plates and steaming bowls
of saimin.

MIYO'S   Japanese $$
our pick Map p170; ☎ 935-2273; Waiakea Villas,
400 Hualani St; mains $8-12; ⊗ lunch & dinner
Mon-Sat

While slightly scruffy in broad daylight,
Miyo's resembles a rustic Japanese teahouse, with shoji doors opening toward
Waiakea Pond. The tasty home cooking
features the classics, from grilled *saba* to
tonkatsu, with traditional sides plus fresh

WHO INVENTED THE LOCO MOCO?

Everyone agrees that the *loco moco* (rice topped with a hamburger patty, fried egg and
an obscene dollop of brown gravy) was invented in Hilo. But the details of who, when and
where (and why that wacky name) are fuzzy. Most believe that the *loco moco* arose in 1949
at a downtown Hilo restaurant called Lincoln Grill (which closed in 1963), where the Lincoln
Wreckers, a teenage sports organization, hung out. The boys would play pinball machines
and cards, drop nickels in the Wurlitzer jukebox and try to fill up on 15¢ hamburgers or 20¢
saimin. Wanting a meal both satisfying and cheap, they nominated a guy nicknamed 'Crazy'
(for his wild football moves) to ask the proprietors to make them a new dish.

They got a big bowl of rice smothered with a hamburger steak and brown gravy for 25¢.
This 'in-house' special for the Wreckers boys eventually made the menu. By 1951 it was
named *loco moco*, in honor of Crazy (since *loco* means crazy in Spanish). When Lincoln Grill
closed, the Wreckers moved their hangout to May's Grill, another long-gone restaurant,
which innovated the dish into its full incarnation by adding two over-easy fried eggs.

Today, *loco moco* is among Hawaii's favorite fast foods (neck and neck with Spam *musubi*).
Aficionados enthusiastically debate the importance of each component: rice, hamburger
patty, eggs, gravy.

In Hilo, you can order a *loco moco* at any drive-in, but the most popular is **Café 100** (p182),
which has even trademarked the name.

green salad. Especially recommended are the daily fish specials (try the locally caught whole fish).

SOMBAT'S FRESH THAI CUISINE Thai $$
Map p170; ☎ 936-8849; 88 Kanoelehua Ave; dishes $8-16; ☺ 10:30am-2pm Mon-Fri, 5-8:30pm Mon-Sat

Eat healthy Thai classics made with local produce and fresh herbs (grown by the chef without pesticides). Sauces are never cloying, and the menu offers many veg options, such as a refreshing green-papaya salad. The location is ho-hum, in a sadly deserted commercial building. Ideal for takeout.

KUHIO GRILLE Diner $$
Map p170; ☎ 959-2336; Suite A106, Prince Kuhio Plaza, 111 E Puainako St; mains $8.50-17; ☺ 6am-10pm Sun-Thu, to midnight Fri & Sat

When in Hilo, eat as the Hiloans eat – at this unanimous-favorite, family-run diner. The fluffy pancakes, fried-rice *loco moco* and especially the 1lb *laulau* (bundle of pork or

---

COOL LICKS

On hot Hilo days (and they *do* exist), beat the heat with ice cream or shave ice. For locally made premium ice cream, the island's best-known brand is **Tropical Dreams** (www.tropicaldreamsicecream.com), based in Waimea. It makes two lines: Hilo Homemade (premium ice cream in classic flavors) and Tropical Dreams (superpremium ice cream in novel fusion flavors). Try the former at **Gammy's** (Map p170; ☎ 933-1520; 41 Waianuenue Ave; single scoops $3; ☺ 8am-7pm Mon-Sat, 10am-7pm Sun) downtown or **Hilo Homemade Ice Cream** (Map p170; ☎ 217-9650; 1477 Kalaniana'ole Ave; single scoops $2.75; ☺ 11am-6pm) near the beaches. Try the latter at **Tropical Dreams** (Map p174; ☎ 935-9109; 174 Kamehameha Ave; single scoops $2.50; ☺ 7am-5pm Mon-Thu, 10am-9:30pm Fri & Sat). Check the website for islandwide locations.

Better yet, go local and try ice shave at **ourpick** **Itsu's Fishing Supplies** (Map p170; ☎ 935-8082; 810 Pi'ilani St; shave ice $1.50, plate lunches $4-6.75; ☺ 8am-5pm Mon-Fri). The 'rainbow' (tri-flavor) is the local favorite choice for shave ice, which Hiloans call 'ice shave.'

---

chicken and salted butterfish, wrapped in taro and *ti* leaves and steamed) plates do lip-smacking justice to local *grinds* (food).

REUBEN'S Mexican $$
Map p174; ☎ 961-2552; 336 Kamehameha Ave; combination plates $10-18; ☺ 11am-9pm Mon-Thu, to 10pm Fri, noon-10pm Sat

While Californians (not to mention Mexicans) might be blasé, locals love this longtime eatery that resembles a Oaxaca cantina. Favorites include classic enchiladas and *chiles rellenos* (chilies stuffed with cheese), freshly fried chips and eye-watering salsa.

QUEEN'S COURT American/Hawaiian $$$
Map p170; ☎ 935-9361, 800-367-5004; www .castleresorts.com; ground fl, Hilo Hawaiian Hotel, 71 Banyan Dr; lunch mains $8-12, dinner buffets $27.50-31; ☺ breakfast, lunch & dinner

Frequented by local businessfolk, retirees and big eaters, this hotel restaurant is like a familiar favorite aunt. It won't wow you with cutting-edge cuisine, but the weekend seafood or Hawaiian buffets are well prepared and all-you-can-eat. The weekday prime rib and crab buffet will also satisfy.

CAFÉ PESTO Hawaii Regional $$$
Map p174; ☎ 969-6640; S Hata Bldg, 308 Kamehameha Ave; pizzas $12-20, dinner $20-30; ☺ 11am-9pm Sun-Thu, to 10pm Fri & Sat

Café Pesto is a safe choice, whether for business lunches, shared pizzas or dinner with your mother-in-law. Set downtown in a lovely historic building, the versatile kitchen features local ingredients in risottos, stir-fries, pastas and salads. Its supposedly wood-fired pizzas need crust makeovers, however.

HILO BAY CAFÉ Hawaii Regional $$$
ourpick Map p170; ☎ 935-4939; Waiakea Center, 315 Maka'ala St; mains $15-26; ☺ 11am-9pm Mon-Sat, 5-9pm Sun

Foodies adore this urban-chic eatery incongruously located near a Wal-Mart. The eclectic menu features local ingredients, from organically grown produce to free-range meats. The youthful chef's creative combinations include seared macadamia-crusted scallops, blackened pork tenderloin with risotto cake, and Guinness onion rings with balsamic ketchup. Limited veg selection.

ISLAND VOICES

NAME: WAYNE SUBICA
OCCUPATION: LOCAL HISTORIAN AND AUTHOR, OWNER OF HAWAI'I PLANTATION & INDUSTRIAL MUSEUM
RESIDENCE: HILO

When did you start collecting plantation-era antiques? I was a soil conservationist (under the US Department of Agriculture) for 35 years starting in 1964. I worked with the greatest island people – the farmers – who would give me old stuff: clocks, farm tools, a kerosene stove, washboards. I recognized these things from my childhood. I appreciated the quality of the workmanship. Old things were made with quality, made in America, made to last.

Why did you start a museum? When my grandkids were younger, I realized that all the soda fountains were gone. So I built one at my house. I found old signs, an ice-cream counter from a fountain in Pahoa, a malt maker, a National cash register and eight stools for my eight grandkids. Neighbors would come to see it and tell me, 'Wayne, open one [sic] museum!'

What appeals to you about downtown Hilo? Downtown Hilo still has the old, plantation-days, mom-and-pop atmosphere. Inside an air-conditioned mall, you could be anywhere in the United States. Downtown, I like to walk around, look at the early 1900s buildings, talk to the old-timers who are still around and listen to their stories.

Why have the new malls superseded downtown? Parking is free downtown but people always say, 'I couldn't find parking.' Locals go to the mall, where they can find parking within sight of their destination. I tell them, 'Come downtown, walk around, check it out.' In committees on revitalizing downtown Hilo, even the mayor recommends tearing down some old buildings and putting up parking lots and buildings on stilts – because this is a tidal-wave zone.

Are young people interested in history? Kids enjoy seeing the old things, like an icebox that uses only ice, or a crank phonograph that played without electricity. They can relate to their parents' and grandparents' stories about plantation camps, but it's mainly old-timers who are interested. After visiting the museum, they donate old photos, furniture, uniforms and so forth – because their kids don't want the stuff. They might not want it today, but eventually they will. That's why we must preserve it.

🌺 SEASIDE RESTAURANT Seafood $$$
our pick Map p170; ☎ 935-8825; 1790 Kalaniana'ole Ave; meals $20-26; ☷ dinner Tue-Sat
Nowadays, once-lowly mullet is appearing on gourmet menus. But this family-run restaurant has raised its mullet (plus *aholehole*, rainbow trout and catfish) in Hawaiian-style fishponds since 1921. Fresh fish can't get any fresher. However, don't expect a fancy dining experience. It's a humble place with plain dinnerware and homey full meals of fish (try the *ti*-leaf–wrapped steamed mullet), rice, salad, apple pie and coffee.

If you prefer to eat in, Hilo has no shortage of raw materials for memorable meals. First try the farmers market (p175) for produce and Suisan Fish Market (Map p170; ☎ 935-9349; 93 Lihiwai St; ☷ 8am-5pm Mon-Fri, to 4pm Sat) for fresh fish, including many varieties of *poke*.

O'Keefe Bakery (Map p174; ☎ 934-9334; www.okeefe bakery.com; 374 Kino'ole St; ☯ 6am-5pm Mon-Fri, to 3pm Sat) bakes artisan breads and cookies.

Recommended grocery stores include the following:

Abundant Life Natural Foods (Map p174; ☎ 935-7411; 292 Kamehameha Ave; ☯ 8:30am-7pm Mon, Tue, Thu & Fri, 7am-5pm Wed & Sat, 10am-5pm Sun)

EDIBLE GIFTS

Locals never arrive empty-handed when they return from trips or pay a house visit. Rather they bring gifts, typically of the edible variety. Here are their Hilo favorites.

Once you taste the exquisite chocolate and macadamia confections by **Big Island Candies** (Map p170; ☎ 935-8890, 800-935-5510; www.bigislandcandies.com; 585 Hinano St; chocolate-dipped macadamia shortbread cookies $6.75-17; ☯ 8:30am-5pm), the standard retail stuff will never quite do. The company started as a tiny mom-and-pop outfit in 1977, but it's big-time now, with a factory store that's a major tourist attraction. Come to watch an immaculate assembly line hand-dipping cookies in chocolate (and for generous samples).

Two Hilo-born ladies make island-style Japanese *mochi* (sticky rice dessert) and *manju* (azuki-bean-filled cake) at their aptly named **Two Ladies Kitchen** (Map p174; ☎ 961-4766; 274 Kilauea; 8-piece boxes $6; ☯ 10am-5pm Wed-Sat). The delicate varieties include golden *liliko'i* (passion fruit) or purple sweet-potato *mochi* and their specialty: fresh strawberries wrapped in sweet bean paste and sticky rice. A must-try.

You haven't tasted buttermilk doughnuts until you've tried the moist, fist-size beauties from **Sputnik's** (Map p170; ☎ 961-2066; 811 Laukapu St; doughnuts 80¢; ☯ 6:30am-2pm Mon-Fri), a third-generation family business. But go before 11am because they bake fewer than 100 doughnuts daily and they're often sold out by then!

A downtown hole-in-the-wall, **Hilo Seeds & Snacks** (Map p174; ☎ 935-7355; 15 Waianuenue Ave; snacks under $5; ☯ 9:30am-5pm Mon-Fri) carries many varieties of 'crack seed,' the indescribable salty-sweet Chinese dried-fruit delicacy that locals find mouthwateringly addictive. Ask the friendly owner for advice.

Longtime downtown store carries wholesome, organic brands. Its side café (which closes about 1½ hours ahead of the store) serves smoothies and wholesome sandwiches, from tamari-baked tofu to curried albacore tuna.

Island Naturals (Map p170; ☎ 935-5533; Waiakea Center, 303 Maka'ala St; smoothies $3-3.75; deli dishes per lb $7; ☯ 8:30am-8pm Mon-Sat, 10am-7pm Sun) Amid the malls near the airport, Island Naturals is a large, well-stocked store with a smoothie counter and a gourmet deli.

our pick **KTA Super Store** Downtown (Map p174; ☎ 935-3751; 323 Keawe St; ☯ 7am-9pm Mon-Sat, to 6pm Sun); Puainako Town Center (Map p170; ☎ 959-9111; 50 E Puainako St; ☯ 5:30am-midnight) Excellent, locally owned chain carries a wide selection of mainstream groceries plus an impressive deli with fresh *poke*, *bento* (box meals of grilled mackerel or salmon, teriyaki beef or sushi) and other ready-to-eat items, which sell out by mid-morning.

DRINKING & ENTERTAINMENT

Nightlife in Hilo? If you find some, please let us know. Actually, the East Hawai'i Cultural Center (p176) and Palace Theater (p187) are impressive venues for live music, dance and theater.

Bars & Nightclubs

KOPE KOPE ESPRESSO CAFÉ

Map p170; ☎ 933-1221; www.kopekope.net; Hilo Shopping Center, 1261 Kilauea St; ☯ 6:30am-9pm Mon-Fri, 7:30am-9pm Sat, 7:30am-6pm Sun
For early-to-bed types, Kope Kope is your best bet for live entertainment, from music to swing dancing, starting around 7pm.

CRONIES BAR & GRILL

Map p174; ☎ 935-5158; 11 Waianuenue Ave; ☯ 11am-10pm Mon-Sat, to 11pm Sun
More restaurant than bar (consider the closing time), Cronies is a clean, rather-well-lit place with TVs, occasional live music and affordable drinks. Pleasant bayfront downtown location.

UNCLE MIKEY'S VIDEO DANCE CLUB

Map p170; ☎ 933-2667; www.unclemikeysnight club.com; Waiakea Villas, Bldg 22, 400 Hualani St; admission $10; ☯ 9pm-1:30am Wed, Fri & Sat
Twenty-somethings into dancing might enjoy this club that's jammed on Saturday nights. One dance floor caters to the 18-to-21 set.

Mochi at Two Ladies Kitchen   GREG ELMS

SHOOTERS BAR & GRILL
Map p170; ☎ 969-7069; 121 Banyan Dr; admission $5; 9pm-2am Mon-Wed, 10pm-3am Thu-Sat
By day, Shooters is a dive. By night, it comes to pulsating life when locals gather for DJ dancing. Best suited to those born past 1980.

Theaters & Cinemas

PALACE THEATER
our pick Map p174; ☎ 934-7010, box office 934-7777; www.hilopalace.com; 38 Haili St; movie tickets $7
This beautifully restored 1925 theater is one of the best performing-arts venues in town. In addition to screening artsy and foreign films, the theater presents concerts, dance, musicals and cultural performances. Tickets for live shows generally cost from $15 to $50.

For first-run movies, the best-value option is Kress Cinemas (Map p174; ☎ 935-6777; 174 Kamehameha Ave; tickets $1), located smack downtown. Otherwise, join the local kids at Stadium Cinemas (Map p170; ☎ 961-3456; Prince Kuhio Plaza, 111 E Puainako St; tickets adult/child/matinee $8/5/5.50), in a standard mall setting.

SHOPPING

Locals flock to Prince Kuhio Plaza (Map p170; ☎ 959-3555; 111 E Puainako St; 10am-9pm Mon-Fri, 9:30am-7pm Sat, 10am-6pm Sun), a standard suburban mall with the megachains from Wal-Mart to Borders Books Music & Café. But downtown Hilo has infinitely more character. Check out the art galleries along Kamehameha Ave and at the corner of Mamo St and Kilauea Ave.

SIG ZANE DESIGNS
Map p174; ☎ 935-7077; www.sigzane.com; 122 Kamehameha Ave; 9:30am-5pm Mon-Fri, 9am-4pm Sat
Longtime Hilo resident Sig Zane is internationally famous for his signature print designs, which interpret traditional Hawaiian plants in a modern minimalist style. His cotton and linen aloha shirts are seen on many famous folks statewide. Pricey, but this is real art.

SUDHA'S ART GALLERY
Map p174; ☎ 934-0009; www.sudhaachar.com; 100 Kamehameha Ave; 11am-4pm Tue-Sat
This eclectic collection of fine paintings, sculpture and woodwork shows off the best of local art. The owner is chair of the East Hawai'i Cultural Center (p176) and a respected artist herself.

ALAN'S ART & COLLECTIBLES
Map p174; ☎ 969-1554; 202 Kamehameha Ave; 10am-4:30pm Mon & Wed-Fri, 1-4:30pm Tue, 10am-3pm Sat
Glimpse old Hawai'i in this chock-full secondhand shop: vintage glassware, household doodads, aloha shirts, vinyl LPs and scattered collectible treasures.

PLANTATION MEMORIES
Map p174; 179 Kilauea Ave; 10am-5pm Mon-Sat
Geared to real collectors, this antiques shop contains furniture, store and street signs, old-fashioned tools and contraptions, household knickknacks and vintage bottles – all genuine.

THE CUTLERY
Map p174; ☎ 934-7500; www.upinthecutlery.com; 141 Mamo St; 10am-6pm Mon-Fri
This minimalist little shop owned by Kuhau Zane (son of Sig Zane) sells ultrahip male fashions by local indie designers. But, even in Hilo, coolness don't come cheap. T-shirts start at $60.

DRAGON MAMA
Map p174; ☎ 934-9081; www.dragonmama.com; 266 Kamehameha Ave; 9am-5pm Mon-Fri, to 4pm Sat
Japan is known for exquisite textiles. Case in point: the custom-made futons, comforters and matching covers sold here.

HILO

HILO GUITARS & UKULELES
Map p174; ☎ 935-4282; www.hiloguitars.com; 56
Ponahawai St; ⏲ 10am-5pm Mon-Fri, to 4pm Sat
Wide selection of ukulele, from koa or mahogany classics to far-out brass or electric creations.

MOST IRRESISTIBLE SHOP
Map p174; ☎ 935-9644; 256 Kamehameha Ave;
⏲ 9am-5pm Mon-Fri, to 4pm Sat
This long-running gift shop lives up to its name by offering handcrafted jewelry, kids' books, soaps and candles, koa objects, artsy greeting cards and much more.

SLEEPING

HILO BAY HOSTEL   Hostel $
Map p174; ☎ 933-2771; www.hawaiihostel.net;
101 Waianuenue Ave; dm $25, r with private/shared
bathroom $75/65; ☐
A backpacker's dream, this hostel is virtually faultless. Perfectly situated downtown (within walking distance of almost everything), it occupies an airy historic building with hardwood floors, remarkably clean restrooms and a kitchen in which you could cook Thanksgiving dinner. Staff are friendly but rule sticklers (after the 11am checkout time, you must leave the premises). The crowd is older and diverse, creating a low-key, relaxed vibe.

OLD HAWAIIAN B&B   B&B $
off Map p170; ☎ 961-2816; www.thebigisland
vacation.com; 1492 Wailuku Dr; r incl breakfast
$80-110; ☐
Perfect for discriminating budget travelers, these three pleasant rooms include private entrances and tidy furnishings. The largest 'Hawaiian Room' and smallest 'Bamboo Room' are the best deals. The rooms open to a backyard lanai, with dining table, microwave and refrigerator. Rates rise for one-night stays; military discounts.

UNCLE BILLY'S HILO
BAY HOTEL   Independent Hotel $$
Map p170; ☎ 935-0861, 800-442-5841; www
.unclebilly.com; 87 Banyan Dr; r $89-114; ✂ ☒
A long-standing fixture on Banyan Dr, Uncle Billy's is rather tired, but it's a bargain if you book online. The rooms are clean and decent-sized, and overlook a central courtyard of palms, red ginger and talkative mynah birds. And where else can you snag an oceanfront room for just over $100? Expect a modest hotel in a terrific location – and you'll be happy.

DOLPHIN BAY HOTEL   Independent Hotel $$
ourpick Map p174; ☎ 935-1466; www.dolphin
bayhotel.com; 333 Iliahi St; studios $99-109,
1br/2br $129/149
This family-run hotel attracts many loyal, repeat guests. Since 1968, folks have appreciated the 18 spick-and-span apartment units, all with full kitchens and TV, located within walking distance of downtown. The hotel owner/manager is an avid outdoorsman and he freely shares his firsthand knowledge of the volcanoes. Free coffee and locally grown fruit for breakfast.

HILO HAWAIIAN HOTEL   Hotel $$
Map p170; ☎ 935-9361, 800-367-5004; www
.castleresorts.com; 71 Banyan Dr; r $100-200;
✂ ☐ ☒
While Hilo's long-standing best hotel could use a facelift, it's still pleasant, airy and decent value at its internet rates. The Banyan Dr location is ideal, with lovely Lili'uokalani Park across the street. From the oceanfront rooms, you can admire all of Hilo, from the bay to Mauna Kea. Rooms include the expected amenities, such as phone, cable TV, air-con and fridge.

ORCHID TREE B&B   B&B $$
ourpick off Map p170; ☎ 961-9678; www.orchid
tree.net; 6 Makakai Pl; r incl breakfast $140;
✂ ☐ ☒
Ever notice how some places just feel like *home*? Case in point: two livable units a hop, skip and a jump from Honoli'i Beach. The Koi Room is spacious (500 sq ft) and modern-chic, with a gleaming hardwood floor and koi pond outside. The Hula Room

Hilo Honu Inn   GREG ELMS

is even bigger, containing two beds, plus a lounging area with two plump, inviting sofas. Outside, find a pool and 'surfer shack' patio facing the eastern horizon. Ask the host about surfing lessons! The highway turnoff to this B&B is just past the 4-mile marker (but less than 2 miles from downtown Hilo) on Nahala St.

BAY HOUSE B&B
B&B $$

Map p174; ☎ 961-6311, 888-235-8195; www.bay househawaii.com; 42 Pukihae St; r incl breakfast $150; 🖳

Just across the Singing Bridge, find three immaculate guest rooms within eyeshot (and earshot) of the bay. Tastefully tropical themed, with classy hardwood and granite floors, each room includes a top-quality king bed, TV and private lanai (for that sunrise cup of coffee). The foyer contains a shared kitchenette and sitting area. Charming hosts are longtime residents who respect guests' privacy.

HILO HONU INN
B&B $$$

Map p170; ☎ 935-4325; www.hilohonu.com; 465 Haili St; r incl breakfast $140-250; 🖳

In a lovely retro home, three custom-designed guest rooms accommodate different budgets. A worthy splurge, the Samurai Suite is utterly memorable, with genuine Japanese detailing, plus tatami floor, *furo* (soaking tub), tea room and sweeping (if distant) views of Hilo Bay. The two-room Bali Hai Suite is tropical themed, with a delicious 'rainfall shower,' while the smallest Honu's Nest is comfy for two.

WATERFALLS INN B&B
B&B $$$

Map p174; ☎ 969-3407, 888-808-4456; www .waterfallsinn.com; 240 Kaiulani St; r incl breakfast $160-225; 🏃 🖳

Choose from four spacious, immaculate and finely appointed rooms in a stately 1916 historic home. Gleaming hardwood, marble and granite floors, plus original fixtures, add a touch of elegance. Ideal for guests who prefer privacy over a chatty host. Savor homemade granola and *akala* (Hawaiian raspberry) butter.

AT THE BEACH WITH FRIENDS
B&B $$$

Map p170; ☎ 934-8040; www.bed-and-breakfast -hilo-hawaii.com; 369 Nene St; r incl breakfast $165-185; 🖳

Indulge your beach-house fantasy at this lushly landscaped B&B across from Leleiwi Beach. The well-designed rooms are quiet (with insulated walls and ceilings) and overlook a beautiful anchialine pond and jungly foliage. Guests share a pleasant common area stocked with snacks, books, CDs and other homey touches. Wi-fi, a computer and a printer are available. Generous breakfast spread includes a hearty egg or cheese dish.

SHIPMAN HOUSE B&B
B&B $$$

Map p174; ☎ 934-8002, 800-627-8447; www .hilo-hawaii.com; 131 Kaiulani St; r incl breakfast $219-249; 🖳

The Shipman family's grand Victorian mansion is peerless in historical significance. Queen Lili'uokalani played the grand piano, while Jack London slept in the guest cottage. Surrounded by museum-quality antiques, the three rooms in the main house are sedate and finely (although not luxuriously) furnished. Out back in the cottage, the two rooms are more casual and airy. Welcoming hosts go the extra mile for guests.

Of Hilo's two hostels near Onekahakaha Beach, your best bet is **Hilo Bay Hostel Tropical Gardens** (Map p170; ☎ 217-9650; www.geocities.com /hilobayhostelgardens; 1477 Kalaniana'ole Ave; dm $25, r with shared bathroom $65), a tiny branch of Hilo Bay Hostel sitting smack in a lush tropical garden. Space is limited (four dorm beds and four private rooms), so book in advance. A distant second choice is grungy, forlorn **Arnott's Lodge** (Map p170; ☎ 969-7097; www.arnottslodge.com; 98 Apapane Rd; tent sites $10, dm/r with shared bathroom $20/60, r/ste $70/130; 🖳), a spread-out hostel that's seen better days. Staffers are polite enough but can seem lackadaisical. Tents occupy a crowded open lawn and use outdoor showers.

Other B&B recommendations include the following:

Emeraldview Guesthouse (Map p170; ☎ 961-5736; www.emeraldview.com; 272 Kaiulani St; r incl breakfast $220; 🖳) Pluses include a scenic river view from room lanai, stylishly appointed rooms, fine art from Asia and cooked breakfasts. The minus is the steep price. Host is fluent in Japanese.

Hale Kai Hawaii (off Map p170; ☎ 935-6330; www .halekaihawaii.com; 111 Honoli'i Pl; r incl breakfast $160; 🖳 🛁) Four rooms enjoy panoramic ocean view, including Honoli'i Beach surfing and Hilo in the distance. Guests rave about the breakfasts. Kids 13 and older only. The highway turnoff to this B&B is Pauka'a Dr, just south of the 5-mile marker.

Holmes' Sweet Home (off Map p170; ☎ 961-9089; www.hilohawaiibandb.com; 107 Koula St; r incl breakfast $80-95; 🖳) A friendly, lived-in B&B provides comfy rooms (both wheelchair accessible) with private entrances, and a large common area with full-sized fridge and microwave. The $95 room, with queen and twin beds, high ceiling and double sink, is especially pleasant.

The Inn at Kulaniapia Falls (off Map p170; ☎ 935-6789, 866-935-6789; www.waterfall.net; r $120-140, cottages $175; 🖳) You'll either like or dislike the winding drive up Amau'ulu Rd to this secluded inn. But all will admire the verdant setting, complete with 120ft waterfall. Rooms are exquisitely appointed, with marble-tile bath and balcony. Vibe is more businesslike than homespun.

GETTING THERE & AWAY
Air

The **Hilo International Airport** (ITO; ☎ 934-5838; www.state.hi.us/dot/airports/hawaii/ito) receives mostly interisland commuters.

Bus

The **Mo'oheau bus terminal** (Map p174; 329 Kamehameha Ave) is the main station for the Hele-On Bus (see p290). All intraisland buses stop here. Routes go to Waikoloa, Honoka'a, Kailua-Kona, Pahoa, Hawai'i Volcanoes National Park, Ka'u and other towns in between. Check the website for current schedules (www.hawaii-county.com/mass_transit/heleonbus.html).

Car & Motorcycle

The drive from Hilo to Kailua-Kona (via Waimea) is 92 miles and takes 2½ hours; for other driving times and distances, see p291. See p290 for rental information.

Hilo's typical 'scattered showers' weather might deter you, but **Hilo Harley-Davidson** (Map p170; ☎ 934-9090; 200 Kanoelehua Ave; per day $125) does brisk business with its small fleet of Big Twin/V-Rod bikes. The prime destination? Hawai'i Volcanoes National Park.

GETTING AROUND
To/From the Airport

Rental-car booths and taxis are located right outside the baggage-claim area. The approximate cab fare from the airport to downtown Hilo is $15.

Bicycle

Cycling is more recreation than transportation in Hilo. Rental outfits in Kailua-Kona (p71) are generally bigger and better, but here are two longtime stores:

Da Kine Bike Shop (Map p174; ☎ 934-9861; www.bicyclehawaii.com; 18 Furneaux Lane; ⏰ noon-6pm Mon-Fri, 9am-3pm Sat) Reasonable rates for used bikes; call first for availability. Custom cycling tours.

Mid-Pacific Wheels (Map p170; ☎ 935-6211; www.midpacificwheels.com; 1133-C Manono St; ⏰ 9am-6pm Mon-Sat, 11am-5pm Sun) Large shop rents mountain bikes for $15 to $20 per day.

Bus

The Hele-On Bus makes weekday rounds covering popular destinations, including the following:

No 4 Kaumana Goes five times daily (from 7:35am to 2:20pm) to Hilo Public Library and Hilo Medical Center.

No 6 Waiakea-Uka Goes five times daily (from 7:05am to 3:05pm) to the University of Hawai'i at Hilo and Prince Kuhio Plaza.

No 7 Downtown Hilo Goes a dozen times daily (from 7am to 9pm) to Prince Kuhio Plaza.

Car & Motorcycle

Driving is the predominant mode of transportation in Hilo, and free parking is generally available. Downtown street parking is limited to two hours. Finding a space is easy except during the Saturday and Wednesday farmers market.

Taxi

Call **Marshall's Taxi** (☎ 936-2654) or **Percy's Taxi** (☎ 969-7060).

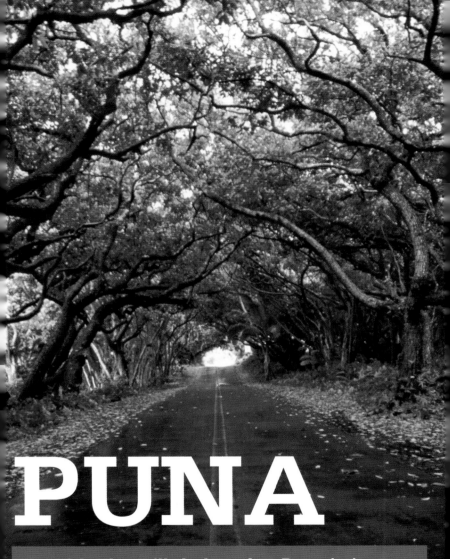

PUNA

Any islander will declare that Puna is its own world, not far away but *far out*. The driving force is change. Here, the original plantation community has been replaced by a new, eclectic population: mainland retirees, nouveau hippies, off-the-grid minimalists, funky artists, New Age seekers, Hawaiian sovereignty activists, organic farmers and, of course, *pakalolo* (marijuana) growers. While different (and sometimes dissonant) from one another, these Punatics relish the laid-back, wristwatch-free lifestyle. They share a deep affinity for the volatile land, which Kilauea Volcano has repeatedly slathered with lava. This sultry place can lure you in – if you're so inclined.

PUNA
ITINERARIES

IN ONE DAY *This leg: 40 miles*

❶ PAHOA (p197) If any Big Island town beckons offbeat, New Age types, it's Pahoa, where people come to escape the straitjacket of closed-toe shoes and 9-to-5 schedules.

❷ LAVA TREE STATE MONUMENT (p132) Start your first morning by touring this unique, if oddly deserted landscape of lava 'trees' and lush greenery.

❸ CAPE KUMUKAHI (p201) Proceed eastward toward the coast, where nothing captures Puna more than the sights along scenic **Red Road (Highway 137)**. Start with the bumpy drive to the **Kumukahi Lighthouse**, walk to the coast and breath the fresh air from **Hawaii's easternmost point**.

❹ KAPOHO TIDE POOLS (p201) Along the way, don't miss a chance to explore lava-rock tide pools, large and small.

❺ AHALANUI BEACH PARK (p201) Next, take a dip in Puna's famous **hot pond** and enjoy a picnic lunch by the ocean.

❻ NEW KAIMU BLACK-SAND BEACH (p203) For a fascinating look at a beach in the making, walk over the 1990 lava flow to the coast near the former village of **Kalapana**. That's what two decades of wave action can do.

❼ PAHOA DINING (p197) End your day with dinner back in Pahoa. The selection of restaurants is limited (and not quite gourmet), but it's ideal for the indecisive – and for rubbing shoulders with the locals. **Luquin's Mexican Restaurant** is a lively hang-out spot, while **Paolo's Bistro** and **Ning's Thai Cuisine** are small-town cozy.

IN TWO DAYS *This leg: 20 miles*

❽ ALOHA OUTPOST INTERNET CAFÉ (p197) Follow the one-day itinerary and then enjoy the luxury of a second day, starting at this local hangout. Expect good strong coffee, a home-cooked breakfast, town gossip and, yes, cheap wi-fi.

❾ MAKU'U CRAFT & FARMERS MARKET (p197) If it's Sunday, head early to the island's funkiest farmers market, where vendors sell crafts, honey, bonsai, shave ice, sarongs, fresh-cooked street food – and even some produce.

❿ EASTSIDE YOGA SHALA (p197) If it's not Sunday, unwind Puna style at the only established yoga studio around, which specializes in serious Ashtanga yoga, and hosts Indian-inspired singing and dancing gatherings on Saturdays.

⓫ A BEAUTIFUL DAY SPA (p195) Wind down even further with a massage or facial at this lovely rustic facility that's an affordable alternative to the chic resort spas.

⓬ DAN DE LUZ'S WOODS (p196) In the afternoon, admire the traditional woodwork of De Luz, an unpretentious island-born craftsman.

⓭ HILO COFFEE MILL (p196) End the day with two local refreshment pit stops. First, sample real Big Island coffee (from around the island) at this mill and café, where coffee is taken very seriously.

⓮ MOUNTAIN VIEW BAKERY (p196) Second, stop for a bag of plain yet strangely compelling 'stone cookies' (as in hard as stone).

FOR ECOTOURISM

❶ **HI'IAKA'S HEALING HAWAIIAN HERB GARDEN (p194)** All of Puna is rural, but along the coast the population is sparse and the spirit of old Hawai'i is palpable. Here, you'll see a variety of native and exotic plants that have medicinal properties.

❷ **ART & ORCHIDS B&B (p195)** An ideal place to stay in Kea'au, this B&B is run by an artist couple who raise egg-laying chickens on a property lush with native ohia, plus palms, bamboo, fruit and hundreds of orchids.

❸ **KAZUMURA CAVE (p196)** Explore the **world's longest lava tube**, a fascinating underground labyrinth created by an ancient lava flow. Tours run from short (one to two hours) to long (three to six hours) and vary in strenuousness.

❹ **HILO COFFEE MILL (p196)** While Kona coffee has the most cachet, beans grown in Hamakua, Ka'u and Puna are now impressing the connoisseurs. Here, you can visit the mill and do your own tastings at the **café**.

❺ **FUKU-BONSAI CULTURAL CENTER (p195)** While bonsai is typically a private, at-home endeavor, this center grows commercial, starter plants for novices. It's an ideal introduction to this intriguing Japanese art.

❻ **AKATSUKA ORCHID GARDENS (p195)** The Big Island's biggest agricultural crop is now tropical flowers and nursery plants. Established in 1974, this pioneering orchid farm is commercial and touristy but spectacular, with hundreds of blooming varieties.

PUNA

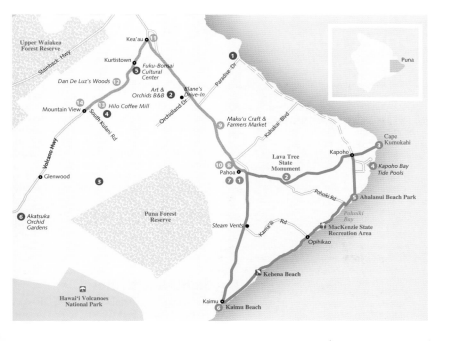

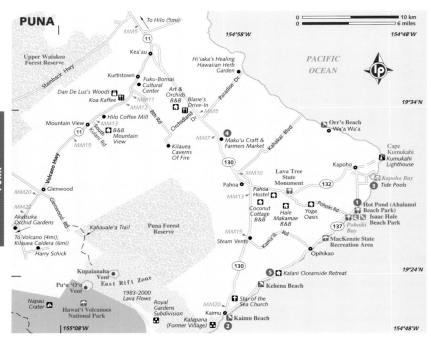

Don't Miss

- **Mountain View Bakery's 'stone cookies'** (p196)
- **Ahalanui hot pond** (p201)
- **Native Guide Hawaii** (☎ 982-7575; www.nativeguidehawaii.com; tour incl lunch $300; ⊙ by appointment) Take a Puna tour with Warren Costa, who's pricey but knowledgeable, pleasant and genuinely local.
- **Prominent artists Jane and Linus Chao's paintings in Bed & Breakfast Mountain View** (p196)
- **Kumukahi Lighthouse and walking beyond to the coast** (p201)
- **New Kaimu black-sand beach** (p203)
- **Dan De Luz's Woods** (p196)
- **The dream beach-house life at Hale O Naia** (p201)
- **Sampling Big Island coffee at Hilo Coffee Mill** (p196)
- **Hanging out with the locals at Aloha Outpost Internet Café** (p197)

KEA'AU

Puna's largest town, Kea'au, is only 2000 strong, but its sprawling subdivisions of Hawaiian Paradise Park, Hawaiian Beaches, Hawaiian Acres and Orchidland Estates are home to 15,000 residents and counting. This bedroom community commutes to Hilo en masse on weekdays: by all means, avoid the rush hour. To get here, exit Volcano Hwy (Hwy 11) at Kea'au–Pahoa Rd (Hwy 130), which is also nicknamed Kea'au Bypass Rd, Pahoa Bypass Rd and Kalapana Hwy.

Puna's varied communities grow increasingly 'alternative' from northwest to southeast. Thus, Kea'au is a relatively standard town, with county gas, electricity, telephone service and so forth. The Kea'au Shopping Center, at the junction of Volcano Hwy and Kea'au–Pahoa Rd, provides basic services, including a post office, an ATM and grocers.

Sights & Activities

Learn about medicinal plants at 🌺 **Hi'iaka's Healing Hawaiian Herb Garden** (☎ 966-6126; www

HIGHLIGHTS

❶ **BEST BEACH:** Ahalanui Beach Park (p201)
❷ **BEST VIEW:** New Kaimu black-sand beach (p203)
❸ **BEST ACTIVITY:** Exploring the Kapoho tide pools (p201)
❹ **BEST ANYBODY GATHERING:** Maku'u Craft & Farmers Market (p197)
❺ **BEST HIPPIE GATHERING:** Ecstatic Dance (p203)

Highlights are numbered on the map on p194.

.hiiakas.com; 15-1667 2nd St, Hawaiian Paradise Park; adult/senior & child $5/3, with guided tour $15/10; ☺ by appointment), a lovingly tended acre of native, Polynesian-introduced and international herbs in a rustic, dirt-road subdivision near the coast. The founding gardener and herbalist sells *noni* (Indian mulberry) and kava concoctions, offers gardening workshops and rents out a whimsical gazebo cottage for internships (per week $550).

Treat yourself to a massage, facial or body wrap at **A Beautiful Day Spa** (☎ 982-7252; www.kipukagraphics.net/scarden/dayspa.html; massages $79-99; ☺ by appointment). Ask about special retreat packages and the cottage for rent.

Eating & Sleeping

🏵 ART & ORCHIDS B&B   B&B $$

our pick ☎ 982-8197; www.artandorchids.com; 16-1504 39th Ave; r incl breakfast $90-115; 🖵

The more you see it, the more you'll like it: three airy, tastefully decorated rooms (go for the apartment-sized Garden Room). Spacious common area with kitchen and phone. Fine glass, mosaic and paper art by the friendly host couple. Generous breakfast including eggs from household chickens. Solar-powered hot water. Free use of washer-dryer. Babysitting services ($20 per hour). You can't top this!

Gourmet palates, you're out of luck. Less picky eaters can try **Blane's Drive-In** (☎ 982-9800; 16-127 Orchidland Dr; mains $3-8; ☺ 6:30am-9pm), halfway between Kea'au and Pahoa, where locals can't get enough artery-clogging *loco moco*

(rice, fried egg and hamburger patty topped with gravy) and plate lunches. For sit-down dining, your only option is **Paradise Bar & Grill** (☎ 966-7589; Kea'au Shopping Center, 16-586 Old Volcano Rd; mains $5-10; ☺ 11am-10pm Mon-Fri, to 11pm Sat & Sun), with standard pub fare and nightly live music. Instead, try Koa Kaffee (p196) in Mountain View or stock up at the town's supermarket and health food store.

HIGHWAY 11 (VOLCANO HIGHWAY)

Between Kea'au and Volcano, the highway whisks past blink-and-miss communities that were once sugar plantations. The area seems sparsely populated, but beyond the highway the land is now a vast grid of residential subdivisions. There's no significant town here, but the handful of worthy attractions are definitely worth a stop.

Sights

🏵 FUKU-BONSAI CULTURAL CENTER
☎ 982-9880; www.fukubonsai.com; Ola'a Rd; admission free; ☺ 8am-4pm Mon-Sat

Visit this working nursery for an excellent introduction to Japanese bonsai, the art of training miniaturized trees into aesthetic shapes. In addition to seeing the hundreds of bonsai on display, you can chat with staff and perhaps buy an indoor bonsai as a home experiment. The turnoff is just past the 9-mile marker. Website is overwhelmingly jammed with info.

AKATSUKA ORCHID GARDENS
☎ 967-8234, 888-967-6669; www.akatsukaorchid.com; Volcano Hwy; admission free; ☺ 8:30am-5pm

Popular among the tour-bus set, these gardens are a must for orchid lovers. Mind you, anyone would admire the hundreds of ever-blooming plants on display. Besides cut and planted orchids, you can buy packaged (inspected for export) seeds and starters for Kona coffee, papaya, guava, hibiscus and other tropical flora. Located past the 22-mile marker.

Eating & Shopping

The residential community of **Mountain View** is only a blip along the Volcano Hwy, but

PUNA

WORLD'S LONGEST LAVA TUBE

Kazumura Cave was formed about 500 years ago by Kilauea Volcano. With almost 41 miles surveyed, it is the world's longest lava tube. (It's also the seventh-longest cave in the USA and the 28th worldwide.) Ancient Hawaiians made much use of the cave, but few modern-day residents have firsthand familiarity with it. In 1966 one of its many openings was designated as a fallout shelter. By the early 1970s, the caving community began noticing Kazumura Cave when new invertebrate species were discovered here.

Today there is much destruction to the cave from overlying roads and subdivisions (eg sewer pipes in the cave, gray-water pollution, garbage dumps), and trash and damage from recreational caving.

Flash photography is allowed on tour, but the bright light tends to wash out the actual depth and detail. Remember to wear sturdy shoes and long pants. Two tours are available:

- **our pick** **Harry Schick** (☎ 967-7208; www.fortunecity.com/oasis/angkor/176; off Volcano Hwy, past 22-mile marker; tours from $10; ⏲ by appointment) Schick accidentally discovered that his property sat above the cave when blasting a cesspool in the mid-1990s. Since then, he's become a self-taught expert on lava caves and gives small tours (four to six people max) at low cost. On the shortest, easiest tour, participants must climb ladders and walk over rocky terrain. Age 10 and above.
- **Kilauea Caverns of Fire** (☎ 217-2363; www.kilaueacavernsoffire.com; off Volcano Hwy, before 11-mile marker; tours $29-79; ⏲ by appointment) For better or worse, this tour company is run as a commercial enterprise, and it shows. There's a small visitor center with flush toilets and large tour groups are allowed.

Other lava tubes to explore include **Pua Po'o** (p219) at Hawai'i Volcanoes National Park and **Kula Kai Caverns** (p239) in Ka'u.

it does boast a handful of worthy stops. Past the 12-mile marker, visit **Dan De Luz's Woods** (☎ 968-6607; Hwy 11; ⏲ 9am-5pm), where the master craftsman, now in his 70s, transforms native hardwoods into graceful bowls, platters and furniture. You'll probably find De Luz in a well-worn T-shirt talking story out front. Adjacent **Koa Kaffee** (☎ 968-1129; Hwy 11; sandwiches $5, dinner $8-10; ⏲ 7am-8pm Mon-Fri, to 9pm Sat & Sun), run by De Luz' wife, is a friendly home-style diner with mostly meaty local *grinds* (food), from Portuguese bean soup to chicken *katsu* (fried fillets).

Sample Hamakua, Puna, Ka'u and other coffees at **Hilo Coffee Mill** (☎ 968-1333; www.hilocoffeemill.com; Hwy 11; ⏲ 10am-4pm Mon-Fri), a tidy café, retail shop and roaster between the 12- and 13-mile markers. The café sells carefully brewed coffee and espresso drinks, while the working mill processes beans for 100 growers from Puna and Ka'u, and 20 from Hamakua. Outdoor patio seating with free wi-fi.

At the 14-mile marker, veer off the highway to stop at old-fashioned **Mountain View Bakery** (☎ 968-6353; Old Volcano Rd; ⏲ 7:30am-1pm Mon-Sat), renowned for its 'stone cookies' – plain, homey, perfect for dipping and hard as stone (not really). Call first as opening days and hours are changeable.

Sleeping

BUTTERFLY INN Inn $
☎ 966-7936, 800-546-2442; www.thebutterflyinn.com; Kurtistown; s/d with shared bathroom $55/65
Since 1987, owners Kay and Patty have welcomed women to stay at their comfortable home in Kurtistown. Two tidy rooms share an ample kitchen, living room, dining deck, bathroom and outdoor hot tub. Single female travelers will appreciate the safe, supportive environment.

BED & BREAKFAST

MOUNTAIN VIEW B&B $
☎ 968-6868, 888-698-9896; www.bbmtview.com; r incl breakfast $55-95
This place offers four comfortable rooms (two with private bathroom) in the warm home of famous Big Island artists Jane and Linus Chao. Hidden on a quiet road a mile from Hwy 11 and surrounded by pretty

landscaping, the couple's large house (built for grown kids who never stayed) is graced with their splendid art and genuine aloha.

PAHOA

Pahoa is an old plantation town, with high wooden sidewalks and peeling paint. But today it's also marked by a bohemian, hippie edge. Expect to see dreadlocks, piercings, tattoos, bare feet, natural foods, alternative lifestyles and mostly haole.

The main town thoroughfare is signposted as Pahoa Village Rd but also goes by Government Main Rd, Old Government Rd, Main St, Puna Rd and Pahoa Rd. In town there's a convenience store, banks with ATMs and a **post office** (☎ 965-1158; 15-2859 Pahoa Village Rd; 8:30am-4pm Mon-Fri, 11am-2pm Sat).

Puna's unofficial hangout and town square is **Aloha Outpost Internet Café** (☎ 965-8333; www.alohaoutpost.com; Pahoa Village Rd; all-day wi-fi $3, internet per 30min $3; 6am-8pm), with plenty of computers and a sweet wi-fi deal. Owner LaMont Carroll is your quintessential Punatic with all the local scoops; also check out the bulletin board. Aloha Outpost is also a legit café, with impressive sandwiches (under $6), fresh baked goods, Tropical Dreams ice cream and espresso drinks.

The other internet café, **Sirius Coffee Connection** (☎ 965-8555; www.siriuscoffeeconnection.com; Pahoa Village Rd; internet per hr $3; 7am-5pm Mon-Fri, 8am-4pm Sat, 8am-3pm Sun), offers excellent coffee and both wi-fi and computers.

Sights & Activities

Now a major attraction, the **Maku'u Craft & Farmers Market** (8am-2pm Sun) is a combination of carnival, flea market, craft fair and, yes, farmers market. Park in expanded lots on the Kea'au–Pahoa Rd between the 7- and 8-mile markers. Bring an appetite for the numerous food vendors, from *hulihuli* (rotisserie) chicken to crepes and shave ice. The comparatively small and deserted **Pahoa Farmers Market** (8am-3pm Sun), behind Luquin's, should switch to a different day.

For lap swimming, try the fantastic outdoor, Olympic-size pool at **Pahoa Community Aquatic Center** (Kauhale St; 9am-4pm), behind the Pahoa Neighborhood Facility; there's also a kiddie pool.

Wake up with Mysore-style Ashtanga yoga at **Eastside Yoga Shala** (☎ 965-0010; www.eastsideyogahawaii.com; Pahoa Village Rd; drop-in class $13), where you can also book an hour-long massage for a reasonable $65. On Saturdays, the studio hosts a free Vedic *kirtan* (sacred Sikh singing) and dance gathering. Check the website for special offerings such as Sanskrit chanting.

Eating & Drinking

For casual café dining (including freshly made sandwiches and espresso), try Aloha Outpost Internet Café (opposite).

PAHOA'S VILLAGE CAFÉ   Café $
☎ 965-7200; 15-2471 Pahoa Village Rd; mains $7-9; 8am-2pm Wed, Thu & Sun, 8am-2pm & 5:30-9pm Fri & Sat
For good American diner food, this pleasant café is it, serving ample breakfast omelettes, crepes and waffles; gourmet veggie sandwiches; and steak dinners for meat eaters.

NING'S THAI CUISINE   Thai $$
☎ 965-7611; 15-2955 Government Main Rd; dishes $4.95-11.95; lunch & dinner Mon-Sat, dinner Sun
Pahoa's tried-and-true Thai restaurant Ning's remains the best, with interesting varieties of curry, perky salads and an emphasis on local, organic ingredients. A top takeout option, too.

Ukulele for sale at Maku'u Market GREG ELMS

Top Picks

PUNA FOR KIDS

- **Kazumura Cave** (p196)
- **Kapoho tide pools** (p201)
- **Ahalanui hot pond** (p201)
- **Maku'u Craft & Farmers Market** (p197)
- **Tropical Dreams ice cream** (p197)

LUQUIN'S MEXICAN
RESTAURANT   Mexican $$
☎ 965-9990; 15-2942 Pahoa Village Rd; mains
$8-15; ☺ 7am-9pm

Always fun and lively, this Pahoa institution is *the* place to hang out and talk story. Connoisseurs might pooh-pooh the island-style Mexican fare, but the kitchen turns out decent classics and nice tofu options for vegetarians. Come to check out a slice of life, Puna style.

PAOLO'S BISTRO   Italian $$
☎ 965-7033; Pahoa Village Rd; mains $11-20;
☺ dinner Tue-Sun

Feel like a welcome houseguest at this cozy, eight-table Northern Italian eatery, a Pahoa favorite for two decades. Pasta, meat and fish dishes are well executed.

KALEO'S BAR & GRILL   Hawaii Regional $$$
our pick ☎ 965-5600; 15-2969 Pahoa Village Rd;
mains $16-25; ☺ dinner Tue-Sun

When Kaleo's opened in 2008, Pahoa finally got an eatery that would impress the food-

ies. Creative mains such as vodka penne pasta with mahimahi are gourmet quality yet portions are satisfying. Live music nightly.

SHAKA'S
☎ 965-1133; 15-2929 Pahoa Village Rd; ☺ from 4pm Mon-Sat

One of the island's best night spots, Shaka's is a casual bar (don't bother dressing up) with pool tables, dance floor and a mixed gay-and-straight crowd. Live entertainment includes DJs, karaoke and live bands from Hawaiian to electronic.

For takeout, **Island Naturals Market & Deli** (☎ 965-8322; 15-1403 Pahoa Village Rd; ☺ 7:30am-8pm Mon-Sat, 9am-7pm Sun) carries gourmet sandwiches, salads, baked goods and hot mains. Also try **Pahoa Natural Groceries** (☎ 965-8322; 15-1403 Government Main Rd; ☺ 7:30am-7:30pm Mon-Sat, to 6pm Sun), the other hub for Pahoa's hippie contingent, which offers pricey but interesting ethnic dishes in a hot-food bar.

Sleeping

The B&Bs listed are excellent but located outside of town. The inn is humbler but phenomenal value.

PAHOA HOSTEL   Hostel $
☎ 965-0317; www.pahoahostel.com; 13-1132 Kahukai St; campsites $10, dm $15; ▣

On an organic farm 6 miles from Pahoa, this place is ideal for low-maintenance,

---

INVASION OF THE EARSPLITTING AMPHIBIANS

Hawaii's most wanted alien is the Puerto Rican **coqui frog**, only an inch long. Why? *Da buggah* is loud! At sunset, coquis begin their nightly chirping (a two-tone 'ko-kee' call), which can register between 90 and 100 decibels from 2ft away. Even at a distance, their chorus maintains 70 decibels, equivalent to a vacuum cleaner. For a demo, visit www.hear.org/Alien SpeciesInHawaii/species/frogs.

Coquis accidentally reached the Hawaiian Islands around 1988, and they've proliferated wildly on the Big Island. Around Lava Tree State Monument, densities are the highest in the state and twice that of Puerto Rico. Besides causing a nightly racket, coquis are disrupting the ecosystem by eating too many of the bugs that feed native birds.

The University of Hawai'i's **College of Tropical Agriculture & Human Resources** (www.ctahr .hawaii.edu/coqui) held the 'First International Conference on the Coqui Frog' in February 2008, illustrating the serious state and county anti-coqui campaign. Likewise, some homeowners are vigilant about eliminating their habitat, spraying foliage with citric acid or hydrated lime, and searching with flashlights to nail each noisemaker within hearing range. But most survive. Chances are, evening frogsong is here to stay.

PUNA

Top Picks

LAVA-ROCK WONDERS
- **Lava Tree State Monument** (below)
- **Kazumura Cave** (p196)
- **Kapoho tide pools** (p201)
- **Ahalanui Beach Park** (p201)
- **New Kaimu black-sand beach** (p203)

backpacker types. Rates include tents, mattresses and linens, plus communal kitchen, nearby phone and internet access, and use of bikes and beach gear. You can also rent a cozy converted bus (sleeps two) in the midst of a banana patch for $20 a night. If you're keen on farming, ask owner Ed Frazer about doing work exchange.

ISLAND PARADISE INN   Inn $
☎ 990-0234; www.islandparadiseinn.com; Pahoa Village Rd; r $40-50; 🖳
A budget traveler's dream, this inn comprises tidy little cottages converted from former plantation workers' houses. All come with kitchen, cable TV, free wi-fi and shared phone, but they vary in size and decor (check the website for descriptions). Run with aloha and TLC, these in-town cottages are truly a find.

HALE MAKAMAE B&B   B&B $$
☎ 965-7015; www.bnb-aloha.com; 13-3315 Makamae St; r incl breakfast $80, 1br/2br $110/135; 🖳
In a clean-cut neighborhood, this B&B is immaculate, family-friendly and quite a bargain (the $20 additional-guest fee is steep). The suites are especially comfy, with well-equipped kitchenettes and enough space to kick back. Hot breakfast is served in a Hawaiian-style breakfast room with a *lauhala* (pandanus leaf) floor and blooming orchids. Hosts are German fluent.

COCONUT COTTAGE B&B   B&B $$
☎ 965-0973, 866-204-7444; www.coconutcottage hawaii.com; 13-1139 Leilani Ave; r incl breakfast $110-140; 🖳
If aesthetics are a high priority, this four-room B&B will surely please. The Garden Bungalow, a studio cottage, is comfiest, with kitchenette and sofas. Bonuses include gazebo hot tub, cotton robes, 500-DVD library, jungly anthurium garden and convenient location just off the Kalapana Hwy.

Getting There & Away

By all means, avoid driving toward Hilo in the early morning and toward Kea'au and Pahoa in the late afternoon. The free Hele-On Bus (p290) travels between Hilo, Kea'au and Pahoa on the No 9 Pahoa route.

HIGHWAY 132

Explore the tip of Puna along the triangle formed by three highways: Hwy 132, Red Rd (Hwy 137) and the Kalapana Hwy (Hwy 130).

Lava Tree State Monument

Driving along Hwy 132 under the Tree Tunnel, a thick canopy of albizia, feels like an escape to a storybook forest – and sets the mood for this park area dedicated to 18th-century 'lava trees.' In 1790, Kilauea Volcano spewed a flood of lava up to 10ft deep through the rain forest, enveloping ohia trees and then receding. The lava hardened around the trees, which burned away, creating molds of lava that still remain.

The lava formations vary in size and shape, blending smoothly with living trees. In the early 2000s, the dense foliage was woefully thinned when locals tried to eradicate the proliferating coqui frog and other invasive species.

Beware of mosquitoes and unsavory characters in this scenic but deserted area. Decently clean restrooms are available.

Kapoho

Hwy 132 goes east until it meets Red Rd at 'Four Corners' near Kapoho. You won't see an actual town anymore, but Kapoho's history makes an interesting tale. It was a farming town until January 1960, when a volcanic fissure let loose a half-mile-long curtain of fiery lava in the midst of a nearby sugarcane field. The main flow of *pahoehoe* (smooth lava) ran toward the ocean, but a pokier offshoot of *'a'a* (rough, jagged lava) crept toward the town, burying orchid farms in its path. Two weeks later the lava buried Kapoho, including nearly 100 homes and businesses.

PUNA

ISLAND VOICES

NAME: ALAN KUWAHARA
OCCUPATION: SECOND-GENERATION ANTHURIUM GROWER, HAWAIIAN GREENHOUSE NURSERY, PAHOA
RESIDENCE: HILO

Where did you grow up? I lived on Oʻahu until the sixth grade, when my father moved our family to Pahoa, where he grew up. My graduating class at Pahoa High School had only 26 students. It was almost like family. We all knew which kid led the exam curve and which brought up the end. We knew who would be on the varsity basketball team. It was great; everyone had a place.

Has Pahoa changed since your childhood here? Pahoa is nothing like the town I knew in the 1960s and 1970s. The locals of my generation have moved out. To folks with kids, Hilo has better schools, better opportunities.

How did you start growing anthuriums? In the early 1960s, my father started growing anthuriums with new methods, such as using artificial shade instead of *hapuʻu* (ferns) or citrus trees. By the 1970s, the anthurium market exploded in popularity. First the Italian importers came, hardly speaking any English but offering to buy the whole supply. Soon came the Germans, then the Swedes, Austrians, and the rest of the Europeans.

Are most anthuriums grown in Puna? I'd say that 95% of the state's anthuriums are grown here. We have relatively cheap land, an ideal climate, a labor force willing to work outdoors, and an ample supply of lava-rock cinders [the growing medium].

What are some challenges of being in agriculture? Your livelihood can change almost instantly. Around 1980, a mysterious epidemic hit the island's anthurium crops. Plants would turn yellow and die. We had to destroy acres. The industry spent millions to discover the cause, a little-known bacterium. When we were struggling, foreign competition from the Philippines, Taiwan and Mauritius filled the gap. They found a ready-made market that we had built.

In a small, family business, the work never ends. And farm costs keep rising, for everything from transportation to shipping boxes to employee benefits. We'd rather see our children enjoy easier lives than continue the business.

Why do you think people like anthuriums? Anthuriums are still special and exotic. People are excited to receive them, especially if they've never seen them before. The flowers last at least two weeks – and up to a month. Nowadays there are many colors – white, purple, green – but at Christmas and on Valentine's Day, everybody wants red.

When the lava approached the sea at **Cape Kumukahi**, it parted around the lighthouse, which alone survived. Old-timers say that the lighthouse keeper offered a meal to Pele, who appeared disguised as an old woman on the eve of the disaster, and so she spared the structure.

You might hear about Champagne Pond, a volcanically heated pond near the lighthouse. Overuse, particularly by tourists and tour groups, has created sanitation problems and incited controversy about the pond's condition. To reach the pond, you need a 4WD. We recommend visiting Ahalanui

DETOUR ➡

KUMUKAHI LIGHTHOUSE & WA'A WA'A

The old lighthouse that Pele spared is just a tall, white-painted metal structure, but it's worth braving the unpaved 1.5-mile road from 'Four Corners' to the lighthouse. **Cape Kumukahi** is the easternmost point in the state. Breathe deeply: the air here is among the freshest in the world.

From the lighthouse, trek 10 minutes over jagged lava toward the sea. You'll reach a rugged beach with **tide pools** amid the rocky coast, where locals might be gathering seafood. The surf is too rough for swimming, but the remote setting is memorable.

For a wild off-road adventure, go north at 'Four Corners' – you'll traverse an epic dirt path through a dense, vine-draped forest of ancient mango trees to **Wa'a Wa'a**. Standard cars can make it, but *barely*. The narrow, cratered road is no picnic, and it's a mud bath after rainfall. If you decide to hoof it, beware of merciless mosquitoes. A contingent does live off the grid here, so mind the numerous 'Kapu' signs (protecting sacred burial sites or private property) and go slow. Remember that you're the outsider. After about 2 miles, you'll be shocked to see houses. After 4 miles you'll reach **Orr's Beach**, scenic but unswimmable, shaded by ironwood trees. Scramble over boulders along the shore, or simply sit, look and listen.

Kapoho tide pools GREG ELMS

Check listings at www.vrbo.com. One gem is **ourpick** **Hale O Naia** (☎ 965-5340; www.hale-o-naia .com; Kapoho Beach Rd; r incl breakfast $90-110, ste $175), which qualifies as a Fantasy Beach House. All units feature gleaming hardwoods, ocean-view lanai, wraparound windows and use of a sauna and whirlpool tub. The sprawling Master Suite is a worthy splurge.

Kapoho Tide Pools

The countless tide pools along Kapoho's lava rock are full of thriving marine life, including coral, eels, Moorish idols, butterfly fish, sea cucumbers and much more. Officially named the Wai Opae Tide Pools Marine Life Conservation District in 2003, these shallow pools are fed by gentle waves, broken far offshore by a shallow shelf. You can hop from pool to pool, **snorkeling** in the deeper ones.

To get here, take Red Rd south 1 mile past 'Four Corners' and turn *makai* (sea-ward) onto Kapoho Kai Dr, which ends at Wai Opae. Turn left and park in the designated lot (open from 7am to 7pm). No facilities.

Ahalanui Beach Park

Among the island's volcanically heated '**hot ponds**,' Ahalanui is the most accessible and well used. Surrounded by palm trees, it's an idyllic spot, but you'll never find solitude

Beach Park's hot pond instead – and leaving Champagne Pond for the locals.

RED ROAD (HIGHWAY 137)

This coastal highway is nicknamed because it was originally paved with red cinders from the 1960 Kapoho lava flow. Although now mostly black asphalt, it's still one of the island's most scenic drives.

Vacation rentals, many in gated communities, are ever-increasing in the prime, ocean-front Kapoho Vacationland subdivision.

PUNA

The 'hot pond' at Ahalanui Beach Park   GREG ELMS

here. The spring-fed thermal pool is deep enough for **swimming**, with water temperatures averaging 90°F. Waves crash over the seawall protecting the pool on the ocean side, bringing in tropical fish during high tide and allowing the water to circulate. Still, heed warning signs about bacterial infection: shower immediately.

The park is officially open from 7am to 7pm, but the gates are never locked and nighttime soaks are possible. There are picnic tables, portable toilets and a lifeguard daily.

Isaac Hale Beach Park

This popular beach at **Pohoiki Bay** (known simply as Pohoiki) is a locals' beach – and you'll feel it, especially when it's jammed on weekends. Waters at Isaac Hale (*ha*-lay) beach are too rough for swimming, but what puts Pohoiki on the map is its surf breaks, the gnarliest on the island. How-ever, the punishing waves and sharp *wana* (sea urchins) make it doable only for advanced surfers.

Another draw is **scuba diving**, as Pohoiki Bay boasts a variety of marine life and terrain, at depths of 20ft to 100ft. While considered the best shore dive in East Hawai'i, the waters can be choppy.

In 2008 the park completed the first phase of a $4.7 million park improvement project, adding restrooms, gazebo-style pavilions, picnic tables, barbecue facilities and concrete walkways. Later construction will include basketball and tennis courts, a large pavilion, camping and possibly a skate ramp. Prior park conditions were shoddy, and camping was not recommended due to long-term squatters and lack of upkeep, but the improvements might change the park's locals-only-keep-away vibe.

MacKenzie State Recreation Area

On the one hand, this park is a spectacular picnic spot, amid groves of ironwood trees overlooking dramatic 40ft cliffs and pounding surf far below. On the other, the place is often eerily quiet and deserted. Locals agree that MacKenzie gives them the creeps. In the 1990s, crime was a problem here, and the reputation still prevails.

It's worth a stop during the day (you might think twice if you're traveling solo),

Island Insights

In 1991 Big Isle surfers lost 20 surf spots to a Kilauea lava flow. Today, Puna's major surf breaks are at **Pohoiki** (above): the beginner's First Bay, intermediate Second Bay and expert Third Bay. The last break is a Big Island monster that can top '15 feet Hawaiian' (meaning a 30ft wave face).

but go elsewhere at night. Camping is allowed, but not recommended. In addition to the spooky vibe, facilities are shabby, trash cans are often overflowing and drinking water is unavailable.

Kehena Beach

Welcome, free spirits! Let it all hang loose at this gorgeous black-sand beach at the base of a steep cliff. This **nude beach** attracts a motley crowd of hippies, locals, old and young. People aren't just lying around but they're merrily frolicking: circles of women might wave their sarongs like flags, or naked men might practice martial arts on the sand. Expect a thick cloud of *pakalolo* smoke everywhere.

On Sundays an open **drum circle** draws musicians of all shapes, sizes and skills. Although the crowd is definitely mixed, the nearby subdivisions of Puna Beach Palisades, Kalapana Seaview Estates and Kehena Beach Estates are all thriving gay communities.

During calm surf, **swimming** is possible, but mind the rip currents and undertows, especially in winter. Do not venture beyond the rocky southern point.

To get here, look for a small parking lot immediately south of the 19-mile marker. The five-minute walk down to the beach crosses jagged lava rock. Don't leave any valuables in your car.

Kalapana (Former Village)

For generations, Kalapana was a tiny, close-knit fishing village near **Kaimu Beach**, the island's most famous black-sand beach. In the 1970s, mainland haole started moving here, drawn by the rural tropical lifestyle, affordable lots and community spirit. When Kilauea began erupting in 1983, the main lava flow moved downslope west of Kalapana. Locals gave offerings to Pele, asking her to spare the village.

But in 1990 the flow changed direction and inched toward Kalapana and its 100 buildings. Residents watched lava engulf the homes they'd built with their own hands; when Star of the Sea Church was threatened, they joined together and moved it to safety less than an hour before the flow obstructed the road. Within

PUNATIC YOGA

Alternative types will find kindred spirits at two longtime yoga retreat centers here. Along Pohoiki Rd, a leafy road that intersects with Hwy 132 and Red Rd, ☀ **Yoga Oasis** (☎ 965-8460, 800-274-4446; www.yogaoasis.org; 13-678 Pohoiki Rd; s/d incl breakfast $75/100, cabins $100-145; 🖵) is a secluded, solar-powered, 26-acre center that feels intimate, with a commune vibe. On average, there are just eight to 12 guests (the maximum is 18). Don't expect posh accommodations; rugs show mildew and cabins are rustic, with simple screens and chickens parading on muddy paths. An outdoorsy yoga studio features an exotic red floor that's springy (gymnastics style). This center is nowhere near the ocean.

Along Red Rd, near Opihikao, ☀ **Kalani Oceanside Retreat** (☎ 965-7828, 800-800-6886; www.kalani.com; campsites $40, s/d $135/145, s/d cottages $150/170) is the island's largest and most commercial center, with a free-spirited, gay-friendly, alternative vibe. Since the 1970s, Kalani has offered yoga (including the nude offshoot), meditation, dance and alternative healing workshops and retreats. Spread over 120 acres, it feels like a casual resort, with a café, 25m pool, sauna and Jacuzzis (clothing optional after 5pm). Individual travelers can rent rooms in two-story cedar lodges, private cottages or tree houses. None of the accommodations have ocean views (or anything even close).

On Sundays from 10am to 1pm, Kalani hosts **Ecstatic Dance**, where hundreds of hippies dance, sit in a trance, hug, moan, go topless, sway, hum and otherwise celebrate the 'divinity' within. And you thought the hippie era was long gone?

If this sounds a tad rustic or communal for you, consider **Tara Yoga Center** (p165), a contemplative retreat on the Hamakua Coast.

the year, the village and beautiful Kaimu Beach were gone.

Interestingly the local Hawaiians were rather accepting of losing their homes to Pele. They acknowledged that things can end and change, and they had less inclination to 'control' nature. It was common to

'New' black sand beach at Kalapana

GREG ELMS

hear Hawaiians say, 'Pele's taking back the land' or 'She gave it to us and now she's reclaiming it.' They would appreciate that an ancient gravesite was spared – due to its mana (spiritual essence) – rather than only lamenting their losses.

Today Hwy 137 ends abruptly at the eastern edge of the former Kalapana, where the few houses standing had been spared. The dead-end is now a modest tourist attraction and an outpost of the Hawaiian sovereignty movement, led here by 'Uncle Robert' Keli'iho'omalu. Makeshift booths sell eruption photos, gifts, shave ice or a drink of 'awa (kava). Across the street, a drive-in eatery serves the usual heaping plates of meaty mains, rice and mac-potato salad.

The main attraction is a short path (clearly marked with red cinders) across the 1990 flow to a **new black-sand beach**, where hundreds of baby coconut palms surround

a fresh crescent of sand, still rather coarse and shiny. The water is too rough to swim. Go to witness a beach in the making.

HIGHWAY 130

Red Rd intersects the many-named Kalapana Hwy (Hwy 130), which leads north to Pahoa. At the 20-mile marker, the historic **Star of the Sea Church** (9am-4pm), nicknamed the 'Painted Church,' is noted for its trompe l'oeil murals that create an illusion of depth and expansiveness. Built in 1929, this tiny Catholic church's first priest was Father Damien, legendary for his work on Moloka'i with people suffering from leprosy. Now deconsecrated, the building will become a community cultural center.

At the 15-mile marker, 3.5 miles south of Pahoa, a faded blue 'Scenic View' highway sign points to nowhere. To solve this mystery, park and follow the well-beaten path around a steaming, shaggy spatter cone. Here, a handful of **steam vents** has been modified into a natural sauna; some have wooden planks to sit on, others have only tarps, and most accommodate one or two people. Warning: bugs are rampant, including countless cockroaches after dark. And while most folks wear swimsuits, many go au naturel.

Island Insights

For a moving account of the Kalapana tragedy, see the film *Kalapana: Death of a Hawaiian Village* at Hilo's **Lyman House Memorial Museum** (p176).

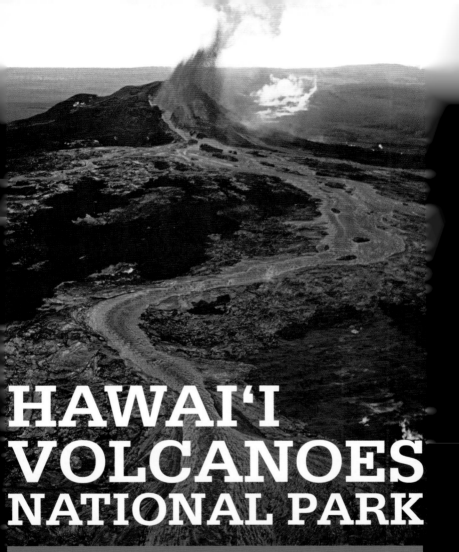

HAWAI'I VOLCANOES NATIONAL PARK

Sulfurous smoke belches from the ground so voluminously it tastes like you're sucking matches. Ribbons of red lava flow from Kilauea – the youngest and most active volcano on the planet – to the sea, boiling it on contact. Elegant palms fringe a white-sand beach backed by jet-black crystallized lava. Above it all looms a snow-capped mountain. It's safe to say there is no place on Earth like Hawai'i Volcanoes National Park, ruled over by goddess Pele. An entire day can easily be spent exploring the sights along Crater Rim Dr, but give it at least two so you can see the lava at night and the surfeit of stars once the sun goes down.

HAWAI'I VOLCANOES NATIONAL PARK
ITINERARIES

IN TWO DAYS *This leg: 75 miles*

❶ KILAUEA CRATER SCENIC DRIVE (p211) Take this 11-mile drive to see Earth science at work, jumping out to visit the Jaggar Museum (p213), to walk through the Thurston Lava Tube (p214) and to do the Kilauea Iki (p218) 4-mile loop hike.

❷ LIVE LAVA FLOW (p217) Lava in the daytime is like a baseball no-hitter: thrilling, but in an intellectual kind of way. For real action, hike out to the flow for sunset and the glowing, flowing hot lava come dark.

❸ SUNRISE AT HALEMA'UMA'U (p219) Arrive at Pele's home for sunrise and you'll surely be the only guest. The rays bouncing off Mauna Kea are dazzling, but the sulfur is noxious. Afterward, drive south on Chain of Craters Road to the Pu'u Loa Petroglyphs (p216).

❹ WINE TASTING (p226) Head to Volcano Winery to savor free samples of macadamia-nut honey wine, before grabbing a bottle of Volcano Red to sip back in the hot tub.

IN FOUR DAYS *This leg: 54 miles*

❺ NAPAU CRATER TRAIL (p222) Follow the two-day itinerary above (plus *lots* of hot-tub time) with the 18-mile round-trip hike to the Pu'u 'O'o vent, where all that lava comes from. Overnight camping is an option.

❻ GALLERY HOPPING (p226) It's like a mini-Soho up here with all the artists-in-residence. While away a rainy day visiting the Volcano Art Center, 2400° Fahrenheit and Volcano Garden Arts.

In 2003 hot lava strictly enforced the No Parking rule on Chain of Craters Rd

© KEVIN EBI / ALAMY

FOR FAMILIES

❶ KILAUEA VISITOR CENTER (p212)
Ramp up the kids by watching the visitor center's movie, with far better eruption footage than you'll see in real life, followed by the **Junior Ranger Program**. Kids learn more about volcanoes at the **Jaggar Museum's (p213)** hands-on 'Science Behind Pele' program, where they can build their own erupting volcanoes and simulate earthquakes.

❷ THURSTON LAVA TUBE (p214) This lava tube – so long and tall you could set up a basketball court inside – is a must-see; bring flashlights to slink down 1000ft of unlit tube. (It gets pretty creepy when you shut off your lights and nervous laughter

starts bouncing off the dark walls.) The smoking, colorful **Sulphur Banks (p212)** is another pit stop kids love, and Pele's home, **Halema'uma'u Crater (p213)**, shouldn't be missed.

❸ HIKING KILAUEA IKI (p218) Outdoor family fun awaits on this easy, 4-mile loop trail dropping down onto the crater floor and past the main steaming vent.

❹ WALKING TO LIVE LAVA (p217) One of the great thrills of a Hawai'i vacation is seeing live lava at night. Hopefully it will be accessible when you arrive. If not, consider a **helicopter tour (p35)**.

HAWAI'I VOLCANOES
NATIONAL PARK

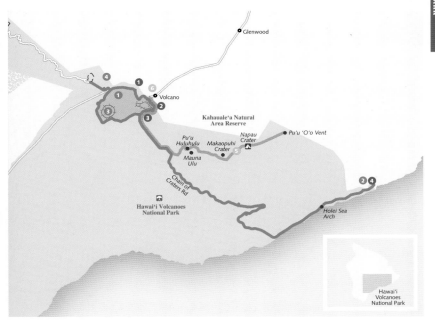

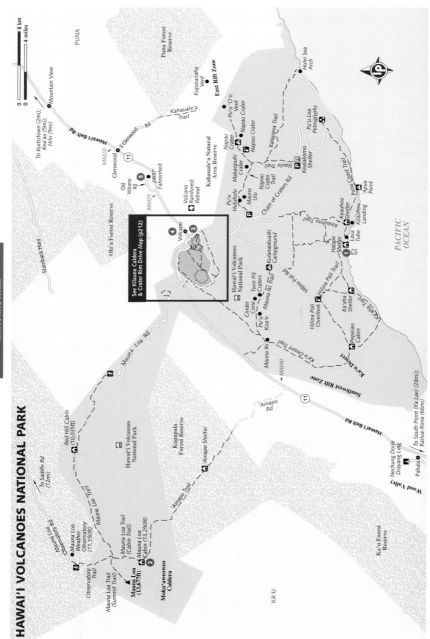

HAWAI'I VOLCANOES NATIONAL PARK

HIGHLIGHTS

❶ **BEST BEACH:** Halape (p223)
❷ **BEST VIEW:** Moku'aweoweo Caldera from Mauna Loa cabin (p220)
❸ **BEST ACTIVITY:** Secret Lava Tube Tour (p219)
❹ **BEST POST-HIKE SPLURGE:** Lomilomi foot massage at Hale Ho'ola (p226)
❺ **BEST SOUVENIR:** Glass sculpture from 2400° Fahrenheit (p226)

Highlights are numbered on the map on p208.

With three active volcanoes and a geological history dating back at least 70 million years, this park is one-of-a-kind and an ideal hiking and camping destination. There are over 140 miles of amazingly varied trails here, from senior citizen cakewalks to ass-kicking summit hikes, plus drive-up campsites and backcountry shelters. The park, established in 1916, is the state's only Unesco World Heritage Site.

Hawai'i Volcanoes National Park (HAVO) encompasses roughly 333,000 acres of land and is growing, as lava pouring from Kilauea adds still more (over 600 acres in the past 15 years). The park recently expanded exponentially when it purchased 116,000 acres of private ranchland on the southeastern flanks of Mauna Loa.

The current eruption along Kilauea's East Rift Zone started on January 3, 1983, making it the longest in recorded history. Twenty-five years of continuous action means a lot of lava – some 2.5 billion cubic yards (that's 50,000 gallons a minute for you math freaks). Though languid, Big Island lava can be deadly stuff, consuming trees, houses, roads and most anything else in its path. The current eruption destroyed the coastal road to Puna (1987), the Waha'ula Visitor Center on the south coast (1988) and the entire village of Kalapana (1990), before turning westward and swallowing up Kamoamoa Beach (1994) and most of sacred Wahaula Heiau. At the time of writing it was flowing over Kaimu–Chain of Craters Rd (Hwy 130) in Puna.

All of this boil, toil and trouble comes from the Pu'u 'O'o vent (Map p208), a smol-

dering cone on the park's northeastern border, along the East Rift Zone. Kilauea is a shield volcano, which means it doesn't have the explosive gases of the more dramatic and deadly strato volcanoes found along the Pacific Ocean's Ring of Fire (Mt St Helens, Mt Pinatubo in the Philippines), which loft ash and flaming rocks into the air. This volcano is instead like a tortoise: the lava slowly creeps along, which is why here you run to, not away from, the volcano.

All those hot lava photos you ogled online before your visit? You probably won't see that. Lava flows are unpredictable, and your vantage point depends on current volcanic activity. Still, you should be able to hike out to watch new lava oozing across the landscape, since authorities make every effort to make the flow accessible. If you're lucky, lava ribbons will be pouring into the sea.

ORIENTATION

The park's main road is 11-mile Crater Rim Dr, which circles Kilauea Caldera. Zooming around, you can see the drive-up sites in an hour. If that's all you have time for, it's worth it, but you'll find yourself wanting more. Views are better going counterclockwise.

The park's other scenic drive is Chain of Craters Rd, which leads south 20 miles to the coast, ending at the site of recent lava activity. Allow about three hours down and back, with stops along the way.

Hiking, turning up early (before 8am) or late (dusk), and exploring beyond the illuminated section of the Thurston Lava Tube are proven strategies for escaping the crowds. Going backcountry and mountain biking are others.

In addition to camping, there is one not terribly inspiring place to stay within the park boundaries; the most seductive accommodations are in and around Volcano Village (p227).

Maps

If you think your old AAA maps are out of date, try a topographical one for the Big Island: cartographers simply can't keep pace with Kilauea, making most maps outdated (especially hiking trails in and around the active rift zones). For day trips, the free driving and trail map at the park entrance will suffice, but if you're backpacking or camping, check out *National Geographic's Trails Illustrated Hawai'i Volcanoes National Park*. For specific hikes, the US Geological Survey's (USGS) 1:24,000 maps *Kilauea*, *Volcano* and *Ka'u Desert* are helpful.

INFORMATION

The **park** (☎ 985-6000; www.nps.gov/havo; 7-day pass per car $10, per person on foot, bicycle or motorcycle $5) never closes, allowing all-night views of the spectacular stars and lava flows. Tip: the entrance fee is good for a week so you can explore for several days for one low price here.

Sold at the entrance, an annual Tri-Park Pass is a steal at just $25, and gives you access to this park, plus Pu'uhonua o Honaunau and Haleakalā on Maui. Annual national park passes are $80. US citizens with disabilities can obtain a Golden Access Passport (free), while the Golden Age Passport ($10) is available to those 62 and older; both allow unlimited, free lifetime access to the entire national park system.

Some of the sites and shorter trails are accessible to people in wheelchairs (the rooms at Volcano House are *not* among these); the best include the Jaggar Museum (particularly the overlook behind the museum; p213), Steam Vents (p213) and Sulphur Banks Trail (p212).

You can obtain the main park brochure in advance, along with its Backcountry Planner, by written request to: Hawai'i Volcanoes National Park, PO Box 52, Hawai'i National Park, HI 96718. Overnight camping permits, however, must be obtained in person at the visitor center no more than 24 hours before you intend to hike.

To make the most of your visit, stop first at the **Kilauea Visitor Center** (Map p212; ☎ 985-6017; ✹ 7:45am-5pm), where bulletin boards have information about the latest volcanic activity, nighttime lecture series, guided tours and what's on for kids. Inside there's a great selection of books (for kids, too), maps and videos on volcanoes, flora and hiking.

The internet provides a wealth of information about the park (surprise, surprise).

Island Insights

Big Islanders know staying informed about live lava flows, weather and trail closures enriches (and sometimes saves) lives. Here's how:

- **Trail closures** www.nps.gov/havo /closed_areas.htm
- **Air quality** www2.nature.nps.gov/air /webcams/parks/havoso2alert/havoalert .cfm
- **Live lava status** http://volcano.wr.usgs .gov/kilaueastatus.php

To enhance your visit, poke around the following sites before turning up:

www.nps.gov/havo Hawai'i Volcanoes National Park official site.

http://hvo.wr.usgs.gov Official site of the Hawaiian Volcano Observatory.

www.volcanoartcenter.org Art and event listings, plus books related to the park.

http://volcano.und.nodak.edu/vwdocs/kids/kids .html Kids can get in on the action at Volcano World's Kids' Door.

DANGERS & ANNOYANCES

To find out about the flow and trail closures, call the park's **hotline** (☎ 985-6000; ✹ 24hr). More up-to-date information is available online at the **Volcano Observatory website** (http://volcano.wr.usgs.gov/hvostatus.php) and at 530AM on your radio. Prolonged periods of drought often close both Mauna Loa Rd and Hilina Pali Rd due to high fire hazards. Meanwhile, Hwy 11 is prone to flooding, washouts and closures during storms.

Although few people have died due to violently explosive eruptions at Kilauea (the last was in 1924), other volcanic activity hasn't been so beneficent. You'll hear about tourists who ventured onto unstable 'benches' of new land that collapsed and campers who slept too close to the Pu'u 'O'o vent and asphyxiated on the fumes. Talk about a buzz kill!

Heed rangers' and park warnings lest you end up like those poor souls. Stick to marked trails and don't venture off on your own – getting lost on lava is easier than you think. Watch your step, especially on the glass-sharp 'a'a (rough, jagged lava); the bloody abrasions aren't pretty.

Take care if you're fortunate enough to see the lava entering the sea – the steam plume is a toxic cocktail of sulfuric and hydrochloric acid, with a dash of silica (ie glass particles). Anyone with respiratory or heart conditions, pregnant women and those with infants or young children should be especially careful. High concentrations of sulfur dioxide permeate the air at Halema'uma'u Overlook and Sulphur Banks, sometimes closing Crater Rim Dr altogether.

Even centuries-old lava gets hot on a hike and it always makes for tricky walking. Hikers should wear hiking shoes with good ankle support, long pants and a hat, and have at least two liters of water per person. Drinking lots of fluids can't be overemphasized: dehydration is a common but preventable malady. For longer hikes, your kit should include a flashlight with extra batteries (or better yet, a wind-up model), binoculars, a first-aid kit, sunscreen and snacks.

Climate

The park entrance sits at a lofty 4000ft, with varying elevation and climates within its boundaries. Smart travelers check the recorded weather forecast (☎ 961-5582) before heading out. Chilly rain, wind, fog and vog (volcanic fog) typify the fickle weather here, which can go from hot and dry to a soaking downpour in a flash. Near Kilauea Caldera, temperatures average 15°F cooler than in Kona, so bring an extra jacket and pair of pants just in case.

SIGHTS
Crater Rim Drive

Kilauea is called the 'drive-up volcano' because you can motor around the entire gaping maw of the caldera on 11-mile Crater Rim Dr, popping out for a gander at steam vents and smoking crater lookouts. Hikes into and around the caldera (see p219) and through lava tubes (p219) are also possible. Start at the visitor center and take the drive counterclockwise for the best views.

The plate tectonics fueling Kilauea also create earthquakes – over 1200 a week as measured by the Hawaiian Volcano Observatory (http://hvo.wr.usgs.gov/earthquakes/; ☼ closed to the public). Though most are too small to be felt, big quakes in 1975 (6.2 magnitude) and 1983 (6.7 magnitude) shook sections of Crater Rim Dr loose, sending them crashing into the caldera. In October 2006, another 6.7 magnitude quake hit offshore near Kiholo Bay (North Kona Coast), causing $2 million in damage, though no loss of life. It's highly unlikely you'll feel a quake here, but you should drive with care as the road is narrow. Also stay alert for the endangered nene (native Hawaiian goose), since cars are its top predator. Feeding the geese is prohibited by law.

Crater Rim Dr is relatively level, making it a good road for cyclists. If you're into pedal power, Volcano Bike Tours (☎ 934-9199, 888-934-9199; www.bikevolcano.com; per person $130) has an 18-mile Crater Rim Dr to Chain of Craters Rd adventure. Independent cyclists can explore either of these routes, plus Escape Road (3.3 miles).

KILAUEA VISITOR CENTER
Map p212; ☎ 985-6017; ☼ 7:45am-5pm
Inside the park visitor center is a theater showing a 25-minute Kilauea Volcano documentary (admission free; ☼ hourly 9am to 4pm). It's worth it for the lava footage – some of the most spectacular ever caught on film. The center is small, but has a good interactive bird exhibit and gift shop.

The Junior Ranger Program gets kids (aged five to 12) excited about geology and teaches stewardship through an activity book, short guided hike and Junior Ranger badge. Hit the gift shop for more activity and coloring books with Hawaiian and natural themes for those heated-to-tears times.

Ranger-led guided walks leave daily from here; see the bulletin board for what's on. You can also join a guided hike with companies Hawaii Forest & Trail or Hawaiian Walkways (see p38).

VOLCANO ART CENTER
Map p212; ☎ 967-7565; www.volcanoartcenter .org; ☼ 9am-5pm
This gallery near the visitor center features high-quality island pottery, paintings, woodwork, sculpture, jewelry, Hawaiian

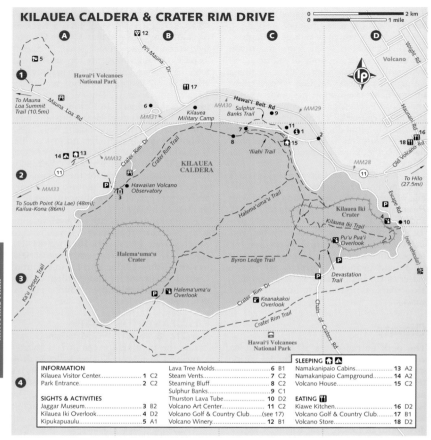

KILAUEA CALDERA & CRATER RIM DRIVE

INFORMATION		Lava Tree Molds	6	B1	Namakanipaio Cabins	13	A2
Kilauea Visitor Center	1 C2	Steam Vents	7	C2	Namakanipaio Campground	14	A2
Park Entrance	2 C2	Steaming Bluff	8	C2	Volcano House	15	C2
		Sulphur Banks	9	C1			
SIGHTS & ACTIVITIES		Thurston Lava Tube	10	D2	EATING 🍴		
Jaggar Museum	3 B2	Volcano Art Center	11	C2	Kiawe Kitchen	16	D2
Kilauea Iki Overlook	4 D2	Volcano Golf & Country Club	(see 17)		Volcano Golf & Country Club	17	B1
Kipukapuaulu	5 A1	Volcano Winery	12	B1	Volcano Store	18	D2

quilts and more. The nonprofit gallery and shop, housed in a historic 1877 Volcano House lodge, is worth a visit just to admire the solid artisanship or learn about upcoming classes, workshops and cultural activities (or to simply warm yourself by the fire). Also see its free monthly publication, *Volcano Gazette*.

SULPHUR BANKS
Map p212

A short stroll from the Volcano Art Center is Sulphur Banks, where rocks are crusted in shades of chartreuse, brick and other J Crew colors due to sulfur-infused steam rising from deep within the earth. This area,

traditionally called **Ha'akulamanu** (Gathering Place for Birds), is one of many areas where Kilauea lets off steam, releasing 2000 tons of sulfuric gases daily. That rotten-egg stench is from the hydrogen sulfide wafting from the vents. Other gases in this noxious mix include carbon dioxide and sulfur dioxide.

The beautiful, wooden, wheelchair-accessible **Sulphur Banks Trail** has just undergone a $1 million renovation. Link up this trail with the **'Iliahi**, **Halema'uma'u** and **Byron Ledge** trails for a multimile hike through verdant storybook forest with lichen-covered lanes and birdsong. For a quick leisurely hike, take the loop along the **Sulphur**

Banks and Crater Rim trails, visiting the **Steam Vents** and **Steaming Bluff** en route (3 miles).

STEAM VENTS
Map p212

When the cool morning air mixes with hot steam, it pumps impressive plumes of (nonsulfurous) steam from a couple of vents here. As opposed to Sulphur Banks, the steam here is created when rainwater percolates into the earth, is heated by the hot rocks below and released upward. Some visitors have taken to using the vents as a wishing well, leaving an unnecessary imprint.

JAGGAR MUSEUM
Map p212; ☎ 985-6049; admission free; ☼ 9am-5pm

The big draws at this one-room museum are the views and the real-time seismographs and tiltmeters recording earthquakes within the park. There's also a mural of the Hawaiian pantheon and a short history of the museum's founder and famed volcanologist, Dr Thomas A Jaggar.

Head around back for an excellent view of Pele's house, at smoking **Halema'uma'u Crater**. From this vantage point you'll see why Halema'uma'u is sometimes referred to as the 'crater within the crater,' since it's plopped in the middle of Kilauea Caldera. The geology behind volcanoes is detailed in a series of interpretive plaques here (or eavesdrop on a tour). When the weather is clear, there's a rapturous view of **Mauna Loa** to the northwest.

This parking lot is a nene hot spot, so drive with care. Heading around the caldera from the museum, you drive through the **Southwest Rift Zone**, with moonscape lava flows from 1971 and 1974 as far as the eye can see. Stop to check out the wide gash slicing through the earth from the caldera summit out to the coast and under the ocean floor.

HALEMA'UMA'U OVERLOOK
Map p212

The phenomenon of our planet is undeniable at the approach to this smoking, gassy crater that feels like a cauldron set upon underworld fires. For at least 100 years (from 1823, when missionary William Ellis first described it), Halema'uma'u was a seething

Don't Miss

- **Camping under a full moon at Halape** (p223)
- **View of Mauna Loa from Devastation Trail** (p214)
- **The unlit extension of Thurston Lava Tube** (p214)
- **Hula overlooking Kilauea Crater** (p224)
- **Pu'u Loa Petroglyphs** (p216)

lake of lava, constantly in flux, boiling over its edges and receding. Look closely and you'll see 'bathtub rings' of old, cold lava inside the crater.

In 1924 the floor of Halema'uma'u subsided rapidly, igniting a series of explosive eruptions. Instead of raining cats and dogs, it rained boulders and mud – for days. When all was quiet again, the crater had doubled in size (to about 300ft deep and 3000ft wide) and lava activity ceased. There have been nearly a score of eruptions since then and it still reeks of sulfur.

The penultimate eruption was early morning on April 30, 1982. Perched over the caldera, geologists at the Hawaiian Volcano Observatory sipped coffee while their instruments went haywire, warning of an imminent eruption. The Halema'uma'u Trail was quickly closed and hikers cleared from the caldera. Before noon, a half-mile fissure had broken open in the crater wall and the caldera floor before spewing out 1.3 million cubic yards of lava.

More recently, a gas explosion on March 19, 2008, shot rocks up and over the crater rim into the parking lot above. Thankfully nobody was hurt, but the extraordinary volcanic activity and high levels of sulfuric gases forced the closure of many Crater Rim sights.

All of the Big Island is Pele's territory, but Halema'uma'u is her home, making it a sacred site for Native Hawaiians. **Ceremonial hula** is performed in her honor on the crater rim (see p224), and those wishing to appease Pele frequently leave offerings of lei or rocks wrapped in *ti* leaves (known as 'rock *laulau*,' like the traditional Hawaiian dish); you'll certainly see some fresh or shriveled flowers along the rim. Some tourists leave offerings as well, but it's better

HAWAI'I VOLCANOES NATIONAL PARK

to leave the goddess worship to those in the know and no evidence of your visit. It's also considered disrespectful and bad luck (not to mention illegal) to take rocks or anything else from the national park.

The overlook is the start of the **Halema'uma'u Trail** (p218).

DEVASTATION TRAIL
Map p212
After the smoking crater, Crater Rim Dr crosses the barren Ka'u Desert and through the 1959 Kilauea Crater eruption area. Hiking across the crater is one of the most popular day hikes (see Kilauea Iki Trail, p218), but Devastation Trail also has its charms. This half-mile hike is best approached from Crater Rim Dr in the south so you can behold Mauna Loa looming over the sulfur-encrusted caldera, but you can connect with any number of trails to the north for an 8-miler or more.

This trail got its name when the 1959 eruption toasted the rain forest here, leaving dead ohia trees, stripped bare and sun-bleached white, and some tree molds. Although horrific sounding, it's fascinating to see the landscape's revival, with ohia trees, native 'ohelo shrubs and ferns colonizing the area anew. The prominent cinder cone along the way is **Pu'u Pua'i** (Gushing Hill), formed during the eruption. The

Along the Devastation Trail   GREG ELMS

northeastern end of the trail looks down into **Kilauea Iki Crater**.

The trail is paved and has parking lots at each end (to make a loop you'll have to walk about half a mile along Crater Rim Dr).

THURSTON LAVA TUBE
Map p212
Continuing around the crater, things get greener, passing through native rain forest thick with tree ferns and ohia. That overflowing parking lot is the access point for the ever-popular **Thurston Lava Tube Trail**. All the tour buses stop here and it's a favorite with kids, so plan to come early or late to enjoy the half-mile loop walk that starts out in ohia forest and passes through an impressive lava tube. The open grove of ohia at the start of the path is a good spot to see and hear the red and rapid-flying *'apapane,* a native honeycreeper.

Lava tubes are formed when the outer crust of a river of lava starts to harden but the liquid lava beneath the surface continues to flow through. After the flow drains out, the hard shell remains. Dating back perhaps 500 years, Thurston Lava Tube is a grand example – it's tunnel-like and almost big enough to run a train through. Bring a flashlight and you can explore the 300yd **unlit extension** – an eerie and electrifying dive into the unknown where few tourists dare to tread. Once deep inside the darkest part of the tube, surrounded by once-molten lava, shut off your light... If you like this one, you'll love the **Secret Lava Tube Tour** (p219).

KILAUEA IKI CRATER
Map p212
On a starry night in November 1959, it felt like Earth was exploding. That was when Kilauea Iki (Little Kilauea) burst open in a fiery inferno, turning the crater into a roiling lake of molten lava and sending 1900ft fountains of lava into the night sky. At its peak, it gushed out two million tons of lava an hour and the island glowed an eerie orange for miles.

From the **overlook** there's a good view of the steaming mile-wide crater below, which was used for filming the 2001 remake of *Planet of the Apes*. Look for tiny hikers making their way across the crater to appreciate its massive proportions. This

Otherwordly lava terrain along Chain of Craters Road

GREG ELMS

4-mile loop trail is the park's most popular **day hike** (see p218), or you can take the half-mile quickie between this and the Thurston Lava Tube parking lots.

Chain of Craters Road

Chain of Craters Rd winds 20 miles and 3700ft down the southern slopes of Kilauea Volcano, ending abruptly at the East Rift Zone on the Puna Coast. This **scenic drive** takes in an impressive array of sights along a paved two-lane road.

From the road you'll have striking vistas of the coastline far below, and for miles the predominant view is of lava, which cooled before reaching the sea. You can sometimes find thin filaments of volcanic glass, known as Pele's hair, in the cracks and crevices. The best time to photograph the unique landscape is before 9am or after 3pm, when sunlight slants off the lava.

Chain of Craters Rd once connected to Hwys 130 and 137, allowing traffic between the volcano and Hilo via Puna. Lava flows closed the road in 1969, but by 1979 it was back in service, albeit slightly rerouted. Then Kilauea's flows cut the link again in 1987, burying a 9-mile stretch of the road.

HILINA PALI ROAD
Map p208
After 2.2 miles of pit craters large and small on Chain of Craters Rd, you come to the turnoff for Hilina Pali Rd. Drive carefully on this narrow, one-lane paved road – especially because your eyes will be popping from the spectacular Mauna Loa and Mauna Kea views. It ends with even more views, this time of the coast, from the **Hilina Pali Overlook**. You may be tempted to hit the **Hilina Pali Trail** (p223), but the water isn't as close as it looks.

After 4 miles along Hilina Pali Rd, you reach the **Kulanaokuaiki Campground** (p225). Just west is the trailhead for the **Mauna Iki Trail** (p219). The **Ka'u Desert Trail** (p224) begins 5 miles further on, where the road ends. These hot, dry trails, for which you'll need to be prepared, are the least exciting of the park's hikes.

MAUNA ULU
Map p208
In 1969, eruptions from Kilauea's East Rift began building a new lava shield that now rises above its surroundings. It was named Mauna Ulu (Growing Mountain). By the

Island Insights

There are only two endemic **Big Island butterflies**: the orange-and-black Kamehameha butterfly and the daintier, white Blackburn butterfly. Keep your eyes peeled on park trails for these native species.

Young ohia tree   GREG ELMS

time the flow stopped in 1974, it had covered 10,000 acres of parkland, added 200 new coastal acres and grown to 2680ft. It also buried a 12-mile section of Chain of Craters Rd in lava.

A trail accessed from the parking area 3.5 miles down Chain of Craters Rd from the intersection with Crater Rim Dr offers partial views of Mauna Ulu.

The **Pu'u Huluhulu Overlook Trail**, a 3-mile round-trip hike, begins at the parking area, crosses over lava flows from 1974, and climbs to the top of the 150ft Pu'u Huluhulu cinder cone, where you're rewarded with panoramic views of Mauna Loa, Mauna Kea, Pu'u 'O'o vent, Kilauea, the East Rift Zone and the ocean. This hike takes about two hours and is recommended if you want a moderate workout with beautiful views. To venture beyond the overlook on this hike requires a free permit from the visitor center (p212).

PU'U LOA PETROGLYPHS
Map p208
The gentle **Pu'u Loa Trail** leads less than a mile to a field of petroglyphs laboriously pecked into *pahoehoe* (smooth-flowing lava) by early Hawaiians. The site, which is along the ancient trail that once ran between Ka'u and Puna, has over 20,000 images of hu-

mans, ships and other objects specialists still can't identify. The marked trailhead begins on the Chain of Craters Rd midway between the 16- and 17-mile markers and makes an interesting 1¼-hour walk.

This is a sacred site and should be treated with respect: it's unlawful to deface, mark or scratch the petroglyphs, so please don't take rubbings and stay on the boardwalk.

At **Pu'u Loa** (Long Hill), toward the southeast, ancient Hawaiians pecked out thousands of dimpled depressions in the petroglyph field to serve as receptacles for their babies' *piko* (umbilical stumps). By placing the *piko* inside and covering them with stones, they hoped to assure their children long, healthy lives.

HOLEI SEA ARCH
Map p208
Just before the 19-mile marker, look for the sign announcing the Holei Sea Arch. Constantly brutalized by unrelenting surf, this section of the coast has sharply eroded *pali* (lava cliffs), called **Holei Pali**. The high rock arch is dramatic, looking like a brace supporting the cliffs, but in fact, it's the other way around. One day, the violent waves, at the behest of sea goddess (and Pele's sister) Namakaokaha'i, will send it crashing into the sea.

THE END OF THE ROAD
Map p208
Quite. The road ends where the lava says it ends, having swamped this coastal section of Chain of Craters Rd repeatedly over the past 25 years. Park rangers try to mark a trail over the hardened lava with small reflectors, leading to a safe observation point. There's a simple info board and portable toilets here, but no water or other facilities.

Mauna Loa Road

If you're looking for a shady, 1-mile loop hike, 'Bird Park,' or **Kipukapuaulu** (Map p212), is it. Technically, a *kipuka* is a patch of land spared by lava that is an oasis for native flora and fauna. This 100-acre sanctuary is a prime specimen, formed about 400 years ago when a major lava flow from Mauna Loa's northeastern rift covered most of the surrounding area except this island forest.

This hike is best done in the early morning or at dusk, when the birds are most active. You'll see honeycreepers – the 'amakihi, 'apapane and 'i'iwi – plus the inquisitive 'elepaio and non-native finches. The trees soar here, so bring your binoculars and park yourself on the benches in the forest for maximum viewing. You won't have to look hard or long to see colorful pheasants ('that's good eating,' according to a local hiker) grazing on the forest floor. You'll also pass a lava tube where a unique species of big-eyed spider was discovered in the dark depths in 1973. A free **flora-and-fauna trail guide** is available at the visitor center inside the park.

Near the start of Mauna Loa Rd there's a turnoff to some **lava tree molds** (skip these if you stopped at the Lava Tree State Monument in Puna; p199). These deep, lava phalluses formed when a lava flow engulfed the rain forest that stood here. Because the trees were so waterlogged, the lava hardened around them instead of burning them on contact. As the trees disintegrated, they left deep holes where the trunks once stood. There's a day use area between here and Bird Park with bathrooms, picnic tables and barbecue grills, plus a grassy expanse for the kids to run off some steam.

Winding up lonely, wooded, 13.5-mile Mauna Loa Rd, you'll pass other heavily forested *kipuka* before coming to Mauna Loa, the world's most massive active volcano. Mauna Loa has erupted more than 18 times in the past century – the last eruption, in March 1984, lasted 21 days. The end of the road is the beginning of the onerous **Mauna Loa Summit Trail** (p220).

HIKING

Dust off the boots and air out the tent because this park has some of Hawaii's best hiking and backpacking. Rain forest, desert, secluded beaches with killer snorkeling,

GO TO THE FLOW

If you're lucky (it's the drive-up volcano, not the dial-up volcano), you can hike to the flowing lava. At the time of writing, the flow was entering the sea near the **Royal Gardens subdivision** (Map p194; ☺ 10am-10pm, last car in 8pm) in Puna, accessible via Hwy 130. The trek toward the flow crosses hardened lava and the 'trail' is unmarked, except for temporary reflectors. Due to unstable land at the coastline and the proximity to molten lava, this can be a dangerous hike. Plan on 20 minutes to several hours for the round-trip, depending on where the lava action is centered – there was talk of opening a coastal viewing site and charging for access at the time of writing. Bring a flashlight, extra batteries and water.

The trail is laid to lead as close to the lava as safety allows, and often toward the point where lava flows into the sea. However, what you'll find at the end of the trek is unpredictable. Maybe you'll see hot lava a few feet away, or just a golden glow and steam rising in the distance.

It's best to start this hike at sunset, when the coast is at its most beautiful and cool. After dark, the lava is most impressive, but the 'trail' will be hard to follow. If that gives you chicken skin, hook up with a tour: **Arnott's Lodge** (p189) and **Hawai'i Forest & Trail** (p38) lead guided treks a few days a week, as do park rangers when the flow is in park domain. Check the boards at the **Kilauea Visitor Center** (p212) for the latest.

The steam plumes are wondrous from afar, but extremely dangerous close up. The explosive clash between seawater and 2100°F molten lava can spray scalding water hundreds of feet into the air and throw flaming lava chunks up to 500yd inland. Unstable ledges of lava crust called lava benches sometimes collapse without warning: in 1993 an islander met a fiery death this way and another 12 were injured. Then in March 1999, a series of explosions blasted lava bombs into the air and collapsed the 25-acre lava bench onlookers had been standing on. Luckily no one was hurt. You should always stay at least 500yd inland on this hike and follow advice and warnings.

Volcanic activity and viewing conditions are always subject to change, so call the park visitor center's **hotline** (☎ 985-6000) or see the **website** (http://volcano.wr.usgs.gov/kilaueastatus.php) for updates.

HAWAI'I VOLCANOES NATIONAL PARK

crater walks and the world's most active volcano all await in the Big Island's heart. The extensive trail network, rising from sea level to over 13,000ft at the snowcapped summit of Mauna Loa, allows you to design your own loops. Just make sure you have a good trail map and a dose of common sense.

The following hikes range from an easy 1-mile walk to multiday backcountry treks. Remember that, except at the cabins and shelters, no drinking water is available. A compass and binoculars will come in handy. All backcountry hikes require a free permit from the visitor center (p212); you can only apply for permits one day before you intend to hike.

Take a hike in the park and you'll experience firsthand the Hawaiian maxim, '*I ka nana no a 'ike*' ('By observing, one learns').

HALEMA'UMA'U TRAIL
Map p212
Proving it's not all about the active flow, this 6-mile loop is one of the park's best day hikes, prized for its variety of ecosystems and colorful old lava flows. The trailhead is located diagonally across the road from the visitor center. Most of this loop is entirely exposed, making it either a hot, dry hike or chillingly damp.

After clearing a moist ohia forest, you descend almost 400ft and head straight across gaping Kilauea Caldera and flows from 1885, 1894, 1954, 1971, 1974 and 1982. The trail, marked by *ahu* (lava-rock cairns), ends about 3 miles from the visitor center at the steaming **Halema'uma'u Overlook**. On the way back, take the `our pick` **Byron Ledge Trail**, heading toward **Pu'u Pua'i** and **Devastation Trail** (p214), which you can add as a side trip. On the last stretch, you'll return to damp, cool forest air.

KILAUEA IKI TRAIL
Map p212
If you can do only one day hike, make it this one with the rest of the day trippers (hitting the trail before 8am is a good way to beat the crowds). The 4-mile, clockwise loop beginning near the Thurston Lava Tube parking lot takes you through a microcosm of the park, quickly descending 400ft through fairytale ohia forest and then cutting across the mile-wide crater, passing close to the

Crossing the Kilauea Iki crater floor

GREG ELMS

HAWAI'I VOLCANOES NATIONAL PARK

main vent. Scattered vents lace the crater surface with ethereal steam plumes, while the wrinkled, often iridescent lava surface is peppered with 'ohelo shrubs, ohia trees and ferns.

The hike northwest across the crater floor is hot, but short (about 1.5 miles) and marked by *ahu*. Don't wander off-trail to explore any steaming vents, lava tubes or caves without an experienced guide.

Keep to the right to ascend the crater wall on the far side. You'll be on **Byron Ledge**, separating Kilauea Iki from Kilauea Caldera, from where there are good views of Kilauea Iki Crater and golden Pu'u Pua'i. From there you'll pass two junctions; if you turn right at both, you'll continue along the Kilauea Iki Trail back to the parking lot (1.1 miles). You can extend your hike by linking this trail with the Byron Ridge or Crater Rim Trails.

CRATER RIM TRAIL
Map p212

To get a real taste of how the volcano has altered the landscape over time, take this 11-mile loop hike. Allow about six hours, with a leisurely picnic lunch thrown in.

Starting at Volcano House, you either skirt the crater rim to the north, gaining a bird's-eye view of the landscape, or drop into misty ohia and fern forest passing Kilauea Iki Crater to the south, crossing a number of historic lava flows along the way. From the Southwest Rift Zone area, you can detour 1.2 miles to see **Halema'uma'u Crater**. Be prepared for changeable weather at this altitude, where a hot sunny stroll can turn cold and wet in an instant.

MAUNA IKI TRAIL
Map p208

If you're craving solitude and a connection with nature, the surprisingly varied 7-mile Mauna Iki Trail is just right (other Ka'u Desert trails are long, hot and mostly dull). The trailhead is reached via narrow Hilina Pali Rd (off Chain of Craters Rd). Look for the trailhead sign shortly after Kulanaokuaiki Campground.

With little to look at and cracks and crevices that force you to watch your step, the varied colors of the *pahoehoe* – from shiny gray to muted brown to metallic red – stand out. From a distance, to your left you'll see the double-peaked **Pu'ukoa'e** (3250ft), and

DETOUR ➡

SECRET LAVA TUBE TOUR

The bacteria hanging on the walls might hold the cure for cancer and the Godzilla-like formations within baffle specialists. Delicate webs like silk hammocks cradle tiny spiders and the sonorous drip of water explains why Native Hawaiians used lava tubes for collecting water. The ancients also used these tubes to bury their *ali'i* (royalty) and as conduits to cross the desert.

These are just some of the fascinations awaiting you on the unique, five-hour **our pick** **Pua Po'o Lava Tube Hike** (admission free; ⏱ 12:30pm Wed). The easy, 4-mile round-trip hike passes through ohia forest to the 500-year-old tube, where you'll don helmet and headlamp for an hour-long exploration of this phenomenal ecosystem. There's some entry and exit scrambling required, but inside is a giant tube with 20ft ceilings and wild sights, including 'soda straw' stalactites and silvery bacteria colonies.

Due to the tube's fragility, only 12 people a week are allowed on this ranger-guided hike and participants are asked to keep the location secret. To sign up, call the **Kilauea Visitor Center** (☎ 985-6017) the Wednesday before you want to make the hike at 7:45am, not later (it's that popular); each caller can reserve for four people and only kids over 10 are allowed. You'll need long pants, water and four AA batteries for the headlamp.

on the right a tawny **cinder cone** with a rust-colored 'chimney' formation on its top.

As you approach a set of **twin pit craters**, you'll see warning signs reading 'Danger, Overhanging Edge, Stay Back.' Carefully peer into the pits, which hide a surprising amount of plant life.

The trail 'ends' around Pu'ukoa'e, though you can connect with other trails, including to **Mauna Iki** (3032ft) lava shield, about 3 miles away. If you continue west along the trail, you'll hit Hwy 11, which is another starting point.

MAUNA LOA SUMMIT TRAILS

Only if you're extremely fit and prepared for winter mountaineering should you try to summit Mauna Loa – the subarctic conditions at this elevation can be daunting. There are three summit trails (all on the map on p208), described here from easiest (relatively speaking) to hardest. Getting a permit at the **Kilauea Visitor Center** (p212) is essential, except for the Mauna Loa Observatory Trail.

Mauna Loa Observatory Trail

This trail is the easiest way to summit 'Long Mountain' because you drive up to 11,150ft on the 19-mile **Mauna Loa Observatory Road** (p150) and then pick up the 6.4-mile trail for the remaining 2527ft to the top. Still, it's a steep, all-day adventure, but one that allows the average hiker to conquer a 13,000ft mountain; it also means you can summit Mauna Loa one day and Mauna Kea the next for a double peak extravaganza.

The drive-hike combination means you have to acclimatize properly, but even that is no guarantee against altitude sickness, symptoms of which include headaches, nausea, vomiting, dizziness, insomnia and lack of appetite. The faster and/or higher you go increases your risk. The only remedy is to descend. Sleeping in your car near the observatory or camping along one of the 4WD roads en route might help. You only need a permit from the Kilauea Visitor Center if you want to overnight at **Mauna Loa cabin** (see p221 for permit information).

Begin early. You don't want to be on the mountain when the customary afternoon clouds roll in. Heavy fog is a real danger here, since it obscures the cairns marking the trail. If fog rolls in, find shelter and wait it out, even if this means spending the night. The trail crisscrosses a series of *'a'a* (rough, jagged lava) and *pahoehoe* (smooth lava) flows, most dating from 1942. After about 4 miles and 2000ft in elevation gain, there's a pit toilet and then the trail connects to the **Mauna Loa Summit Trail**. From the trail junction, it's just over 2.5 miles around the caldera's western side to Mauna Loa summit (13,677ft), or about 2 miles along the caldera's eastern side to Mauna Loa cabin (13,250ft). Perched on the awesome **Moku-'aweoweo Caldera**, the cabin offers respite, but if you're on a day trip, push straight on to the summit. It will take half as long to descend. All told, plan on a 10-hour day.

Mauna Loa Summit Trail

The Summit Trail begins at the end of Mauna Loa Rd, accessed via Hwy 11 between the 30- and 31-mile markers.

This rugged 19.6-mile trail gradually ascends 6600ft and takes a minimum of three days, but four is better for proper acclimatization and time exploring the summit area. Two simple **cabins** are available on a first-come, first-served basis at Pu'u'ula'ula (Red Hill) and the Mauna Loa summit. Potable water might be available and must be treated (inquire at the visitor center).

The trail begins rising through an ohia forest and above the tree line. After 7.5 miles (allow four to six hours), you reach **Pu'u'ula'ula** at 10,035ft. There are fine views of Mauna Kea to the north and Maui's venerable Haleakalā to the northwest.

The 11.6-mile hike from Pu'u'ula'ula to the summit cabin at 13,250ft takes a full day. The route crosses a stark, stirring landscape of multicolored cinder fields, *'a'a* and *pahoehoe,* with gaping fissures cleaving the landscape, spatter cones, and variegated, iridescent lava. After 9.5 miles you come to **Moku'aweoweo Caldera** and a fork in the trail; left takes you to your night's resting place. If you absolutely can't push on, **Jaggar's Cave** (just beyond the fork) can serve as a windbreak – but it's a small niche rather than an actual cave.

The other fork is for the 2.5-mile Summit Trail. The last 2 miles are especially challenging and will seem to last forever. At 13,677ft, temperatures drop to freezing nearly every night and winter snowstorms can last for days, bringing whiteout conditions. Snow can fall any time of year and occasionally it falls as low as Pu'u'ula'ula, covering the upper end of the trail. Consult park rangers about weather conditions before setting out.

'Ainapo Trail

The 'Ainapo Trail is the most challenging of all the summit trails. It combines a lengthy 10.2 miles at altitude and a steep rise up the southeastern flank of Mauna Loa. Prehistoric Hawaiians are thought to have originally used the 'Ainapo Trail for ceremonies honoring Pele.

Aside from being physically difficult, this route also necessitates some major logistical planning, but if you want an adventure that even very few locals have done, this is it. Day hikers do not need a permit, but anyone using the 'Ainapo Trail must call **Kapapala Ranch** (☎ 928-6206) to obtain the combination (which is changed daily) for the access gate. Call the ranch between 7:30pm and 8:30pm the day before you intend to hike, *and* between 4:30am and 7am on the day of your hike. If you plan to overnight at the 'Ainapo Shelter, you must obtain a permit from the **Division of Forestry & Wildlife** (☎ 974-4221; 19 E Kawili St, PO Box 4849, Hilo, HI 96720; ⌚ 8am-4:30pm Mon-Fri) since it's on the Kapapala Forest Reserve. Then if planning to summit Mauna Loa, you must also register at the Kilauea Visitor Center.

To access the trailhead, turn onto 'Ainapo Rd between mile markers 40 and 41, off Hwy 11. This is a serious 4WD road and you'll need a high-clearance vehicle to make it to the trailhead. You'll come to the Kapapala Ranch gate after about 2 miles, from where it's another 6 miles to the trailhead; look for it on the *mauka* (inland) side at the cattle guard. Departure from this public corridor is considered trespassing.

Beginning at 5650ft, you ascend 2100ft in 2.7 miles to reach the 'Ainapo Shelter. This moderate to challenging portion of the trail passes through koa, ohia and subalpine ohia/ shrub forest. The cabin has six bunks, a composting toilet and limited catchment water (treat it before drinking), and maybe some extra goodies from previous hikers. Fires are prohibited. Above the shelter the trail becomes challenging: first an uphill ankle-twister over *'a'a* and then substantial elevation gains (5500ft in 7.5 miles) to the Mauna Loa cabin.

The strategy for anyone attempting this hike should include getting a good trail map, consulting with locals who are familiar with the hike, talking to national park rangers about the portion of the trail within park boundaries, renting a 4WD with high clearance and waiting for good weather. Regardless, you should be equipped for winter mountaineering on this rugged adventure.

HAWAI'I VOLCANOES NATIONAL PARK

Backcountry Trails

These trails over and around the island's volcanoes provide unparalleled adventures. Though the park makes it easy to explore the backcountry with three-sided shelters and cabins dotting the trails, you should be well equipped and prepared. Cabins are available at Kipuka Pepeiao along the Ka'u Desert Trail, at Pu'u'ula'ula (Red Hill) on the Mauna Loa Trail and at the Mauna Loa summit. Lean-tos and campgrounds are on the coast at Keauhou, Halape and Ka'aha. All have pit toilets and limited catchment water that must be treated before drinking. There are also two primitive campgrounds with pit toilets (but no water) at 'Apua Point along the Puna Coast Trail, and Napau Crater campground, 3 miles west of the Pu'u 'O'o vent. Over lava flows you'll be relying on *ahu* to find your way. Misty or 'voggy' conditions make it easy to get disoriented, so pack a compass and don't get macho out there on the lava – it can turn you around before you know it.

Before heading out, overnight hikers are required to register for free permits at the visitor center (p212). Rangers have updates on trail and cabin conditions, plus water levels at each site. Permits are issued on a first-come, first-served basis, beginning no earlier than noon on the day before your intended hike. There's a three-day limit at each backcountry campsite.

Essential backpacking equipment includes a first-aid kit, trail map, flashlight with extra batteries, a minimum of a gallon of water, an extra stash of food, a cooking stove with fuel (open fires are prohibited), biodegradable soap, broken-in boots, sunglasses, sunscreen, rain gear and a hat. Minimum-impact camping is always the rule, so pack out what you pack in. Note that the desert and coastal trails are extremely hot – heat exhaustion can be a real danger. More information on backcountry

Top Picks

RAINY-DAY ACTIVITIES

- **Volcano Garden Arts** (p226)
- **2400° Fahrenheit, where glass treasures are created** (p226)
- **Lomilomi massage at Hale Ho'ola** (p226)
- **Fireside cocktails at Volcano House** (p225)
- **Hit the skate park** (p226)
- **Wine tasting at Volcano Winery** (p226)

hiking, including basic trail maps and hiking books, is available at the Kilauea Visitor Center.

On the Mauna Loa Summit, Observatory and 'Ainapo trails (see p220 and p221), it's critically important to acclimatize. Altitude sickness is a danger. The high altitude can produce extreme environmental conditions, making hypothermia from the cold and wind a hazard. A good windproof jacket, wool sweater, winter-rated sleeping bag, rain gear and high-altitude experience are essential, as are sunglasses and sunscreen.

NAPAU CRATER TRAIL
Map p208

For spectacular views of Pu'u 'O'o, the source of Kilauea's current spectacle, the 18-mile Napau Crater Trail can't be beat. Unfortunately, at press time volcanic activity had forced the closure of the trail beyond the Napau Crater campground until further notice. However, you can still do the first leg of this hike, the Pu'u Huluhulu Overlook Trail (no permit required; p216), and up to the campground (permit required; 7.1 miles). Exercise extreme caution in this area since it's riddled with deep cracks as the cinder cone continues to collapse.

The Napau trailhead is at the 3.5-mile marker along Chain of Craters Rd, near the Mauna Ulu parking area. The trail's first 5 miles follow what was formerly Chain of Craters Rd, before *pahoehoe* swamped it in 1973. Reticulite and Pele's hair (fine strands of volcanic glass) are strewn all over the flows.

You'll pass lava trees and the 150ft Pu'u Huluhulu (Shaggy Hill) cinder cone before veering left (east). On clear days the view is magnificent, with Mauna Loa off to the northwest, Mauna Kea to the north and the volatile Pu'u 'O'o vent to the east. After descending across *pahoehoe* terrain, you'll reach the south rim of Makaopuhi Crater, a jaw-dropping 1 mile wide and 500ft deep.

Upon exiting a cool fern forest, you come to the rock walls of an old depository for *pulu*, the golden, silky 'hair' found at the base of *hapu'u* (tree fern) fiddlehead stems. The ancient Hawaiians used *pulu* to embalm their dead. In the late 19th century, *pulu* was exported for use as mattress and pillow stuffing, until it was discovered that it quickly decomposed and turned to dust. Whoops.

Ten minutes past the '*pulu* factory' are fantastic views of the partially collapsed Pu'u 'O'o cone. Beyond the junction for the Napau Crater lookout is the primitive campground.

CAMPING IN TURTLE TERRITORY

The prime camping spots along the coast are also where critically endangered **hawksbill sea turtles** come ashore every July to October to bury their eggs. Two months later, hundreds of teeny turtles emerge from the sandy pits and waddle to the sea. Not all make it. Only 81 adult female hawksbills have been identified in Hawai'i, so it's imperative – legally, as well as morally – that you follow these guidelines when visiting these protected areas.

- Do not pitch tents in signposted turtle nesting spots (beaches around the protected cove).
- Keep sites free of food scraps – they attract feral predators.
- Pack out your garbage.
- Flashlights, campfires and camera flashes disorient females looking for a place to nest and hatchlings trying to find the ocean. Direct all light away from the water and beaches at night.
- Use red filters on flashlights.
- Follow instructions of park rangers.
- Stay at least 30ft from turtles.

View from Hilina Pali Trail   CONNER GORRY

KAHAUALE'A TRAIL

Map p208

One of those 'insider' hikes, this backdoor trail-of-use toward the Pu'u 'O'o vent was closed indefinitely by the Department of Land and Natural Resources (DLNR) in July 2007 due to hazardous conditions. Even before the lava flow shifted to this part of the East Rift Zone, forcing the closure, several adventure junkies were lost or injured on this hike located outside the park on the Kahauale'a Natural Area Reserve. To find out if it has reopened, see www.nps .gov/havo/closed_areas.htm.

The poorly maintained trail is accessed by turning onto S Glenwood Rd immediately before the 20-mile marker. At the end of the dirt road beyond the Kahauale'a Natural Area Reserve sign, a footpath wanders for about 4.5 miles through lush ohia and *hapu'u* forest, then forges one last mile over desolate volcanic desert toward Pu'u 'O'o. Don't go further than the edge of the forest – the terrain is unstable and treacherous.

KEAUHOU, KA'AHA & HILINA PALI TRAILS

Map p208

Hike into the backcountry coastal sites via the Keauhou and Hilina Pali trails and you'll experience secluded **snorkeling, white-sand beaches** and soaring **cliffs**, plus savagely beautiful landscapes. These routes are hot and fairly strenuous, so bring lots of water. The extensive trail network means you can design your own loop between the three shelters: Ka'aha, Halape and Keauhou. The easiest trail is the gently sloping Keauhou (6.8 miles to the absolutely stunning campsites there), while the shortest is Ka'aha (3.6 miles to rich snorkeling grounds), but it starts with the brutal cliff descent that makes the Hilina Pali Trail the toughest of the three (8 miles to Halape).

Of all the coastal shelters, **Halape** is the most storied. On November 29, 1975, a 7.2 magnitude earthquake shook the Big Island – the strongest in 100 years. Just before dawn, rockslides from the upper slopes sent most of the 36 campers running toward the sea, where the coastline suddenly sank. What moments before was an idyllic, beachfront, palm-fringed campground had been submerged beneath their feet. A series of tsunami swept the campers up, carrying them out to sea and then coughing them back on shore. Miraculously, only two people died.

The earthquake left a sandy, multiscalloped cove and, despite its turbulent past, Halape is a lovely spot. **Swimming** is good in the protected cove, but there are strong currents in the open ocean beyond. Bring your snorkel gear – there's not much coral, but there are bigger reef fish, clownfish and *humuhumunukunukuapua'a* (Hawaiian triggerfish). The 4-mile round-trip **day hike** between Halape and Keauhou is terrific; look for an amazing lava tube *makai* (seaward) about five minutes from the *pali*.

Camping at Halape   CONNER GORRY

Kilauea Iki overlook

GREG ELMS

Halape is one of only eight Big Island nesting sites for the endangered **Hawaiian hawksbill sea turtle** *(honu'ea)*. Hawksbill turtles also nest at Keauhou and 'Apua Point. Please travel responsibly here; see p222.

KA'U DESERT TRAIL
Map p208

If you're determined to do some heavy-duty desert hiking, this trail network, the park's most extensive, allows you to connect a variety of trails (including Mauna Iki, coastal gems such as Ka'aha and the knee-quaking Hilina Pali), cabins and campgrounds for multiday endurance hikes. These hot, lackluster trails are not all that interesting, however, and are recommended only for those who have hiked the park in its entirety and want to complete the circuit.

PUNA COAST TRAIL
Map p208

This trail starts almost at the end of the Chain of Craters Rd, at the Pu'u Loa Petroglyphs. This hot and barren hike crosses miles of *pahoehoe* from Mauna Ulu's early 1970s eruptions. Unless you find volcanic textures interesting, there's little to recommend it. Still, this 6.5-mile trail is flat and well marked and could be incorporated into a multiday loop between the Ka'aha, Halape, Keauhou and 'Apua campsites.

FESTIVALS & EVENTS

Regular park programs include **After Dark in the Park** (Kilauea Visitor Center Auditorium; suggested donation $1; ☻ 7pm Tue), a series of free talks by specialists on cultural, historic and geological matters.

Annual special events (free with park admission) include the following:

Kilauea Volcano Wilderness Runs (☎ 985-8725; www.volcanoartcenter.org) Four separate events in late July, from a 5-mile walk or run to a full marathon around the craters and calderas. For information, including how to volunteer, contact the Volcano Art Center.

Aloha Festivals Ka Ho'ola'a o Na Ali'i (www.aloha festivals.com) A brilliant royal court procession on the Halema'uma'u Crater rim kicking off the Aloha Festivals, held from August to early October, islandwide.

Na Mea Hawai'i Hula Kahiko Series (www.volcano artcenter.org; ☻ 10am) A series of outdoor *kahiko* (ancient) hula performances overlooking Kilauea Crater. Held four times yearly; see the Performances & Events section of the website for details.

EATING & DRINKING

Except for picnics, the only place to sate yourself within the park is at Volcano House (p225). The bland cafeteria food is overpriced, but the views are priceless; sip a hot chocolate overlooking the caldera at the **snack bar** (☻ 9am-5pm) or a cocktail at **Uncle George's Lounge** (☻ 4:30-9pm). Afterward, warm yourself by the living-room fire (which has been burning since the 1870s!).

SLEEPING

Unless you're camping, stay in Volcano Village (p227), where you have a wide variety of choices. In addition to backcountry shelters and campsites (see p221), the park has two free drive-up campgrounds that are relatively uncrowded outside summer (no registration required). Sites are first-come, first-served, with a three-night limit. Nights can be crisp and cool at this elevation.

KULANAOKUAIKI CAMPGROUND
Campground

our pick Map p208; Hilina Pali Rd; free

This campground off Chain of Craters Rd has several campsites, plus toilets and picnic tables, but no water. Tip: follow the cairns over the hill for secluded sites catching the Mauna Loa sunrise.

NAMAKANIPAIO CAMPGROUND
Campground

Map p212; btwn the 32- and 33-mile markers off Hwy 11; free

The park's busiest campground is 3 miles west of the visitor center. Tent sites are in a small, unshaded meadow with little privacy. There are full facilities.

NAMAKANIPAIO CABINS
Cabins $

Map p212; ☎ 967-7321; cabins $55, additional person $10, maximum 4 per cabin

Every plywood A-frame cabin here has a double bed, two bunks and lights; showers and toilets are shared. Volcano House (which takes bookings for the cabins) provides sheets, but bring something to warm you through cold nights. Did someone say whiskey? Check-in requires deposits for keys ($12) and linens ($20). Unit No 1 is

best, followed by Nos 2, 9 and 10. A half-mile track connecting to Crater Rim Trail is across the road.

VOLCANO HOUSE
Independent Hotel $$$

Map p212; ☎ 967-7321; www.volcanohousehotel .com; 1 Crater Rim Dr; r $100-230; P

Do you need to be looking into Kilauea Caldera? If not, skip this historic, somewhat dowdy hotel. The views are one-of-a-kind, but the digs are more glorified motel than glorious hotel. If you're determined, splurge on a Crater View room; the downstairs units (Nos 26 to 29) with sliding wooden doors onto a shared patio are best. Cheap rooms overlook the parking lot. Stairs throughout mean wheelchair-bound folks should book elsewhere.

GETTING THERE & AROUND

The park is 29 miles (45 minutes) from Hilo and 97 miles (two hours) from Kailua-Kona via Hwy 11. Volcano Village is a couple of miles east of the park entrance.

The free **Hele-On Bus** (☎ 961-8744; www.co .hawaii.hi.us/mass_transit/heleonbus.html) running between Hilo and Ocean View leaves Hilo for Volcano Village (one hour) weekdays at 5:30am, 2:40pm and 4:30pm. You can request a stop at the park entrance. The return trip is made from the village at 6:30am, 8:10am and 5:30pm.

In the park, cyclists are permitted on Crater Rim Dr, Chain of Craters Rd, Hilina Pali Rd and Escape Rd.

AROUND HAWAI'I VOLCANOES NATIONAL PARK

VOLCANO

Slow down: this is Volcano, elevation 3750ft, population 2900. Just 2 miles from the park, a cool mist envelops Volcano in a mystic hush. Even the foulmouthed toughs and winos on the public bus simmer down when approaching this enchanting town, hedged in by giant *sugi* (Japanese evergreen trees), ohia forest and tree ferns. Many artists and writers find inspiration in this small, soulful place; unfortunately, so did Donald Trump, who proclaimed Volcano the best real-estate investment in the USA, something you'll hear locals grumble

about. Pull out your wet-weather gear: It can be cold and rainy for long stretches.

Information

Almost everything you need can be found along Old Volcano Rd. Many businesses here don't accept plastic. When you need cash, there are ATMs at **Kilauea General Store** (☎ 967-7555; 19-3972 Old Volcano Rd; 🕑 6:30am-7:30pm) and **True Value Hardware** (☎ 967-7969; 19-4084 Old Volcano Rd; 🕑 8am-4:30pm). These two shops sell basic camping gear, too, excluding tents.

There's internet access at **Lava Rock Café** (☎ 967-8526; 19-3972 Old Volcano Rd; internet per 20min $3, daily/weekly wi-fi card $10/25; ⏰ 7:30am-5pm Mon, to 9pm Tue-Sat, to 4pm Sun) and a small **post office** (☎ 967-7611; 19-4030 Old Volcano Rd; ⏰ 7:30am-3:30pm Mon-Fri, 11am-noon Sat) a block west.

Sights & Activities

Make a stop at the island's unique **Volcano Winery** (Map p212; ☎ 967-7772; www.volcanowinery.com; 35 Pi'i Mauna Dr; ⏰ 10am-5:30pm) for some wine tasting in the shadow of Mauna Loa. For our palate, the Volcano Red ($17 per bottle) is tops.

If golf turns you on, hit the 18-hole, par-72 course at the **Volcano Golf & Country Club** (Map p212; ☎ 967-7331; www.volcanogolfshop.com; Pi'i Mauna Dr; greens fee $68). The setting is lush beneath Mauna Loa and Mauna Kea (snowcapped in winter), and the straight-forward course is well maintained.

After a hard day hiking, relax with a traditional Hawaiian massage, facial or steam bath. All are on the extensive spa menu at **Hale Ho'ola Hawaiian Healing Arts Center & Spa** (☎ 756-2421; www.halehoola.net; 11-3913 7th St; 30/60/90/120min treatments from $45/75/95/140). Special massages for kids *(na keiki)* and elders *(kupuna)* are also offered. Turn right onto Pearl Ave near the 26-mile marker and right on 7th St to get here.

Free nature walks are offered by the **Volcano Art Center** (☎ 967-8222; www.volcanoartcenter.org; 19-4074 Old Volcano Rd; ⏰ 9:30am Mon). If you want to get more involved, you can volunteer on **'forest workday'** (⏰ 9am-noon 3rd Sun of month).

Volcano's famous **farmers market** (Cooper Community Center, Wright Rd; ⏰ 6-10am Sun) draws folks from far and wide for organic everything, gourmet meals, local crafts and used books. The whole community comes out – including skaters grinding at the rad **skate park** (admission free).

Part of Volcano's charm is in its art scene, from formal galleries to roadside sculptures (look for the installation at the intersection of Alii Kane Rd and Hwy 11 after the 23-mile marker). You can easily spend an afternoon studio hopping here; try the following places:
2400º Fahrenheit (Map p208; ☎ 985-8667; www.2400F.com; ⏰ 10am-4pm Thu-Mon) Drop in here to watch Michael and Misato Mortara blow some cool, hot glass. This is a great studio visit for kids. Between the 23- and 24-mile markers off Hwy 11.
Volcano Garden Arts (☎ 967-7261; www.volcanogardenarts.com; 19-3834 Old Volcano Rd; admission free; ⏰ 10am-4pm Tue-Sun) Get inspired at Ira Ono's working studio, with gallery, installations, gardens and art classes.

Eating & Drinking

Volcano is a small town with big dining.

VOLCANO GOLF & COUNTRY CLUB   Diner $
Map p212; ☎ 967-8228; Pi'i Mauna Dr; breakfast $2-6.50, lunch $5.75-9.25; ⏰ 7am-2pm Mon-Fri, 6:30am-2pm Sat & Sun
It's fun to eavesdrop on locals talking story and comparing handicaps while watching golfers miss putts, but the food here is unimaginative diner fare: pancakes for breakfast, burgers for lunch. The golfer's/hiker's takeout menu (*bento* boxes, bagel creations) is handy though.

LAVA ROCK CAFÉ   Comfort Food $
☎ 967-8526; 19-3972 Old Volcano Rd; dishes $6-12; ⏰ 7:30am-5pm Mon, to 9pm Tue-Sat, to 4pm Sun
This joint is nearly always jumping with locals and visitors sidling up to huge burgers and fresh salads and soups. For breakfast, try the French toast with the house specialty *liliko'i* (passion fruit) butter. Kids' menu available.

THAI THAI RESTAURANT   Thai $$
our pick ☎ 967-7969; 19-4084 Old Volcano Rd; mains $13-20; ⏰ 4-9pm
Locals claim it's the best Thai on the island, and we're loathe to argue. The classic *lab* or green papaya salad ($10 to $20) and curries are all proven 'ono kine grinds (good food). This place earns bonus points for its big portions and excellent vegetarian selection, but gets crowded and stressed out (reservations recommended). Solo traveler's tip: eat at the bar.

KIAWE KITCHEN   Bistro $$
☎ 967-7711; cnr Old Volcano & Haunani Rds; mains $13-20; ⏰ lunch & dinner
The house special at this popular café is anything wood-fired (thin-crust pizzas, gourmet meats), plus high-quality potent potables, including Big Island microbrews. It's not

cheap (a basic 10in pizza is $16), but it *is* tasty; try the crab-stuffed portobello or linguine with clam sauce ($21). Small outdoor patio is best for conversation or romance.

KILAUEA LODGE
Eclectic $$$$

☎ 967-7366; www.kilauealodge.com; 19-3948 Old Volcano Rd; mains $20-45; ☽ dinner

If you want fine dining ambience, this restaurant with couches around a stone fireplace is your only option. Stick to the exotic game (venison, ostrich) or stay local (Parker Ranch steaks, catch of the day). This is not the place for vegetarians – 20 bucks for eggplant casserole?!

For groceries, including (limited) fresh veggies, try **Volcano Store** (☎ 967-7210; cnr Old Volcano & Haunani Rds; ☽ 5am-7pm) and **Kilauea**

General Store (☎ 967-7555; 19-3972 Old Volcano Rd; ☽ 6:30am-7:30pm).

Sleeping

Lovely B&Bs and rental cottages grow around Volcano like mushrooms; to focus your search, consult an islandwide booking service (see p273). All the mist makes Volcano damp: if you have respiratory problems, make sure your room has a dehumidifier.

KULANA ARTIST SANCTUARY
Artist Colony $

☎ 985-9055; www.discoverkulana.com; Volcano Village; camping per person $15, s/d $25/40

Growing apace with the founder's vision for a nurturing, creative environment, Kulana

ISLAND VOICES

NAME: IRA ONO

OCCUPATION: VISUAL AND PERFORMANCE ARTIST, CARETAKER AT VOLCANO GARDEN ARTS

RESIDENCE: VOLCANO

What kind of a name is Ono? Are you delicious? Many years ago I was at a craft show selling my pieces and I had a sign that said 'Ira's Ono Ceramics.' And this little Hawaiian kid came up to me and asked, 'Are you Mr Ono?' I looked at him and said, 'I guess I am.'

What brought you to Volcano? In 1968 I was a starving artist from New York. I kept heading west until I landed in Maui, where the living was easy and rent was cheap. In 1980 I came over here looking to buy land and this was where I could afford. I love it. I love the access to the park. It's inspirational.

I've noticed. There are lots of artists here. Yes, we have a lovely community of artists. Here we host art classes, folk festivals, poetry nights… Artists are always dropping in – there are some women doing ceramics in the greenhouse right now. We're also building a ceramics studio and out buildings for artists-in-residence.

How has Volcano changed since you've lived here? About five years ago, we were discovered. There was a feeding frenzy, land speculation. But it's flattened out. Now Volcano is scientists, bird people, artists and dope growers.

What's the next big thing on the Big Island? Tea. Everyone's growing it. We're putting a tea pavilion in that circle of pine trees. That grove is 60 years old. We're going to serve high tea in there.

is a budding intentional community with a positive, women-centric vibe. Guests in the two cabins share the main house bathroom, kitchen and library, and are required to participate in easy caretaking tasks (a couple of hours a week). Note Kulana's motto – 'no smoking, alcohol, drugs or drama' – and review its online guidelines. Discounts for stays of two nights or more; artist-in-residence rates also available.

HOLO HOLO IN
Hostel $

☎ 967-7950, 967-8025; www.enable.org/holoholo; 19-4036 Kalani Honua Rd; dm $19, r with shared/private bathroom $50/65; 🖳

This small hostel has clean, darkish dorms downstairs, plus four private rooms (two with private bathrooms) upstairs. The mattresses are good, if soft, and plenty of blankets are provided. There's a shared kitchen, free internet and a well-stocked library. There's also the pitter patter of little feet and the odd (rare) temper tantrum. Call for reservations after 4:30pm; the hostel is locked from 11am to 4pm daily, when guests must vacate. Cash or checks only.

THE ARTIST COTTAGE
Cottage $$

our pick ☎ 967-7261; www.volcanoartistscottage .com; 19-3436 Old Volcano Rd; cottage $109; P 🖳

To all the artists and writers reading this: set your creative retreat here. The refurbished cabin is adorable – sky-lit bedroom, Zen bathroom with giant walk-in shower, original art – but also functional. There's a full kitchen for nibbling away creative blocks, wi-fi, an admirable library and stereo. It's small though – best for one or an intimate pair. Need outdoor space? No worries: these digs are on the grounds of **Volcano Garden Arts** (p226).

VOLCANO COUNTRY COTTAGES
Cottages $$

☎ 967-7960, 888-446-3910; www.volcanocottages.com; 19-3990 Old Volcano Rd; cottages d $132, additional person $15, incl breakfast; P 🖳

Centrally located in Volcano Village, each of these fabulously appointed cottages has koa beds with high-quality linens and full kitchen with modern appliances (except for the studio, which has no kitchen). Privacy is assured, and outdoor space, too (lanai or lawn), plus 24/7 dehumidifiers in each unit mean no clammy sheets. There's wi-fi and

a hot tub nestled among giant *sugi* and ohia trees. Gather the tribe and rent all four for a memorable retreat, but not during the Merrie Monarch Festival, when a hula *halau* (school) books it.

VOLCANO RAINFOREST RETREAT
Cottages $$$

Map p208; ☎ 985-8696, 800-550-8696; www .volcanoretreat.com; 11-3832 12th St; cottages incl breakfast $140-260; P

With four beautiful cottages nestled in the forest, this is one of Volcano's most romantic B&Bs (reservations a must). Each unit is designed to harmonize with nature and emphasize spiritual and restorative practices (hence the Japanese-style soaking tubs and Jacuzzi). From stargazing in bed to sleeping in the tree line, these are sublime accommodations. Energy healing, personal-growth workshops and guided spiritual retreats also available.

KILAUEA LODGE
Inn $$$

☎ 967-7366; www.kilauealodge.com; 19-3948 Old Volcano Rd; r $155-170, cottages $170-195, incl breakfast; P

The Lodge's grandiose entrance belies the cozy and intimate atmosphere of this longtime favorite. Request the Hale Aloha Building, with its grand room warmed by a fire. Snag room No 6 (wheelchair accessible) or No 9 and you'll have a patio overlooking a patch of rain forest. Head upstairs for high-ceilinged rooms (a shame they're carpeted) dappled with light from the stained-glass windows, and featuring exquisite quilts and koa furnishings. The Honeymoon Suite has its own fireplace and balcony, but even newlyweds have to share the garden hot tub.

Steaming Halema'uma'u Crater   GREG ELMS

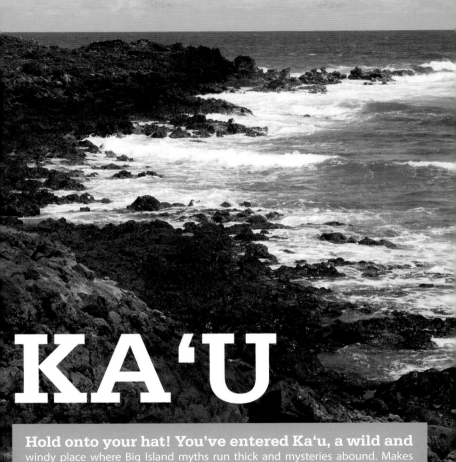

KA'U

Hold onto your hat! You've entered Ka'u, a wild and windy place where Big Island myths run thick and mysteries abound. Makes sense, since it all began at Ka Lae (South Point), believed to be the landing site of the Polynesians in Hawaii. Sure, you can spend a day at Green Sands Beach or Road to the Sea and think there isn't much to this arid lava land but a couple of hard-to-reach swaths of sand. But linger in this southernmost region of the USA and you'll see why locals are so rabid to protect it. And protect it they do: Ka'u folks have squashed coastal resorts and lobbied for the national park to acquire 116,000 acres, and are pioneers of 'off-the-grid' living.

KA'U
ITINERARIES

IN TWO DAYS *This leg: 30 miles*

❶ SOUTH POINT (p236) Ramble down to the country's southernmost point to kick off day one. We dare you to try the 40ft **cliff jump (p237)**. Alternatively, take some sunset cocktails here – a couple of beach chairs facing west await. Can you find them?

❷ GREEN SANDS BEACH (p236) Detour from South Point and hike into this famous olive-green scoop of sand early in the morning or at dusk and it might be just you, the water and (oh, yes) the wind.

❸ NA'ALEHU (p234) On day two, stop at **Hana Hou Coffee Shop (p235)** for fresh cinnamon buns, plus free samples across the

street at the **Punalu'u Bakeshop (p235)**. Don't miss the **koi pond** at the former and the **garden trail** at the latter.

❹ PUNALU'U BEACH PARK (p233) Continue to this **black-sand beach** for some turtle watching. Easily accessible, there are almost always turtles stuffing themselves on seaweed and trundling up to bake in the sun here.

❺ NECHUNG DORJE DRAYANG LING (p233) End day two with a visit to this **Buddhist temple** tucked in Wood Valley. Even the 4-mile drive up through the forest is meditative.

IN FOUR DAYS *This leg: 55 miles*

❻ KULA KAI CAVERNS (p239) Follow the two-day itinerary then plunge into a **caving adventure**. Soda straws, moonmilk puffballs, pillars and columns: a lava tube's exoticism comes alive on these tours.

❼ MANUKA STATE WAYSIDE PARK (p240) Enjoy some outdoor relief after the lava tubes' dark recesses at this forested state park with a 2-mile **loop trail** through native forest full of rare native plants.

❽ ROAD TO THE SEA (p240) You'll need a 4WD to make it to these secluded **beaches**, but it'll be worth it when you finally strip off your clothes in a mad dash toward the water.

❾ DESERT ROSE CAFÉ (p239) Hungry yet? Get stuffed at this local joint after a long day of frolicking Ka'u style. If it's Saturday, get ready to karaoke, baby.

You'll need a 4WD to reach South Point, the southernmost spot in the USA

GREG ELMS

FOR BEACH HERMITS

❶ ROAD TO THE SEA (p240) Only those with a 4WD can get to the beaches on this isolated stretch of the Ka'u coast. **Camping** here is a possibility, though the whipping wind might wipe the freckles right off your face.

❷ POHUE BAY (p238) You have to hike over hot 'a'a (rough, jagged lava) to get to one of the island's most pristine and private beaches, but trust us, it will be worth it. Even some locals have never romped on this one.

❸ GREEN SANDS BEACH (p236) All that shimmering green olivine is still a damned

pretty site – despite the kamikaze tourism that dominates here. Pack a picnic, ignore the hordes, and enjoy this unique and colorful beach. Remember: karma and custom warn against taking some of that remarkable sand with you (and we know how tempting it can be!).

❹ KAWA BAY (p234) This off-the-beaten-track spot, where you can **fish**, **surf**, **camp** or just hang out and catch a killer sunset, is as local as it gets. You won't find a more welcoming pocket on this beach-starved stretch of coast.

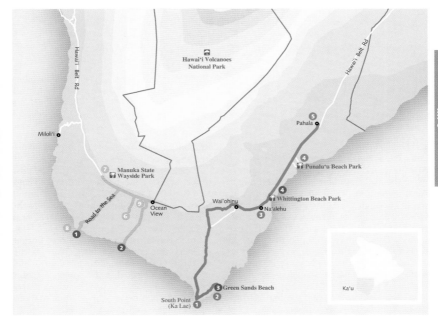

KA'U

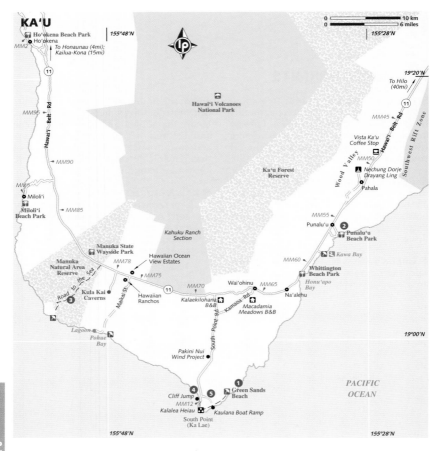

KA'U

PAHALA

Pahala is a funky little town just past the 51-mile marker. Once sugarcane country, when the mill closed for good in 1996, Ka'u Agribusiness switched to macadamia-nut trees. The highway is thick with them and there are scads of farm tours to choose from. This is also the Ka'u coffee belt. Java junkies take note: some specialists rate it higher than Kona for flavor.

Coming from the south, enter Pahala via Maile St to see what this town is about: the shuttered mill, rickety homes, 'Beware of Dog' signs and junked cars rusting in front yards. Alternatively, you can enter Pahala via Kamani St, which passes the hospital before heading directly into small-town USA.

Pahala has a fire house, gas station, post office, school, one bank (with ATM) and **Ka'u Hospital** (☎ 928-2050). Like most small towns, it also has down-home good cooking at **PT Café** (☎ 928-8200; 96-3163 Pikake St; meals $4-10; ⏰ 6:30am-7pm Thu-Mon, to 3pm Tue & Wed). Hunker down with a grass-fed-beef burger or local *'ahi* (yellowfin tuna) plate at the outdoor tables with the old-timers. The menu is solid, but skip the coffee. A better bet is outdoor **Vista Ka'u Coffee Stop** (⏰ when it feels like it), just before the 49-mile marker, with a long vista toward the sea.

HIGHLIGHTS

❶ **BEST BEACH:** Green Sands (p236)
❷ **BEST VIEW:** Turtles dotting Punalu'u Beach (below)
❸ **BEST ACTIVITY:** Off-roading along the Road to the Sea (p240)
❹ **BEST THRILL:** Cliff jumping at South Point (p237)
❺ **BEST RAINY-DAY ACTIVITY:** Braiding a lei with master Kilohana Domingo (p238)

Highlights are numbered on the map on p232.

PUNALU'U

Seeing animals in the wild is a thrill, and this small **our pick** black-sand beach is a prime spot for it. One of the few hawksbill nesting sites on the island, Punalu'u has delivered these or green sea turtles every time we've turned up, so chances are you'll see some of these cute little *buggahs*, too. The bay here, once a major Hawaiian settlement and then a sugar port, is full of tasty *limu* (seaweed). After gorging themselves on the leafy greens, the *honu* (sea turtles) trundle up to the beach to rest. It's quite an inspiring spectacle, which, under no circumstances, should be disrupted by you or your children (a visit here is a good ecological educational opportunity). These are an endangered species protected by law and should not be approached. Take care, too, walking on the sands, which are sometimes used as nesting sites.

For more turtle time, you can camp at Punalu'u Beach Park, a county park located just south with full facilities. The flat, grassy sites overlooking the beach are beautiful, but there's zero privacy. This is a night-time hangout for young, drunken thugs, who have become aggressive toward campers, so beware. Come daybreak, it's overrun with picnickers and grannies on bus tours. Permits are required; see p273.

In addition to turtles, you might also see a panicked swimmer being rescued via helicopter, like we did during research. Even locals treat this beach with guarded respect, since the chilly, spring-fed waters roil with

DETOUR ➡

WOOD VALLEY

About 4 miles inland from Pahala is the remote Buddhist temple and retreat center, **Nechung Dorje Drayang Ling** (Immutable Island of Melodious Sound). The temple was built in 1902 by Japanese sugarcane laborers. Originally located a few miles nearer Pahala, it was relocated to its present spot after a severe storm in 1917.

The storied temple became one of the first places for the study of Tibetan Buddhism in the USA. Based on early Western pilgrimages to Tibet in the 1970s, several high lamas were asked to bring their wisdom to the West. An initial visit to O'ahu by His Holiness, Dudjom Rinpoche, brought this message: 'The main responsibility for religious people is to spread the teachings of peace, brotherhood and happiness to all sentient beings. Not to disturb existing religions, but spread goodwill to all faiths.'

Soon after, nonprofit organizations and volunteers helped to restore the abandoned temple. In 1973 a Tibetan lama, Nechung Rinpoche, took up residence here, and in 1980 the Dalai Lama visited to dedicate the temple. Since then, many Tibetan lamas have conducted programs here and the Dalai Lama himself returned for a visit in 1994.

The **retreat center** (☎ 928-8539, 928-6271; www.nechung.org; Nechung Dorje Drayang Ling; s/d/tr with shared bathroom $65/75/100, 2br ste $135-150), nestled in a tranquil forest with peacocks roaming freely about, provides an ideal location for contemplation. Here you'll find a meditation hall with two peaceful guest rooms (one done up Japanese style, the other Hawaiian). The ground floor also has a few simpler, smaller rooms ($50 per person) and the suite has its own bathroom. There's a full kitchen and dining room. Two-day minimum stay required. There's a library of books on Buddhist culture, and you're welcome to join in morning services. Day visitors are welcomed on weekends ($5 donation). For those seeking a peaceful retreat, this temple is a special place.

fierce rip currents and strong undertows. Be cautious here.

The northern pocket of the beach is lined with coconut palms and backed by a duck pond. The ruins of the Pahala Sugar Company's old warehouse and pier lie slightly to the north. The Kane'ele'ele Heiau ruins sit on a small rise.

To reach the beach, take either the turnoff to SeaMountain (now *there's* a scary place!) or the one marked Punalu'u Park, less than 1 mile east.

WHITTINGTON BEACH PARK & AROUND

For a killer south-coast view, pull off at the scenic lookout above Honu'apo Bay just before Na'alehu. From here you can see the cement pilings of the old Whittington Pier, which was used for shipping sugar and hemp until the 1930s, but now has a sexier, scientific purpose: the fiber-optic cable measuring the rising Lo'ihi Seamount, Hawai'i's active underwater volcano, is attached to the pier's crumbling pylons.

The turnoff to Whittington Beach Park is 1 mile beyond the lookout. There's no beach and the ocean is usually too rough for swimming, but *honu* can sometimes be seen offshore; apparently they've been frequenting these waters for a long time (Honu'apo

means 'caught turtle' in Hawaiian). The eponymous fishpond is at the north end of the bay. On Sunday afternoons there's a drum circle here.

Camping here (technically) requires a county permit (see p273). The park's proximity to the highway means little privacy, but the shady campsites and picnic pavilions make it a pretty choice spot – itinerant locals hanging here seem to think so. There is no potable water.

Surf's up! at **our pick** Kawa Bay, reached via a drivable dirt road between the 58- and 59-mile markers (stay straight rather than taking any lefts). This is Ka'u's best surfable break (known locally as Windmills). Respect the space of locals here.

NA'ALEHU
Tiny Na'alehu, population 875, is famous for being the southernmost town in the

The former Whittington Pier and current Whittington Beach Park   GREG ELMS

USA. The cultural vibe here is potent and the pastel plantation houses dotting the hills make a quaint scene. It sure feels like old Hawai'i in all-volunteer Na'alehu Internet (☎ 929-8322; donation per hr $3; ⊗ 1-5pm Mon-Fri). Star Wash (per load $3) is next door.

Otherwise Na'alehu is the Ka'u district's commercial center, with a grocery store, Ace Hardware (☎ 929-9030; ⊗ 8am-5pm Mon-Sat, 9am-3pm Sun), a library, police station, post office, gas station and an ATM. There are public tennis courts and a playground at Na'alehu Park.

Eating

SHAKA RESTAURANT   Comfort Food $
☎ 929-7404; www.shakarestaurant.com; Hwy 11; breakfast & lunch $5-8, dinner $10-20; ⊗ 10am-8:30pm
This laid-back diner has pizza, pub grub (the deep fryer here is working overtime) and a *na keiki* (children's) menu, plus breakfast until 5pm for you slackers. Try a Ka'u iced coffee to shake that hangover, or a hair of the dog at the full bar. Major sporting events are shown here.

HANA HOU COFFEE SHOP   Diner $
☎ 929-9717; 95-1148 Spur Rd; meals $6-15; ⊗ 8am-3pm Mon-Wed, to 8pm Thu-Sat, to 6pm Sun
More fuel than food, the diner meals here are filling, but just so-so, especially for the price (*loco moco* for $9.50?!). The bring-your-own wine option is cool, though. The real draw here is the home-baked yummies, such as cinnamon rolls, mac-nut pie, macaroons and rum cake.

The well-stocked **ourpick** Na'alehu Market (☎ 929-7527; ⊗ 8am-7pm Mon-Sat, 9am-6pm Sun) is the best between Hilo and Kailua-Kona. The Punalu'u Bakeshop & Visitor Center (☎ 929-7343; Hwy 11, near Ka'alaiki Rd; ⊗ 9am-5pm) has free samples and an interpretive garden out back for walking off the calories.

WAI'OHINU

It seems each Ka'u town is smaller than the last, and if you blink you'll miss sleepy little Wai'ohinu ('sparkling water'), tucked into a green dip in the road around the 66-mile marker. The village's claim to fame is its landmark Mark Twain monkeypod tree, planted by the author in 1866. The original tree fell in a 1957 hurricane, but hardy new trunks have sprung up and it's once again full grown. There's gas and a general store here.

Sleeping

If you want to drop out for a couple of days, there are some accommodation gems hiding away near Wai'ohinu.

MARGO'S CORNER   Campground/Cottages $$
ourpick ☎ 929-9614; www.margoscorner.com; Wakea St, PO Box 447, Na'alehu, HI 96772; tent sites per person $30, cottages $90-130, additional person $30, all incl breakfast; 🖳
Flying high the rainbow flag, this gay-friendly guesthouse is a standard stopover on the Ka'u camping-cycling route. Of the two cottages, the Adobe Suite, with its wall of windows, double beds in Star Trek–like berths and private sauna, is superior. The garden setting is peaceful and even campers are offered breakfast, plus hot showers! Smoking is prohibited. Margo's is a couple of miles southwest of Wai'ohinu center, off Kama'oa Rd.

MACADAMIA MEADOWS B&B   B&B $$
☎ 929-8097, 888-929-8118; www.macadamia meadows.com; 94-6263 Kama'oa Rd; d $100-130, ste $150, all incl breakfast; 🏊
Staying at a mac-nut or coffee farm is all the rage, and this contemporary home just down Kama'oa Rd is the place to do it. The somewhat dark rooms are clean and nicely appointed (cable TV, microwave, refrigerator, private entrances and lanai), and two adjoin – ideal for families or groups. There's a tennis court and pool, plus an educational farm tour.

SOUTH POINT BANYAN TREE HOUSE   Vacation Rental $$$
☎ reservations 715-302-8180; www.southpoint bth.com; cnr Pinao St & Hwy 11; house $185
These fabulous digs float between the branches of a giant banyan tree. Fully equipped and flooded with light, the house is a private escape in a jungle of mango, lychee and *'ulu* (breadfruit) trees (just ignore the chattering parrot). Did someone say honeymoon?

KA'U

HONU HAUNT

Lovely beaches and warm tropical waters attract more than tourists; they also attract *honu* (sea turtles). Revered by Native Hawaiians, these magnificent creatures can be seen feeding, sunning – even nesting – on Big Island beaches. Often considered a personal 'aumakua (family deity or guardian spirit), you'll also see *honu* images in petroglyphs, tattoos, on mugs, bumper stickers, luggage tags…

In old Hawaii, sea turtles were a prized source of food, but their capture and consumption were governed by strict religious and traditional codes. In recent times, governance has once again become necessary to prevent further damage to the ancestral beaches turtles depend upon to reproduce. Development, tourism, over-hunting and harvesting of their shells have all contributed to the dwindling populations.

Green turtles are now common in Hawaii (look for them eating seaweed in shallow, rocky areas), but the *honu'ea* (hawksbill sea turtle), the rarest in the Pacific Ocean, can also be seen at Punalu'u or the coastal sites in Hawai'i Volcanoes National Park (p224). You'll recognize it by its delicately patterned shell and beaked nose. Before you get too close to these sacred and endangered creatures, consider that only one in 5000 survives the hatch, matures and returns to reproduce. Please keep your distance (this means kids, too!).

The unique Hobbit House (☎ 929-9755; www.hi-hobbit.com/Hawaii/bnb; d per night 3/2 nights $170/200), another fabulous honeymoon spot, is perched atop a bluff with sweeping ocean views. Great for a romantic and whimsical stay; minimum two nights.

If you have no choice, there's spartan and charmless (but dirt cheap) Shirakawa Motel (☎ 929-7462; www.shirakawamotel.com; 95-6040 Hwy 11; d $50, r with kitchenette $60). Still family-run, this weather-beaten but serviceable place is surrounded by exotic plants and exuberant orchards. The neighbor's dog is nasty, however.

SOUTH POINT

South Point is the southernmost spot in the USA, but more importantly it's where the Polynesians first landed in Hawaii, according to most theories (it's also where some folks think the aliens are going to beam us up). In Hawaiian, it's known as Ka Lae, which means simply 'the point.'

A turbulent, windy place, South Point must have looked positively heavenly to the ancient seafarers. Ka Lae was one of the earliest Hawaiian settlements, thanks to the rich fishing grounds offshore and the fresh water available at Punalu'u. These waters still sustain life and the cliffs are dotted with families fishing the weekend away. The turnoff to South Point Rd is between the 69- and 70-mile markers on Hwy 11. Ten miles on, you come to a fork: left leads to the Green Sands Beach Trail, right to Ka Lae. There are finally (thankfully) toilets at Ka Lae and at the Kaulana boat ramp.

Beaches

GREEN SANDS BEACH

You've likely already heard about this beach, traditionally known as Papakolea. It's not *that* green, but it is a secluded patch of beach requiring a 2.5-mile hike or 4WD (from Kaulana boat ramp). It's become a tourist attraction of late; go early, late or when it's overcast to beat the crowds (and heat). The olive-green tableau is formed by semiprecious olivine crystals (a type of volcanic basalt) eroded from the cliffs, worn smooth by the relentless surf and then mixed with black sand. You can swim here, but take care when the surf's up.

To get here, go left at the first fork you come to on South Point Rd. After about

The revered *honu* CONNER GORRY

1 mile, you'll dead-end at a shack where locals might try charging $5 for 'secure parking' in an impromptu lot. No one can legally charge 'admission' to the public-access shoreline, so pay or don't, but do it with aloha.

From here, drop down to the Kaulana boat ramp and walk 2.5 miles along the rutted road to the beach. If you've got a high-clearance 4WD, you can drive it in about 25 minutes. Just beyond the boat ramp the trail passes the site of Kapalaoa, an ancient fishing village. Eventually you'll scramble down some cliffs to the beach. Pick a calm day to visit or face high surf and wicked winds.

Sights

PAKINI NUI WIND PROJECT

After 5 miles of scattered houses and cows on South Point Rd, this wind farm rises into view, with rows of high-tech windmills dotting the pastures down to the sea. In 2006 General Electric jumped on the renewable energy bandwagon, essentially replacing the Kama'oa Wind Farm here, adding 14 1.5-megawatt turbines (and 21 megawatts of wind-generated power to the grid).

About 4 miles south of the wind farm, look for the white orb plopped in a field. Until 1965, this and the outlying buildings were a Pacific Missile Range station that tracked missiles shot from California to the Marshall Islands.

KA LAE

Ten miles down South Point Rd you hit a fork: right leads to a parking lot and the craggy coastal cliffs of Ka Lae. The confluence of ocean currents just offshore makes this area one of Hawai'i's most bountiful fishing grounds – one reason Ka'u residents so doggedly protect this stretch of coast.

At the northern end of the parking lot, right on the cliff's edge, are wooden platforms with hoists and ladders for the small boats anchored below; look for *honu* in the relatively calm waters here or humpback whales further out (from January to April). This is where daredevils take the 40ft cliff jump and is a popular fishing spot for red snapper and *ulua* (jack fish).

To plant yourself at actual South Point, take the well-worn path south from the parking lot toward the beacon. Sit quietly.

Imagine what it must have been like to land here, fighting violent surf after months at sea. Feel the mana. Full moon is a special time to visit.

Right behind here is Kalalea Heiau, usually classified as a *ko'a* (a small stone pen designed to encourage fish and birds to multiply). Inside is a fishing shrine where ancient Hawaiians left offerings to Ku'ula, the god of fishermen, in hopes of currying favor for a bountiful catch. An outcropping on the western side of the heiau is pocked with canoe mooring holes, chipped long ago into the lava rock. Strong currents would pull the canoes out into deep turbulent waters, where enterprising ancient Hawaiians could fish, still tethered to shore.

Sleeping

KALAEKILOHANA   B&B $$$
our pick ☎ 939-8052; www.kau-hawaii.com; Ka Lae; r incl breakfast $189; 🖳
Ho'okipa (hospitality) is the watchword at this upscale – and yet down-home – B&B. Upstairs, four airy rooms feature gleaming hardwood floors, top-quality linens, open 'rainfall' shower and French doors that open to large lanai. Downstairs, guests are welcome to join hosts Kilohana Domingo and Kenny Joyce in free Hawaiian language or *kanikapila* (informal jam session) nights. Highly recommended are Domingo's personalized workshops on lei making and other native crafts.

OCEAN VIEW

You may have heard lore about this last gasp for food and gas around the 76-mile marker before the drive up to Honaunau. Known as Ocean View, it's divided into greener

Top Picks
KA'U FOR KIDS
- **Kite flying at South Point** (p236)
- **Ogling Punalu'u Beach Park's** *honu* **(sea turtles)** (p233)
- **Hana Hou Coffee Shop's homemade pies** (235)
- **Exploring the lava tubes at Kula Kai Caverns** (239)

ISLAND VOICES

NAME: KILOHANA DOMINGO
OCCUPATION: CO-OWNER OF KALAEKILO-HANA B&B AND MASTER LEI MAKER
RESIDENCE: SOUTH POINT

Why do you live in Ka'u? I grew up in Kealakekua, where my father was a ranch hand. It was simple living but there was always food on the table and lots of time for going fishing, hunting or *holoholo* (ambling around for fun) up *mauka* (inland). I took these experiences for granted until I left to attend Kamehameha Schools in Honolulu. Ka'u was a frontier where no one wanted to live. But I appreciate its quiet beauty – isolated, undiscovered, still 'country.'

As a B&B owner, how do you define ho'okipa (hospitality)? My father had a habit of giving things away and taking the time to show visitors around. If people stopped by, he immediately offered them something to eat and welcomed them as if they hadn't seen each other for a long time. *Ho'okipa* means treating guests the best way you can – to treat them like family.

Is there a proper way to pick plants for lei making? Before I start picking, I give a chant: to get permission, announce my presence and express gratitude. Then the rules are simple: take only what is needed. Don't pillage. The plant shouldn't look as if it's been picked.

How do you advise novice lei makers? I let people do what comes naturally. Some people choose big, showy branches. Others prefer a compact, neater look. The braiding 'hand' might be tight or loose. Once I was teaching a couple and the man took *all* of the red flowers. He had a right to do so, but it did reveal something. In the end, whoever you are, it shows in your lei.

Hawaiian Ocean View Estates (HOVE) up *mauka* (inland) and arid Hawaiian Ranchos *makai* (seaward). This is Hawai'i's frontier, where people come to find themselves or get lost, scratching an existence out of the hard, hot lava. If you linger, you'll find a friendly, tight-knit community, with many alternative energy and antidevelopment activists, plus the odd kook or two. There's gas, a post office and The Wash (☎ 929-7072; wash or dry $2; ☺ 6am-9pm).

Beaches

POHUE BAY

You're going to love this: a pristine beach with good swimming in turquoise blue waters, a (nearly) freshwater lagoon and privacy to spare. To reach Pohue Bay takes a hot one-hour walk over loose lava – start early to beat the heat and wind, and bring plenty of water.

The easiest way to get here is via Maikai St in Hawaiian Ranchos. From Hwy 11, turn *makai* at Prince Kuhio Blvd, then take your first left onto Maile St and your second right onto Maikai St. Follow this to the end, when you'll come to a lava rock wall. This is the beginning of the 2.5-mile, easy-to-follow trail going from dirt to a 4WD road and chunky *'a'a*. After 40 minutes you'll come to a gate. Pass through the gate and you're at a fork: right leads five minutes to the lagoon surrounded by pandanus plants and coconut palms. With barbecue facilities and an outhouse, camping is a distinct possibility here. The left fork leads 10 minutes to wonderful Pohue Bay and a beach epitomizing paradise.

There's plenty of shade and exploration opportunities, plus a three-sided shelter.

A prerequisite for this trip is respecting the land and community hosting you. This is Ka'u after all: you will know if you're not wanted.

Activities

With six of the 10 longest lava tubes in the world, the Big Island is a caving hot spot and Ka'u is fast becoming its capital. Adventures are top-notch at ☀ **our pick** Kula Kai Caverns (☎ 929-9725; www.kulakaicaverns.com; PO Box 6313, Ocean View, HI 96737; adult/child tours from $15/10). These tours are led by experts who've mapped over 20 miles of Big Island caves. Possibilities run the gamut, from a 45-minute illuminated cave exploration to the 'complete cave experience' ($195). Reservations are essential.

Eating

OCEAN VIEW PIZZARIA   Pizzeria $
☎ 929-9677; Ocean View Town Center; small/large pizzas $12/14, sandwiches $7-8.50; ⏱ 11am-7pm Sun-Thu, to 8pm Fri & Sat
Surprisingly, there's some tasty pizza in li'l ole Ocean View. Linger over a large veggie pie with a chocolate milkshake while catching up on local gossip. It also makes hearty sandwiches.

Other recommendations include the following:
Anuenue Natural Foods (☎ 929-7550; Ocean View Town Center; ⏱ 9am-5:30pm Mon-Fri, to 5pm Sat, 8am-5pm Sun) Good for staples, organic produce and fresh juice.
Desert Rose Café (☎ 939-7673; Pohue Plaza; ⏱ 7am-9pm) Cool hangout spot with real espresso, great breakfasts and Saturday night karaoke.
Malama Market (Pohue Plaza; ⏱ 6:30am-8pm) Produce, steaks, *hulihuli* (rotisserie-cooked) chicken ($7) and everything in between.

Sleeping

☀ **LOVA LAVA LAND**   Eco-Resort $
our pick ☎ 352-9097; www.lovalavaland.com; Hawaiian Ranchos; yurt $55, VW buses $35; ▯
This innovative 'eco-resort' is completely off-the-grid (solar power, catchment water, composting toilet), but you wouldn't know it with the fully equipped kitchen, kicking wi-fi and hot showers. The yurt is a snazzy love nest, with a double bed, hardwood floors and moon roof, or you can get cozy in a tricked-out VW bus (it helps to be under 6ft tall) – all in the middle of a lava flow, c 1914. Discounts for longer stays.

**BOUGAINVILLEA
BED & BREAKFAST**   B&B $
☎ /fax 929-7089, 800-688-1763; www.bougainvillea bedandbreakfast.com; PO Box 6045, Ocean View, HI 96737; s/d incl breakfast $80/90; ▨
This comfortable B&B is a terrific spot to acquaint yourself with the pleasures of Ocean View. Each room has a private entrance, therapeutic beds and TV/VCR. Rooms 3 and 4 are best, with a shared lanai looking onto South Point. All rooms are wheelchair accessible. There's a pool,

Vacationing off the grid in a solar-powered VW bus at Lova Lava Land   GREG ELMS

KA'U

Master lei maker Kilohana Domingo   GREG ELMS

Jacuzzi and communal kitchenette, plus barbecue and horseshoes.

Other recommended Ocean View digs include the following:

Hiroko's Hideaway (☎ 939-7132; www.hirokos-hide away.com; HOVE; 2br house per week/month $500/1500) Charming but cluttered house with nice lanai.

Leilani Bed & Breakfast (☎ 929-7101; www.leilani bedandbreakfast.com; 92-8822 Leilani Pkwy; s/d incl breakfast $85/95) Unique lava-rock home with three well-appointed rooms, plus lovely common and outdoor areas.

❀ Ohana House Rural Retreat (☎ 929-9139; www.alternative-hawaii.com/ohana; PO Box 6351, Ocean View, HI 96737; house $75, cottage $50, s/d cabin per week $100/200) Energy abounds at this solar-powered retreat with lots of flexible accommodations, from a house for 10 to a rustic cabin.

Getting There & Away

The free **Hele-On Bus** (☎ 961-8744; www.co.hawaii .hi.us/mass_transit/heleonbus.html) runs one bus at 3:30pm daily between Pahala and Ocean View (No 23 Ka'u route), continuing on to the South Kohala resorts. From Ka'u to Hilo, take the No 7 Downtown Hilo bus; it originates in Wai'ohinu, but you can call to request pick-up in Ocean View.

ROAD TO THE SEA

The Road to the Sea is the road less traveled with reason: the 4WD lava road crosses enough loose 'a'a and ledges to shake your fillings loose. If you brave the journey, however, you'll be on some of the island's most isolated beaches. The mana is palpable here, but so is the wind.

To get here, turn *makai* at the row of three mailboxes between the 79- and 80-mile markers (look for the 'Ka Ulu Malu Shady Grove Farm' sign). Set your odometer as soon as you turn. The road is private and barking dogs might give chase. From here you'll cover 6 miles over rudimentary, seemingly never-ending lava. To reach the first and smaller of the two beaches takes 20 to 30 minutes, depending on how rough you like your ride.

To reach the second beach, drive a half-mile back inland. Skip the first left fork (it's a dead end) and take the second left fork instead. Look for arrows painted on the lava rock. The road jogs inland before heading toward the shore again, and the route isn't always readily apparent. There are many places you can lose traction or get lost. Almost 1 mile from the fork, you'll reach a red *pu'u* (hill). Park here and walk down to the ocean. If you decide to walk the whole distance, it's about 1.5 miles. Bring as much water as you can carry, as it's hot and shadeless, with no potable water.

Both nameless beaches have exquisite black-and-green sand, similar to Green Sands Beach (p236). There's a bit of shade and the cliffs looming over the beach are stunning. At the north end there are a few palms and a lime-green brackish pool, a beautiful place for a soak. Trekking at low tide presents some intriguing possibilities to discover new coves. These waters have excellent fishing, especially off the cliffs at the second beach. This is an all-day adventure.

MANUKA STATE WAYSIDE PARK

Manuka State Wayside Park is a 13.5-acre arboretum off Hwy 11, just north of the 81-mile marker, with a 2-mile nature walk among 48 native Hawaiian and 130 introduced species of trees and bushes. There are a couple of heiau (temples) and other ruins within the park. This is but a small swath of the 25,500-acre Manuka Natural Area Reserve, which reaches from the slopes of Mauna Loa down to the sea.

You can camp with a permit here (see p273), but it's lackluster and there's no drinking water.

BIG ISLAND
MYTHS & LEGENDS

Of chiefs and heroes, of gods and ghosts, ancient Hawaiians created a captivating library – all by oral tradition. Unlike impromptu fictional tales, the traditional myths and legends were detailed historical narratives. They mixed real events and genealogies with the imaginary exploits of the immortals. The stories reflect the traditional religious worldview, which was essentially reverence for nature, plus absolute acceptance of one's place in nature. When the Hawaiians converted en masse to Christianity in the 1800s, their stories (and the gods themselves) lost much of their visceral power. But a few of the ancient gods remain influential – and on Hawai'i, Pele still reigns supreme.

THE ORIGIN OF HUMANKIND

The Hawaiian **Kumulipo** (The Source of Life) is an epic genealogy *oli* (chant) and creation myth. Kahuna (priests) would memorize its 2101 lines and recite it during important events. As it's told, in the beginning there was only darkness, an infinite nothingness. But within that void, a spark of intelligence arose, lying there for aeons in time and space. Then the womb of the Earth Mother, known as Papa, appeared. The sunlight of the Sky Father, Wakea, followed. As male light penetrated female darkness, this union of opposites created a whole universe of harmonized opposites.

The first life forms are plants, then fishes, birds, insects, mammals and finally humankind, in remarkably accurate Darwinist order. From their deep intimacy with nature, the Hawaiians seem to have grasped the basic concepts of biological evolution.

The genealogy records royal births until the late 1700s. Royal bloodlines can be traced back to the beginning of time, when gods were still on Earth and the first humans arose. Thus, humankind descended from the gods (with kings and chiefs being the purest descendents), as did everything in nature, from rocks and trees to fish and birds. Everything was godly, sacred and interrelated.

Among the last times that the whole Kumulipo was recited was during Captain Cook's arrival in Kealakekua Bay in 1779, when he was deemed the incarnation of the god Lono.

THE HAWAIIAN PANTHEON

In Hawaiian myths, the gods are typically chiefs in faraway lands who come as visitors to the lands where they're worshipped. Among the large pantheon, the four major gods were Kane, the creator and thus associated with fresh water, sunlight and fertility; Ku, the god of humankind, war and virility; Lono, the god of peace and agriculture; and Kanaloa, the god of the ocean and sea winds.

Ku and the female god Hina are the original ancestral gods of the Hawaiian people. Ku was the patron spirit of chiefs and actively worshipped for bountiful crops, victorious battles, long life and overall prosperity. All *luakini* heiau (temples of human sacrifice) were dedicated to him, the only god honored with the utmost gift of a human's life. Ku is particularly significant to Hawai'i because Kamehameha the Great built Pu'ukohola Heiau (p119) to honor him. The people (including his rivals) believed that if Kamehameha completed the massive heiau, he was guaranteed to rule all of the Islands. Thus, as the heiau grew more and more imposing, he had a great psychological advantage over the other chiefs.

Lono was worshipped mainly during the *makahiki* (fall harvest festival of sports and games). Captain Cook's landing in Kealakekua Bay in 1779 coincided with the *makahiki*, and Cook was deified as the incarnation of Lono when he first arrived.

While Kane was the leading god when the missionaries first arrived, his significance lessened over time. Kanaloa eventually became a Christian devil type of figure, probably due to the missionaries' influence. Known as the 'kava ('awa) drinker,' Kanaloa lived for a while in Waipi'o Valley. According to myth, he and his followers revolted following a prohibition on the narcotic 'awa beverage, and they were thus banished to the underworld.

While these gods' names occasionally appear in hula, stories, songs and place names, they've become rather obscure to most island residents.

Ki'i adorning Pu'ukohola Heiau   ERIC WHEATER

PELE, THE FIERY VOLCANO GODDESS

No deity wields such influence on the Big Island as Pele, the tempestuous, violent and powerful volcano goddess. Her exalted lineage includes her mother, Haumea, goddess of creation and childbirth; and her grandmother, the Earth Mother, Papa (see the box on p242). Her appearance (in the form of gushing lava eruptions) is loud and brazen, a catalyst for great destruction and creation. She lives in Halemaʻumaʻu Crater on Kilauea (p213), where hula *halau* (schools) and other locals pay their respects.

Migration to Hawaiʻi

Born on a distant island, the adventurous beauty Pele left her homeland and sailed north with her little sister Hiʻiaka (still in an egg) tucked under her armpit. Some say that her older sister Namakaokahaʻi (Goddess of the Sea) banished Pele after she seduced her husband – a plausible conjecture, as you'll soon see.

When she arrived in the northernmost Hawaiian Islands, she sought a safe home by trying to dig a pit deep enough to protect her sacred fire. But each time she dug a suitable home, her angry older sister flooded it with seawater.

Pele traveled from island to island, until she reached the island of Hawaiʻi, where Mauna Loa, the earth's largest volcanic mountain, was high enough above the sea to protect her precious fire. Here she made her permanent home.

A Love Triangle: Lohiʻau and Hiʻiaka

Once, while dreaming, Pele's spirit journeyed to the island of Kauaʻi, where she fell in love with a handsome mortal chief named Lohiʻau. In the form of a gorgeous woman, she took him as her lover. Upon awakening, she asked her favorite sister, Hiʻiaka (Spirit of the Dance), to go and fetch Lohiʻau. Hiʻiaka, a gentle nature lover imbued with healing powers, was the only person brave enough to volunteer for the dangerous journey, which was rife with monsters and evil spirits.

Suspicious even of her beloved sister, Pele made Hiʻiaka promise not to encourage any advances by Lohiʻau. In return, Hiʻiaka received Pele's vow not to harm her beloved ohia groves or her best friend, Hopoe, a forest spirit.

EARTHLY MANIFESTATIONS OF THE GODS

To the ancients, god and nature were synonymous. Thus, they associated their gods with *kinolau* (earthly counterparts) that could be animate or inanimate, such as rocks, animals, trees, wind and rain. Virtually all things in the earthly world were the *kinolau* of a deity, therefore all things were considered to have mana (spiritual essence) to one degree or another.

On the Big Island, different gods are associated with particular elements, landmarks or regions:

Pele: Volcanoes, fire, Mauna Loa and Kilauea, leeward Hawaiʻi
Poliahu: Snow, ice, Mauna Kea
Kamapuaʻa: Rain, moisture, living flora, windward Hawaiʻi
Hiʻiaka and Pele: Red ohia lehua flower

Mauna Kea, an especially important sacred place, is more than Poliahu's home. It is considered the mountain of Wakea (Sky Father), the place between heaven and earth.

Another group of earthly spirits were the *ʻaumakua* (guardian spirits of deceased humans), which protected living family members. *ʻAumakua* adopted earthly forms such as sharks, geckos, birds or fish. In return for their protection, the living were duty-bound to reciprocate and protect their guardian spirits on earth.

In this way, the Hawaiians' religious beliefs led them to treat nature and living creatures as sacred. Now-trendy concepts such as conservation, preservation and nonpollution were nothing new to the ancients.

Island Insights

To preserve their mythology, ancient Hawaiians trained kahuna (priests) to memorize lengthy stories almost word for word. The story of Kamapua'a entails 16 hours of recitation. Religious invocations required perfect recitation to be effective, so those that took two days to complete were quite an oratory feat! When the Hawaiians learned from the missionaries how to read, they displayed a remarkable ability to recite entire books or passages from the Bible.

The journey to Kaua'i was long and perilous. When she finally arrived, Lohi'au had died of grief over Pele's disappearance. But Hi'iaka revived him and they departed for Hawai'i. By then, Pele was agitated from impatience; she assumed that Hi'iaka had betrayed her and thus spewed hot lava over the ohia groves and Hopoe.

Actually, Hi'iaka had spurned Lohi'au's advances despite her attraction to him. But when she saw the charred remains of her precious forest and friend, she embraced Lohi'au in full view of Pele. Now furious, Pele attacked them with lava and fire. Hi'iaka, an immortal, survived, but Lohi'au was killed.

But one of Pele's brothers, sailing from Tahiti to Hawai'i, noticed Lohi'au's spirit flying overseas toward the ancestral homeland, where all dead spirits go. He caught Lohi'au's spirit and revived it. (Pele's siblings were always atoning for her impetuous rages.) Lohi'au and Hi'iaka reunited and together returned to Kaua'i.

Pele Meets Her Match: Kamapua'a

Kamapua'a is among the most memorable gods for his rebellious 'bad boy' reputation and his striking manifestation as a handsome chief (albeit with pig bristles growing on his back) or a gigantic eight-eyed hog – or as various fishes or plants, when needed. His love-hate relationship with Pele is a grand example of the Hawaiian's worldview of opposite pairings.

Kamapua'a was larger than life, both as a pig (the largest land animal known to the Hawaiians) and as a chauvinistic male, and thus an audience favorite. Like real pigs, Kamapua'a preferred cool, damp environments, like the dripping gulches and waterfall-strewn valley on the windward side – which was just the opposite of Pele's ideal, high-and-dry setting.

When Kamapua'a first spied Pele, he was immediately attracted and tried to pursue her. But she spurned him, calling him a pig and other insulting names. They infuriated each other. She would thrash him with scorching lava and fire, and chase him to the sea, but he would transform himself into the *humuhumunukunukuapua'a* (triggerfish) and thus survive her attacks.

He would retaliate with rainstorms and armies of tusked hogs that demolished her lands. When the downpours once nearly extinguished her fires, Pele's brothers ordered her to yield to him. In a place on the Puna coast, where the land is wild and disheveled, as if the site of a great battle, Kamapua'a finally had his way with her.

Ultimately they became lovers, but forward-thinking ones who eschewed togetherness for individual autonomy. They divided the island between them, with Pele taking the dry, leeward side (Ka'u and Kona) and Kamapua'a taking the wet windward side (North Kohala, Hamakua and Hilo). Of course, only by accepting Kamapua'a's rains and seeds could Pele's new lands become fertile.

Pele's Nemesis: Snow Goddess Poliahu

Fire and ice. This archetypal opposition (not to mention epic sibling rivalry) comes to life with red-hot Pele pitted against her sister Poliahu, the magnificent snow goddess who resides on Mauna Kea. Pele was resentful of Poliahu's incomparable beauty and her beguiling effect on handsome chiefs. The two battled back and forth, spewing fiery lava and icy snow at each other.

Long ago, when Mauna Kea was an active volcano, Pele caused it to let loose a great fountain of lava, melting Poliahu's snow and scaring her away in panic. But Pohiahu took revenge by covering Mauna Kea with

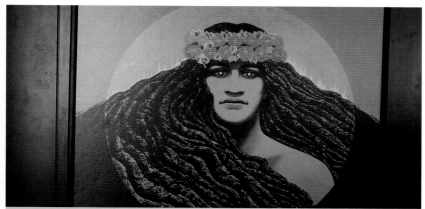

Painting of the goddess Pele at the Jaggar Museum, Hawai'i Volcanoes National Park   GREG ELMS

deep snow and ice, dousing Pele's fire on the mountain forever. (Indeed, Mauna Kea did erupt through glacial ice caps 10,000 years ago and, over the centuries, became extinct.)

By letting loose all that lava in her cat-fights with Poliahu, Pele ended up expanding the Big Island. Once, Poliahu and her friends descended to the Hamakua Coast for *he'e holua* (grass sledding), a thrilling sport that Pele loved. Racers would run like crazy to the start of a steep hillside track, hurl themselves onto their sleds and speed downhill toward the sea.

Disguised as a young woman, Pele approached and the unsuspecting Poliahu invited her to participate. When the ground grew hot, however, Poliahu realized her mistake. Suddenly Pele caused Mauna Loa to explode with fiery fountains, forcing Poliahu to flee to the top of Mauna Kea, chased by flames.

To retaliate, Poliahu bombarded the mountains with freezing snow. Pele's currents of lava cooled and hardened immediately, thus sealing the chasms that expelled the molten rock. But, by then, rivers of lava had flowed down the Hamakua Coast, forming the Laupahoehoe region.

Today, Poliahu continues to rule Mauna Kea, keeping the mountaintop freezing with ice and snow, which melts into windward rivers that give the Hilo, Hamakua and North Kohala regions their dewy emerald appeal.

The Wrath of Pele

Irresistibly seductive and extremely jealous, Pele was brutal to the men she took as lovers. If she caught a man cheating on her, she immediately smothered him in scalding lava. The next two stories illustrate Pele's violence and, if there is a silver lining, her fortuitous contribution to Hawaii's flora.

OHIA & LEHUA
On the slopes of Mauna Loa and Kilauea, Pele's territory, the ohia lehua tree thrives. Ohia refers to the tree; lehua is the flower.

Top Picks
MYTHS & LEGENDS BOOKS

- ■ *Pele*, written and illustrated by Herb Kawainui Kane
- ■ *Powerstones: Letters to a Goddess*, by Linda Ching and Robin Stephens
- ■ *The Legends & Myths of Hawai'i*, by King David Kalakaua
- ■ *Madame Pele: True Encounters with Hawai'i's Fire Goddess*, compiled by Rick Carroll
- ■ *Hawai'i Island Legends: Pikoi, Pele & Others*, compiled by Mary Kawena Pukui
- ■ *Hawaiian Mythology*, by Martha Beckwith

BE KIND TO STRANGERS

In some accounts, she is a beautiful young woman. In others, she is old and wrinkled, clad in a white *holoku* (long missionary-style dress), perhaps accompanied by a white dog. Typically, she asks for some assistance, which, if not given, brings harm or bad luck. Superstitions about **Pele** abound – and countless accounts 'prove' her existence.

Many of these stories depict a strange woman who appears 'out of nowhere' and then disappears. After the 1960 Kilauea eruption that destroyed Kapoho (p199), a story circulated about how the Kumukahi Lighthouse keeper had offered a meal to an elderly woman who appeared at his door on the eve of the catastrophe – and how the lighthouse was spared.

Some eyewitness accounts come from nonlocals who are skeptical rather than superstitious. In one account described in Herb Kawainui Kane's book *Pele*, two geologists with the US Geological Survey's Hawai'i Volcanoes Observatory in July 1975 flew a helicopter over Mauna Loa when it erupted for the first time in 26 years. From above, they saw three people at a rest cabin near the summit crater, Moku'aweoweo.

It's a strenuous climb to Mauna Loa's 13,677ft summit and the trail was closed for safety, so it was startling to see them there. Two were standing in front of the cabin and the third, a woman, was on the porch. Another helicopter flew in to rescue the three stranded hikers. But they found only two hikers, who said that they had been alone at the cabin and that they had not seen any woman there. Both geologists also noticed that the woman had been barefooted!

Certainly, in this modern age, Big Islanders heed the Pele superstitions with a grain of salt. Modern science has convincingly explained the once-mysterious volcanic phenomena associated with Pele. But she remains a potent figure – not only to Hawaiians and other locals, but to anyone who witnesses the indomitable force of a lava-spewing volcano.

Ohia was once a young man who was inseparable from his beautiful lover, Lehua. One day Pele noticed Ohia and, disguised as a pretty young thing, tried to seduce him. He was in love with Lehua and ignored Pele. Livid with jealousy, she killed both of them.

Her sisters reprimanded her and she regretted her impulsiveness. So she turned Ohia's body into a rugged, masculine tree and Lehua's body into the vividly colored, feminine flower of that tree. Thus the two lovers were reunited for eternity.

Legend holds that if you pick a lehua blossom, it will rain – the tears of separated lovers.

NAUPAKA

Along the Hawaiian coastline, the *naupaka kahakai* (beach *naupaka*; literally '*naupaka* by the sea') grows wild. The white flowers of this sprawling, pulpy-leaved plant are notable because they have petals only on

the lower half. Even odder, there is a different type of *naupaka* that grows only in the mountains – and its flowers are just the opposite, with petals only on the upper half!

According to legend, Pele noticed two young lovers, utterly devoted to each other. She found the man desirable and tried to seduce him with her great beauty. But, no matter what she did, he was uninterested. (This plot is starting to sound familiar, eh?) Angered by his rejection, she chased him up to the mountains, bombarding him with molten lava.

Pele's sister Hi'iaka sympathized with the helpless man and saved him from death by transforming him into the mountain *naupaka*. Then Pele pursued the young woman, chasing her to the sea. Again, Hi'iaka intervened and turned her into the beach *naupaka*.

If the mountain *naupaka* and beach *naupaka* flowers are reunited, the two young lovers are also together again.

HISTORY & CULTURE

Hawai'i is a knockout. Her physical presence – lava-
spewing volcanoes, lush zigzagging valleys and even the spectacle of palatial
resorts – is riveting. But Hawai'i's true distinction from any ol' tropical beauty
lies in her fascinating past. An isolated society, omnipotent kings, bloody
battles, European explorers, immigrants and intermarriage – her story's got
the makings of a true epic. Today, Hawai'i's complex post-European history
remains controversial, but it has undoubtedly produced a unique culture. The
local languages, customs, arts and foods reflect its diverse population, from the
Native Hawaiians to the immigrants who have come seeking 'the good life.'

HISTORY

ANCIENT HAWAI'I

Ancient Hawaiians believed that the ruling aristocracy of hereditary kings and chiefs were direct descendents of the gods. Thus, no one dared question their authority and mana (spiritual essence). In the social order, the highest class was the *ali'i nui* (high chiefs), who ruled one of the four major islands. One's rank as an *ali'i* was determined by the mother's family lineage, making Hawai'i a matriarchal society.

The second class comprised *ali'i 'ai moku* (district chiefs), who ruled island districts, and *ali'i 'ai ahupua'a* (lower chiefs), who ruled *ahupua'a*, pie-shaped subdistricts extending from the mountains to the ocean. Also ranked second were kahuna (priests), experts in important skills such as canoe building, religious practices, healing arts and navigation.

The third, and largest, class was the *maka'ainana* (commoners), who were not chattels of the *ali'i* and could live wherever they pleased, but who were obligated to support the *ali'i* through taxes paid in kind with food, goods and labor.

The final *kauwa* (outcast) class was shunned and did not mix with the other classes, except as slaves. No one resented their position, for people accepted the 'natural order' and based their identity on the group rather than on their individuality.

Although the hierarchy might sound feudal in the European sense, Hawaiian society was quite different because *ali'i* did not 'own' land. It was inconceivable to the Hawaiian mind to own land or anything in nature. Rather the *ali'i* were stewards of the land – and they had a sacred duty to care for it on behalf of the gods. Further,

the ancients had no concept of trade (for profit) or a monetary system. They instead exchanged goods and services through customary, reciprocal gift-giving and, of course, obligations to superiors.

Strict religious laws, known as the *kapu* (taboo) system, governed what people ate, who they married, when they fished or harvested crops, and practically all human behavior. The *kapu* often discriminated against women, who could not dine with men or eat bananas, coconuts, pork and certain types of fish. (Of course, the ancients didn't consider it discrimination but simply the natural order.) For more on ancient Hawaiians' spiritual beliefs, see p241.

FROM HAWAIIAN KINGDOM TO US TERRITORY

Kamehameha the Great

Kamehameha I, 'The Lonely One,' was born in North Kohala around 1753. He was born into the *ali'i* class, and became a strong warrior under the guidance of his powerful uncle and chief, Kalaniopu'u. As a teen, he allegedly lifted the gargantuan Naha Stone (see the box on p183), which, according to prophecy, meant that he would ultimately rule the land. He was no stranger to warfare or Western arrival, and he was present with his uncle at Kealakekua Bay in 1779, when Captain Cook was killed in battle.

Until the 1790s, the major islands of Hawai'i, Kaua'i, Maui and O'ahu were independently ruled by *ali'i 'ai moku*. Kamehameha fought for eight years to become *ali'i 'ai moku* of Hawai'i and he finally

1778	1810	1820
British Captain James Cook becomes the first Westerner to 'discover' the Hawaiian Islands when he lands at Waimea Bay on Kaua'i. In 1779 Captain Cook is killed at Kealakekua Bay on Hawai'i.	Kamehameha the Great unites the major Hawaiian Islands under one kingdom, which is called Hawai'i after his home island. He took 20 years to accomplish this singular feat.	First missionaries arrive at Kailua Bay on the Kona Coast. By then, Kamehameha I was dead and the *kapu* (taboo) system abolished, so Hawaiians readily convert to Christianity.

Statue of King Kamehameha I   GREG ELMS

power struggles among the *ali'i*. While all-powerful under the *kapu* system, he was also fair, diplomatic and greatly admired by his people. He established his royal court on Maui at Lahaina (where it remained until 1845, when King Kamehameha III moved the capital to Honolulu on O'ahu). When he died in 1819 at his Kamakahonu home in Kailua-Kona (see p58), two loyal chiefs buried him in a secret place to prevent rivals from stealing his bones, which were believed to hold great mana.

When Kamehameha died, his 23-year-old son Liholiho (Kamehameha II) became *mo'i* and his wife, Queen Ka'ahumanu became *kuhina nui* (regent) and co-ruler. Both of them were greatly influenced by Westerners and eager to renounce the *kapu* system. In a shocking snub to tradition, the two broke a strict taboo against men and women eating together and later ordered many heiau (temples) and *ki'i* (idols) destroyed. Without the oppressive but stabilizing ancient traditions, Hawaiian society was in chaos. The door was wide open for the American missionaries who would arrive only 11 months later.

Captain Cook & the European Invasion

When British naval explorer Captain James Cook sighted the island of O'ahu on January 18, 1778, the Hawaiian civilization's 500 years of isolation were forever lost. This singular event transformed Hawai'i in ways inconceivable at the time. Cook was sailing to the Pacific Northwest in search of the elusive Northwest Passage and accidentally 'discovered' the Islands.

Cook landed in Waimea Bay on Kaua'i, where he and his men were roundly

succeeded in 1790. To further his dominion (as chiefs are wont to do), he began a monumental campaign to conquer all of the Islands.

In 1791 he built a massive *luakini* heiau (sacrificial temple) at Kawaihae (p119), where he prayed and sacrificed more than a few enemies to please the great war god Ku. In 1810, after two decades of warfare (plus some diplomatic efforts), he fulfilled the prophecy and became the first *mo'i* (ruling chief) of the Kingdom of Hawai'i, named after his native island.

During his nine-year reign, King Kamehameha I brought relative peace and stability to a society previously in flux with constant

1828	1835	1863
First coffee trees are planted in Kona by missionary Samuel Ruggles. King Kamehameha's confidant and physician Don Francisco de Paula y Marin brought the plant to O'ahu around 1813.	First successful commercial sugar plantation is established on Kaua'i. Early Polynesians brought sugarcane to the islands, but they only chewed it for its juices and never refined it.	Reverend Elias Bond establishes the Kohala Sugar Company, the island's first sugar plantation, to create jobs for Hawaiians, many of whom were leaving for better opportunities on O'ahu and Maui.

HISTORY & CULTURE

Island Insights

The word **kapu** (taboo) originally had multiple meanings, as it referred to all of the various prohibitions on behavior. Today it generally means 'no trespassing' or 'off-limits.' It appears mostly on makeshift signs posted on private property: 'KAPU. KEEP OUT. THIS MEANS YOU.'

welcomed. In return, the Hawaiians contracted venereal diseases, which quickly spread throughout the Islands, killing hundreds of Hawaiians. When Cook returned to Hawai'i in February 1779, he anchored in idyllic Kealakekua Bay to repair his two ships and to refresh supplies. But, later that month, Cook tried to take a chief hostage in retaliation for a stolen boat. A battle ensued, killing Cook, four of his men and 17 Hawaiians.

When Cook's men returned without him, the news spread throughout Europe and America, leading to a flood of foreigners eager to explore the Hawaiian Islands.

Traders, Whalers & Soul Savers

As a prime Pacific way station for traders and whalers, by the 1820s Hawai'i had a foreign resident population of about 500. British, American, French and Russian traders would travel to the Pacific Northwest for furs and stop in Hawai'i to restock their ships and buy 'iliahi (fragrant sandalwood), a valuable commodity in China. Then they would trade the furs and sandalwood for exotic Chinese silks, spices and furniture. Due to the greed of both traders and Hawaiians, 'iliahi was virtually decimated and remains rare today.

By the 1840s Hawai'i also became the whaling capital of the Pacific, as hundreds of whaling ships stopped at Hawaiian ports annually. Here, they restocked and transferred their catch to ships bound for the US eastern seaboard, which meant they could stay in the Pacific for much longer periods, thereby boosting their annual catch and profits.

The first missionaries to Hawai'i chanced upon a fortuitous time and place to arrive. The American Congregationalists from Boston landed in Kailua Bay on April 19, 1820, just 11 months after King Kamehameha died in almost the exact spot. The Hawaiians had just abolished the ancient religion, so the missionaries found a receptive audience of souls to save.

They prohibited hula dancing because of its 'lewd and suggestive movements,' denounced the traditional Hawaiian chants and songs that honored 'heathen' gods, taught women to sew Western-style clothing and abolished polygamy, which was accepted and necessary in the isolated island group.

The Hawaiians had no written language, so the missionaries established a Hawaiian alphabet using Roman letters and zealously taught them how to read and write. This fostered a high literacy rate and publication of 100 Hawaiian-language newspapers. Eventually, however, the missionaries banned the Hawaiian language in schools, to distance Hawaiians from their 'hedonistic' cultural roots.

Many missionaries became influential advisors to the monarch and received large tracts of land in return, prompting them to leave the church altogether and turn their land into sugar plantations. It is often said that the missionaries came to do good – and did very well.

1882	1893	1900
Macadamia trees arrive on Hawai'i. Native to Australia, initially they are planted only as an ornamental tree. The rich, buttery nuts aren't eaten till the 1920s.	The Hawaiian monarchy, under Queen Lili'uokalani, is overthrown, ending 83 years of rule. In 1895 Hawaiian royalists attempt a counterrevolution, and the deposed queen is placed under house arrest for nine months.	Hawaii becomes a US territory and then takes 59 years to reach statehood – longer than any other territory in the union. Many blame the delay on racial prejudice against Hawai'i's Hawaiian and Asian populations.

THE STAR COMPASS

The first humans on the Hawaiian Islands arrived around AD 500, the end of a 2000-year period of migration by ancient seafarers originally from Southeast Asia. They traveled eastward into Polynesia (a vast triangle of Pacific islands with New Zealand, Easter Island and Hawai'i at its three points), settling first in Samoa and Tonga and then spreading to the furthest reaches.

Talk about uncharted waters! They sailed in double-hulled canoes 60ft long and 14ft wide, sans any modern navigational tools, whether compasses, radar, radios or satellites. Instead they relied on the 'star compass,' a celestial map based on keen observation (and perfect memory) of star paths.

They had no idea what, if anything, they would find thousands of miles across the open ocean. Experts estimate that Hawai'i's discoverers came from the Marquesas Islands and sailed for four months straight (with no stops to restock food and water). They brought plants and animals that would be useful for settlement – now that's positive thinking.

Westerners generally assumed that ancient Polynesians drifted to Hawai'i by accident. But prevailing winds and ocean currents preclude such a northerly path. In 1976 the **Polynesian Voyaging Society** (www.pvs.hawaii.org) proved that ancient Polynesians were phenomenal wayfinders by re-enacting an ancient journey to Tahiti and back. The group built a replica of an ancient Hawaiian long-distance sailing canoe named *Hokule'a* (Arcturus, Hawai'i's zenith star) and, after months of intense training, made the 4800-mile round-trip voyage.

This historic achievement was followed by numerous incredible voyages to far-flung islands, such as Rarotonga, the Marquesas, Rapa Nui (Easter Island), Aotearoa (New Zealand) and the Northwestern Hawaiian Islands. Most recently, in 2007, *Hokule'a* sailed 9570 miles to Micronesia and Japan.

King Sugar

When foreigners quickly saw that Hawai'i was ideal for growing sugarcane, they established small plantations using Hawaiian labor. But by then the native population had severely declined, thanks to introduced diseases such as typhoid, influenza, smallpox and syphilis. To fill the shortage, workers were imported from overseas starting in the 1860s, first from China, and soon after from Japan and the Portuguese islands of Madeira and the Azores.

The influx of imported foreign labor and the rise of the sugar industry had a major impact on the Islands' social structure. Caucasian plantation owners and sugar agents rose to become the elite upper economic and political class, while the Hawaiians and foreign laborers became the lower class, without much of a middle class in between.

The sugar industry boomed during the American Civil War (1861–65), when Hawai'i became the northern states' sugar source. After the war, the industry languished until 1875, when the USA ended foreign import taxes and sugar production instantly skyrocketed, rising from 21 million pounds in 1874 to 114 million pounds in 1883.

1925	1941	1946
The first flight between the mainland and Hawaii is made. Eleven years later, Pan American launches the first commercial mainland–Hawaii flights.	Japanese forces attack Pearl Harbor and the USA enters WWII. The Japanese in Hawaii are spared from internment camps because they are necessary laborers in the sugar fields.	Tsunami generated by an earthquake in Alaska kills 159 people across the Islands. The Big Island is hardest hit, with 122 deaths, primarily in Hilo and Laupahoehoe.

The Great Mahele

By the time of the reign of King Kamehameha III (Kauikeaouli), foreigners were vying to end the absolute monarchy. They wanted governmental powers and the right to own land. The king struggled against such demands but in 1840 signed Hawai'i's first constitution, which allowed limited citizen representation.

Eight years later, in a momentous blow to the Hawaiian monarchy, foreigners introduced the Great Mahele, a sweeping land reform act. This act took all the lands in the kingdom and redistributed them in three parts: crown lands (kings and heirs), chief lands and government lands (for the benefit of the general public). The traditional concept of land stewardship gave way to the Western ideal of fee-simple land ownership.

In 1850 the subsequent Kuleana Act awarded 30,000 acres of government lands to Hawaiian commoners (and gave foreigners the right to purchase some lands), but most of the land set aside for Hawaiians ended up in foreign hands anyway.

Overthrow of the Monarchy

In 1887 the members of the Hawaiian League, a secret antimonarchy organization run by sugar interests, wrote a new constitution and, by threat of violence, forced King David Kalakaua to sign it. This constitution, which became known as the 'Bayonet Constitution,' essentially stripped the monarch's powers, effectively making King Kalakaua a figurehead. It also limited voting rights, effectively allowing only wealthy businessmen and landowners to vote.

When Kalakaua, Hawai'i's last king, died in 1891, his sister and heir, Princess Lili'uokalani, ascended the throne. She tried to restore the monarchy but, on January 17, 1893, the Hawaiian League's leaders, supported by both US Minister John L Stevens and a 150-man contingent of US marines and sailors, forcibly arrested Queen Lili'uokalani and took over 'Iolani Palace in Honolulu in a tense but bloodless coup d'état. The Kingdom of Hawai'i was now the Republic of Hawai'i.

ANNEXATION, WAR & STATEHOOD

American interests continued to push hard for annexation, while Hawaiians fought to prevent this final, formal acquisition. In 1897 more than 21,000 people (almost half of the population of Hawai'i) signed an anti-annexation petition and sent it to Washington. In 1898 President William McKinley nevertheless approved the annexation, perhaps influenced by the con-

Island Insights

Five sugar companies, known as the **Big Five**, rose to dominate not only the industry, but virtually all economic and political realms in Hawai'i. Essentially an oligarchy, Castle & Cooke, Alexander & Baldwin, C Brewer & Co, American Factors and Theo H Davies & Co – all controlled by white businessmen – were bitter business rivals but established an alliance to keep the balance of power in their favor. Alexander & Baldwin, which owns Matson Navigation Company (the state's primary ocean shipper), remains influential and among the state's biggest landowners.

1959	1960	1963
On August 21, 1959, Hawaii becomes the 50th US state. Opponents had argued that island labor unions were communist and that the Islands were too remote.	Hilo is devastated by a massive tsunami generated off the coast of South America. More than 100 buildings are destroyed and 61 people killed.	Hilo's Merrie Monarch Festival launches and becomes a premier hula competition, giving Hilo's tourist industry a massive boost each spring.

PROMISED LAND

It seemed promising when the US Congress passed the **Hawaiian Homes Commission Act** in 1920, which set aside almost 200,000 acres of government land for Native Hawaiians to lease for $1 per year. But myriad problems have plagued the program. Much of the set-aside lands are remote and lack basic infrastructure, such as roads and access to water and electricity – and the managing agency is too strapped to make improvements. Also, regardless of the 'free' land, the lessee still must afford a house. Many applicants are not financially prepared even if the agency does offer them a home.

So applicants are stuck on a waiting list for years, even decades. Today there are over 19,000 residential applicants waiting across the state. Only about 8300 leases have been granted since 1920. Some are elderly by the time they receive a lease, and others never make it.

current Spanish-American War, which highlighted Pearl Harbor's strategic military location.

Statehood was a tough sell to the US Congress, but a series of significant historical events paved the way. In 1936 Pan American airlines launched the first commercial flights from the US mainland to Hawai'i, thus launching the transpacific air age and the beginning of mass tourism. Wireless telegraph, followed by telephone, service between Hawai'i and the mainland alleviated doubts about long-distance communication. Most importantly, WWII proved both the strategic military role of Pearl Harbor and the loyalty and heroism of Japanese immigrants.

During WWII the Japanese were initially banned from joining the armed forces, due to great suspicion about their loyalty. In 1943 the US government yielded to political pressure and formed an all-Japanese combat unit, the 100th Infantry Battalion. While only 3000 men were needed for this unit, more than 10,000 men volunteered.

When the war ended, another all-Japanese unit, the 442nd Regimental Combat Team, formed with 3800 men from Hawai'i and the mainland, received more commendations and medal awards than any other army unit. The 100th Infantry Battalion also received special recognition when it helped to rescue the so-called 'Lost Battalion,' stranded behind enemy lines in France.

While still a controversial candidate, especially to Southern conservatives, both Democrat and Republic, the Islands were finally admitted as the 50th US state in 1959.

TOURISM & THE NEW ECONOMY

After statehood, tourism exploded, thanks to the advent of jet airplanes, which could transport thousands of people per week to the Islands. Hotel construction also boomed and tourism quickly became the second-largest industry, behind sugar production.

Over the next 30 years, tourism became the state's leading, multibillion-dollar industry. By the 1990s it was clear that the industry was out of control, but efforts to limit its growth have proven futile.

Contrast the plight of sugar: in 1960 the sugar industry was the state's largest, with

1981	1983	1992
The Ironman Triathlon, founded in Honolulu in 1978, moves to Kona. In 1995 Kailua-Kona native Lokelani McMichael, at age 18, becomes the youngest female to finish the race (then and now).	Kilauea Volcano starts its latest eruption, which is ongoing. The longest eruption in recorded history, it destroys the coastal road to Puna and the village of Kalapana, among other sites.	The world's largest optical telescope is installed at Mauna Kea on Hawai'i. Today there are 13 observatories on the mountain.

Top Picks

HISTORY READING ROUNDUP

- **Ancient Hawai'i** (Herb Kawainui Kane) This renowned artist-historian's gorgeously illustrated book makes it easy to imagine old Hawai'i. This one's a keeper.
- **A Concise History of the Hawaiian Islands** (Phil Barnes) Both concise and complete in less than 100 pages, this excellent account spans from ancient Polynesian discovery to the 1990s.
- **Hawai'i: A History of the Big Island** (Robert Oaks) For a history specifically on Hawai'i, this well-researched book delves into King Kamehameha's reign, plantation days, statehood and tourism.
- **Shoal of Time: A History of the Hawaiian Islands** (Gavan Daws) History buffs, this is the classic textbook covering the period from Captain Cook's arrival to statehood (and it's required reading for many high-school students).
- **Hawaii's Story by Hawaii's Queen** (Queen Lili'uokalani) This is the queen's own account of the dastardly circumstances surrounding her 1893 overthrow.

26 plantations and 228,000 acres of cultivated land. In the 1980s and '90s, plantations began to fold at an alarming rate, unable to compete with cheaper foreign markets. Today there are just two working plantations, neither on the Big Island.

Other crops, predominantly nursery flora (such as anthuriums and orchids), coffee, macadamia nuts, fruits and vegetables, are now key to the economy, but nothing will ever compare with sugar.

THE HAWAIIAN RENAISSANCE

In the post-WWII era, Hawaii became America's tropical fantasyland. The tiki craze, Hollywood surfer movies, aloha shirts and Waikiki were all Westernized, commercial images, but they made Hawaii iconic to the masses. (To this day, mainlanders idealize a *Brady Bunch* luau.) Simultaneously, no one spoke Hawaiian in public – and the native people felt a sense of disillusionment, even shame.

The 1970s introduced a cultural awakening, due largely to two events. In 1974 a small group called the Polynesian Voyaging Society committed themselves to building and sailing a replica of a voyaging canoe. When, in 1976, they succeeded in sailing the *Hokule'a* on a round-trip to Tahiti (see the boxed text on p251), everyone was newly intrigued by traditional Hawaiian knowledge.

The same year, a small grassroots group of Hawaiians from Moloka'i, the Protect Kaho'olawe 'Ohana (PKO), began protesting the bombing of Kaho'olawe, an island taken by the US government during WWII and used as a practice bombing site.

The political actions of the PKO, which included illegal occupation of the island, spurred new interest in reclaiming not only Kaho'olawe and other military lands, but also Hawaiian cultural practices, from hula to lomilomi massage. Public schools started teaching Hawaiian language and culture classes, while Hawaiian-immersion charter schools proliferated. Hawaiian music topped the charts, turning island-born musicians into now-legendary superstars (see p259). Small but vocal contingents began pushing for Hawaiian sovereignty, from complete secession from the USA to a nation-within-a-nation model.

1996	2000	2008
Ka'u Agribusiness Company, Hawai'i's last sugar mill, closes after rising labor costs drive the industry to Mexico and the Philippines.	Senator Daniel Akaka first introduces the Native Hawaiian Government Reorganization Act ('Akaka Bill'), which recognizes Hawaiians' indigenous status and allows limited self-governance. The bill has repeatedly stalled in Congress and remains on the floor.	The controversial Hawaii Superferry starts service between O'ahu and Maui. Service to Kaua'i is postponed after strong protests by island residents. Big Island service is projected to start in 2009.

THE CULTURE

ISLAND IDENTITY

Nicknamed the Orchid Island, Hawai'i has much in common with the other Hawaiian Islands, due to their 2500-mile distance from the nearest continent and collective mixed-race society. All locals take great pride in their localness, which is especially obvious outside the Islands. When fellow islanders meet on the mainland, they typically find instant camaraderie (and let loose that pidgin!). When one of Hawaii's own makes the national stage – such as Barack Obama, golfer Michelle Wie, and the UH Warrior football team in the 2008 Sugar Bowl – they make front-page news. Win or lose, locals are loyal to their 'ohana (family).

Make no mistake, however, about the uniqueness of each island. The Big Island is, obviously, big. Its sheer geographical size makes for a critical mass of local residents. Overall, Hawai'i is much less touristy than the other Islands. In Hilo, folks can go about their business fo' days without seeing tourists.

Hawai'i's vastness also means that real estate is cheaper here than on O'ahu, Maui and Kaua'i. When other islanders move here, the main reason is the affordability (while other reasons include jobs, the University of Hawai'i at Hilo and the slow pace). In 2006 the median single-family property cost $418,000 on the Big Island and $692,000 on Maui, with O'ahu and Kaua'i also fetching prices well above $600,000. Of course, Big Island land values run the gamut, with Puna representing the bargain rack, and Kohala and Kailua-Kona the upmarket labels.

Indeed, around the island it's not just land values but also *vibe* that varies. While Honolulu folk view Hilo, the capital town, as 'country' or even *da boonies* (the boondocks), everything's relative. Here, Hilo is 'town,' where people wear unwrinkled aloha shirts and wristwatches, work in government offices, attend the island's two largest public high schools and lead ordinary lives. With only a modest tourist trade and a population of almost 60% Japanese or mixed race, Hilo's plantation roots are clear.

In contrast, Kailua-Kona, while also a long-standing town, has become the island's economic powerhouse and tourist mecca, busy and 'haole-fied.' Due to the influx of new residents, it's less of a tight community, unless you're already locally rooted. Traffic along the Queen Ka'ahumanu Hwy

WHO ARE YOU?

- **Haole** White person (except local Portuguese). Often further defined as 'mainland haole' or 'local haole.'
- **Hapa** Person of mixed ancestry, most commonly referring to *hapa* haole who are part white and part Asian.
- **Hawaiian** Person of Native Hawaiian ancestry. It's a faux pas to call any Hawaii resident 'Hawaiian' (as you would a Californian or Texan), thus ignoring the existence of an indigenous people.
- **Kama'aina** Person who is native to a particular place. A Hilo native is a *kama'aina* (literally 'child of the land') of Hilo and not of Kailua-Kona. It assumes a deep knowledge of and connection to the place. In the retail context, '*kama'aina* discounts' apply to any resident of Hawaii (ie anyone with a Hawaii driver's license).
- **Local** Person who grew up in Hawaii. Locals who move away retain their local 'cred,' at least in part. But longtime transplants (see below) never become local. To call a transplant 'almost local' is a welcome compliment, despite its emphasis on the insider-outsider mentality.
- **Neighbor Islander** Person who lives on any Hawaiian Island other than O'ahu.
- **Transplant** Person who moves to the Islands as an adult.

Note: in this book, **Hawai'i** (with the *'okina* punctuation mark) refers to the island of Hawai'i (Big Island) and also to pre-statehood ancient Hawai'i. **Hawaii** (without the *'okina*) refers to the state. We use this distinction to avoid confusion between the island and the state, but locally the *'okina* spelling is officially used for both.

Island Insights

Politically, the vast majority of island (and state) voters are middle-of-the-road Democrats who tend to vote along party, racial, ethnic, seniority and local/nonlocal lines. Mainland transplants, generally haole, are more often the island's vocal advocates for progressive causes: sustainable development, affordable housing, limiting big-box retailers, recycling, alternative energy. Certainly, there are locals who are passionate activists and forward thinkers, but many are rather tolerant and not inclined to be activists.

is a nightmare, and Kailua residents often gripe about the county's shortsightedness in improving Kona's jammed roads when Hilo is sitting pretty with a well-planned system.

LIFESTYLE

Daily life is generally simple, laid-back and family oriented. The workday starts and ends early, and even workaholics tend also to be backyard gardeners. The typical local enjoys golf and travels regularly, even multiple times per year, to Las Vegas (favored for its manmade glitz, slot machines and constant contingent of fellow locals). In rural towns and in deep-rooted Hilo, it's impossible to be anonymous. At the mall or at a PTA meeting, locals are sure to bump into old classmates or relatives.

Of course, regional differences can be stark. Puna is teeming with off-the-grid types who raise their kids under tarps, eschewing conventional amenities from toothbrushes to hot showers. In Hilo, such a lifestyle is practically unheard of (and certainly not one willingly embraced).

While even the Big Island might seem compact, its relative size has inured its residents to long (two hours or more) drives. Of course, it was once a major event for Kailua-Kona residents to drive to Hilo to shop for goods found only in the 'city' (such as bicycles and boy scout uniforms). Today, the roles are reversed and Hiloans regularly cruise to Kona to stock up at Costco.

Locals tend toward more conventional 'American dream' lives, meaning marriage, kids, a modest home, stable work and free nights and weekends. Mainland transplants are here for other reasons: retirement, a dream B&B or coffee estate, art, youthful experimentation. Here, they are free to be unconventional.

But all Big Islanders are generally down-to-earth types, blasé about mainland fashion trends or the latest high-tech gizmo. Even in Hilo or Kailua-Kona, it takes eagle eyes to spot a Prius or an iPhone.

Big Islanders regularly travel to Honolulu, mainly to shop (a popular hobby among locals) and to visit family and friends. As for the other Neighbor Islands, locals tend to prefer visiting the mainland (particularly Vegas), Japan and Southeast Asia in tour groups. Perhaps it's a case of island nonchalance, but locals tend to visit Maui and Kaua'i mainly for golf or family visits, not for pure destination travel.

Since its 1980s heyday, *pakalolo* (marijuana) has been Hawai'i's most lucrative crop. But pot growing has markedly dropped (and moved indoors) since then, with about $46 million worth of plants confiscated in 2006, compared with $1 billion in 1987. The real troublemaker drug is 'ice' (crystal methamphetamine), which has been rampant on the island since the '90s, especially in rural Hawaiian communities.

POPULATION

Hilo remains the island's largest town, with 41,000 residents, followed by Kailua-Kona at 10,000. But the Big Island's growth resembles suburban sprawl, so regional numbers are key. If you count Kailua-Kona's suburbs to the north and east, its population of almost 30,000 rivals Hilo's.

By 2010 the Big Island population is projected to reach almost 177,000, led by rampant growth in Puna's extensive grid of subdivisions. Considering the already brutal commuter traffic between Puna and Hilo, that projection is dire indeed.

In the Big Island's ethnic mix, there's no real majority. Haole comprise the largest ethnic group at 34%, an ever increasing percentage. Hawaiians (including part-Hawaiians) are the second-largest group at 27%, followed by the Japanese at just over

FIFTY YEARS OF STATEHOOD

In Hawaii, statehood remains a hot-button issue. On August 21, 2009, residents will commemorate 50 years of statehood – perhaps with celebration, perhaps with protest. At the time of research for this book, little had been planned. Governor Linda Lingle had formed a 25-member statehood commission to plan an appropriate (read uncontroversial) celebration.

As *Honolulu Advertiser* columnist David Shapiro wrote in his blog, 'It's a continuation of the walking-on-eggshell jitters that have gripped the officials worried about potential conflicts between those who want to wave the flag on this landmark anniversary and a vocal minority of Native Hawaiians who regard statehood as the theft of their nation.'

Some argue that statehood was supported by 93% of local residents who voted in 1959, including most Native Hawaiians (and that most current residents do value American citizenship). But others counter that the statehood vote allowed only two choices: remain a territory or become a state. Other options – such as a nation-within-a-nation – were never offered. And no one can deny that Hawaiians have legitimate issues about their troubles, from loss of land to general marginalization, since US rule.

Such strife is a recurrent theme, as seen in ardent support of and opposition to the **Hawaii Superferry** (see p289) and more observatories on Mauna Kea. A fine balance, indeed.

11% and Filipinos at 7%. Mixed-race people (not including part-Hawaiians) comprise 18% of the population.

The number of 'pure' Native Hawaiians has dropped steadily ever since Captain Cook's arrival, and while a sizable number identify themselves as Hawaiian or part-Hawaiian, experts estimate the number of pure Native Hawaiians to be under 5000 nationwide.

Note that regions vary greatly in ethnic composition. In Hilo, almost 27% of the population is Japanese and 16% is white. But the North Kona to Kailua-Kona region comprises a whopping 47% whites and only 7% Japanese. Still, half of all marriages throughout Hawaii are mixed race.

MULTICULTURALISM

Nowadays, Big Island immigrants are predominantly white, so the island's diversity is based on historic minorities: Native Hawaiians and plantation immigrants (predominantly Japanese, Portuguese, Filipino and Chinese). This unique ethnic mix differs from mainland minority/majority populations, which are either black or Mexican Hispanic.

During plantation days, whites were the wealthy plantation owners, and their legendary surnames (from Lyman to Shipman to Parker) remain household words. Their ingrained privilege is one reason why some resentment toward haole lingers. Granted,

those prominent families were often close allies of the high-ranking Hawaiians – or even related by marriage. As time passes and the plantation era fades away, the traditional stereotypes, hierarchies and alliances soften, too. But for years, the immigrants would capitalize on plantation nostalgia during political elections, emphasizing their insider status as former plantation laborers.

That said, no ethnic group ever kept exclusive; instead groups freely adopted and shared cultural customs, from food to festivals to language. Folks of all colors dance hula, weave *lauhala* (pandanus leaves), craft hardwood bowls, play the ukulele and study the Hawaiian language. Cultural festivals, such as Chinese New Year or Japanese Obon, attract mixed crowds.

Island Insights

A Hawaii wedding is far from novel, yet still much desired. To add a bit of uniqueness, get hitched on the Big Island instead of on Maui! On both islands, resident marriages numbered just under 1000 in 2006. But nonresident marriages totaled a whopping 8563 on Maui that year, while only 1764 such couples married on the Big Island. On Maui (and also Kaua'i), nonresident marriages constitute almost 90% of the island total.

WHAT MAKES BIG ISLAND LOCALS TICK?

- Sunny days (especially in Hilo)
- Nostalgia for the 2007 UH Warrior football season
- Las Vegas
- Winning a jackpot in Vegas
- Winning a free trip to Vegas
- Costco (never mind what nonlocals think)
- Snow on Mauna Kea
- New Year's Eve home fireworks
- High-school commencement ceremonies
- Finding the perfect, storefront parking space
- Golf, whether on the course or on TV
- Catching waves at the go-to surf spots
- Massive potluck spreads

Due to intermarriage, you cannot always assume a person's race or ethnicity by surname. Many Hawaiians have Caucasian or Asian surnames, for example. If you observe Kamehameha School students, who must prove any quantum of Hawaiian ancestry, you'll see features that appear Chinese, Japanese or Caucasian, among the Hawaiian faces. It's also common, in multiethnic families, for siblings to vary in skin, eye and hair colors, which locals find amusing.

Generally, locals feel bonded with other locals. While tourists and transplants are welcomed with open arms, they must earn the trust and respect of the locals. It is unacceptable for an outsider to assume an air of superiority and to try to 'fix' local ways. If white, such people will inevitably fall into the category of 'loudmouth haole.'

In populated areas, prejudice against haole is minimal, but threats and even violence are possible at remote beaches and parks.

RELIGION

Although Hawaiians abandoned their ancient religion for Christianity after King Kamehameha died, some took the traditions underground. Today, you see glimpses of the old religion in local ceremonies. Christian sermons often include both Hawaiian and English words, and public ceremonies, such as a groundbreaking, feature a kahuna to bless the land.

Ancient historical sites – *pu'uhonua* (places of refuge), heiau, petroglyphs – are usually religious sites, chosen for the mana of the land. Certain natural sites, such as Halema'uma'u Crater and Mauna Kea, are

A traditional ceremony at Halema'uma'u Crater   ANN CECIL

Top Picks

PERFORMING-ARTS VENUES

- **Kahilu Theatre** (p134)
- **Volcano Art Center** (p211)
- **Palace Theater** (p187)
- **East Hawai'i Cultural Center** (p177)
- **Aloha Theatre** (p83)

also considered sacred. Hawaiians' activism against development is rooted in *aloha 'aina* (love of the sacred land).

Today, most residents do not claim adherence to a particular faith, and the religious milieu is tolerant rather than dogmatic. The largest religious group is Roman Catholic, due to the significant Filipino population, followed by the Church of Jesus Christ of Latter-Day Saints, which has attracted many South Pacific converts. Mainstream Protestant Christianity is struggling with declining membership, while evangelical churches are burgeoning. Buddhism is prevalent among the Japanese, and their temples are often important community centers.

ARTS
Music

Hawaiian music runs the gamut. It would take a textbook to cover every genre, from traditional Hawaiian *mele* (songs) to *ha'i* (Hawaiian falsetto singing) to contemporary vocalists who meshed Hawaiian and English lyrics, such as Hawaii's best-known singer, Israel Kamakawiwo'ole. One commonality for modern` Hawaii music is found in three instruments, described following.

The Hawaiian steel guitar *(kika kila)* might be less of a household word than the other two, but it's fundamental to the signature Hawaiian sound. Most cite Joseph Kekuhu as the inventor of the iconic lap guitar in the 1880s; by the 1900s, he and other Hawaiians burst onto the international scene, introducing both the instrument and *hapahaole* (Hawaiian music with English lyrics) to Americans and Europeans.

The ukulele is the most widely popular (to the point of Hollywood cliché) Hawaiian instrument. While always present in the background to accompany *'auana* (modern hula dance), it's also a solo instrument for bestselling musicians such as Eddie Kamae and Jake Shimabukuro (who became a YouTube hit with his mesmerizing cover of George Harrison's 'While My Guitar Gently Weeps').

Slack key guitar *(ki ho'alu*, which means 'loosen the key') is not an instrument but a method whereby the strings are slacked from their standard tuning. Since Gabby Pahinui first recorded his slack key tunes in the 1940s for the public, it's become the most famous and commercially successful Hawaiian genre. In fact, since the Grammy Award for Best Hawaiian Music Album was established in 2005, every winner has been a slack key compilation featuring living legends. Interestingly, the same company, Daniel Ho Creations (www.danielho.com), produced all three winners from 2006 to 2008.

Hawaiian vocalists are known for a distinctive falsetto style called *ha'i*, which

Top Picks

BIG ISLAND MUSICIANS

- **Kekuhi Kanahele** Stirring Hawaiian compositions by a hula and chant master
- **Darlene Ahuna** Longtime favorite falsetto known for her renditions of hula classics
- **Brittni Paiva** Young ukulele, guitar and bass talent who debuted as a teen in 2004
- **Cyril Pahinui** Slack key virtuoso featured on multiple Grammy-winning albums
- **Kainani Kahaunaele** Pure, traditional *mele* (songs) by a Hawaiian language instructor at the University of Hawai'i at Hilo
- **Keoki Kahumoku** Slack key and ukulele master featured on all four Hawaiian Music Grammy winners
- **The Lim Family** Much-loved Kohala family known for its up-tempo 'swing' sound, first recorded in 1979
- **John Keawe** Much renowned slack key guitarist and composer from Hawi, known for his simplicity and precision

stresses the breaks between lower and upper registers. Among females, the unquestioned leader remains the late Genoa Keawe, whose impossibly long-held notes in the song 'Alika' set the standard (and set it high). Other notables include jazz-turned-Hawaiian songbird Amy Hanaiali'i Gilliom and the 20-something superstar Raiatea Helm, both Grammy nominees.

Since the early 1900s, Hawaii music has shifted between Westernized and Hawaiian sounds. Nowadays, the trend is toward Hawaiian lyrics, both new compositions and traditional chanting with little accompaniment, often featuring the commanding vocals of gifted *kumu* hula (hula teachers).

To hear a diverse selection of Hawaii music, stream the radio station at www.hawaiianrainbow.com. An excellent resource and online CD retailer is www.mele.com.

Hula

Modern audiences assume that hula is entertainment or creative expression. But ancient Hawaiians regarded hula as much more. They had no written language, so hula and chanting served as essential communication to record historical events, myths and legends. It was also a religious offering to the gods.

Today's commercial hula shows, which emphasize swaying hips and nonstop smiling, might be compelling but they're not 'real' hula. Serious students join a hula *halau* (school), where they undergo rigorous training and adopt hula as a life practice.

But hula *halau* have embraced the utterly modern concept of…competition. In major competitions in Hawaii and California, dancers vie in *kahiko* (ancient) and '*auana* (modern) categories. *Kahiko* performances are raw and primordial, accompanied only by chanting, and they use a bent-knee stance to allow dancers to absorb Earth's energy. *Kahiko* dancers' costumes show primary colors and often lots of skin. Accompanied by harmonious singing and stringed instruments, '*auana* seems more like mainstream hula, with Western-influenced dresses and pants, sinuous arm movements and smiling faces.

The state's biggest hula competition is Hilo's Merrie Monarch Festival (see boxed text, p182), held during Easter week, but a newer competition in Waikoloa called Moku O Keawe (p109) is also good and less jammed. Don't miss the stunning outdoor shows offered quarterly at Hawai'i Volcanoes National Park (p224).

Literature

Hawaii's first examples of literature were ancient Hawaiian myths and legends, origi-

Competitors at the renowned Merrie Monarch Festival

MADE IN HAWAII

The best Hawai'i souvenirs are made locally and reflect the native culture. Look for the following Hawaiian arts and crafts around the island.

The finest examples of traditional woodworking are pricey collectibles, but budget shoppers can find inexpensive desk accessories and kitchen utensils. Today's woodworkers use a variety of hardwoods, from koa to Norfolk pine. At **Dan De Luz's Woods** (p196), there's a handy display of classic calabashes, each made from a different island wood.

It might be short-lived, but a lei makes an uplifting, in-the-moment souvenir. In daily life, locals continue to wear lei for special events, such as weddings and public ceremonies. Ancient lei were subtle in their beauty, made of modest berries, fragrant maile leaves and other greenery. Today's popular tourist lei feature fragrant or showy flowers, such as plumeria or dendrobium orchids. Florists sell popular and affordable lei, but to see master-crafted specimens, visit the island on May Day (May 1), when Hilo's **Palace Theater** (p187) holds a free festival and lei contest.

Christian missionaries introduced patchwork quilting to Hawaiians, who designed their own elegant, non-scrap appliqué method. Classic Hawaiian quilts feature a single, stylized floral shape appliquéd on a white background cloth. Painstakingly handstitched throughout, a genuine Hawaiian quilt costs thousands of dollars. Fine fabric shops islandwide offer excellent examples of handmade quilts (plus all the raw materials if you are handy with a needle and thread yourself); for a list, see http://planetpatchwork.com/passtvq/tvq24/hawaii.htm.

Thanks to a small group of master weavers, lauhala (pandanus leaf) weaving remains viable. Look for genuine, handmade baskets, hats, place mats and other household items at **Kimura Lauhala Shop** (see the box on p77), the only specialty lauhala shop on the island.

Beware of cheap monkeypod bowls, kukui (candlenut) lei, mass-produced quilts and lauhala knockoffs – all imported from the Philippines and sold at tourist traps.

See examples of all four types of arts and crafts at the **Lyman House Memorial Museum & Mission House** (p176).

---

nally transmitted by oral tradition (see the Myths & Legends chapter, p241). But in modern times, novels by nonlocal writers, such as James Michener's *Hawaii*, dominated Hawaii literature.

In the 1970s and 1980s, novels and poems by local authors expanded the definition of Hawaii literature. Maui-born Milton Murayama's *All I Asking For Is My Body* (first published in 1975), a 1980 American Book Award winner, is a realistic account of the Japanese-American experience around WWII. He wrote using the local vernacular, as does prolific Hilo-born author Lois-Ann Yamanaka, whose breakthrough collection of poems, *Saturday Night at the Pahala Theatre* (1993 Pushcart Prize winner) proved that pidgin English can be literary. A good intro to the pidgin vernacular and local personalities is *Growing Up Local: An Anthology of Poetry and Prose from Hawai'i*, a compendium published by Bamboo Ridge Press, a pioneer in the genre.

While vernacular literature is viscerally moving and tends to appeal to indie tastes,

another branch of contemporary literature is written in standard English and in more of a *New Yorker* literary style. O'ahu-born, San Francisco–based writer Kaui Hart Hemmings is currently garnering much critical kudos for her 2005 debut collection of short stories, *House of Thieves*, and 2007 novel *The Descendents*, both of which characterize the complicated lives of modern, upper-class Honolulu society.

Finally, if you prefer family epics, read the 500-page *Shark Dialogues*. This 1994 novel by Kiana Davenport, an O'ahu-born, Boston-based writer, deftly intertwines the plot with Hawaiian history, from a runaway Tahitian princess to a leprosy-afflicted grandfather.

Cinema & TV

The Hawaii Film Office is always wooing Hollywood to shoot on location throughout the state. Production revenues give a multimillion-dollar boost to the economy and also highlight Hawaii as a desirable destination. Granted, nowadays the Islands usually serve as stand-ins for Africa, Vietnam and South American countries, but when Hollywood's love affair with Hawaii first bloomed in the 1930s, films, such as Bing Crosby's *Waikiki Wedding* and Elvis Presley's *Blue Hawaii*, were actually set in Hawaii.

Of the hundreds of feature films shot in the Islands, the vast majority were on Kaua'i and O'ahu. But, in 2007, the Big Island substituted for Peru in *Indiana Jones and the Kingdom of the Crystal Skull* (2008), the third sequel to the 1981 classic *Raiders of the Lost Ark*. You know the chase scene in the 'Peruvian' jungle? It was shot in lush rainforests and along coastal cliffs on private property in Puna. Among the big-name films shot here is the 1995 Kevin Costner hit *Waterworld*, which featured the black-sand beach at Waimanu Bay (p162). In 2001, *Planet of the Apes*, directed by Tim Burton and starring Mark Wahlberg, used a desolate lava field in Kalapana (p203) to stage a major battle scene starring horse-riding apes.

While Hawaii has hosted over two-dozen major TV series since 1968, including *Hawaii Five-O* and *Magnum PI*, few have featured the Big Island. Most were filmed on O'ahu, which garnered much attention during the ABC's 2004–08 hit series *Lost*. But the Big Island did host *Amazing Race 4* (2003), in which the challengers swam near Ka Lae (p237) and found a clue box at Hawai'i Volcanoes National Park. For more information about the industry, contact the Hawaii Film Office (www.hawaiifilmoffice.com).

LEARN THE LINGO

While English is the standard language used in Hawaii, you'll quickly realize that it's a far cry from mainland English. Here, locals use a combination of pidgin, Hawaiian and English (with a dose of Japanese and Chinese, too).

It sounds more challenging than it is. Local kids grow up with this hodgepodge but they're taught in public schools to use standard English in academic and professional settings. Most agree with this distinction, but a once-renegade, now-respected group called **Da Pidgin Coup at the University of Hawai'i** (www.hawaii.edu/satocenter/dapidgincoup.html) advocates recognition of pidgin (which it calls Hawai'i Creole English) as a legitimate language.

The best-known champion of pidgin use is Lee Tonouchi, a writer, playwright and lecturer at Kapiolani Community College on O'ahu, who was hired in the English Department with an application written entirely in pidgin. His books include *Da Word* (short stories), *Living Pidgin: Contemplations on Pidgin Culture* (essays) and *Da Kine Dictionary* (pictorial dictionary). In addition to Tonouchi's titles, find Douglas Simonson's classic *Pidgin To Da Max*, a laugh-out-loud cartoon dictionary.

Lonelyplanet.com offers a free downloadable **Hawaiian Language & Glossary** supplement at www.lonelyplanet.com/hawaiian-language. For now, here are some common words and phrases:

Pidgin

brah – shortened form of *braddah* (brother)
chicken skin – goose bumps from cold, fear, thrill
coconut wireless – the 'grapevine'; local gossip channels
da kine – whatchamacallit; used whenever you can't think of the appropriate word
Fo' real? – Really? Are you kidding me?
Howzit? – Hey, how's it going? As in 'Eh, howzit brah?'
high makamaka – stuck-up, snooty, pretentious; literally 'high eyes,' meaning head in the air
rubbah slippahs – rubber slippers, flip-flops
talk story – chitchat or any casual conversation
to da max – used as an adjective or adverb to add emphasis, as in 'Da waves was big to da max!'

Hawaiian

aloha – love, hello, welcome, goodbye
hale – house
kane – man
kapu – taboo, restricted
mahalo – thank you
makai – a directional, toward the sea
mauka – a directional, toward the mountains
pau – finished, completed
pono – goodness, justice, responsibility
wahine – woman

FOOD & DRINK

Forget pineapple toppings and blue cocktails. Real Hawaii cuisine is no cliché. It's a multicultural taste explosion, influenced by the Pacific Rim but rooted in the natural island bounty. The first Polynesians brought nourishing staples such as *kalo* (taro), *mai'a* (banana) and *niu* (coconut), plus chickens and pigs. The Hawaiians and plantation-era immigrants added distinct flavors – from Japanese teriyaki to Chinese noodles to Hawaiian *kalua* pork – that complemented island-grown produce and fresh-caught fish. Over time the cuisines melded and became 'local.' For the full experience, try Hawaii Regional Cuisine and also everyday *grinds*, from saimin noodles to shave ice.

STAPLES & SPECIALTIES

The island diet is quite Americanized, and you'll immediately see the usual fast-food chains, supermarkets stocked with national brands, and familiar menus of pancakes and Caesar salads. But Hawai'i is no white-bread wasteland either. Look for distinctions in the details. First, the primary starch is sticky, medium-grain, white rice. Jasmine rice is tolerated with Thai food, but flaky rice is considered haole food (and Uncle Ben's is inedible!).

Second, the top condiment is soy sauce (ubiquitously called by its Japanese name, shoyu), which combines well with sharp Asian flavors, such as ginger, green onion and garlic.

Third, meat, chicken or fish is often integral to a dish. For quick, cheap eating, locals devour anything tasty, from Portuguese sausage to hamburger steak to corned beef. But the dinner table highlight is always seafood, especially succulent, fresh-caught 'ahi (yellowfin tuna) – where the red color is 100% natural.

Fourth, island-grown produce is a given, especially because it's readily available at farmers markets, local supermarkets and… the backyard. Locals are avid gardeners and enjoy a surplus of homegrown tangerines, bananas, star fruit and avocados.

Finally, while the Big Island boasts world-class papayas, macadamias and coffee, plus delicious island-style Japanese and Thai cuisines, its attempts at nonlocal classics (such as pizza, bagels, croissants and Southern barbecue) are disappointing. Stick with *local* local food.

Top Picks

HAWAIIAN COOKBOOKS

- **Kona on My Plate** Kona Outdoor Circle
- **Aloha Cuisine** Sam Choy
- **What Hawaii Likes to Eat** Muriel Miura and Betty Shimabukuro
- **Hawaii Cooks With Taro** Marcia Zina Mager and Muriel Miura
- **101 Great Desserts from Hawaii's Favorite Restaurants** Cheryl Chee Tsutsumi
- **The Island Plate** Honolulu Advertiser Food Editor Wanda Adams

Hawaii Regional Cuisine

If pineapple-topped entrées epitomized Hawaii cuisine till the late 1980s, locals are partly to blame. Fine dining in Hawaii meant copycat 'continental' fare that hid the basic appeal of local ingredients: locally caught fish, locally grown produce and locally raised meat.

While there were many decent, mid-range Japanese and Chinese eateries, Hawaii lacked an actual unique local cuisine. Further, the local appetite for cheap, filling food (never mind that it's made with canned goods) did nothing to push the gourmet envelope.

In the late '80s, Hawaii's top chefs finally shone the spotlight on the Islands. They partnered with local farmers, ranchers and fishers to gather the freshest ingredients, and they found inspiration in the varied ethnic cuisines. Often they transformed their favorite childhood dishes into grown-up masterpieces. The movement was dubbed 'Hawaii Regional Cuisine,' and the pioneering chefs became celebrities.

On the Big Island, big-name chefs Roy Yamaguchi (p110), Alan Wong (p100) and Peter Merriman (p133 and p110) have outposts that attract foodies, no matter that they're not actually manning the kitchen.

A newer trend is the Japanese-fusion cuisines that also feature island ingredients: Sansei Seafood Restaurant & Sushi Bar (p110), Fujimamas (p65) and Kenichi Pacific (p74 and p114) are standouts.

FRESHNESS IS THE KEY

While Hawaii Regional Cuisine started as a four-star phenomenon, it is defined not by fanciness but by simplicity. Look for fresh, local, seasonal, organic ingredients, hand-picked if possible.

The 'locavore' trend, spurred by Hawaii Regional Cuisine, might help struggling island farms survive. Regrettably, much of the state's basic food supply is imported, including 80% of fresh milk. In fact, when O'ahu's last dairy closed in early 2008, only two Big Island dairies (one in Hamakua and one in North Kohala) were left statewide.

But local producers are rallying with top-quality, name-recognizable crops. Across the state, foodies rave about Hamakua mushrooms, Ka'u oranges, Puna papayas,

Vegetable stand at the Hilo Farmers Market

GREG ELMS

Kamuela tomatoes, Big Island beef, and Kona farmed *kampachi* (yellowtail) and shellfish.

Local Food

Cheap, filling and tasty, local food is the stuff of cravings and comfort. Such food might be dubbed 'street food' but street vendors are uncommon, except at farmers markets. No list is complete without the classic plate lunch, a fixed-plate meal containing 'two scoop rice,' macaroni-potato salad and your choice of a hot protein dish, such as *tonkatsu* (breaded pork cutlets), fried mahimahi or teriyaki chicken. Often eaten with disposable chopsticks on disposable plates, they are tasty and filling. Typically fried, salty, gravy-laden and meaty, plates now include grilled fish, brown rice and green salad.

The local palate prefers hot rice or noodle entrées to cold cuts and sliced bread. Thus another favorite is saimin, a soup of chewy Chinese egg noodles and Japanese broth, garnished with colorful toppings such as green onion, nori (dried seaweed), *kamaboko* (steamed fish cake), egg roll or *char siu* (Chinese barbecued pork). And you can't go home without trying the Big Island invention called *loco moco*, a bowl of rice, two eggs (typically fried over-easy) and a hamburger patty, topped with gravy and a dash of shoyu. The current go-to spot for *loco moco* is Café 100 (p182) in Hilo.

Many local favorites come from Japanese cuisine, tweaked to be sweet and strongly flavored. For a sampling, head to an *okazu-ya*, a hole-in-the-wall Japanese delicatessen with an eye-popping selection of finger foods and savory dishes: *musubi* (rice balls), *maki* (rolled) sushi, fried noodles, tofu patties, shrimp and vegetable tempura, *nishime* (root-vegetable stew), teriyaki beef, broiled mackerel. Favorite *okazu-ya* include Hilo Lunch Shop (☎ 935-8273; 421 Kalanikoa St, Hilo; ☷ 5:30am-1pm) and Kawamoto Store (☎ 935-8209; 784 Kilauea Ave, Hilo; ☷ 6am-12:30pm). Arrive by mid-morning for the full selection. In a hurry, pick up a *bento* (prepackaged Japanese-style box lunch with rice, meat or fish, plus pickles, cooked vegetables and other Japanese garnishes) at deli counters and corner stores.

Consider yourself lucky if you snag an invitation to a *pupu* (appetizer) party at a local home. Go casual and expect an endless spread of grazing foods (forget the cheese and crackers), such as fried shrimp, *edamame* (boiled soybeans in the pod) and *maki* sushi. A must-try is *poke* (*po*-keh), Hawaii's soul food – a savory dish of bite-sized raw fish (typically *'ahi*), marinated in a shoyu/sesame-oil sauce and tossed with *ogo* (seaweed) and *inamona*, a flavoring made of roasted and ground *kukui* (candlenut).

Nowadays kids veer toward mainstream candy and gum, but the traditional local treat is mouthwatering Chinese crack seed, preserved fruit (typically plum, cherry, mango or lemon) that, like Coca-Cola or curry, is impossible to describe. It can be sweet, sour, salty or licorice-spicy. Sold prepackaged at grocers or by the pound at specialty shops, crack seed is as the name indirectly suggests, addictive.

THE OTHER PINK MEAT

If **Spam** disgusts you, brace yourself. Hormel's iconic canned ham is a local favorite comfort food. Here in the Spam capital of the USA, locals consume almost seven million cans per year.

Bear in mind, presentation is key. Spam is always eaten sliced and sautéed to a light crispiness, typically in sweetened shoyu. It serves as a tasty form of meat: Spam and eggs, Spam and rice, Spam and vegetables.

The affinity for Spam arose during the plantation era, when canned meat was cheap and easy to prepare for *bento* (box) lunches. Locals still can't get enough of that salty taste and uniform texture. Created in the 1960s or '70s, Spam *musubi* – a rice ball topped with fried Spam and wrapped with sushi nori (dried seaweed) – is an island classic, sold by the thousands daily at grocers, lunch counters and convenience stores.

If you acquire a taste for Spam, plan a trip to Honolulu for the annual **Waikiki Spam Jam** (www.spamjamhawaii.com). Yes, really.

Native Hawaiian

Utterly memorable in rich, earthy flavors and native ingredients, Hawaiian food is like no other. Today, several dishes are staples in the local diet, but they're generally harder to find than other cuisines. The best venues for good, authentic Hawaiian food are plate-lunch shops, diners, fish markets and supermarket delis. Commercial luau buffets include all the notable dishes, but the quality can be mediocre.

Perhaps the most famous (or infamous) Hawaiian dish is poi, steamed and mashed wetland taro, which was sacred to Hawaiians. Locals savor the bland to mildly tart flavor as a starchy palate cleanser, but its slightly sticky and pasty consistency can be off-putting to nonlocals. Taro is highly nutritious, low in calories, easily digestible and versatile to prepare. Also try taro chips

Spam *bento* boxes   GREG ELMS

(made with dryland/upland 'Chinese' taro) at local grocers.

Locals typically eat poi as a counterpoint to strongly flavored fish dishes such as *lomi-lomi* salmon (minced, salted salmon tossed with diced tomato and green onion) and *poke*. In case you're wondering, salmon is an import, first introduced to Hawaiians by whaling ships.

No Hawaiian feast is complete without *kalua* pig, which is traditionally roasted whole underground in an *imu*, a sealed pit of red-hot stones. Cooked this way, the pork is smoky, salty and succulent. Nowadays *kalua* pork is typically oven-roasted and seasoned with salt and liquid smoke. At commercial luau, a pig placed in an *imu* is only for show (and it couldn't feed 300-plus guests anyway).

A popular restaurant dish is *laulau*, a bundle of pork or chicken and salted butterfish, wrapped in taro leaves and steamed in *ti* leaves. When cooked, the melt-in-your-mouth taro leaves blend perfectly with the savory meats.

Another food hardly seen on menus is raw *'opihi* (limpet), which you can pick yourself (if they're 1.5in or larger) from remote coasts such as Halape (p223) and Road to the Sea (p240).

DRINKS

Since the plantation era, smooth and mellow Kona coffee has brought the Big Island international fame. But only recently has café culture taken root, with baristas brewing espresso at deli counters, indie hangouts and, of course, Starbucks. (Hilo's drive-through Starbucks does brisk business.) Local old-timers balk at paying $3 plus for coffee, but today's youth are eager converts to lattes and cappuccinos.

In 2007 Ka'u shocked everyone when two of its farms placed sixth and ninth among the world's 10 best in a Specialty Coffee Association of America cupping competition. (The other winners were all from Central and South America.) Today Honoka'a, Puna and Ka'u coffee are sharing the spotlight.

They say that tea, grown experimentally by University of Hawai'i researchers since 1999, is the next big thing. Private farms are popping up in the Hamakua and Volcano upcountry; see www.maunakeatea.com and www.teahawaii.com for more.

While fresh fruit is plentiful at farmers markets, fresh fruit juice tends to be pricey and sold mainly at health food markets and eateries. Forgo the supermarket cartons and cans, which tend to be sugary drinks.

Unique to Hawaii are two botanical 'tonics,' nowadays marketed mainly to tourists: 'awa (kava), a mild sedative, and noni

Island Insights

Hawaii is the only US state that commercially grows coffee and chocolate.

(Indian mulberry), which some consider a cure-all. Both are pungent, if not repulsive, in smell and taste, so they are typically mixed with other juices.

Among alcoholic beverages, beer is your average person's drink. While national brands such as Coors are popular, two microbreweries are thriving. Kona Brewing Company (p64) and Hilo's Mehana Brewing Company (p178) both started up in the mid-1990s and now distribute their brews across the state and even internationally.

Wine remains more exclusive in its audience. The wine lists at upscale restaurants and specialty wine shops are geared mainly toward tourists and mainland transplants. In Honolulu, wine has grown trendy among the upper-income, professional crowd, but the Big Island is a down-home place, still ruled by the beer-and-*pupu* contingent. The island's sole winery, Volcano Winery (p226), is boldly untraditional in its guava or macadamia-honey concoctions.

As for umbrella drinks, rum and vodka are transformed into the mai tai, piña colada and Blue Hawaii for tourists (and the eager 21-year-olds) only.

Don't Miss

- **Unidentifiable fruit at South Kona Fruit Stand** (p91)
- **Atebara's potato chips** A Hilo tradition, sold at grocery and convenience stores islandwide.
- **Superb *malasada* (Portuguese sugar-coated doughnuts) at Tex Drive-In** (p155)
- **Maku'u Craft & Farmers Market** (p197)
- **Restaurant Miwa's excellent *teishoku* (multicourse Japanese meals)** (p183)
- **Café 100's legendary *loco moco*** (p182)
- **Fruit smoothies at What's Shakin'** (p166)
- **The extensive vegetarian menu at O's Bistro** (p65)
- **Memorable cuisine at Thai Thai Restaurant** (p226)
- **Aloha Festivals Poke Contest** (p117)
- **Ocean View Pizzaria's tasty pizza and sandwiches** (p239)
- **Fresh poke, bento and other local takeout food at KTA Super Stores** (p186 and other locations islandwide)

CELEBRATIONS

To celebrate is to feast. Whether a 300-guest wedding or an intimate birthday party, a massive spread is mandatory. If not, why bother? Most gatherings are informal, held at parks, beaches or homes, featuring a potluck buffet of homemade dishes. On major American holidays, mainstream foods (eg Easter eggs and Thanksgiving turkey) appear alongside local fare such as rice (instead of mashed potatoes), sweet-potato tempura (instead of yams) and hibachi-grilled teriyaki beef (instead of roast beef).

Now that agritourism and gourmet cuisine are trendy, food festivals are garnering much attention. The oldest and most community-oriented is the Kona Coffee Cultural Festival (p64), which honors the pioneering Kona coffee farmers. Craft beer fits right into

OF FEASTS & FANTASIES

Like aloha shirts and hula girls, the **luau** is a Hawaii icon – and among the top 10 tourist must-sees. In ancient Hawaii, a luau commemorated auspicious occasions, such as births, war victories or successful harvests.

Today, only commercial luau offer the elaborate Hawaiian feast and hula dancing that folks expect. A $70 to $100 ticket buys you a highly choreographed Polynesian dance show and an all-you-can-eat buffet. Some, such as the **Kona Village Resort's luau** (p101), focus primarily on Hawaiian traditions. Others, such as the Sheraton Keauhou's **Kamaha'o** (p74), are professional, acrobatic stage productions enacting Hawaiian myths and legends.

The buffet includes Hawaiian standards such as poi and *kalua* pig, plus please-all selections such as roast beef, teriyaki beef and pineapple cake. Foodies with picky tastes will enjoy the offerings at superior hotels, such as the **Fairmont Orchid** (☎ 326-4969; adult/child $99/65; ☒ 6pm Tue & Sat) and the two mentioned above, although all the stage shows might be on par.

Private luau celebrations, typically for weddings or first birthdays, are more like normal family gatherings. The menu might be more daring – and include raw *'a'ama* (black crab) and *'opihi* (limpet) – and the entertainment more low-key. Forget the fire-eaters.

the made-in-Hawaii movement, and the biggest beer bash is the Kona Brewers Festival (p64). Most resort events are pricey foodie galas, but the Aloha Festivals Poke Contest (p117) is a $5 immersion into Hawaii's soul food. To promote the Big Island's ranching industry, a Waikoloa gala dubbed A Taste of the Hawaiian Range (p109) lets guests sample over 50 chef-made creations featuring range-fed meats and local produce.

WHERE TO EAT & DRINK

Except at the South Kohala and North Kona resort restaurants, all Big Island dining is casual. (Even the top resorts are known to waive the dress code for shorts-clad guests, although shoes and shirts are expected.) Destination eateries tend to cluster in the resort areas and larger towns, meaning Hilo and Kailua-Kona. But Waimea established its foodie status two decades ago when Merriman's opened in 1988. A surprise dining destination is Hawi (p124), where Bamboo and Sushi Rock illustrate the variety of unfussy, indie eateries.

On the road, takeout food will save time and money. If you're a meat eater and not counting calories, go for the local-style plate lunches, *loco moco* and saimin at drive-ins (which are often drive-throughs) and diners.

Often, there's a local-tourist divide in restaurant choices. This is especially clear in tourist towns such as Kailua-Kona. If atmosphere is key, then the steep prices for oceanfront dining might be worth it. Lo-

cals tend to focus on tasty food, generous portions and good value, so they're often found at diner-style restaurants, typically with Formica tables and vinyl chairs, sans view and decor.

HABITS & CUSTOMS

Home cooking is integral to the local lifestyle, perhaps owing to the slower pace and plentiful food supply. Meals are early and on the dot: typically 6am breakfast, noon lunch and 6pm dinner. At home, locals rarely (perhaps never) serve formal sit-down meals with individual courses. Even when entertaining, meals are typically served potluck style with a spread of flavorful dishes that to the unfamiliar palate will seem ridiculously clashing.

If you're invited to a local home, show up on time and bring dessert. Remove your shoes at the door. And don't be surprised if you're forced to take home a plate or two of leftovers.

Except at top resort restaurants, the island dress code means that T-shirts and flip-flops are ubiquitous. But the older local generation tends toward neat, modest attire.

Big Island restaurants typically open and close early – late-night dining is limited to bars and the rare 24-hour diner, such as Hilo's Ken's House of Pancakes (p183). In general, locals tip slightly less than mainlanders do, but still up to 20% for good service and at least 15% for the basics.

EATING WITH CHILDREN

Hawai'i is a family-oriented and unfussy place, so all restaurants welcome children. Even the finest resort restaurants, such as Pahui'a (p100) and Brown's Beach House (p114), accommodate kids (often with dedicated menus). Of course, no one appreciates noisy interruptions during a four-star, wallet-emptying meal.

If restaurant dining is inconvenient, no problem: eating outdoors is among the simplest and best island pleasures. Pack *bento* and farmers market fruit for a picnic, or eat plate lunches at open-air drive-ins. Also, consider accommodations that include a kitchen.

The food itself should pose little trouble, as Big Island grocers stock mainstream national brands. A kid who can't live without Honey Nut Cheerios will not go hungry here. But the local diet will probably tempt kids, with its plethora of sweet treats and variety of cuisines. Basics, such as infant formula and baby food, are widely available at grocers and drugstores. For more on traveling with kids, see p278.

VEGETARIANS & VEGANS

On Hawai'i, the vegetarian population is negligible, and most are mainland transplants, not locals. Veganism is rare and considered rather extreme. Nevertheless it's quite easy to survive sans meat or animal products here. That's due to the island's substantial produce industry, which is best experienced at the many farmers markets.

When dining out, vegetarians will find impeccable options at the top Hawaii Regional Cuisine restaurants; O's Bistro (p65) offers an especially abundant vegetarian menu. For budget meals, try the healthy 'California cuisine'–inspired cafés popping up around the island, where whole-grain breads, meal-sized salads, grilled vegetables, lentils and couscous are not hippie food anymore. Try Pico's Bistro (p127), Pau (p132), Lilikoi Café (p133) and the deli counters at the island's many health food stores; none of these is exclusively vegetarian, much less vegan, but their meatless offerings will probably suit most. Asian eateries offer varied tofu and veggie options but beware of meat- or fish-based broths.

FOOD GLOSSARY

Local cuisine is multiethnic and so is the lingo. In addition to the following food glossary, we offer a free downloadable Hawaiian Language & Glossary at www.lonelyplanet.com/hawaiian-language, which provides more Hawaiian and pidgin terms as well as pronunciation tips.

adobo – Filipino chicken or pork cooked in vinegar, shoyu, garlic and spices
arare – shoyu-flavored rice crackers; also called *kaki mochi*
'awa – kava, a native plant used to make an intoxicating drink
bento – Japanese-style box lunch
broke da mout – delicious; literally 'broke the mouth'
char siu – Chinese barbecued pork
crack seed – Chinese-style preserved fruit; a salty, sweet and/or sour snack
donburi – meal-sized bowl of rice and main dish
furikake – Japanese condiment typically containing dried seaweed, sesame seeds and bonito flakes
grind – to eat
grinds – food; see also *'ono kine grinds*
guava – fruit with green or yellow rind, moist pink flesh and lots of edible seeds
gyoza – grilled dumpling usually containing minced pork or shrimp
haupia – coconut-cream dessert
hulihuli chicken – rotisserie-cooked chicken
imu – underground earthen oven used to cook *kalua* pig and other luau food
inamona – roasted and ground *kukui* (candlenut), used to flavor *poke*
kalo – Hawaiian word for taro
kalua – Hawaiian method of cooking pork and other luau food in an *imu*

kaukau – food
kamaboko – cake of pureed, steamed fish; used to garnish Japanese dishes
katsu – deep-fried fillets, usually chicken; see also *tonkatsu*
laulau – bundle of pork or chicken and salted butterfish, wrapped in taro and *ti* leaves and steamed
li hing mui – sweet-salty preserved plum; type of crack seed; also refers to the flavor powder
liliko'i – passion fruit
loco moco – dish of rice, fried egg and hamburger patty topped with gravy or other condiments
lomilomi salmon – minced, salted salmon, diced tomato and green onion
luau – Hawaiian feast
mai tai – 'tiki bar' drink typically containing rum, grenadine, and lemon and pineapple juices
malasada – Portuguese fried doughnut, sugar-coated, no hole
manapua – Chinese steamed or baked bun filled with *char siu*
manju – Japanese bun filled with sweet bean paste
mochi – Japanese sticky-rice dumpling
nishime – Japanese stew of root vegetables and seaweed
noni – type of mulberry with smelly yellow fruit, used medicinally
nori – Japanese seaweed, usually dried
ogo – crunchy seaweed, often added to *poke; limu* in Hawaiian
'ohelo – shrub with edible red berries similar in tartness and size to cranberries
'ono – delicious
'ono kine grinds – good food
pho – Vietnamese soup, typically beef broth, noodles and fresh herbs
pipikaula – Hawaiian beef jerky
poi – staple Hawaiian starch made of steamed, mashed taro
poke – cubed, marinated raw fish
ponzu – Japanese citrus sauce
pupu – snacks or appetizers
saimin – local-style noodle soup
shave ice – cup of finely shaved ice sweetened with colorful syrups
shoyu – soy sauce
soba – buckwheat noodles
star fruit – translucent green-yellow fruit with five ribs like the points of a star and sweet, juicy pulp
taro – plant with edible corm used to make poi and with edible leaves eaten in *laulau;* see also *kalo*
teishoku – fixed, multicourse Japanese meal
teppanyaki – Japanese style of cooking with an iron grill
tonkatsu – breaded and fried pork cutlets, also prepared as chicken *katsu*
tsukemono – Japanese pickled vegetables
ume – Japanese pickled plum

NAME THAT FISH

See the Hawai'i Seafood Buyers' Guide at www.hawaii-seafood.org for more info.

'ahi – yellowfin or bigeye tuna, red flesh, excellent raw or rare
aku – skipjack tuna, red flesh, strong flavor; *katsuo* in Japanese
kajiki – Pacific blue marlin; *a'u* in Hawaiian
mahimahi – dolphin fish or dorado, pink flesh, popular cooked
nairagi – striped marlin; *a'u* in Hawaiian
onaga – red snapper, soft and moist
ono – wahoo, white-fleshed and flaky
opah – moonfish, firm and rich
'opakapaka – pink snapper, delicate flavor, premium quality
'opelu – mackerel scad, pan-sized, delicious fried
shutome – swordfish, succulent and meaty
tako – octopus, chewy texture

PLANNING YOUR TRIP

The Big Island makes for an easy tropical getaway, where world-class beaches come with comfy US standards of living. Thus it's very popular and requires budget travelers to plan ahead.

Many do a two-island hop with Hawai'i and O'ahu, especially if they arrive first in Honolulu. Once on the Big Island, remember its relative geographical size. Circling the island in a day is certainly possible, but why waste your vacation in a car?

Definitely consider the island's geographic variety; if you're seeking a particular setting or climate, choose apt accommodations so you won't be disappointed. For a variety of recommended itineraries, see p18.

WHEN TO GO

With mild temperatures year-round, there's no real off-season regarding climate. But it is cooler and rainier in winter (mid-December through March), the season most prone to torrential rainstorms that can cause major flooding. That said, winter does offer the thrill of whale watching. Summers are generally hotter and drier, with calmer surf. See Climate (p279) for more information.

A primary consideration should be the tourist season: avoid the winter high season, when prices soar at many hotels and condos, particularly those in Kailua-Kona and South Kohala. Instead, plan to go during fall (September through early December) or spring (mid-April through June), when prices drop and holiday vacationers are gone. Most activities, such as snorkeling, diving and hiking, are doable year-round; only whale watching is seasonal, while lava viewing is totally unpredictable.

During major holidays such as Thanksgiving, Christmas, and New Year (see p281), vacancies are scarce. But the Big Island's busiest tourist week falls around Easter, during the Merrie Monarch Festival (p182); if you arrive in Hilo sans accommodations during the festival, be prepared to sleep in your car! In Kailua-Kona, the annual Ironman Triathlon World Championship (p34) in October guarantees few vacancies and snarled traffic along the Kona Coast. Other major festivals and events are listed on p274.

COSTS & MONEY

The Big Island can be an extravagant four-star destination or a no-frills hostelling adventure, depending on your travel style. In general, the priciest accommodations are the luxury resorts along the Gold Coast, but upscale inns and B&Bs have proliferated across the island.

Usually accommodations will be your biggest expense, followed by airfare and car rental. While accommodations run the gamut, most hotel, condo and B&B rates fall in the midrange category, from \$125 to \$200; for an ocean view, expect to pay \$200 or more. Decent digs under \$100 are rather scarce, especially as more innkeepers and B&B owners now target the higher-end

---

DON'T LEAVE HOME WITHOUT...

- Specialty items that you can't live without (from maternity swimsuit to fave yoga mat)
- Broken-in hiking boots or shoes
- UV-protection sunglasses, especially for ocean glare
- Wide-brimmed sunhat
- Long pants for lava caving
- Heavy jacket and gloves for Mauna Kea
- Travel umbrella
- Binoculars for whale watching and birding
- Snorkel gear if you're particular about fit and quality
- Identification cards (eg student, automobile association, AARP) for possible discounts

PLANNING YOUR TRIP

DOS & DON'TS

- Avoid honking your car horn unless absolutely necessary.
- Be courteous and 'no make waves' (be cool and low-key).
- Try pronouncing individual Hawaiian words, as sincere effort is appreciated, but avoid a barrage of pidgin, which might seem to mock the local vernacular.
- Dress informally, if you want to blend in.
- Regard any ancient Hawaiian site or artifact with respect.
- Mention Las Vegas as a conversation starter, but only if you're likewise a fan.
- Remove your shoes before entering local homes (and many B&Bs and condos).
- Always give a thank-you wave (or the *shaka* hand sign) if a driver lets you merge into their lane.
- Never use the term 'Hawaiian' as a catchall for island residents; Hawaiians constitute the native race.
- Never drop in on a local surfer's wave.
- If called a haole, don't assume that it's an insult.
- Tread lightly at 'locals only' beaches; they're usually small and cannot sustain tourist traffic.

market. Big-name resorts start between $350 and $550, but skyrocket to ridiculous figures for the best oceanfront rooms and during the peak winter season.

Airfares vary too greatly for any generalities, but we can offer a tip on timing: fares definitely increase during the winter high season. For land transportation, there is no question – you must rent a car. The Big Island's Hele-On Bus (p290) is extremely limited. If you book ahead for nonpeak periods, you can clinch sweet weekly deals of $130 for economy cars and $160 for full-size cars, albeit plus high taxes and fees. Weekly rates easily top $300 for last-minute and high-season bookings. To go off-road, you'll need to shell out big bucks for a 4WD (see p290). Rates fluctuate wildly based on availability; book early to guarantee a good deal.

As for food costs, you can fill up for under $20 per day if you forage at farmers markets, supermarkets and takeout counters, but dining exclusively at resorts and gourmet restaurants will set you back $75 (at the *very* least) per day.

CHOOSING ACCOMMODATIONS

In this book, accommodations are listed in price order, from lowest to highest, in the Sleeping section of each regional chapter. Price indicators are $ (under $90), $$ ($90 to $160), $$$ ($160 to $230) and $$$$ (over $230). Room rates are listed for single (s) or double (d) occupancy; if there's no rate difference for one or two people, the general room (r) rate is listed. Unless otherwise noted, breakfast is not included, bathrooms are private and the room is available year-round. Listed rates do not include taxes of 11.41%. Smoking is prohibited indoors. For a key to the icons used in this book, see Quick Reference on the inside front cover.

At many hotels and condos, rates rise during the winter high season (mid-December through March) and during major holidays, festivals and events. In high-demand times, the best accommodations are booked months (even a year) in advance. See below for specific information about each lodging type.

Regarding bargaining or haggling: don't bother. In Hawaii it's just not a widespread practice. Hotel or condo staffers have no authority to grant special discounts, while innkeepers and B&B owners might simply refuse the room.

For a range of accommodations listings, see **Vacation Rentals By Owner** (www.vrbo.com). Before choosing, check recent reviews at **Trip Advisor** (www.tripadvisor.com), the leading accommodations-rating website.

B&Bs, Inns & Guesthouses

The B&B market is thriving on Hawai'i, especially as visitors nowadays want personalized, small-scale experiences. Quality ranges from simple extra rooms to upscale designer suites – and you can usually predict the quality level by the price.

The terminology can be fuzzy, but in this book, B&Bs either serve full or continental breakfasts or provide groceries for guests

BOOK ACCOMMODATIONS ONLINE

For more accommodation reviews and recommendations by Lonely Planet authors, check out www.lonelyplanet.com/hotels. You'll find the true, insider lowdown on the best places to stay. Reviews are thorough and independent, and best of all, you can book online.

to prepare on their own. While also located in private homes, inns do not include breakfast. Both B&B and inn rooms might include a kitchenette, private access and other apartment amenities. Guesthouses (also called *'ohana*) are freestanding, fully equipped cottages.

While B&B and inn rooms sometimes drop under $100, most cost between $125 and $175. Many require a minimum stay of two or three days and offer discounts for extended stays. Some refuse child guests to maintain a quiet, immaculate or 'romantic' setting. Guesthouses typically start at about $150; note the extra-guest cost, typically $15.

To research B&Bs yourself, start with the Hawaii Island Bed & Breakfast Association (www .stayhawaii.com; PO Box 1890, Honoka'a, HI 96727). The Big Island's tightly run B&B association lists 40 to 50 licensed, county-inspected B&Bs. While they vary in swankiness, all are comfortable and upscale. The list is very reliable and includes numerous B&Bs reviewed in this book.

For B&B, inn and guesthouse listings, try the aforementioned Vacation Rentals By Owner (www.vrbo.com), which provides an extensive, if overwhelming, selection. With these listings, caveat emptor: there is no quality guarantee, so you're on your own if problems arise.

You can also book all three types of accommodations through an agency such as Hawaii's Best Bed & Breakfasts (☎ 800-262-9912;

www.bestbnb.com), based on O'ahu but with good Big Island coverage. This is a great resource for guesthouses, ranging from cozy cottages to fantasy beach villas. The selection is limited but handpicked and high quality.

Camping & Cabins

By far the best camping is found at Hawai'i Volcanoes National Park (p225), where sites are free and available on a first-come, first-served basis.

State and county parks run the gamut. In general, remote sites are cleaner and safer, while accessible spots, especially county beach parks, can be deserted pit stops for drunkards and druggies. When reserving a permit, ask whether drinking water is available.

STATE PARKS

Permits are required and cost $5 per family campsite; $20 per night for the four-person, A-frame cabins at Hapuna Beach State Recreation Area (p117); and $55 per night for the eight-person cabins at Kalopa State Recreation Area (p163). The other locations, such as MacKenzie State Recreation Area (p202) and Manuka State Wayside Park (p240), are scenic but creepily deserted.

For details on rules, reservations and permits, check with the Division of State Parks (☎ 974-6200; www.hawaiistateparks.org; PO Box 936, Hilo, HI 96721; ☺ 8am-noon Mon-Fri). The max stay at any site is five nights, which should satisfy most campers.

COUNTY PARKS

Permits are required for the 10 county campgrounds, most located on the Big Island's 'second-tier' beaches. Daily fees are $5 for adults, $2 for teens and $1 for children 12 and under; internet booking costs $1 more. Camping is allowed for up to two weeks, except between June and August, when the limit is one week only.

HOW MUCH?

- **Six-pack of local craft beer** $10
- **Pound of Kona coffee** $25–40
- **Half-day snorkeling cruise** $100
- **Round of resort golf** $200
- **Admission to Hawai'i Volcanoes National Park** $10

For additional price information, see the inside front cover.

(Continued on p276)

FESTIVALS & EVENTS
CALENDAR

FEBRUARY

Waimea Cherry Blossom Festival (p132)
first Saturday in February
Celebrate the Japanese tradition of *hanami* (cherry-blossom viewing) with craft fairs, food booths, live music and dance, and other cultural demonstrations.

Laupahoehoe Music Festival (p164)
mid-February
Enjoy an informal all-day jam session at Laupahoehoe Beach Park, featuring Big Island talent from The Lim Family to Bruddah Smitty.

MARCH

Na Mea Hawai'i Hula Kahiko Series (p224)
early March (also May, June and August)
Gather at the rim of Kilauea Crater to witness ancient-style hula and chanting. This extraordinary event occurs four times per year.

Kona Brewers Festival (p64)
second Saturday in March
Sample craft beers from Hawaii, California and the Pacific Northwest, plus gourmet *pupu* (appetizers) made by top local eateries.

Merrie Monarch Festival (p182)
late March or early April
Hilo's premier attraction is this intense, three-day hula competition featuring the state's finest hula *halau* (schools). The chanting and music alone are worth the admission price. Advance planning is necessary.

MAY

May Day Lei Day Festival (p181)
first Sunday in May
See masterful lei displays and lei-making demonstrations, plus live music and hula, at Hilo's beautifully restored Palace Theater.

Hamakua Music Festival (p155)
mid-May (also early October)
A fundraiser for music education, this bi-annual concert brings world-class musicians (primarily Hawaiian, jazz and classical) to small-town Honoka'a.

Honoka'a Western Weekend (p155)
late May
Enjoy an island-style Wild West with a week of *paniolo* (Hawaiian cowboy) events, including a parade, barbecue, block party and rodeo.

JUNE

Waiki'i Music Festival (p149)
mid-June
Set outdoors at Waiki'i Ranch on the slopes of Mauna Kea, this two-day, all-day family event brings top Hawaiian musicians, a craft fair, food booths and children's games.

JULY

Fourth of July Rodeo (p132)
July 4
Come for thrilling rodeo events, from cattle roping to bull riding, as local *paniolo* compete and show their stuff.

Big Island Hawaiian Music Festival (p181)
mid-July
A must for Hawaiian-music fans, this two-day concert features virtuoso performances in ukulele, steel guitar, slack key guitar and falsetto singing – for an incredible $10 per half-day concert!

Kilauea Volcano Wilderness Runs (p224)
late July
Nowhere else can you race on an active volcano! All levels are accommodated in four events ranging from a 5-mile walk in Kilauea Iki Crater to a 26-mile run through the Ka'u Desert.

SEPTEMBER

Aloha Festivals (p224)
late August to early October
Originally established in 1946, this state-wide Hawaiian cultural celebration now spans two months during the *makahaki* (ancient Hawaiian harvest festival of sports and games) season. The Big Island's festivities start with an elaborate presentation of the Hawaiian royal court at Halema'uma'u Crater and continue with dozens of island-wide events. For more information, see www.alohafestivals.com.

OCTOBER

Ironman Triathlon World Championship (p34)
third Saturday in October
Witness human glory and grit when this legendary swim-bike-run race comes to Kailua-Kona with 2000 participants and thousands of spectators and volunteers.

NOVEMBER

Kona Coffee Cultural Festival (p64)
early November
Celebrate Kona coffee and the pioneering family farms that built the industry. Dozens of events include coffee tastings, farm tours and a cupping competition to choose the year's finest estate crop.

Waimea Ukulele & Slack Key Guitar Institute (p132)
early November
Aspiring musicians can study with Hawaii's foremost musicians in a variety of workshops, while everyone can enjoy concerts and *kanikapila* (jam sessions).

DECEMBER

Mochi Pounding Festival (p165)
last weekend in December
Join the local community for Japanese *mochi* (sticky-rice cake) pounding, a New Year's tradition. The once-tiny neighborhood gathering now draws over 400 spectators for an all-day party with live music, crafts, plate lunch and more.

The Volcano Rainforest Retreat   GREG ELMS

(Continued from p273)

To obtain a permit, contact the **Department of Parks & Recreation** (☎ 961-8311; www.co.hawaii.hi.us/parks/parks.htm; Suite 6, 101 Pauahi St, Hilo, HI 96720; ⏱ 7:45am-4pm Mon-Fri).

Condominiums

Condominiums can offer much more than comparable hotel rooms: they're generally larger, often with separate bedroom(s), kitchen and washer-dryer. They're also more likely to include free wi-fi, plus a bunch of homey amenities, such as books, DVDs, towels, appliances and beach equipment. If you're lucky, you'll land a renovated unit with hardwood floor, 400-count sheets and even a computer for guests. But therein lies the frustrating thing about condos: each unit is individually owned and, even within the same complex, inconsistencies abound.

For saving money, condos are best for those staying a week or longer, otherwise the mandatory cleaning fee (which averages $75 to $100 for a studio or one-bedroom unit) negates any savings. Most condos require three- to seven-day minimum stays. Prices drop if you stay longer: the weekly rate is typically six times the daily rate and the monthly is three times the weekly.

Most condos are rented through agencies, which are listed in the Kailua-Kona chapter (p67) because of their overwhelming concentration there. Also check **Vacation Rentals By Owner** (www.vrbo.com). If you know exactly which complex you want, do a Google search to find owners' listings.

Hostels

Hostels are rather scarce on the Big Island, but with at least one option in each major region (Hilo, Kailua-Kona, Honoka'a and Volcano), you can tour the island by hostelling. The reviewed and recommended hostels are spartan but clean and safe, typically with a common kitchen and internet access. Dorm beds cost about $20 to $25 per night.

Hotels & Resorts

Hotels suit those who want a full-time staff, daily housekeeping and amenities such as pools and restaurants. They range from rustic motels to luxury mega-hotels, often called 'resorts,' that epitomize the commercial tropical paradise. ('Resorts' also refers to general resort areas, such as Waikoloa and Mauna Lani.)

One fundamental rule applies to hotels: never pay rack rates. Major hotels (particularly the largest and priciest) commonly undercut their published 'rack rates' to remain as close to capacity as possible. Rates fluctuate madly based on occupancy, so book a room well in advance through the hotel's website (for discounted internet rates) or through packagers such as **Orbitz** (www.orbitz.com).

Within a given hotel, rates depend mainly on the view. An ocean view can cost 50% to 100% more than a parking-lot view (euphemistically called a 'garden' or 'mountain' view).

TRAVEL LITERATURE

The Hawaiian Islands have always intrigued visitors, including writers who try to capture their uniqueness and complexity. Surprisingly there is little contemporary travel writing about the Big Island beyond travel guides and histories. The following are among the best accounts by either visitors

Top Picks

SOUVENIRS

- **Dietrich Varez' prints** From Volcano Art Center (p211).
- **Aloha shirts** Produced by Sig Zane Designs (p187).
- **Confections** From Big Island Candies (p186).
- **Lauhala (pandanus leaf) items** At Kimura Lauhala Shop (p77).
- **Cool T-shirts** At Destee Nation (p67).
- **100% Big Island Coffee** Available islandwide.
- **Locally made jewelry** At Elements (p127).
- **CDs by local musicians** See p259 for recommendations.
- **Your own handmade arts and crafts** From various workshops in Hilo (p177) and Holualoa (p77).
- **Books, toys and nifty gifts** At Basically Books (p172).

or transplants. For fiction recommendations, see p260.

Letters from Hawaii (Mark Twain, 1866) Observant, irreverent, wise and witty, Twain's 25 letters from four months in the 'Sandwich Islands' in 1866 reveal both his pre-fame literary genius and the exoticism of 19th-century island life.

Travelers' Tales Hawai'i: True Stories (various authors, revised edition 2005) Featuring writers such as John McPhee, Jan Morris, Barbara Kingsolver and Maxine Hong Kingston, this varied collection of fine essays on Hawaii is an entertaining introduction to its culture and quirks.

Memoirs of a Buddhist Woman Missionary in Hawaii (Shigeo Kikuchi, 1991) Written when she was 90, this book details life in Na'alehu from the early 1900s through WWII, when the author and her minister husband persevered through tough times to introduce Shin Buddhism to Hawai'i and the West.

Affordable Paradise (H Skip Thomsen, third edition 2005) While geared toward those seeking an affordable move to the Big Island, this part-memoir, part-advice book is a compelling account of Hawai'i's lifestyle and changing demographics.

INTERNET RESOURCES

Alternative-Hawaii (www.alternative-hawaii.com) Colorful one-stop site for 'eco-cultural' events, beaches, sights and reviews.

Big Island Visitors Bureau (www.bigisland.org) Mainstream coverage provides a good, if overwhelmingly jammed, starting point.

KonaWeb (www.konaweb.com) Mom-and-pop site covers entire island, with handy links and decent (if subjective) content.

Lonely Planet (www.lonelyplanet.com) Concise basic information on Hawaii and travel planning, plus hotel reviews.

Ulukau: The Hawaiian Electronic Library (www.ulukau.org) Online Hawaiian-to-English (and vice versa) dictionaries and key Hawaiian texts.

CLIMATE CHANGE & TRAVEL

Climate change is a serious threat to the ecosystems that humans rely upon, and air travel is the fastest-growing contributor to the problem. Lonely Planet regards travel, overall, as a global benefit, but believes we all have a responsibility to limit our personal impact on global warming.

Nearly every form of motorized travel generates CO_2 (the main cause of human-induced climate change), but planes are far and away the worst offenders, not just because of the sheer distances they allow us to travel, but also because they release greenhouse gases high into the atmosphere. The statistics are frightening: two people taking a round-trip flight between Europe and the USA will contribute as much to climate change as an average household's gas and electricity consumption over a whole year.

Climatecare.org and other websites use 'carbon calculators' that allow travelers to offset the level of greenhouse gases they are responsible for with financial contributions to sustainable travel schemes that reduce global warming – including projects in India, Honduras, Kazakhstan and Uganda.

Lonely Planet, together with Rough Guides and other concerned partners in the travel industry, support the carbon offset scheme run by climatecare.org. Lonely Planet offsets all of its staff and author travel. For more information, check out our website, www.lonelyplanet.com.

DIRECTORY & TRANSPORTATION

CONTENTS

PRACTICALITIES

BUSINESS HOURS

In this book, reviews do not include opening hours if they follow the typical time frames listed below. But if a business's opening hours differ by over 30 minutes in either direction, the review does specify them.

Banks 8:30am-4pm Mon-Fri, some to 6pm Fri & 9am-noon or 1pm Sat

Bars & Clubs to midnight daily, some to 2am Fri & Sat

Information (including businesses) 8:30am-4:30pm Mon-Fri, some post offices 9am-noon Sat

Restaurants breakfast 6-10am, lunch 11:30am-2pm, dinner 5-9:30pm

Shops 9am-5pm Mon-Sat, some also noon-5pm Sun; major shopping areas and malls keep extended hours

CHILDREN

The island social scene is very informal and family-oriented, so travelers with kids will feel welcome almost everywhere. The balmy climate allows ample outdoor time, which is ideal for staving off restlessness and cabin fever. It also means that you should pack lightly and leave at home any dressy attire and cold-weather gear (wee ones should not ascend to the summit of Mauna Kea anyway).

Practicalities

When choosing sights and activities, note that reduced rates often apply to kids; ask before you pay. Most restaurants are diner-casual and appropriate for all ages. Don't assume that the high-end resort restaurants are averse to families; they often offer impressive kids' menus. Most sit-down restaurants provide high chairs.

At hotels, kids through high-school-age youngsters typically stay free if they share their parents' room and don't require extra beds. Rollaway beds generally incur an additional fee (about $20 to $30 per bed). But B&Bs, particularly the upscale ones wary of noise and mess, might preclude babies and little kids. If you find a B&B that allows tots, keep yours under control to ensure that they'll continue their family-friendly policy. Note that while older kids might be acceptable, they'll probably incur extra-guest fees, which can skyrocket the price for large families.

Major retail stores often provide diaper-changing stations in women's restrooms. While relatively common among today's mothers, breastfeeding is generally done in private and not smack in the middle of a restaurant dining room.

To rent infant equipment, such as cribs, strollers and car seats, try **Baby's Away** (☎ 987-9236, 800-996-9030; www.babysaway.com). Most car-rental companies (see p290) lease child-safety seats (per day $8, per week $40 to $45) if you reserve in advance. The best childcare options are available at the major resorts, which typically offer established programs that highlight Hawaiian culture and outdoorsy activities.

For general advice, see Lonely Planet's *Travel with Children*.

Sights & Activities

If parents want to introduce their kids to ocean sports, the Big Island's clear, calm and warm waters are ideal. Little-kid beaches include Onekahakaha Beach (p173) and Spencer Beach Park (p118). Kahalu'u Beach Park (p71) is ideal for multiple-kid families because it offers both shallow snorkeling and offshore bodyboarding and surfing, while Kauna'oa Bay (p116) is a bit more exclusive but perfectly glassy and pristine. The warm lava-rock pond at Ahalanui Beach Park (p201) is also ideal for tots. Always use secure waterproof diapers.

Rainy days require indoor distractions, which on the Big Island are most prevalent in Hilo, where there are numerous kid-oriented, interactive museums. The standby shopping malls and movie theaters are always options, too.

For more ideas, see the Top Picks For Kids boxes in almost every regional chapter, plus a few indoor suggestions for Hilo (p181) and Kailua-Kona (p62).

GET PLUGGED IN

- **Electricity** Voltage is 110/120V, 60 cycles, as elsewhere in the USA.
- **Measurement** Distances are measured in feet, yards and miles; weights in ounces, pounds and tons; liquid volumes in cups, pints, quarts and gallons.
- **Newspapers** The island's two major newspapers are the *Hawai'i Tribune-Herald* and *West Hawai'i Today*.
- **Radio** The Big Island broadcasts about 18 FM and six AM radio stations.
- **TV** All the major US TV networks and cable channels are represented.
- **Video/DVD** Video systems use the NTSC standard, which is incompatible with the PAL system. If DVDs are encoded, they'll be region code 1.

CLIMATE

The Big Island is a split personality in its climate: on the leeward (western) side, it's hot and dry, while the windward (northeastern) side is exposed to trade winds that bring abundant rainfall all year round. Winter rainstorms can affect the entire island, however.

Elevation is another major climatic factor. Driving just 5 miles from Kailua-Kona to Holualoa, you'll notice the air becomes noticeably cooler and moister. Of course, the elevation difference is most marked on Mauna Kea, the only place that requires insulating clothing.

Contrary to common belief, Hawaii does experience seasons, relatively speaking. Winter (December to March) is rainier than summer, and it's the season most likely to see major storms and flooding. Still, 'rainy' days typically include periods of sun. Even in Hilo, showers are interspersed with sunshine, hence the frequent rainbows.

For information on seasonal differences, see p271; for climate charts, see p280.

COURSES

If you're interested in learning Hawaiian arts and crafts, hula or music, you can find informal mini workshops at the large hotels and condos. Often free, these are geared to tourists and generally lighthearted, if not truly hokey, rather than serious.

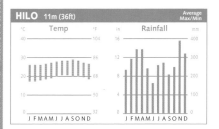

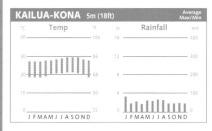

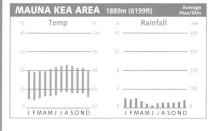

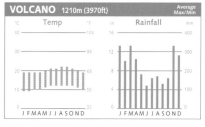

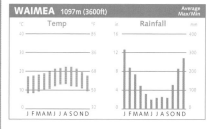

For a deeper experience, you'll probably need to pay for instruction, but workshops and courses tend to be affordable and worth the cost. Note that hula classes at formal *halau* (schools) are not for novice drop-ins. For musicians, the Waimea Ukulele & Slack Key Guitar Institute (p132) is a fantastic chance to learn from the state's masters.

Hawai'i boasts a handful of outstanding art centers. Dabblers can create personal souvenirs while serious students can learn from top-notch professionals. Check these places' websites for current offerings.

Donkey Mill Art Center (www.donkeymillartcenter.org; p77)

East Hawai'i Cultural Center (www.ehcc.org; p177)

Volcano Art Center (www.vlcanoartcenter.org; p211)

CUSTOMS

Visitors to the USA (including Hawaii) can bring 1L of liquor and 200 cigarettes duty free; age minimums of 21 years for liquor and 18 years for tobacco apply. Additionally, visitors can bring up to $100 worth of gift merchandise duty free into the USA.

Hawaii has stringent restrictions against importing any fresh fruits and plants. Think twice about traveling with your pet because the rabies-free state enforces strict pet quarantine laws, but you may be able to slice the time and expense to 30 days ($655) or five days ($225). For complete details, contact the **Hawaiian Department of Agriculture** (☎ 808-483-7151; www.hawaiiag.org).

DANGERS & ANNOYANCES

The majority of visitors leave with pleasant memories, but if you're an unfortunate accident or crime victim, contact the **Visitor Aloha Society of Hawaii** (VASH; ☎ 808-926-8274; www.visitoralohasocietyofhawaii.org).

Drug addition on the island generally involves 'ice' (crystal methamphetamine) or *pakalolo* (marijuana). Visitors can avoid any drug trouble by being on guard in rural areas, where ice addicts tend to congregate. Pot is a different story; it's found everywhere, especially on the Puna coast.

Scams

Be wary of tourist-information booths that actually lure visitors into buying timeshares.

Sellers use freebies, from luau to cruises, to attract an audience for their 'no obligation' pitch. Don't waste your time.

While relatively innocuous, the fake 'Hawaiian' souvenirs sold at cheap tourist traps hurt genuine makers and sellers. If the label states 'Made in China' (or any other foreign origin), why bother?

Theft & Violence

In general, crime is much lower on Hawai'i than on the mainland. Populated areas, such as towns and popular sights, are relatively safe. Across the island, residents still tend to leave their houses and cars unlocked if they're home (but we recommend that visitors be prudent and always lock up).

The main crimes against tourists are car break-ins, especially at roadside parks, campgrounds and parking lots that are slightly deserted – too far from town for police patrol, yet close enough to be a druggie hangout. The very remote beaches, trails and campgrounds tend to be cleaner and safer because they are less accessible.

At beaches and other popular destinations deemed 'locals only,' haole tourists might encounter resentment and even violence. Avoid confrontation (you'll be outnumbered) and heed 'Kapu' (No Trespassing) signs on private property.

Tsunami

Like all islands, Hawai'i is always at risk of tsunami. Of all natural disasters, tsunami have killed more people statewide than all others combined. The largest tsunami ever to hit the island occurred in 1946, when waves reached 55ft and 159 people died. Today Hawai'i has a siren warning system aired through yellow speakers mounted on telephone poles. They're tested on the first working day of each month at 11:45am.

If you're at the coast when a tsunami occurs, immediately head upland (to state the obvious). The front section of local telephone books has maps of areas susceptible to tsunami and safety evacuation zones.

DISCOUNTS

Unfortunately for visitors, the biggest savings come from 'kama'aina discounts' given to state residents (or anyone with a valid Hawaii driver's license). For non-residents, children, student, senior, military and automobile-club discounts might apply. Remember to bring your ID cards for proof of membership.

FOOD

In this book, reviews are listed in price order, from lowest to highest, in the Eating sections of each regional chapter. Price indicators are $ (under $12), $$ ($12 to $20), $$$ ($20 to $28) and $$$$ (over $28) for the price of one main dish. The price estimates do not include taxes, tips or beverages. Recommended grocers are listed below the restaurants. For more on Hawaii's unique cuisine, see the Food & Drink chapter (p263).

GAY & LESBIAN TRAVELERS

The state of Hawaii is very popular with gay and lesbian travelers. This is not surprising, considering the state's strong legislation to protect minority groups and a constitutional guarantee of privacy that extends to sexual behavior between all consenting adults. That said, overt 'couple' behavior, whether handholding or kissing, is rarely seen at all, much less between gays. Locals tend to keep their private lives to themselves. Being out is fine; being way out is too much.

The Puna region attracts a particular type of gay man (and hippie chick, for that matter). It contains a sizable gay population, the long-standing gay-friendly Kalani Oceanside Retreat (p203; a wellness center with numerous workshops geared toward men) and Kehena Beach (p203), an anything-goes nude beach.

Most gay-Hawaii websites are mediocre and limited in coverage, but Out in Hawaii (www.outinhawaii.com) contains a handy list of gay-friendly accommodations. *Out Traveler: Hawaii* (2008), by Matthew Link, a former Big Island resident, is worth a read.

HOLIDAYS

The following state holidays will affect visitors only slightly, except for the three major ones: Thanksgiving, Christmas and

DIRECTORY & TRANSPORTATION

New Year's Day. During those holidays, air travel will be pricey and packed. For other significant dates, see the Festivals & Events Calendar (p274).

New Year's Day January 1
Martin Luther King Jr Day Third Monday in January
Presidents Day Third Monday in February
Kuhio Day March 26
Good Friday Friday before Easter Sunday
Memorial Day Last Monday in May
King Kamehameha Day June 11
Independence Day July 4
Statehood Day Third Friday in August
Labor Day First Monday in September
Election Day Second Tuesday in November
Veterans Day November 11
Thanksgiving Fourth Thursday in November
Christmas Day December 25

INTERNATIONAL TRAVELERS
Consulates

In the state of Hawaii, all consulates are located in Honolulu.

Australia (☎ 524-5050; 1000 Bishop St)
Germany (☎ 946-3819; 252 Paoa Pl)
Italy (☎ 531-2277; Suite 201, 735 Bishop St)
Japan (☎ 543-3111; 1742 Nuuanu Ave)
Netherlands (☎ 531-6897; Suite 702, 745 Fort St Mall)
New Zealand (☎ 547-5117; Suite 414, 900 Richards St)
Philippines (☎ 595-6316; 2433 Pali Hwy)

Visas

US entry requirements remain in flux post–September 11, so all foreign visitors should confirm visa rules before traveling. The introductory portal for US visa information is **Destination USA** (www.unitedstatesvisas.gov), but for complete information and forms see **US Department of State** (www.travel.state.gov). Note that **US Citizenship & Immigration Services** (www.uscis.gov) is geared toward immigrants, not temporary visitors.

Except for visitors from Canada, Mexico, Bermuda and the Visa Waiver Program countries (see below), foreign visitors to the USA need a visa. (Of course, all non–US citizens need passports.) Basic requirements include a valid passport, recent photo, travel details and possibly proof of financial stability. See the US DoS website for details.

The Visa Waiver Program allows citizens of the following 27 countries to enter the USA for stays of 90 days or fewer without obtaining a US visa: Andorra, Australia, Austria, Belgium, Brunei, Denmark, Finland, France, Germany, Iceland, Ireland, Italy, Japan, Liechtenstein, Luxembourg, Monaco, the Netherlands, New Zealand, Norway, Portugal, San Marino, Singapore, Slovenia, Spain, Sweden, Switzerland and the UK. To qualify, you need an exit ticket that's nonrefundable in the USA and a machine-readable or digital-chip passport. And as of January 2009, you'll need to register online (https://esta.cbp.dhs.gov/) three days before your visit.

Your home country determines the validity period for a US visitor visa, while US officials set the length of your stay at the port of entry. To remain in the USA longer than the date stamped on your passport, you must go to the Honolulu office of the **Citizenship & Immigration Service** (☎ 532-3721; 595 Ala Moana Blvd) before the stamped date to apply for an extension.

Upon arriving in the USA, all foreign visitors must have their two index fingers scanned and a digital photo taken. For more information, see the Travel Security & Procedures section of the **Department of Homeland Security** (www.dhs.gov) site.

INTERNET ACCESS

Nowadays many hotels, condos and B&Bs offer high-speed internet access. At B&Bs, access is usually wireless, but a surprising number of hotels and condos offer only wired in-room connections. Ask about rates because they can be exorbitant, especially at the luxury resorts.

In this book, accommodations reviews with the 🖳 symbol refer to those that provide either high-speed access (wireless or wired) or computers for guest use. This applies to both free and fee access.

Most towns have internet cafés or business centers offering wi-fi and computers (average rate of $2.50 per 15 minutes). Don't expect numerous venues, however. The Hilo Public Library (p172) has free computer terminals for those with library cards ($10), but time limits apply.

This book recommends internet access spots for each town, but also check out **Wi-Fi Free Spot** (www.wififreespot.com), a handy but not exhaustive wi-fi directory.

LEGAL MATTERS

You are entitled to an attorney from the moment you are arrested. The **Hawaii State Bar Association** (☎ 537-9140, 800-808-4722; www .hsba.org) is one starting point to find an attorney. If you can't afford one, the state must provide one for free.

In Hawaii, anyone driving with a blood alcohol level of 0.08% or higher is guilty of driving 'under the influence.' Possessing marijuana and narcotics is illegal. Hitchhiking and public nudity (eg at nude beaches) are crimes rarely punished. That said, the former is always risky and the latter should be avoided at mainstream family beaches.

While the **Department of Commerce & Consumer Affairs** (☎ Big Island 974-4000; www.hawaii .gov/dcca) deals primarily with residents' issues, visitors who want to lodge a complaint against a business should contact the department's Consumer Resource Center.

MAPS

If you plan to stick to towns and highways, the maps in this book will probably suffice. But if you want to explore unpaved roads or find secluded B&Bs, the atlas-style **Ready Mapbook** (www.hawaiimapsource.com) is indispensable. The vast Big Island requires two books, for East and West Hawai'i ($11 each).

For ocean sports, see **Franko's Map of Hawai'i** (www.frankosmaps.com; $6), a fold-up, waterproof map showing snorkeling and diving spots (with a guide to tropical fish). *Nelles Map of Hawai'i* ($6), a fold-up road map, is a minimalist alternative to the *Ready Mapbook*. The *UH Press Map of Hawai'i* ($4) by James Bier is a topographic map that details every bay, beach and gulch on the island. All of these maps are readily available at local bookstores and other retailers.

Only geographers, backcountry explorers and map fiends would need topographic maps. If needed, first try **TopoZone** (www.topo zone.com). Hawai'i Volcanoes National Park sells detailed but sometimes dated maps by the **United States Geological Survey** (USGS; ☎ 888-275-8747; www.usgs.gov).

MONEY

Prices quoted in this book are in US dollars ($), the only currency used in Hawaii. The dollar (commonly called a buck) is divided into 100 cents. Coins come in denominations of one cent (penny), five cents (nickel), 10 cents (dime), 25 cents (quarter) and the rare 50-cent piece (half dollar). Notes come in one-, five-, 10-, 20-, 50- and 100-dollar denominations.

See Quick Reference (inside front cover) for exchange rates and the Planning Your Trip chapter (p271) for basic costs info.

ATMs, Cash & Checks

Found everywhere, ATMs have largely negated the need for traveler's checks. But ATM withdrawals using out-of-state cards do incur surcharges of $1.50 to $2.

Hawaii's two largest banks, **Bank of Hawaii** (www.boh.com) and **First Hawaiian Bank** (www.fhb .com), both have extensive ATM networks that will give cash advances on major credit cards and allow cash withdrawals with affiliated ATM cards. Most ATMs accept bankcards from both the Plus and Cirrus systems. Look for ATMs outside banks and inside supermarkets, shopping centers, convenience stores and gas stations.

Foreign currency can be exchanged for US dollars at Honolulu International Airport and at main bank branches on Hawai'i.

Out-of-state personal checks are generally not accepted.

Credit Cards

Major credit cards are widely accepted on the Big Island, although they're typically not accepted by B&Bs and condos, particularly those booked by owners and agencies, and smaller eateries.

Tipping

In restaurants, tip at least 15% for good service and 10% if it's mediocre. Leaving no tip is rare and requires real cause. Taxi drivers and hairstylists are typically tipped 10% and hotel bellhops $1 per bag.

Traveler's Checks

Traveler's checks seem archaic but they do offer protection from theft and loss. They're accepted like cash by most vendors, but mom-and-pop shops and eateries might not take them.

Keep a record of all check numbers separate from the checks themselves. For refunds on lost or stolen traveler's checks, call American Express (☎ 800-992-3404) or Thomas Cook (☎ 800-287-7362).

PHOTOGRAPHY

All camera supplies (such as print and slide film, digital memory and batteries) are available on the Big Island. Disposable underwater cameras (average price $15) are ideal for capturing those snorkeling and kayaking adventures.

To burn a CD or DVD of your images, most internet cafés and business centers will charge you for computer time and for the CD (about $1) or DVD (about $3). Film users, develop each roll as you finish it because the island's high temperature and humidity accelerate the deterioration of exposed film. Longs Drugs stores charge reasonable prices for film developing.

Don't pack unprocessed film (including the roll inside your camera) into checked luggage because exposure to high-powered x-ray equipment will cause it to fog. While the scanners used for carry-on baggage are less powerful, carry your film separately and submit it to airport security officials for a 'hand check' to be on the safe side.

For a quick course on taking good shots, consult Lonely Planet's *Travel Photography*.

POST

The US postal service (USPS; ☎ 800-275-8777; www .usps.gov) delivers mail to and from Hawaii. Its service is reliable, albeit slower than in the continental USA.

First-class airmail between Hawaii and the mainland usually takes three to four days. For first-class mail sent and delivered within the USA, postage rates are 42¢ for letters up to 1oz (17¢ for each additional ounce) and 27¢ for standard-size postcards.

International airmail rates for letters up to 1oz are 72¢ to Canada or Mexico and 94¢ to other countries.

You can receive mail c/o General Delivery at most post offices on the Big Island, but you must first complete an application in person. Bring two forms of ID and your temporary local address. The accepted application is valid for 30 days; mail is held for up to 15 days. Many accommodations will also hold mail for incoming guests.

SHOPPING

Souvenirs range from genuine, handmade collectibles to plastic hula dolls and cheapo fakes. Avoid the latter. There are lots of little items that are nevertheless legitimately Hawai'i-made.

First, shop at respected venues, such as artist-owned galleries, to develop an eye for the real deal. For starters, go to Volcano Art Center (p211), Sudha's Art Gallery (p187), Isaacs Art Center (p130) and Holualoa's gallery row (p76). To see fine examples of traditional Hawaiian woodworking, visit Dan De Luz at his low-key shop in Mountain View (p195). Among the most affordable souvenirs are *lauhala* (pandanus leaf) crafts from Kimura Lauhala Shop (p77). Elements (p127) is an artisan-owned boutique filled with locally made jewelry at all price points.

Macadamia nuts and Kona coffee are obvious choices, but also consider Big Island Candies confections (p186), delicious Portuguese sweet bread *(pao doce)* from Punalu'u Bakeshop (p235) and Ka'u honey (sold at farmers markets). Browse the food aisles at Longs Drugs and you'll find a tantalizing array of local treats, from crack seed to homemade cookies to Hilo's legendary Atebara's potato chips.

Flowers, such as orchids, anthuriums and proteas, can fly with you to the US mainland if they are inspected and approved by the US Department of Agriculture at either Hilo airport (☎ 933-6931) or Kona airport (☎ 326-1252). To avoid any hassles, you can pay a premium to have nurseries such as Akatsuka Orchid Gardens (p195) send you cut flowers or live plants.

See p277 for more souvenir ideas and p261 for more on Hawaiian arts and crafts.

One last point: haggling is rarely done except maybe at farmers markets (although prices are so low, it'll seem mighty petty).

TELEPHONE

Always dial '1' before toll-free (☎ 800, 888 etc) and domestic long-distance numbers.

Also, while the area code ☎ 808 applies to all Islands, it must be dialed for interisland calls.

Pay phones are readily found in shopping centers, beach parks and other public places. Local calls include all calls within the island and cost 25¢ or 50¢. Interisland calls are long-distance and costlier. Hotels often add a hefty service charge of $1 or more per call made from a room phone.

Private prepaid phone cards are readily available (check convenience stores, supermarkets and pharmacies).

Cell (Mobile) Phones

Verizon has the most extensive cellular network across the Islands, but AT&T and Sprint also have decent coverage. Coverage on Hawai'i is good in major towns but spotty or nonexistent in rural places. But in early 2008 the major providers expanded coverage on the island, improving service in Puna, Waikoloa and other sketchily served places. Don't expect service in the remote backcountry, however.

Asian and European phones won't work in the USA unless they are quad-band (supporting all four major GSM bands: 850, 900, 1800 and 1900) phones.

International Calls

To make international calls direct from Hawaii, dial ☎ 011 + country code + area code + number. (An exception is to Canada, where you dial ☎ 1 + area code + number, but international rates still apply.)

For international operator assistance, dial ☎ 0. The operator can provide specific rate information, including the cheapest time periods for calling.

If you're calling Hawaii from abroad, use the international country code for the USA (☎ 1), followed by the area code ☎ 808 and the seven-digit local number.

TIME

Hawaii does not observe daylight saving time, probably because it has 11 hours of daylight in midwinter (December) and 13½ hours in midsummer (June). In midwinter, the sun rises around 7am and sets around 6pm. In midsummer, it rises before 6am and sets after 7pm. During standard time (winter), Hawaii time differs from Los Angeles by two hours, from New York by five hours, from London by 10 hours and from Tokyo by 19 hours. During daylight saving time (summer), the difference is one hour more for countries that observe it.

Upon arrival, set your internal clock to 'Hawaiian time,' meaning slow down (and remove your wristwatch).

TOURIST INFORMATION

Before arrival, check the websites listed on p277. The Big Island Visitors Bureau (☎ 800-648-2441; www.bigisland.org) is handy for general information and a comprehensive events calendar. On the island, you can visit branches in Hilo (p172) and Waikoloa (p107).

The statewide Hawaii Visitors & Convention Bureau (☎ 800-464-2924; www.gohawaii.com; Suite 801, 2270 Kalakaua Ave, Waikiki, HI 96815) provides only general info, but might be handy for island hoppers.

At the airport (and brochure stands islandwide), pick up the free tourist guides 101 Things to Do (www.101thingstodo.com) and This Week (www.thisweek.com), which contain handy current info, maps and discount coupons.

TOURS

Here, 'tours' refers to group sightseeing options. For activity tours (such as snorkeling cruises, cycling trips and helicopter rides), see the Outdoor Activities & Adventures chapter (p24) and the regional chapters for details.

Bus tour companies offer all-day, circle-island tours, meaning stop-and-click sightseeing. Forgo them unless you're a nondriver stuck in Kailua-Kona or Waikoloa with only one day on the island. Rates range from $60 to $78 for adults and $50 to $60 for kids. It's hard to tell 'em apart:

Jack's Tours (☎ 961-6666, 800-442-5557; www .jackshawaii.com) Hilo-based and priciest.

Polynesian Adventure Tours (☎ 329-8008, 800-622-3011; www.polyad.com) Similar to Roberts Hawaii.

Roberts Hawaii (☎ 329-1688, 866-898-2519; www .robertshawaii.com) Large, Honolulu-based company with cheapest rates.

See p288 for group package tours, which can be a steal. Such tours merely package air, hotel and car bookings, so you're not stuck with a group during your stay. See p289 for cruises to the Hawaiian Islands.

An excellent option for learning is **Elderhostel** (☎ 800-454-5768; www.elderhostel.org), which offers tours (including accommodations, meals and lectures) for those aged 55 and older. Most of the themed trips are multi-island and focus on Hawaiian history, culture and geography.

TRAVELERS WITH DISABILITIES

Major hotels are equipped with elevators, phones with TDD (telecommunications device for the deaf) and wheelchair-accessible rooms (which must be reserved in advance). But few islandwide generalizations can be made. For more information, visit the website of the **Disability & Communication Access Board** (DCAB; ☎ 586-8121; www.hawaii .gov/health/dcab; Room 101, 919 Ala Moana Blvd, Honolulu, HI 96814), which provides information on airports, transportation, medical and other support services.

Seeing-eye and guide dogs are not subject to the general quarantine rules for pets if they meet the Department of Agriculture's minimum requirements; see www .hawaiiag.org/hdoa/ai_aqs_guidedog.htm for details. All animals must enter the state at Honolulu International Airport.

Wheelchair Getaways of Hawaii (☎ 800-638-1912; www.wheelchairgetaways.com) rents wheelchair-accessible vans. While many outdoor attractions are challenging for people in wheelchairs, Pu'uhonua o Honaunau National Historical Park (p91) offers sturdy beach wheelchairs at the visitors center.

For general information, see the website and quarterly magazine of the **Society for Accessible Travel & Hospitality** (SATH; ☎ 212-447-7284; www.sath.org; Suite 610, 347 Fifth Ave, New York, NY 10016).

VOLUNTEERING

The **Mauna Kea Visitor Information Station** (☎ 808-961-2180; www.ifa.hawaii.edu/info/vis/volunteers.html; 177 Maka'ala St, Hilo, HI 96720) runs an outstanding program that trains volunteers to lead summit tours, staff the visitor center, maintain the summit trail and assist with stargazing. The Saddle Rd drive can be a drag, but free transportation from Hilo is provided.

At **Hawai'i Volcanoes National Park** (☎ 808-985-6000; www.nps.gov/havo/supportyourpark/volunteer.htm) volunteers are needed for diverse jobs, from backcountry work with hawksbill turtles to assistance in the library and museum.

A one-stop resource for statewide volunteering opportunities is **Malama Hawaii** (www .malamahawaii.org), a network of community and nonprofit groups. The website posts volunteer programs and a calendar of fundraisers, workshops and lectures.

For more on volunteering, see the Green Big Island chapter (p47).

WORK

US citizens can legally work in Hawaii, but short-term employment will probably mean entry-level jobs in restaurants and hotels. With specific outdoor skills (eg scuba diving), you can explore employment with activity operators. The same goes for those with massage or cosmetology training, who might find work at resort spas. If you're qualified for serious 'professional' jobs, decent opportunities are scarce and comparatively low paying, and might require local connections.

But the entire state tends to need teachers and nurses. Also, residential construction is booming, and there's a shortage of licensed carpenters, plumbers, painters, electricians and roofers.

Check the listings in newspaper classifieds and also the **Big Island Craigslist** (http://honolulu.craigslist.org/big) site.

GETTING THERE & AWAY

AIR

Virtually all travelers to the Big Island arrive by air, and the vast majority stops first at Honolulu International Airport. If you have a layover in Honolulu, make sure the ticket agent marks your baggage with Hilo or Kona as the final destination.

US domestic and international airfares vary too much for generalizations about the cheapest carriers or months. But you can count on across-the-board fare hikes from mid-December to mid-March.

Airports

Big Island visitors arrive in either Hilo or Kona. While most first stop in Honolulu, direct flights from the mainland are increasing. Most arrive in Kona.

Hilo International Airport (ITO; ☎ 934-5838; www .state.hi.us/dot/airports/hawaii/ito)

Honolulu International Airport (HNL; ☎ 836-6413; www.honoluluairport.com)

Kona International Airport at Keahole (KOA; ☎ 329-3423; www.hawaii.gov/dot/airports/hawaii/koa)

Airlines

As most incoming flights from overseas and the US mainland arrive on O'ahu at Honolulu International Airport, travelers must catch an interisland flight from there to the Big Island. Airfares fluctuate due to intense price competition among the carriers, but one-way fares generally range from $50 to $90.

Following are the three interisland carriers:

go! (airline code YV; ☎ 888-435-9462; www.iflygo.com) Discount airline. Flies frequently from Honolulu to Kaua'i, Maui and the Big Island.

Hawaiian Airlines (airline code HA; ☎ 800-367-5320; www.hawaiianair.com) Major airline with domestic US and international flights. Flies over 100 daily routes on 717s between Honolulu, Kaua'i, Maui and the Big Island.

Island Air (airline code WP; ☎ US mainland 800-323-3345, Neighbor Islands 800-652-6541; www .islandair.com) Commuter airline; pricier than the other two carriers. Flies small 37-passenger planes between Honolulu, Moloka'i, Lana'i, Maui, Kaua'i and the Big Island.

The following airlines fly directly from the US mainland, Canada or Japan to Kona International Airport:

Air Canada (airline code AC; ☎ 888-247-2262; www .aircanada.com)

American Airlines (airline code AA; ☎ 800-223-5436; www.aa.com)

Delta (airline code DL; ☎ 800-221-1212; www.delta .com)

Japan Airlines (airline code JL; ☎ 800-525-3663; www .japanair.com) From Japan.

Northwest Airlines (airline code NW; ☎ 800-225-2525; www.nwa.com)

United Airlines (airline code UA; ☎ 800-241-6522; www.ual.com)

US Airways (airline code US; ☎ 800-428-4322; www .usairways.com)

WestJet (airline code WS; ☎ 888-937-8538; www .westjet.com) From Canada.

Airlines flying into Honolulu include the following:

Air New Zealand (airline code NZ; ☎ 800-262-1234; www.airnz.co.nz)

Air Pacific (airline code FJ; ☎ 800-227-4446; www .airpacific.com)

Alaska Airlines (airline code AS; ☎ 800-252-7522; www.alaskaair.com)

ANA (airline code NH; ☎ 800-235-9262; www.ana.co.jp /eng)

China Airlines (airline code CI; ☎ 800-227-5118; www .china-airlines.com)

Continental (airline code CO; ☎ 800-523-3273; www .continental.com)

Korean Airlines (airline code KE; ☎ 800-438-5000; www.koreanair.com)

Philippine Airlines (airline code PR; ☎ 800-435-9725; www.philippineair.com)

Qantas Airways (airline code QF; ☎ 800-227-4500; www.qantasusa.com)

Tickets

Ah, the art and science of finding the lowest airfares. The internet is by far your best tool. First try the travel websites that broadly search multiple airlines and online booking sites; **Kayak** (www.kayak.com) and **Farecast** (www.farecast.com) are two good ones.

Otherwise, go to the booking sites directly and compare prices between them. Good ones to try include www.travelocity .com, www.expedia.com, www.orbitz.com and www.cheaptickets.com.

THINGS CHANGE...

The information in this chapter is particularly vulnerable to change. Check directly with the airline or a travel agent to make sure you understand how a fare (and ticket you may buy) works, and be aware of the security requirements for international travel. Shop carefully. The details given in this chapter should be regarded as pointers and are not a substitute for your own careful, up-to-date research.

DIRECTORY & TRANSPORTATION

US MAINLAND
It's hard to estimate average fares between Hawaii and the US mainland because prices vary by hundreds of dollars, depending on your travel dates. For advance bookings during off seasons, round-trip fares to Kona drop to the low $400s from the west coast and below $600 from the east coast.

Booking a direct flight to the Big Island might cost more, but you'll save time and reduce the chance of missing baggage. Direct flights depart from west coast cities such as Los Angeles and San Francisco. Fortunately the number of direct flights continues to increase.

Package tours, which can include airfare, hotel and car, can be a bargain for traveling couples who would stay at affiliated hotels anyway. But single travelers will find no savings because they base rates on double occupancy. Pleasant Hawaiian Holidays (☎ 800-742-9244; www.pleasantholidays .com) departs from numerous US mainland cities. Sun Trips (☎ 800-786-8747; www .suntrips.com) offers packages from Oakland, California.

An interesting option for flexible summer travelers is Airtech (☎ 212-219-7000; www.airtech.com) and its Space-Available FlightPass, a standby ticket that can be the cheapest way to fly between the west coast and Kona (as well as to Honolulu, Kaua'i and Maui). That said, its Kona flights are available only in summer and they aren't as cheap as those to Honolulu and Maui.

The nonstop flight time to Hawaii is about 5½ hours from the west coast and 11 hours from the east coast.

AUSTRALIA
Hawaiian Airlines flies nonstop between Sydney and Honolulu. Qantas flies to Honolulu from Sydney and Melbourne (via Sydney, but without changing planes).

For bookings, try Flight Centre (☎ 1300-133-133; www.flightcentre.com.au) and STA Travel (☎ 1300-733-035; www.statravel.com.au).

CANADA
Air Canada and WestJet offer direct flights to Honolulu and Kona from Vancouver; Calgary, Edmonton and Toronto connect via Vancouver.

Hawaiian Airlines also flies from Vancouver, Calgary, Edmonton and Toronto, with stopovers in Phoenix and Honolulu.

Booking agencies include Travel Cuts (☎ 866-246-9762; www.travelcuts.com) and Travelocity (☎ 877-282-2925; www.travelocity.ca).

JAPAN
Japan Airlines flies directly between Tokyo and Kona, but if you fly to Honolulu first, your starting point can also be Osaka, Nagoya or Fukuoka. Fares vary according to departure city and season but they always rise during Golden Week in May, Obon in August and around the New Year.

ANA flies to Honolulu from Tokyo, Sapporo and Kumamoto. Continental and Northwest have several flights to Honolulu from Tokyo and Osaka; ticket prices are comparable to those offered by Japan Airlines.

For bookings, start with STA Travel (☎ 03-5391-2922; www.statravel.co.jp).

NEW ZEALAND, MICRONESIA & SOUTH PACIFIC ISLANDS
Continental has nonstop flights from Guam to Honolulu, and Air New Zealand flies from Auckland.

Hawaiian Airlines flies to Honolulu from Tahiti and American Samoa. Air New Zealand offers round-trip tickets from Fiji to Honolulu via Auckland. It also flies to Honolulu from Tonga, the Cook Islands and Western Samoa.

Agents serving New Zealand include Flight Centre (☎ 0800-243-544; www.flightcentre .co.nz) and STA Travel (☎ 0800-474-400; www.sta travel.co.nz).

UK & CONTINENTAL EUROPE
United, American and all of the national carriers fly between Honolulu and various European cities. The most common route to Hawaii from Europe is west via New York, Chicago or Los Angeles. If you're interested in heading east with stops in Asia, it may be cheaper to get a round-the-world (RTW) ticket instead of returning the same way.

London is arguably the world's headquarters for bucket shops specializing in discount tickets. Two good, reliable agents for cheap tickets in London are STA Travel (☎ 0870-162-7551; www.statravel.co.uk) and Trailfinders (☎ 0845-058-5858; www.trailfinders.com).

SEA
Cruises

The colossal cruise ships seen throughout Hawaii are predominantly island-hoppers that originate in Honolulu. But there are occasional ships that originate in California or Vancouver. On either type of cruise, don't expect to spend more than one day each in Kailua-Kona and Hilo.

The North American cruises range from 10 to 19 days; the average 15-day tour from California costs about $1500 to $1900 per person and includes daylong stops on O'ahu, Maui, Kaua'i and the Big Island. Cruise lines include the following:

Holland America Cruise Line (☎ 877-724-5425; www.hollandamerica.com) Departures from San Diego or Vancouver.

Princess Cruises (☎ 800-568-3262; www.princess .com) Rates are generally steeper than Holland's; departures from Los Angeles and Vancouver.

The only company running interisland cruises is **Norwegian Cruise Line** (☎ 800-327-7030; www.ncl.com) and its *Pride of America* liner, distinctly painted with Old Glory. Seven-day trips (starting in Honolulu and stopping in Maui, Kaua'i, Hilo and Kona) range from about $1200 (no view) to $1650 (balcony).

Ferry

In early 2008, the **Hawaii Superferry** (www.hawaii superferry.com) launched its first commuter ferry, the *Alakai*, amid vigorous controversy by diverse opponents. At the time of research, only the O'ahu–Maui route was active; the Kaua'i route was suspended due to local opposition.

Opponents argue that the large vessels will harm marine life, spread environmental pests across the Islands and worsen traffic jams. But supporters counter that whale-watching ships and barges are more dangerous to whales and also more likely to transport invasive species – and that traffic is really caused by poor planning and inadequate roads. Big Island service is slated to launch in 2009, upon acquisition of a second ferry.

The *Alakai*, which can hold 866 passengers and 282 cars, features cushy furnishings and panoramic views from the deck. Travel time from Honolulu to the Big Island's Kawaihae harbor will run about four hours; Hilo was not an option because the trip would take six hours. Big Island round-trip fares are expected to run just over $50 per person and about the same per vehicle (more for pickups and vans), about half the cost of flying.

GETTING AROUND

At press time, there were no commercial flights between Kailua-Kona and Hilo since Island Air eliminated that route in March 2008.

TO/FROM THE AIRPORTS

Almost all visitors rent cars from agencies located at the Kona or Hilo airports. Those forgoing rentals can catch cabs; see the Kailua-Kona (p70) and Hilo (p190) chapters for details. There are no value-priced airport shuttles from either airport.

BICYCLE

Few circle the island as solo cyclists. The going can be tough, with unpredictable downpours, blinding heat, strong headwinds, narrow roads and oblivious drivers.

Dedicated bicycle lanes are rare. In fact, most visiting cyclists tour with a group (accompanied by vans toting their gear). But the adventurous and truly fit can certainly go it alone. Just bear in mind that distance cyclists are a rare breed.

In town, cycling can be fun and convenient for those comfortable riding in traffic. Kailua-Kona and Hilo are not cycling towns and local drivers lack that innate awareness of vehicles smaller than cars.

The best place to rent bikes is Kailua-Kona (p71), but Hilo (p190) is decent enough. Bringing your own bike to Hawaii costs upwards of $100 on flights from the mainland; interisland flights charge an additional $25 or more. The bicycle can be checked at the airline counter as baggage, but don't expect kid-glove treatment. At the very least, wrap the handlebars and pedals in foam or fix the handlebars to the side and remove the pedals.

In general, bicycles are required to follow the same state laws and road rules as cars.

See the Outdoor Activities & Adventures chapter (p34) for more info.

BUS

Let's face it: bus transit is a last-resort transportation mode on the Big Island. Many locals *never* ride the pubic buses, even if it's *free*. Still, buses do pack in hotel workers and folks without wheels. For visitors, touring the island by bus is too limiting. But, in a pinch, the county-run **Hele-On Bus** (☎ 961-8744; www.co.hawaii.hi.us/mass_transit/hele onbus.html; ⏲ 7:45am-4:30pm Mon-Fri) does offer limited service islandwide from Monday to Friday, plus minimal runs on Saturday. Schedules are available at the Big Island Visitors Bureau (p172 and p107) and the information kiosk at Hilo's Mo'oheau bus terminal (p190). The regional chapters in this book summarize main routes, but always check the website for current information. Most routes originate from Mo'oheau terminal.

Note that boarding with luggage, surfboards, bicycles or other unwieldy objects costs $1. Also, many stops are unmarked.

CAR

Automobile Associations

The **American Automobile Association** (AAA; ☎ 800-736-2886; www.aaa-hawaii.com), which has its only Hawaii office in Honolulu, provides members with maps and other information. Members get discounts on car rental, air tickets, some hotels and some sightseeing attractions, as well as emergency road service and towing (☎ 800-222-4357). For information on joining, call ☎ 800-564-6222. AAA has reciprocal agreements with automobile associations in other countries, but bring your membership card from home.

Driver's License

An international driving license, obtained before you leave home, is necessary only if your country of origin is a non-English-speaking one.

Fuel & Towing

Fuel is readily available everywhere except in remote areas such as Saddle Rd. Expect to pay at least 20¢ more per gallon than on the mainland. For example, when mainland gas costs an average of $3.55 per gallon, you'll pay about $3.75 in Hawaii. Still, for Europeans and Canadians, it will be less expensive than at home.

If you get into trouble with your car, towing is mighty expensive and therefore to be avoided at all costs. Figure the fees at about $65 to start, plus $6.50 per mile you must be towed. How to avoid it? Don't drive up to Mauna Kea in anything but a 4WD, for instance, and never drive 4WD vehicles in deep sand.

Insurance

Liability insurance covers people and property if you cause a collision. For damage to the rental vehicle, a collision damage waiver (CDW) is available for about $15 a day. If you have collision coverage on your vehicle at home, it might cover damages to car rentals. Also, your credit card might offer reimbursement coverage for collision damages if you rent the car with that credit card; however, most credit-card coverage isn't valid for rentals of more than 15 days or for exotic models, vans and 4WD vehicles.

Rental

Car-rental companies are located at Kona and Hilo airports. Reserve well in advance to clinch low rates (and continue to check rates online, as they occasionally drop as time passes). Most rental companies enforce a minimum age of 25; if they allow rentals by 21- to 24-year-olds, they typically charge an extra fee of $25 per day.

If you book early during nonpeak periods, weekly rates fall to $130 for compact and $160 for full-size cars, plus taxes and fees that add 16% to 30% to the base estimate. Rates rise to between $300 and $400 weekly for high-season and last-minute bookings. Rates for 4WD vehicles range from $60 to $100 per day, but all agencies except Harper Car & Truck Rentals prohibit driving to the Mauna Kea summit. Bottom line: check the total price, *including taxes and fees*, when shopping around and book early to guarantee good rates.

Rental rates generally include unlimited mileage, though if you drop off the car at a different location from where you picked it up, there's usually a hefty additional fee. Having a major credit card greatly simplifies the rental process. Without one, some companies will not rent to you, while others require prepayment, a deposit of $200 per week, pay stubs, proof of return airfare and possibly more.

The following major agencies are familiar and reliable:

Alamo (☎ 800-327-9633; www.alamo.com)
Avis (☎ 800-331-1212; www.avis.com)
Budget (☎ 800-527-0700; www.budget.com)
Dollar (☎ 800-800-4000; www.dollarcar.com)
Enterprise (☎ 800-325-8007; www.enterprise.com)
Hertz (☎ 800-654-3011; www.hertz.com)
National (☎ 888-868-6207; www.nationalcar.com)
Thrifty (☎ 800-847-4389; www.thrifty.com)

ROAD DISTANCES & TIMES

To circumnavigate the island on the 230-mile Hawai'i Belt Rd (Hwys 19 and 11), you'll need about six hours.

From Hilo

Destination	Distance (miles)	Time
Hawai'i Volcanoes NP	28	¾hr
Hawi	86	2¼hr
Honoka'a	40	1hr
Kailua-Kona	92	2½hr
Na'alehu	64	1¾hr
Pahoa	16	½hr
Waikoloa	80	2¼hr
Waimea	54	1½hr
Waipi'o Lookout	50	1¼hr

From Kailua-Kona

Destination	Distance (miles)	Time
Hawai'i Volcanoes NP	98	2½hr
Hawi	51	1¼hr
Hilo	92	2½hr
Honoka'a	61	1½hr
Na'alehu	60	1½hr
Pahoa	108	3hr
Waikoloa	18	¾hr
Waimea	43	1hr
Waipi'o Lookout	70	1¾hr

Harper Car & Truck Rentals (☎ 969-1478, 800-852-9993; www.harpershawaii.com; 456 Kalaniana'ole Ave, Hilo) has a main office in Hilo but also rents from the Kona airport. Only Harper puts no restrictions on driving its 4WDs to Mauna Kea's summit or almost anywhere on the island, except Waipi'o Valley and Green Sands Beach. But any damage to a vehicle entails a high deductible. Rates are generally steeper than the national companies'; the $110 to $135 per day for a 4WD (plus taxes and fees) is hard to swallow unless you're traveling with a family or group.

If you're under 21, your only option is **Affordable Rent-A-Car** (☎ 329-7766; 74-5543 Kaiwi St, Kailua-Kona), but prices are outrageous at $65 per day for drivers between 18 and 21. The agency requires pick up and drop off in Kailua-Kona.

Road Conditions & Hazards

During major rainstorms, roads and bridges can flood; especially prone to flooding are the Ka'u bridges and downtown Hilo. The Hamakua Coast can see landslides near gulches.

Driving off-road (eg Road to the Sea) or to the Mauna Kea summit is not for newbie 4WD drivers. In such remote areas, you'll be miles from any help.

Street addresses on major roads in West Hawai'i might seem oddly long and complicated, but there's a pattern. In hyphenated numbers, such as 75-2345 Kuakini Hwy, the first part of the number identifies the post office district and the second part identifies the street address. Numbers increase as you travel south.

Road Rules

As in North America, drivers keep to the right-hand side of the road. Turning right at a red light is permitted (after stopping and yielding to oncoming traffic, of course) unless a sign prohibits it. Seat belts are required for drivers and front-seat passengers.

Note the strict rules for child passengers: kids aged three and under must use infant/ toddler safety seats; kids aged four to seven must use a booster seat (unless the child is 4ft 9in tall and can properly use a seat belt). Most car-rental companies can rent child-safety seats if reserved in advance.

Speed limits are posted *and* enforced. If stopped for speeding, expect a ticket; the police rarely give mere warnings. Accidents are common on Big Island highways and most are caused by excessive speed.

While drivers tend to speed on highways, in-town driving is courteous and rather leisurely. Locals don't honk (unless a crash is imminent), they don't tailgate and they let faster cars pass. Do the same, and you'll get an appreciative thank-you wave or *shaka* sign (local hand greeting) in return.

HITCHHIKING

Hitchhiking is officially illegal statewide; however, this rule is not rigidly enforced. It's not a common practice among locals. In places such as offbeat, hippie-mecca Puna, folks are more likely to offer rides. But hitching is always a risk, especially for solo travelers. Instead, try to meet fellow travelers at hostels or campgrounds and to check bulletin boards for rideshares.

MOPED & MOTORCYCLE

For motorcycle rentals, the go-to place is Harley-Davidson, with a 22-bike fleet in Kailua-Kona (p70) and a couple of bikes in Hilo (p190). Moped rentals are scarce, though you'll find them along Kailua-Kona's Ali'i Dr. (They say the low moped rates can't cover their insurance and other costs.)

You need a valid motorcycle license to rent one, but a standard driver's license will suffice for mopeds. The minimum age for renting a moped is 16; for a motorcycle it's 21.

There are no helmet laws in the state of Hawaii, but rental agencies often provide free helmets and smart riders will use them.

HIGHWAY NICKNAMES

Locals call highways by nickname, not by number. That's confusing enough, but some highways have multiple nicknames! Here's a cheat sheet:

- **Hwy 11** Volcano Hwy (from Hilo to Hawai'i Volcanoes National Park); Mamalahoa Hwy (from Hawai'i Volcanoes National Park to Honalo); Kuakini Hwy (from Honalo to Kuakini Hwy junction); Queen Ka'ahumanu Hwy (from Kuakini Hwy junction to Palani Rd)
- **Hwy 19** Bayfront Hwy (in and around Hilo); Hawai'i Belt Rd or Mamalahoa Hwy (from Hilo to Waimea); Kawaihae Rd (from Waimea to Kawaihae); Queen Ka'ahumanu Hwy (from Kawaihae to Kailua-Kona)
- **Hwy 130** Kea'au–Pahoa Rd (also called Kalapana Hwy, Kea'au Bypass Rd or Pahoa Bypass Rd)
- **Hwy 137** Red Rd
- **Hwy 180** Mamalahoa Hwy
- **Hwy 190** Mamalahoa Hwy
- **Hwy 200** Saddle Rd
- **Hwy 250** Kohala Mountain Rd
- **Hwy 270** Akoni Pule Hwy

Note: Hwy 132 in Puna has no nickname.

TAXI

Locals rarely use taxicabs so you'll find them mainly in Kailua-Kona and Hilo. Fares are based on mileage regardless of the number of passengers. Since cabs are often station wagons or minivans, they're good value for groups. The standard flag-down fee is $3, plus 30¢ per additional 0.125 miles. Cabs are easily found at either airport during normal business hours, but they don't run all night or cruise for passengers; in town you'll need to call ahead.

See Kailua-Kona (p71) and Hilo (p190) for recommended cab companies.

BEHIND THE SCENES

LUCI YAMAMOTO *Coordinating Author*

Luci Yamamoto is a fourth-generation native of Hawai'i. Growing up in Hilo, she viewed the cross-island drive to Kailua-Kona as a rare, all-day adventure. She left for college in Los Angeles and law school in Berkeley – and then even the Big Island seemed small indeed. Since becoming a Lonely Planet author and covering Hawai'i, Kaua'i and Honolulu, she's opened her eyes to the true greatness of her home island. For this book, Luci wrote the Kailua-Kona, North Kohala, South Kohala, Hilo, Puna, Big Island Myths & Legends, History & Culture, Food & Drink, Planning Your Trip and Directory & Transportation sections.

CONNER GORRY

An island girl at heart, Conner knows some of the best: Manhattan, Moloka'i, Cuba, Kaua'i. But oh, Hawai'i. Since the moment she smelled Hilo and beheld the Pu'u 'O'o while writing the first Lonely Planet guide to the Big Island, she's felt just like Twain, longing for 'the privilege of living forever away up on one of those mountains in the Sandwich Islands overlooking the sea…' She happily consumed over half a dozen cans of Spam during the research and writing of this book, for which Conner wrote the Outdoor Activities & Adventures, Green Big Island, Kona Coast, Waimea, Mauna Kea, Hamakua Coast, Hawai'i Volcanoes National Park and Ka'u sections.

LONELY PLANET AUTHORS

Why is our travel information the best in the world? It's simple: our authors are independent, dedicated travelers. They don't research using just the internet or phone, and they don't take freebies, so you can rely on their advice being well researched and impartial. They travel widely, to all the popular spots and off the beaten track. They personally visit thousands of hotels, restaurants, cafés, bars, galleries, palaces, museums and more – and they take great pride in getting all the details right and telling it like it is. Think you can do it? Find out how at www.lonelyplanet.com.

THIS BOOK

This third edition of *Hawai'i the Big Island* was written by Luci Yamamoto and Conner Gorry. Contributions were also made by Jake Howard and Emily K Wolman. The previous edition was written by Luci Yamamoto and Alan Tarbell. This guidebook was commissioned in Lonely Planet's Oakland, California, office and produced by the following:

Hawaii Product Development Manager & Commissioning Editor Emily K Wolman
Coordinating Editor Michelle Bennett
Coordinating Cartographer Andrew Smith
Senior Editor Helen Christinis
Managing Cartographer Alison Lyall
Assisting Editor Stephanie Pearson
Assisting Cartographer Tadhgh Knaggs
Series Designer Gerilyn Attebery
Layout Designer Megan Cooney
Cover Designers & Image Researchers Yukiyoshi Kamimura, Marika Kozak, Nic Lehman, Michael Ruff, Kate Slattery
Indexer Ken DellaPenta
Project Manager Eoin Dunlevy
Language Content Coordinator Quentin Franyne

Thanks to Glenn Beanland, Michaela Caughlan, Monique Choy, Heather Dickson, Ryan Evans, Jessica Ferracane, Rana Freedman, Jennifer Garrett, Suki Gear, Aimée Goggins, Brice Gosnell, Bronwyn Hicks, Lauren Hunt, Lisa Knights, Marina Kosmatos, Naomi Parker, Paul Piaia, Raphael Richards, Frank Ruiz, Becky Ryan, Christina Tunnah, Vivek Waglé

Internal photographs by Greg Elms for Lonely Planet Images except for: p7, Greg Vaughn/Alamy; p9 (top) Ann Cecil/Lonely Planet Images; p10 Photo Resource Hawaii/Alamy; p13 V1/Alamy; p14 Phil Degginger/Alamy; p15 (bottom) John Elk III/Lonely Planet Images; p16 RHK UW Productions/Alamy; p30 Conner Gorry; p39 Conner Gorry; p41 Conner Gorry; p43 Keauhou Beach Resort; p44 Conner Gorry; p46 Conner Gorry; p51, Wolfgang Kaehler/Alamy; p63, Luci Yamamoto; p75, Produce to Product Inc; p78, Luci Yamamoto; p79, Douglas Peebles Photography/Alamy; p101, Conner Gorry; p102, Conner Gorry; p103, Glow Images/Alamy; p116, Conner Gorry; p122, Luci Yamamoto; p123, Luci Yamamoto; p125, Luci Yamamoto; p128, Roger Fletcher/Alamy; p136 Karl Lehmann/Lonely Planet Images; p137, Dave Jepson/Alamy; p138, Abbot Low Moffat III/freelance; p144, 'Imiloa Astronomy Center; p148, Abbot Low Moffat III/freelance; p150, Corbis Premium RF/Alamy; p152, Lawrence Worcester/Lonely Planet Images; p159, Conner Gorry; p162 Douglas Peebles Photography/Alamy; p167, Photo Resource Hawaii/Alamy; p177, Luci Yamamoto; p185, Luci Yamamoto; p191, Photo Resource Hawaii/Alamy; p200, Luci Yamamoto; p205 ER Degginger/Alamy; p206, Kevin Ebi/Alamy; p223 (top & bottom), Conner Gorry; p227, Conner Gorry; p236, Conner Gorry; p238, Luci Yamamoto; p241, Greg Vaughn/Alamy; p242, Eric Wheater/Lonely Planet Images; p258, Ann Cecil/Lonely Planet Images; p260, Big Island Visitors Bureau; p263, Holger Leue/Lonely Planet Images; p274 (#1), Big Island Visitors Bureau; p274 (#2), Emily Riddell/Lonely Planet Images; p275 (#1), Ann Cecil/Lonely Planet Images; p275 (#2), Michael Darden/Kona Coffee Cultural Festival

All images are copyright of the photographer unless otherwise indicated. Many of the images in this guide are available for licensing from Lonely Planet Images: www.lonelyplanetimages.com.

THANKS from the Authors

Luci Yamamoto
Mahalo to my insiders: Hawai'i expert Bobby Camara, *Hawaii-Tribune Herald* editor David Bock, Big Island Visitor's Bureau's Jessica Ferracane, columnist Gloria Baraquio and 'Imiloa's Gloria Chun Hoo. Cheers to my fascinating Island Voices interviewees: Kilohana Domingo, Renee Kimura, Alan Kuwahara, Wayne Subica, Shiro Takata and Barbara Uechi. I owe much to LP specialist author Nanette Napoleon, whose prior writings on Hawaii history greatly influenced mine, and to LP commissioning editor Emily K Wolman and co-author Conner Gorry for making an excellent team. Aloha and special thanks to my family in Hilo (still home!), Santa Cruz and Vancouver, for the obvious reasons.

Conner Gorry
Mahalo to Emily K Wolman at LP for pulling me back into the fold, and to previous *Big Island* author Alan Tarbell. On the road, Joseph Aguiar was the best adventure partner ever, and my sister Carolyn was, as always, a rock. Big up to Anitra and the Ocean View crew; Eden in Waipi'o; James from South Kona; and Christina, Garrett and Sandy in Volcano. Thanks to all my Island Voices interviewees, plus Donna Kimura, Jessica Ferracane and Gloria Chun Hoo. One day, beyond January 20, 2009, my dream to discover Big Island love with my husband will come true. *Te quiero más que nunca.*

THANKS from Lonely Planet

Many thanks to the travelers who used the last edition and wrote to us with helpful hints, useful advice and interesting anecdotes: Rachel Asquith, Wendy Bat-Sarah, Chris Bennack, Walter Bono, Francesca Brice, Mark Caudill, Jon Coloma, Chanin Cook, Claudia Crenshaw, Juliane Crump, Bianca Falace, Maurice Friedman, Jack Gordon, Kirby Guyer, Gregory Hall, Aline Huntly, Jan-Peter Idel, Tom Kerr, Deb Kim, Robert Masters, Judy Mendoza, Danny Miller, Barbara Murphy, Niall Murphy, Elke Obermeier, Chris Ploegaert, Walter Rask, Emma Rayson, Hayley & Shelley Reynolds, Rosemarie Richards, Emilio Salami, Sheree Silvey, Lorraine & Murray Sinderberry, Gail Smith, Scott O Sutton, Michelle Tinsay, E Van Garner, Joy Vanbuhler, Andrea Voigt, Ian Walker, Kl Waugh, William Wilson, Satoshi Yabuki

Send Us Your Feedback

We love to hear from travelers – your comments keep us on our toes and help make our books better. Our well-travelled team reads every word on what you loved or loathed about this book. Although we cannot reply individually to postal submissions, we always guarantee that your feedback goes straight to the appropriate authors, in time for the next edition. Each person who sends us information is thanked in the next edition – and the most useful submissions are rewarded with a free book.

To send us your updates – and find out about Lonely Planet events, newsletters and travel news – visit our award-winning website: **www.lonelyplanet.com/contact**.

Note: we may edit, reproduce and incorporate your comments in Lonely Planet products such as guidebooks, websites and digital products, so let us know if you don't want your comments reproduced or your name acknowledged. For a copy of our privacy policy, visit **www.lonelyplanet.com/privacy**.

THE LONELY PLANET STORY

Fresh from an epic journey across Europe, Asia and Australia in 1972, Tony and Maureen Wheeler sat at their kitchen table stapling together notes. The first Lonely Planet guidebook, *Across Asia on the Cheap,* was born.

Travelers snapped up the guides. Inspired by their success, the Wheelers began publishing books to Southeast Asia, India and beyond. Demand was prodigious, and the Wheelers expanded the business rapidly to keep up. Over the years, Lonely Planet extended its coverage to every country, and into the virtual world via www.lonelyplanet.com and the Thorn Tree message board.

As Lonely Planet became a globally loved brand, Tony and Maureen received several offers for the company. But it wasn't until 2007 that they found a partner whom they trusted to remain true to the company's principles of traveling widely, treading lightly and giving sustainably. In October of that year, BBC Worldwide acquired a 75% share in the company, pledging to uphold Lonely Planet's commitment to independent travel, trustworthy advice and editorial independence.

Today Lonely Planet has offices in Melbourne, London and Oakland, with over 500 staff members and 300 authors. Tony and Maureen are still actively involved with Lonely Planet. They're traveling more often than ever, and they're devoting their spare time to charitable projects. And the company is still driven by the philosophy of *Across Asia on the Cheap:* 'All you've got to do is decide to go and the hardest part is over. So go!'

INDEX

ACCOMMODATIONS

ACTIVITIES

BEACHES

GREENDEX

GOING GREEN

It seems like everyone's going 'green' these days, but how can you know which businesses are actually eco-friendly and which are simply jumping on the sustainable bandwagon?

The following listings have all been selected by Lonely Planet authors because they demonstrate an active sustainable-tourism policy. Some are involved in conservation or environmental education, and many are owned and operated by local and indigenous operators, thereby maintaining and preserving Hawaiian identity and culture.

We want to keep developing our sustainable-tourism content. If you think we've omitted someone who should be listed here, or if you disagree with our choices, email us at talk2us@ lonelyplanet.com.au. For more information about sustainable tourism and Lonely Planet, see www.lonelyplanet.com/responsibletravel.

MAP LEGEND

ROUTES

Primary	One-Way Street
Secondary	➜ MM29 .... Mile Marker
Tertiary	Walking Tour
Lane	Walking Trail
Unsealed Road	Walking Path
	Track

TRANSPORT

Ferry	Rail

HYDROGRAPHY

River, Creek	Reef
Intermittent River	Glacier
Swamp	Water

BOUNDARIES

State, Provincial	Regional, Suburb
Marine Park	Cliff

AREA FEATURES

Airport	Land
Beach	Market
Building	Park, Reserve
Forest	Sports

POPULATION

⊙ CAPITAL (NATIONAL)	**◉ CAPITAL (STATE)**
● Large City	**● Medium City**
● Small City	● Town, Village

SYMBOLS

Sights/Activities

- Beach
- Bodysurfing
- Buddhist
- Canoeing, Kayaking
- Christian
- Diving
- Golf
- Monument
- Museum, Gallery
- Point of Interest
- Pool
- Ruin
- Snorkeling
- Surfing, Surf Beach
- Trail Head
- Windsurfing
- Winery, Vineyard
- Zoo, Bird Sanctuary

Eating

- Eating

Drinking

- Drinking
- Café

Entertainment

- Entertainment

Shopping

- Shopping

Sleeping

- Sleeping
- Camping

Transport

- Airport, Airfield
- Bus Station
- Cycling, Bicycle Path
- General Transport
- Parking Area
- Petrol Station
- Taxi Rank

Information

- Bank, ATM
- Hospital, Medical
- Information
- Internet Facilities
- Police Station
- Post Office, GPO

Geographic

- Lighthouse
- Lookout
- Mountain, Volcano
- National Park
- Beach Park
- Picnic Area
- Shelter, Hut
- Spot Height
- Waterfall

Published by Lonely Planet Publications Pty Ltd
ABN 36 005 607 983

LONELY PLANET OFFICES

Australia
Head Office
Locked Bag 1, Footscray, Victoria 3011
☎ 03 8379 8000, fax 03 8379 8111
talk2us@lonelyplanet.com.au

USA
150 Linden St, Oakland, CA 94607
☎ 510 250 6400, toll free 800 275 8555
fax 510 893 8572, info@lonelyplanet.com

UK
2nd Fl, 186 City Rd
London EC1V 2NT
☎ 020 7106 2100, fax 020 7106 2101
go@lonelyplanet.co.uk

Cover photographs: Lava flowing in Hawai'i Volcanoes National Park, G Brad Lewis/Getty Images (front); Big Island beach landscape, Karl Lehmann/Lonely Planet Images (back top), *kahiko* hula on the rim of Halema'uma'u Crater, Ann Cecil/Lonely Planet Images

Printed by Hang Tai Printing Company.
Printed in China.